The OECD and the International Political Economy Since 1948

Matthieu Leimgruber · Matthias Schmelzer
Editors

The OECD and the International Political Economy Since 1948

palgrave
macmillan

Editors
Matthieu Leimgruber
Department of History
University of Zürich
Zürich, Switzerland

Matthias Schmelzer
DFG-Kolleg on Post-Growth Societies
Friedrich Schiller University Jena
Jena, Germany

ISBN 978-3-319-60242-4 ISBN 978-3-319-60243-1 (eBook)
DOI 10.1007/978-3-319-60243-1

Library of Congress Control Number: 2017944556

Printed on acid-free paper

This Palgrave Macmillan imprint is published by Springer Nature
The registered company is Springer International Publishing AG
The registered company address is: Gewerbestrasse 11, 6330 Cham, Switzerland

Acknowledgements

This collective volume is one of the outcomes of the OECD History Project that was hosted at the University of Geneva and the University of Zürich from 2012 to 2016 (www.oecdhistoryproject.net). It brings together a selection of contributions presented at the international conference, Warden of the West: The OECD and the Global Political Economy, 1948 to Present, that we convened in August 2015 at the University of Zürich. As all such endeavors, it could not have been realized without the comments, criticism, and help of many, to all of whom we would like to express our sincerest gratitude.

First, Ludovic Fulleringer and Samuel Beroud contributed much, through their suggestions and their own research, to make this volume possible. Their comments have been tremendously helpful during the entire process, from early conceptual discussions to final realization. Next, we would like to thank all contributors to this volume for their patience with our detailed and demanding revisions, comments, and more revisions. Also, we would like to thank all the participants in the 2015 Warden of the West conference, in particular the colleagues who generously acted as commentators: Vincent Gayon, Rüdiger Graf, William Hynes, Sandrine Kott, Corinne Pernet, Tobias Straumann, Jakob Tanner, and Richard Woodward. Furthermore, we are indebted to all the researchers that have contributed over the years in our discussions at the OECD History Project for their insights into the history and functioning of this elusive organization. Nina Kunz has also proofread all chapters and brought them stylistically closer together. Last but not least, we would like to thank the history department at the University of Zürich and the Paul Bairoch Institute for Economic History at University of Geneva for hosting the OECD History Project, and the Swiss National Science Foundation for its generous financial support.

Zürich and Berlin, November 2017

Matthieu Leimgruber
Matthias Schmelzer

Contents

Contributors

Samuel Beroud University of Geneva, Geneva, Switzerland

Iris Borowy College of Liberal Arts, Shanghai University, Shanghai, China

Regula Bürgi FHNW School of Education, Solothurn, Switzerland

Peter Carroll University of Tasmania, Hobart, Australia

Emmanuel Comte Department of History, University of California, Berkeley, United States

William Glenn Gray Department of History, Purdue University, West Lafayette, United States

Patricia Hongler Department of History, University of Luzern, Luzern, Switzerland

Wolfram Kaiser School of Social, Historical and Literary Studies, University of Portsmouth, Portsmouth, United Kingdom

Matthieu Leimgruber Department of History, University of Zürich, Zurich, Switzerland

Rianne Mahon Balsillie School of International Affairs and Department of Political Science, Wilfrid Laurier University, Waterloo, Canada

Andrej Marković Department of History, University of Zurich, Zurich, Switzerland

Ivan Obadić European University Institute, Firenze, Italy

Simone Paoli University of Padova, Padua, Italy

Matthias Schmelzer University of Jena, Jena, Germany

Daniel Stinsky Maastricht University, Maastricht, Netherlands

Kazuhiko Yago Waseda University, Tokyo, Japan

Abbreviations

BIAC	Business and Industry Advisory Committee (OECD)
BIS	Bank for International Settlements
CEEC	Committee of European Economic Co-operation
CERI	Centre for Educational Research and Innovation (OECD)
COMECON	Council for Mutual Economic Assistance
CSTP	Committee for Scientific and Technical Personnel (OECD)
DAC	Development Assistance Committee (OECD)
DAG	Development Assistance Group (OEEC)
ECA	Economic Cooperation Administration
ECSC	European Coal and Steel Community
EDRC	Economic and Development Review Committee (OECD)
EEC	European Economic Community
EFTA	European Free Trade Association
EPA	European Productivity Agency (OEEC)
EPC	Economic Policy Committee (OECD)
EPU	European Payments Union (OEEC)
ERP	European Recovery Program
FAO	Food and Agriculture Organization of the United Nations
G10	Group of Ten of the International Monetary Fund
GATT	General Agreement on Tariffs and Trade
IBRD	International Bank for Reconstruction and Development
ILO	International Labor Organization
IMF	International Monetary Fund
MDGs	Millennium Development Goals
MSAC	Manpower and Social Affairs Committee (OECD)
NATO	North Atlantic Treaty Organization

ODA	Official Development Assistance
OECD	Organization for Economic Co-operation and Development
OEEC	Organization for European Economic Co-operation
PISA	Programme for International Student Assessment (OECD)
PPP	Polluter Pays Principle
TUAC	Trade Union Advisory Council (OECD)
UNCTAD	United Nations Conference on Trade and Development
UNDP	United Nations Development Programme
UNECE	United Nations Economic Commission for Europe
UNESCO	United Nations Educational, Scientific and Cultural Organization
UN	United Nations
WHO	World Health Organization
WP3	Working Party 3 of the EPC (OECD)

List of Figures

List of Tables

Introduction: Writing Histories of the OECD

Matthieu Leimgruber and Matthias Schmelzer

Even though ubiquitously mentioned in current affairs and in academic writing, the Organization for Economic Co-operation and Development (OECD) has remained one of the most elusive and under-researched international organizations. Founded in 1948 as the Organization for European Economic Co-operation (OEEC), a Western European institution charged with monitoring Marshall Plan aid, the organization was reorganized in 1961 as an Atlantic (including the US and Canada), and then triadic (Japan joined in 1964, Australia and New Zealand by 1974) platform. Though the 24 members of the Organization also included Yugoslavia as an associate member (a border case which is specifically dealt with in this volume), it was within and through the OECD that Western capitalist countries discussed their economic policies both in the Cold War setting and vis-à-vis the emerging power-bloc of decolonizing countries in the Global South. After the end of the Cold War, the organization expanded its membership to include a dozen more

M. Leimgruber (✉)
Department of History, University of Zürich, Rämistrasse 64,
CH-8001 Zurich, Switzerland
e-mail: matthieu.leimgruber@uzh.ch

M. Schmelzer
University of Jena, Humboldtstr. 34, 07743 Jena, Germany
e-mail: m.schmelzer@knoe.org

M. Leimgruber and M. Schmelzer (eds.), *The OECD and the International Political Economy Since 1948*, DOI 10.1007/978-3-319-60243-1_1

emerging market economies as well as former Soviet Bloc countries (for a full list, see below Table 1). By the turn of the millennium, the OECD had established its reputation as a key knowledge hub in the current era of globalization.

Throughout its history, the OECD has worked on almost every subject of interest to national governments ranging from growth statistics (GDP, economic outlook) to education (PISA rankings) to the environment (Polluter Pays Principle). It has developed a series of unique modes of governance, and it has with varying success played a role as a think tank and promoter of the industrialized Western countries in the Cold War and post-colonial setting, and of capitalist development more generally. OECD reports are widely used by researchers and journalists alike as a recognized expert opinion on current affairs, its statistics are taken as objective and reliable, and its advice is extensively reported on in the public. OECD officials have regularly described their tasks as assembling, producing, and diffusing "knowledge relevant to *rational* policy-making in *every* major field of economic activity," as advising "better policies for better lives," and have thus interpreted the OECD as "speaking truth to power."[1]

Yet what exactly is this organization, which was often dubbed the "Club of the Rich"?[2] How does it function, what is its history, and how did it become the quintessential expert organization? Answers to these questions are not easy to find. Most researchers regard the OECD more as a resource—providing statistics, expert opinions, and authoritative reports—than as a field of enquiry. The history of the OECD and its predecessor, the OEEC, has only recently moved into the limelight of international relations and social sciences.[3] What is more, even those researchers have tended to idealize the OECD's work as a rational process of providing and sharing knowledge, organizing dialogue, and acting as a neutral think tank.

Providing a proper historical overview of the Organization is further complicated by the fact that researchers—if they study the OECD at all—tend to look at it through the lens of a theme, nation state, or very specific time frame and thus tell very different stories. Furthermore, the OECD is more multi-thematic than most other international organizations—while its core focus is clearly economic, it has played a key role in fields as diverse as education, agriculture, fisheries, transport, the environment, social welfare, and development aid. Finally and relatedly, the OECD has used various overlapping modes of governance, ranging from

Table 1 Members of the OEEC and OECD, 1948–2016

Original members of the OEEC		
1	Austria	1948
2	Belgium	1948
3	Denmark	1948
4	France	1948
5	Germany	1948
6	Greece	1948
7	Iceland	1948
8	Ireland	1948
9	Luxembourg	1948
10	Netherlands	1948
11	Norway	1948
12	Portugal	1948
13	Spain	1948
14	Sweden	1948
15	Switzerland	1948
16	Turkey	1948
17	United Kingdom	1948
18	Italy	1949
Additional members of the OECD, 1961–1973		
19	Canada	1961
20	United States	1961
21	Japan	1964
22	Finland	1969
23	Australia	1971
24	New Zealand	1973
Post-1989 enlargement of the OECD		
25	Mexico	1994
26	Czech Republic	1995
27	Hungary	1996
28	Korea	1996
29	Poland	1996
30	Slovakia	2000
31	Chile	2010
32	Estonia	2010
33	Israel	2010
34	Slovenia	2010
35	Latvia	2016

Note The Socialist Federal Republic of Yugoslavia had an observer status in the OEEC since 1950. It was then an associate member of the OECD from 1961 until its dissolution in 1992 (see the chapter by Andrej Markovic and Ivan Obadic in this volume). Before joining the OECD, the US and Canada were observers (1950) and then associate members (1955) of the OEEC international law to international high-level meetings as well as the collection of statistics.

Building on emerging new research on the OEEC/OECD, this volume presents a historically grounded analysis of its first half-century of existence, from 1948 to the 1980s. Our perspective is influenced by recent trends in international, transnational, or global history, the entanglements and transfers of globalizing interconnections, and in governance structures.[4] Within this general trend, the topic of international organizations, which had long been reserved to political science and international relations scholars, has attracted increasing attention by historians. Recent syntheses on the issue have stressed the importance of international organizations as agents of globalization. More particularly, these accounts highlight the importance of international organizations as meeting points for transnational communities of bureaucrats and experts and the complexity of the internal dynamics of international bureaucracies and their relation to member states and other international actors.[5] Besides analyzing the national debates in the plenary sessions of international organizations, historians have started to focus on the work of the secretariats, commissions, or technical agencies, the experts and officials that work in these international bureaucracies, and their relationships to and fluctuating careers in academia, governments, and international organizations. Even though historical research on international organizations is still in its infancy, historians have not only analyzed European integration and the EEC/EU, the study of which has developed into a booming research field, but in recent years more and more international organizations have come under scrutiny. These studies have largely focused on international organizations in the areas of social, developmental, cultural, or technical cooperation and have paid less attention to those organizations dealing with macroeconomic as well as financial questions. Only recently has this started to change with new research on the Economic and Financial Organization (EFO) of the interwar League of Nations, the World Bank, the International Monetary Fund (IMF), the Bank for International Settlements (BIS), and the GATT.[6]

The next section demonstrates why we think it is essential to adopt a long-term historical perspective to understand the key characteristics of both the OEEC *and* the OECD. We then provide a succinct state of the art of the actual research on the OECD, which encompasses both social science and historical approaches. In the third and last section, we present the thematic structure of this volume and highlight some key findings for each chapter.

A Historically Grounded Perspective on the OEEC/OECD

As stated in the preceding section, researchers have tended to idealize the OECD's work as a rational process of "epistemic learning" that is "campaigning on expertise."[7] The OECD has been described as a "communication system," an "orchestrator of global knowledge networks," or an "ideational artist" and has been analyzed as a relatively non-hierarchical, knowledge-based forum for the production and exchange of expertise among civil servants and economists from member states.[8] Highlighting the OECD soft power functions may shed light on its distinctive modes of governance, but this perspective impedes a more thorough understanding of the OECD's role among postwar multilateral organizations. Focusing on soft power dimensions, many scholars tend to downplay or even ignore the use and diffusion of power and (geo-)political interests within and through the OECD as well as its competition and collaboration with other international organizations. By focusing almost exclusively on the post-1989 period and by basing their studies on published materials and interviews, these accounts have established a static view of the OECD. If the longer-term history of the OECD is addressed at all, it tends to be narrated as a linear success story that conspicuously resembles the organization's own view of its past, as it was, for example, depicted around its 50th anniversary in 2011—starting from successful Western European cooperation in the context of the Marshall Plan, the organization developed first into a transatlantic and then seamlessly into a global knowledge hub, advising industrialized countries and advancing development aid to the Global South.[9] This narrative obscures the foundational role the OECD's entanglements in the (post-)colonial period and its key function as a Cold War economic institution.

Three claims form the core of our historical perspective. Firstly, the history of the OECD is better understood if one analyzes it as the organization's continuous endeavor to *reinvent* itself after it had lost its original purpose at the end of the Marshall Plan. In this process, the OECD developed into a warden of liberal capitalism and played a key role in defining the "West"—a role that it had to redefine again after the fall of the Berlin Wall. The OECD functioned both as a custodian—a keeper and promoter of the key tenets of economic expertise—and a flexible tool that member countries could mobilize for analyzing certain problems, negotiating inter-capitalist economic tensions, pre-negotiating a common stance to present in less exclusive fora (i.e., the UN), defining a common and specifically "Western" identity, or defusing developments that were averse to international free trade capitalism. This broad perspective enables an understanding of the dynamic changes of the OECD's role within the framework of postwar developments (e.g., Cold War, decolonization, rise of economic expertise) and how the Organization responded to challenges to the hegemony of "the West" or of its larger member countries.

Secondly, during much of its history, the OECD was not (or not primarily) a *think tank* but served other important functions. Rather than imposing contemporary conceptions of the OECD as an expert talking shop about its past, we need a thorough analysis of how the think tank functions emerged and evolved, when and how they did shape the OECD, how they were used, and in which changing contexts. Indeed, the OEEC was founded to administer European Marshall Plan aid, and as an early embryo of Western European integration—it only later shifted toward being a knowledge-based expert organization. And when this expert outlook became increasingly prominent from the early 1960s onward, it was consciously constructed and defended by the OECD Secretariat. Throughout its history the OECD was first and foremost an international organization made up of nation states, and employed many economists but still acted very much in the framework of international power relations and inter-state negotiations. Analyzing the OECD as a Cold War institution—as shown in the following chapter, it served as an "economic NATO" during the 1950s and 1960s—helps in understanding the OECD more generally, also at present, in its *geopolitical* dimension and its search for a new, post-Cold-War role.

And finally, the OECD is characterized by its survival strategies in competition with other international organizations, by its fundamental (geo)political and identity-defining role, by formal and informal hierarchies, by restricted spaces within the organization, and by internal rivalries, both between countries and between its different directorates. As will be shown throughout this volume, the historical significance of the OECD can thus only inadequately be understood if we consider it as a non-hierarchical and knowledge-based expert talking shop. The twelve original contributions gathered here do not analyze the OEEC/OECD in an insular manner, but in its multiple relations to member states and other international organizations. In particular, they insert the organization's history within key trends of the twentieth century, most importantly decolonization, the rise of the West, and the Cold War. And, by consciously focusing not only on the OECD archives but also on other source material such as national archives of key member countries, or archives from other international organizations, the contributions analyze the workings of this organization in some of the hitherto neglected key areas at the heart of the OECD's outlook: international economic governance.

What Do We Know About the OEEC/OECD? A Short State of the Art

Although the scarcity of publications on the OEEC as an organization is striking, this organization was at the heart of the well-researched European Recovery Program (ERP).[10] Long-standing controversies between traditionalists, revisionists, post-revisionists, and corporatists have discussed the intentions, importance, and effects of the Marshall Plan.[11] Yet, most of this research has disregarded the role of the OEEC. An exception is Alan Milward's *Reconstruction of Western Europe*, which deals extensively with the first years of the OEEC. Milward's argument—that the American authorities' failure to turn the OEEC into an early prototype of a European supranational government had led to the "depoliticization" and "collapse" of the organization already by 1949—is partly responsible for the relative neglect of the OEEC's history.[12] Since the 1990s, however, historical scholarship has explored the continued flourishing of this organization by analyzing its specific contributions to European reconstruction, liberalization, and technical cooperation. On the occasion of the 50th anniversary of the Marshall Plan, the OECD commissioned an edited volume covering many fields of OEEC activity and also discussing the relation to some of its member countries.[13] Further, several monographs and articles analyze the European Productivity Agency (EPA), the European Payments Union (EPU), the integration of Germany into this Western European organization, the OEEC's involvement in managing its member countries colonial relations, the organization's work on economic statistics and growth theories, and the free trade negotiations in the late 1950s.[14] Yet the period of transition from a Western European organization to an Atlantic and then triadic (Euro-Atlantic-Pacific) capitalist think tank has not been analyzed.[15]

As a matter of fact, it is only very recently that political scientists and sociologists have addressed the study of the OECD. Former OECD administrators have written several monographs on the general history and functioning of the Organization and on its various fields of activity, such as development cooperation, science, education, environment, trade and finance, social indicators, and the International Energy Agency.[16] These partly self-congratulatory accounts do not qualify as independent analysis and generally overstate the importance of the OECD. They nevertheless provide a rich source of information and interesting inside narratives on the workings of the bureaucracy and its committees and expert groups.

The lack of research on the OECD and its neglect by historians can to some extent be explained by the OECD's specific mode of governance, its politically neutral and non-controversial image, and the relative absence of historical interest by the OECD itself. Because of its self-representation as a soft power organization, the OECD has often escaped the attention of historical and political science scholars who have focused on traditional forms of economic and political power. Only after the constructivist turn and the new interest in economic expertise has this neglect been overcome among political scientists and scholars in international relations. Next, while other international organizations, such as the UN, IMF, or the World Bank, have sparked great societal hopes or opposition and thus become the target of heated public and scholarly debates, the OECD has yet to enjoy comparable exposure. The OECD is largely seen as a politically neutral think tank and a provider of statistics and detached expert advice that lacks significant sources of power and thus merits no critical scrutiny, even though its numbers and studies are cited regularly in newspapers and scholarly articles. Finally, contrary to other organizations such as the UN, the International Labour Organization (ILO), or the IMF, the OECD has not set up and financed a large research project on its own history and its extensive historical archives are not described, as of early 2017, as a satisfactory finding aid. (For a brief presentation of available resources, see the short archival guide in this volume.)

The few *scholarly* studies on the OECD that appeared before 1990 were largely factual descriptions of the structure of the organization or dealt with specific questions such as export credits or the 1977

McCracken report.[17] Early political science studies already noted the particular communicative and monitoring functions of the organization and its lack of legal or financial power.[18] It was not before the early 2000s, however, that international political economy scholars started to pay serious attention to the OECD and published several edited volumes and articles on the OECD. These studies are similar in four respects: they are generally very theoretical and focus on defining, identifying, and explaining the specific modes of OECD governance; in contrast to historical research on the OEEC and to earlier studies they have emphasized the importance and effectiveness of the OECD's soft power influence; they mostly deal with post-1989 developments; and they have not used archival sources but solely rely on published material and sometimes on interviews.

Political and social scientists working in the perspective of the sociology of organizations have analyzed the OECD as an "ideational artist," arbitrator, and authority, as an "orchestrator of global knowledge networks" and "norm entrepreneur," and have generally emphasized the "discursive power" of the organization.[19] The few attempts to substantiate these allegations provide no definite answer. On the one hand, a collective research project on the OECD's impact on national welfare policies found little clear-cut evidence to support the influence usually attributed to the OECD in theoretical and cursory accounts.[20] On the other hand, several studies focusing on the OECD's role in specific policy fields have revealed the many-faceted and varying ways in which the Organizations has indeed influenced member country governments, other international organizations, or public debates. Comparative research into soft regulation in the OECD, the IMF, and the EU, for example, has argued that the so-called open method of coordination currently used in the EU had been adopted from the OECD.[21] Other examples can be found in the areas of financial liberalization,[22] environmental policies,[23] public management reform,[24] educational policies,[25] trade,[26] capital movements,[27] science policy,[28] international taxation,[29] development policies,[30] crisis management,[31] nuclear engineering,[32] and labor market reform.[33]

More recently, scholars have called for a "public administrative turn" in the study of international organizations. A comparative research project has studied the OECD, GATT, and the European Commission as "compound bureaucracies," focusing on the OECD staff and the influence of bureaucratic practices on their work.[34] Further, researchers in international political economy have stressed the importance of the

OECD in the creation of technocratic networks of experts that help member states manage the increasingly complex "transnational global governance."[35] And in the run-up to the OECD's 50th anniversary in 2011, two edited volumes have presented research on many of the different issues the OECD works on.[36]

Yet because these studies have not used the vast archives of the OECD and have focused on the period since the late 1980s, we still lack a clear understanding of the long-term evolution of the structure and functioning of the organization and its modes of governance. The historical literature on the OECD is extremely sparse. It includes accounts on the OECD's science statistics,[37] its work on colonial relations and development aid,[38] the competition between OECD and ILO in analyzing the "crisis of the welfare state" in the 1970s,[39] a sociological analysis of the production of the 1977 McCracken report,[40] contributions on the role of the OECD in the regulation of multinational enterprises,[41] its early fight against tax evasion,[42] as well as an overview of OECD work in some of its fields by public administration scholars.[43] Furthermore, Matthias Schmelzer's recent monograph analyzes the history and role of the OEEC and OECD with a focus on its key policy goal: the shaping, upholding, and diffusion of growth policies after 1945.[44] Related work has analyzed the OECD's late-1960s discussion on the so-called "problems of modern society" and the connections between the OECD and the Club of Rome.[45] These and other historical works form the backbone of the overview of the OEEC/OECD's trajectory that is presented in the next chapter.

This volume delineates fundamental features of the OEEC/OECD, presents innovative analyses of its manifold initiatives, and identifies key contexts, countries, institutions, and protagonists which contributed to structure its actions from 1948 onward. By shedding light on these various dimensions, we hope that it will be used as a roadmap for ongoing and future research.

The Structure and Content of This Volume

Following a full historical overview of the OEEC/OECD trajectory, which serves as a common background for the individual case studies gathered in this volume, this book is structured in three parts. The first part, entitled "Being part of the West," discusses processes of inclusion and exclusion, of membership, identity, and otherness. These issues are key to understanding the importance of the OEEC/OECD—an organization fundamentally understood by its members as an exclusive "club"—and thus play a key role in all chapters of this volume. Membership in this grouping is only by invitation, and is a complicated procedure. The significance of being among "OECD countries" has historically evolved and has oscillated between a regional demarcation (first "Western Europe", then "the West" or "the Global North") and a functionalist understanding (capitalist or free, developed or rich, and "democratic," though Southern European dictatorships and military regimes in Greece and Turkey were also members). In all this, the "other" against which this grouping was constructed played a key role, in particular Cold War opponents and the countries in the colonized and then decolonizing Global South. How did these processes of construction work? What did it mean to be a member of the Club? And how did this play out in relation to outsiders?

By focusing on the intricate relationships of collaboration and competition between the OEEC and the UN Economic Commission for Europe (ECE) in the late 1940s and early 1950s, Daniel Stinsky shows how the OEEC's foundation played a key role in the construction of Western Europe not only as a geopolitical, but also as an economic, unit. There were, indeed, competing forms of European integration, and the OEEC was just one of them. The others were the more restrictive and supranational European Coal and Steel Community (forerunner of the EEC), but also, as shown by Stinsky, the pan-European UNECE, which straddled the Iron Curtain. Even though the OEEC, and then the OECD, was an immanently Western organization, it kept multifaceted bridges across the Iron Curtain. An interesting case in point is Yugoslavia, which for various reasons became an associated member of this Western Club. As argued by Andrej Markovic and Ivan Obadic, Belgrade's readiness for cooperation was founded, among other reasons, on its concern about deteriorating conditions for trade with the Western European countries, especially after the creation of the EEC and European Free Trade Area (EFTA). Their chapter emphasizes how the cooperation between Yugoslavia and the OEEC/OECD provided Belgrade with an important mechanism for the transfer of knowledge essential to both the modernization of Yugoslavia's economy and the adoption of Western concepts by Yugoslav planners and economists who tried to manage the economy more effectively.

By analyzing the factors that led to Japanese, Australian, and New Zealand membership in the OECD in the 1960s and early 1970s and the initial reactions of officials working with the Paris-based OECD, Peter Carroll highlights that membership in the OECD can be characterized, in part, as a search for economic security on the basis of expanded access to, and influence within, a powerful international organization. While East-West relations continued to play a key role, with the onset of decolonization in the late 1950s the Global South moved center stage within the OECD's strategy. As Patricia Hongler argues, the OECD's Development Assistance Committee (DAC) worked as a place in the 1960s where the West positioned itself as a competent center of rationality versus an emotional and needy Global South. By focusing on the first UN Conference on Trade and Development (UNCTAD) in 1964, she portrays the DAC as an exclusive donors' club that produced knowledge about development assistance without entering into dialogue with the receivers of aid. Her chapter shows how important North-South relations were to the OECD.

The second part, "Managing the economy," focuses on the OECD's key area of work, economic policies. While the OECD's economic activities have largely been overlooked in the historical literature on this organization, it is clear that, not least through its focus on promoting economic growth but also more generally, the OECD acted—or tried to act—as a warden of the world capitalist economy. Its key tasks were not only the complex management of the economic relations of its member countries, with a particular focus on economic planning and the liberalization of trade and capital flows, but also the establishment of new forms of governance that enabled its member countries to "open up" sensitive information on economic policy-making and tried to harmonize the national economic policies of its member countries. Of course, the specific economic ideology dominant within the Secretariat in Paris and the various committees of the OECD as well as their recommendations and policies have varied fundamentally not only between various parts of the Organization, but also, most importantly, over time. While economic planning, inspired by Keynesian policies, shaped the early decades of the OECD's history, from the mid-1970s onward neoliberal ideas became more prominent—a shift discussed in the three chapters of this part.

To begin with, Wolfram Kaiser analyzes the OECD's role in steel, a core industrial policy field that came to be at the heart of European economic integration. Taking a long-term perspective that brings us up to the late 1980s, the author analyzes how competition and cooperation with other international organizations, including the UNECE and the ECSC, shaped OECD policies. Due to its limited legal competences, financial resources, and spatial scope, the OECD had to be especially flexible in the steel sector in carving out a changing role and identity for itself. This chapter also underscores how the OEEC/OECD, while remaining in the backseat in comparison to ECSC, offered a platform to discuss steel issues across the Atlantic as well as with emerging Asian producers such as Japan and, from the 1970s onward, South Korea. The following two contributions analyze the role and functions of two specific OECD committees. In his contribution, Kazuhiko Yago presents the work of the famed "Working Party No. 3 on Policies for the Promotion of Better International Payments Equilibrium" of the OECD Economic Policy Committee. Besides growth management, monitoring financial and monetary stability was of paramount importance for the Paris Organization, and this task was performed by the WP3. With its restricted and selected membership, this Committee played an important role as an informal meeting point for key central bankers and finance ministry officials dealing with the adjustments of balance of payments issues under fixed exchange rates. With the unraveling of the Bretton Woods order during the 1970s, the WP3 lost much of its pre-eminence. William Gray analyzes the annual reviews of economic performance organized by the Economic and Development Review Committee (EDRC) and during which OECD countries submitted themselves to the scrutiny of their peers. These peer review rituals served several functions: they encouraged accountability among members, offered members a forum to present and discuss domestic issues, and let smaller countries tread on a stage that was mostly occupied by the largest powers.

In his chapter, Samuel Beroud analyzes the changing economic paradigms that guided OECD policies during and after the crisis of the 1970s by retracing the emergence of positive adjustment measures. By analyzing these attempts to bolster OECD members' economies in the face of inflation and economic crisis, Beroud highlights the unraveling of Keynesian demand-based expertise within the Organization and its gradual shift toward supply-side solutions. However, this change would not be finalized until the mid-1980s and his study forewarns us about too hasty conclusions about the rise of neoliberalism among international bureaucracies.

The third and final part of the volume, "Coping with socio-ecological challenges," analyzes other key areas of OECD activity dealing with the social or ecological contexts that emerged in the background of the core economic policy focus of the Organization. These contributions also examine how the OECD found (or lost) its place in the ever more crowded arena of international organizations working in the fields of migration, education, environmental policy, or gender and development. In their contribution on migration policy, Emmanuel Comte and Simone Paoli underscore the recurring tensions that pitted the Southern European countries of the OEEC/OECD against their Northern counterparts. The Organization was thus unable to liberalize labor migration flows and gradually lost its precedence in this domain to the ascendant EEC. In a second contribution dealing with issues linked to human capital, Regula Bürgi retraces the foundation in 1968 of the Center for Educational Research and Innovation, a joint venture between the OECD Secretariat, member countries, and the US Ford Foundation. These early activities in the domain of education modernization and planning led to the gradual rise to prominence of the OECD vis-à-vis less successful competitors such as UNESCO. It also set the institutional basis for comparative education statistics and performance rankings such as the PISA surveys.

With her focus on environmental issues, Iris Borowy analyzes how the OECD engaged with ecological challenges but also worked to channel responses to these challenges in ways that would make them compatible with growth and market principles. In this context, the shaping and diffusion of new norms and standards, such as the Polluter Pays Principle, played a key role. In the last contribution to this volume, Rianne Mahon examines how women experts and civil servants active in the field of development, the so-called "femocrats," raised awareness for gender issues within the OECD bureaucracy, and especially its Development Assistance Committee. This case study underscores the relative permeability of the Organization to advocacy networks and the ability of these networks to shape a space of their own within the OECD bureaucracy.

Notes

1. *OECD at Work* (Paris: OECD, 1969), 1 (emphasis added); Ron Gass, "Speaking Truth to Power," *The OECD Observer* 296 (2013).
2. The idea of "Club of the Rich" doesn't necessarily refer to the OECD. This term was also used by countries from the Global South to describe

the Group of 10 countries of the IMF. More recently, the OECD has sometimes also been described as "a club of mainly rich countries". See "What countries can learn from PISA tests?", *The Economist*, 10 December 2016.

3. See in particular Richard Woodward, *The Organisation for Economic Co-Operation and Development (OECD)* (London and New York: Routledge, 2009); Rianne Mahon and Stephen McBride, eds., *The OECD and Transnational Governance* (Vancouver: University of British Columbia Press, 2008); Kerstin Martens and Anja P. Jakobi, eds., *Mechanisms of OECD Governance: International Incentives for National Policy Making* (Oxford: Oxford University Press, 2010); Peter Carroll and Aynsley Kellow, *The OECD. A Study of Organisational Adaptation* (Cheltenham: Edward Elgar, 2011); Jarle Trondal et al., *Unpacking International Organisations. The Dynamics of Compound Bureaucracies* (Manchester: Manchester University Press, 2010). See also the Fall 2011 issue of the *Review of International Political Economy* and the Spring 2014 issue of the *Journal of Comparative Policy Analysis,* most importantly Judith Clifton and Daniel Díaz-Fuentes, "The OECD and Phases in the International Political Economy, 1961–2011," *Review of International Political Economy* 18, no. 5 (2011): 552–569.
4. See the programmatic essay by Patrick O'Brien, "Historiographical Traditions and Modern Imperatives for the Restoration of Global History," *Journal of Global History* 1, no. 1 (2006): 3–39.
5. See, for example, Akira Iriye, *Global Community: The Role of International Organizations in the Making of the Contemporary World* (Berkeley and Los Angeles: University of California Press, 2002); Madeleine Herren, *Internationale Organisationen seit 1865. Eine Globalgeschichte der internationalen Ordnung* (Darmstadt: Wissenschaftliche Buchgesellschaft, 2009); Bob Reinalda, *Routledge History of International Organizations: From 1815 to the Present Day* (London and New York: Routledge, 2009).
6. Michele Alacevich, *The Political Economy of the World Bank: The Early Years* (Stanford: Stanford University Press, 2009); Patricia Clavin, *Securing the World Economy: The Reinvention of the League of Nations, 1920–1946* (Oxford: Oxford University Press, 2013); Harold James, *International Monetary Cooperation since Bretton Woods* (Washington: Oxford University Press, 1996); Francine McKenzie, *Accidental Organization: The GATT and Global Geopolitics, 1947–1994* (forthcoming).
7. See Niklas Noaksson and Kerstin Jacobsson, "The Production of Ideas and Expert Knowledge in OECD: The OECD Jobs Strategy in Contrast with the EU Employment Strategy" (Stockholm: SCORE, 2003); Carroll and Kellow, *OECD*; J.M. Dostal, "Campaigning on Expertise: How the OECD Framed EU Welfare and Labour Market Policies and Why Success

Could Trigger Failure," *Journal of European Public Policy* 11, no. 3 (2004): 440–460.

8. Gunnar Sjöstedt, "OECD-Samarbetet: Funktioner och effekter" (Stockholms Universitet, 1973); Tony Porter and Michael Webb, "The Role of the OECD in the Orchestration of Global Knowledge Networks," in *The OECD and Transnational Governance*, ed. Rianne Mahon and Stephen McBride (Vancouver: University of British Columbia Press, 2008), 43–59; Martin Marcussen, "The OECD as Ideational Artist and Arbitrator: Reality or Dream?," in *Decision Making Within International Organizations*, ed. Bob Reinalda and Bertjan Verbeek (London and New York: Routledge, 2004), 90–105.
9. See for example http://www.oecd.org/about/, and the OECD-made promotional film "OECD at 50: How's Life?" (2011), https://www.youtube.com/watch?v=MIEzs_AlxPE. See also Carroll and Kellow, *The OECD*.
10. Wendy Asbeek Brusse and Richard T. Griffiths, "Exploring the OEEC's Past: The Potentials and the Sources," in *Explorations in OEEC History*, ed. Richard T. Griffiths (Paris: OECD, 1997), 15–32. See also the annotated bibliography: *The European Reconstruction 1948–1961: A Bibliography on the Marshall Plan and the Organisation for European Economic Co-operation and Development* (Paris: OECD, 1996). Open access versions of both volumes are available on the OECD website.
11. While traditionalists have interpreted the Marshall Plan as a successful financial aid program that saved OEEC countries from economic disaster and communist expansion and launched the unprecedented growth of the 1950s, revisionists have highlighted the strategic hegemonic and imperialist motives behind the United States' operations in Europe in the Cold War context. Since the 1980s, the post-revisionist and corporatist interpretations of the ERP, which were based on the newly opened governmental archives, have focused on other strategic and slowly evolving American interests besides communist containment and have stressed the United States' interest in European integration, the integration of trade unions, and the promotion of productivity. The main controversies since then have discussed whether the ERP succeeded in contributing to the rise in European production, investment and trade, or whether European reconstruction was already on its way before and independently of the ERP funding. See in particular Lawrence S. Kaplan, "The Cold War and European Revisionism," *Diplomatic History* 11, no. 2 (1987): 143–156; Barry J. Eichengreen, *Europe's Post-war Recovery* (Cambridge University Press, 1995); Michael J. Hogan, *The Marshall Plan: America, Britain, and the Reconstruction of Western Europe, 1947–1952* (Cambridge: Cambridge University Press, 1987); Imanuel Wexler, *The Marshall*

Plan Revisited: The European Recovery Program in Economic Perspective (Westport: Greenwood Press, 1983).

12. Alan Milward, *The Reconstruction of Western Europe, 1945–51* (Berkeley and Los Angeles: University of California Press, 1987), 56–125, 168–211.
13. Richard T. Griffiths, ed., *Explorations in OEEC History* (Paris: OECD, 1997).
14. Bent Boel, *The European Productivity Agency and Transatlantic Relations, 1953–1961* (Copenhagen: Museum Tusculanum Press, 2003); Werner Bührer, *Westdeutschland in der OEEC: Eingliederung, Krise, Bewährung 1947–1961* (München: Oldenbourg-Verlag, 1998); Jacob J. Kaplan and Günther Schleiminger, *The European Payments Union: Financial Diplomacy in the 1950s* (Oxford: Oxford University Press, 1989); Patricia Hongler, "Die OEEC und ihre unsichtbare Kolonialgeschichte. Lektüre einer Kakaostudie von 1956," in *Neue Beiträge zur Wirtschaftsgeschichte/ Nouvelles contributions à l'histoire économique*, ed. Thomas David, Tobias Straumann, and Simon Teuscher (Zürich: Chronos, 2015), 235–250; Hans Evers, *Die Entwicklungsgebiete im Rahmen der OEEC und ihre Förderung*, Forschungsberichte des Landes Nordhein-Westfalen Nr. 1071 (Köln: Westdeutscher Verlag, 1962); Matthias Schmelzer, *The Hegemony of Growth. The Making and Remaking of the Economic Growth Paradigm and the OECD, 1948–2010* (Cambridge: Cambridge University Press, 2016), Part 1; Matthias Schmelzer, "Die Vermessung, der Wirtschaft': Konstruktionen und Kontroversen in der internationalen Standardisierung der volkswirtschaftlichen Gesamtrechnung, 1940er- und 50er-Jahre," in *Die Innenwelt der Ökonomie: Wissen, Macht und Performativität in der Wirtschaftswissenschaft,* ed. Jens Maeße, Hanno Pahl, and Jan Sparsam (Wiesbaden: Springer VS, 2016), 287–310; Gabriele Brenke, "Europakonzeptionen im Widerstreit. Die Freihandelszonen-Verhandlungen 1956–1958," *Vierteljahrshefte für Zeitgeschichte* (1994): 595–633.
15. One exception is Richard T. Griffiths, "'An Act of Creative Leadership': The End of the OEEC and the Birth of the OECD," in *Explorations in OEEC History*, ed. Richard T. Griffiths (Paris: OECD, 1997), 235–256; Schmelzer, *Hegemony,* Chaps. 3 and 4. See also Julie Rausis, "Intégrer le nouvel ordre économique international. La Suisse face à la réforme de l'Organisation européenne de coopération économique (OECE), 1958–1961." MA thesis, University of Geneva, Paul Bairoch Institute of Economic History, 2014.
16. For general accounts see Jean Bonvin and Christian Morrisson, *L'Organisation de coopération et de développement économiques (OCDE)* (Paris: Presses universitaires de France, 1998); Miriam Camps, *"First World" Relationships: The Role of the OECD* (Paris: Atlantic Institute

for International Affairs, 1975); Henri Chavranski, *L'OCDE: au coeur des grands débats économiques*, (Paris: Documentation Française, 1997); Jean-H. Guilmette, *The Power of Peer Learning: Networks and Development Cooperation* (Ottawa: IDRC, 2008); Hugo J. Hahn and Albrecht Weber, *Die OECD, Organisation für Wirtschaftliche Zusammenarbeit und Entwicklung* (Baden-Baden: Nomos-Verlagsgesellschaft, 1976); OEEC, *The Organisation for European Economic Co-operation. History and Structure* (Paris: OEEC, 1960); *OECD, OECD. History, Structures, Aims* (Paris: OECD, 1973); Scott Sullivan, *From War to Wealth: Fifty Years of Innovation* (OECD, 1997). On particular fields of activity see Helmuth Führer, *The Story of Official Development Assistance: A History of the Development Assistance Committee and the Development Co-operation Directorate in Dates, Names and Figures* (Paris: OECD, 1996); Jorge Braga de Macedo, Colm Foy, and Charles Oman, eds., *Development Is Back* (Paris: OECD, 2002); Goran Ohlin, "The Organization for Economic Cooperation and Development," *International Organization* 22, no. 1 (1968): 231–243; Angus Maddison, "Confessions of a Chiffrephile," *Banca Nazionale Del Lavoro Quarterly Review* 189 (1994): 123–185; Alexander King, "Scientific Concerns in an Economic Environment: Science in OEEC-OECD," *Technology in Society* 23, no. 3 (2001): 337–348; Bill L. Long, *International Environmental Issues and the OECD, 1950–2000: An Historical Perspective* (Paris: OECD, 2000); David E. Christian, "International Social Indicators: The OECD Experience," *Social Indicators Research* 1, no. 2 (1974): 169–186; George S. Papadopoulos, *Education 1960–1990: The OECD Perspective.* (Paris: OECD, 1994); David Henderson, "The Role of the OECD in Liberalising International Trade and Capital Flows," *The World Economy* 19 (1996): 11–28; David John Blair, *Trade Negotiations in the OECD: Structures, Institutions, and States* (London: Kegan Paul International, 1993); Richard Scott, *The History of the International Energy Agency: The First Twenty Years* (Paris: International Energy Agency, 1994); Craig S. Bamberger, *The History of the International Energy Agency, 1974–2004* (Paris: International Energy Agency, 2004).

17. Henry C. Aubrey, *Atlantic Economic Cooperation: The Case of the OECD* (New York: Praeger, 1967); Miriam Camps, *"First World" Relationships: The Role of the OECD* (Paris: Atlantic Institute for International Affairs, 1975); Michele Fratianni and John C. Pattison, "The Economics of the OECD," Carnegie-Rochester Conference Series on Public Policy 4, no. 1 (1976): 75–140; Michael Henderson, "The OECD as an Instrument of National Policy," International Journal 36, no. 4 (1981): 793–814; A.M. Moravcsik, "Disciplining Trade Finance: The OECD Export Credit

Arrangement," *International Organization* 43, no. 1 (1989): 173–205; Robert O. Keohane, "Economics, Inflation, and the Role of the State: Political Implications of the McCracken Report," *World Politics* 31, no. 1 (1978): 108–128.

18. Gunnar Sjöstedt, "OECD-Samarbetet: Funktioner och effekter" (Stockholms Universitet, 1973); Michael Henderson, "The OECD as an Instrument of National Policy," *International Journal* 36, no. 4 (1981): 793–814.
19. Martin Marcussen, "The OECD in Search of a Role: Playing the Idea Game," in *ECPR Joint Session of Workshops, Grenoble*, 2001; Martin Marcussen, *OECD Og Idéspillet—Game Over?* (Copenhagen: Hans Reitzels Forlag, 2002); Martin Marcussen, "The OECD as Ideational Artist and Arbitrator: Reality or Dream?," in *Decision Making Within International Organizations*, ed. Bob Reinalda and Bertjan Verbeek (London: Routledge, 2004), 90–105; T. Porter and M. Webb, "The Role of the OECD in the Orchestration of Global Knowledge Networks," in *International Studies Association Annual Meeting, Montreal*, 2004; J.M. Dostal, "Campaigning on Expertise: How the OECD Framed EU Welfare and Labour Market Policies–and Why Success Could Trigger Failure," *Journal of European Public Policy* 11, no. 3 (2004): 440–460. See also Robert Wolfe, "From Reconstructing Europe to Constructing Globalization: The OECD in Historical Perspective," in *The OECD and Transnational Governance*, ed. Rianne Mahon and Stephen McBride (Vancouver: University of British Columbia Press, 2008), 25–42.
20. Klaus Armingeon and Michelle Beyeler, eds., *The OECD and European Welfare States* (Cheltenham: Edward Elgar Publishing, 2004); Dostal, "Campaigning on Expertise."
21. Armin Schäfer, *Die neue Unverbindlichkeit: Wirtschaftspolitische Koordinierung in Europa* (Frankfurt a.M.: Campus-Verlag, 2004); Armin Schäfer, "A New Form of Governance? Comparing the Open Method of Co-ordination to Multilateral Surveillance by the IMF and the OECD," *Journal of European Public Policy* 13, no. 1 (2006): 70.
22. Rawi Abdelal, *Capital Rules. The Construction of Global Finance* (Cambridge: Harvard University Press, 2009).
23. Per-Olof Busch, "The OECD Environment Directorate. The Art of Persuasion and Its Limits," in *Managers of Global Change: The Influence of International Environmental Bureaucracies*, ed. Frank Biermann and Bernd Siebenhüner (Cambridge: MIT Press, 2009), 75–99; Markku Lehtonen, "OECD Peer Reviews and Policy Convergence. Diffusing Policies or Discourses?," in *International Organizations in Global Environmental Governance*, ed. Frank Biermann, Bernd Siebenhüner, and Schreyögg (London: Routledge, 2009), 71–90.

24. Leslie A. Pal, *Frontiers of Governance: The OECD and Global Public Management Reform* (Basingstoke: Palgrave Macmillan, 2012).
25. Myuung-Shin Kim, *Bildungsökonomie und Bildungsreform: Der Beitrag der OECD in den 60er und 70er Jahren*, vol. 17 (Königshausen & Neumann, 1994); Kjell Rubenson, "OECD Education Policies and World Hegemony," in *The OECD and Transnational Governance*, 2009, 242–259; Pedro N. Teixeira, "A Portrait of the Economics of Education, 1960–1997," *History of Political Economy* 32, no. Suppl. 1 (2000): 257–287.
26. Blair, *Trade Negotiations in the OECD.*
27. Abdelal, *Capital Rules.*
28. Edgeir Benum, "Making Research Count: Norway and the OECD Connection 1965–1980," *Minerva* 45, no. 4 (2007): 365–387.
29. Richard Eccleston and Robert Woodward. "Pathologies in International Policy Transfer: The Case of the OECD Tax Transparency Initiative," *Journal of Comparative Policy Analysis: Research and Practice* 16, no. 3 (2014): 216–229. See also endnote 42, below.
30. Ken Masujima, "'Good Governance' and the Development Assistance Committee: Ideas and Organizational Constraints," in *Global Institutions and Development: Framing the World?* ed. Morten Boas and Desmond McNeill (London: Routledge, 2003), 151–163; Arne Ruckert, "Making Neo-Gramscian Sense of the Development Assistance Committee: Toward an Inclusive Neoliberal World Development Order," in *The OECD and Transnational Governance*, ed. Rianne Mahon and Stephen McBride (Vancouver: University of British Columbia Press, 2008), 96–113; Guido Ashoff, *Entwicklungshilfeausschuss der OECD und die deutsche Entwicklungszusammenarbeit: ein Verhältnis auf dem Prüfstand* (Bonn: Weltforum-Verlag, 2000).
31. Benjamin Cohen, "When Giants Clash: The OECD Financial Support Fund and the IMF," in *Institutional Design for a Complex World: Bargaining, Linkages and Nesting*, ed. Vinod K. Aggarwal (Cornell University Press, 1998); Nicholas Bayne, *Hanging In There. The G7 and G8 Summit in Maturity and Renewal* (Aldershot: Ashgate, 2000).
32. Jean-Marc Wolff, *Eurochemic 1956–1990: Thirty-five Years of International Co-operation in the Field of Nuclear Engineering* (Paris: OECD, 1996).
33. Dostal, "Campaigning on Expertise"; Virginia A. Leary and Daniel. Warner, *Social Issues, Globalisation and International Institutions: Labour Rights and the EU, ILO, OECD and WTO* (Leiden: Nijhoff, 2006); James Salzman and Julio Bacio Terracino, "Labour Rights, Globalization and Institutions: The Role and Influence of the Organisation for Economic Cooperation and Development," in *Social Issues, Globalisation and International Institutions*, ed. Virginia A. Leary and Daniel Warner (Martinus Nijhoff Publishers, 2006), 311–402; J. Timo Weishaupt,

From the Manpower Revolution to the Activation Paradigm: Explaining Institutional Continuity and Change in an Integrating Europe (Amsterdam: Amsterdam University Press, 2011).

34. Jarle Trondal et al., *Unpacking International Organisations. The Dynamics of Compound Bureaucracies* (Manchester: Manchester University Press, 2010); Jarle Trondal, Martin Marcussen, and Frode Veggeland, "Re-discovering International Executive Institutions," *Comparative European Politics* 3, no. 2 (2005): 232–258; Martin Marcussen and Jarle Trondal, "The OECD Civil Servant: Caught Between Scylla and Charybdis," *Review of International Political Economy* 18, no. 5 (2011): 592–621.
35. Richard Woodward, *The Organisation for Economic Co-operation and Development*; Richard Woodward, "The Organisation for Economic Cooperation and Development," *New Political Economy* 9, no. 1 (2004): 113–127; Rianne Mahon and Stephen McBride, eds., *The OECD.*
36. Kerstin Martens and Anja P. Jakobi, eds., *Mechanisms of OECD Governance: International Incentives for National Policy Making* (Oxford: Oxford University Press, 2010). See also the fall 2011 issue of the *Review of International Political Economy*, most importantly Judith Clifton and Daniel Díaz-Fuentes, "The OECD and Phases in the International Political Economy, 1961–2011," *Review of International Political Economy* 18, no. 5 (2011): 552–569.
37. Benoît Godin, *Measurement and Statistics on Science and Technology: 1920 to the Present* (London: Routledge, 2005); Benoit Godin, *The Making of Science, Technology and Innovation Policy: Conceptual Frameworks as Narratives, 1945–2005* (Montréal: Institut national de la recherche scientifique, 2009).
38. Matthias Schmelzer, "A Club of the Rich to Help the Poor? The OECD, 'Development', and the Hegemony of Donor Countries," in *International Organizations and Development, 1945 to 1990*, ed Marc Frey, Sönke Kunkel, and Corinna Unger (Basingstoke: Palgrave Macmillan, 2014), 171–195.
39. Matthieu Leimgruber, "The Embattled Standard-bearer of Social Insurance and Its Challenger: The ILO, the OECD and the 'Crisis of the Welfare State', 1975–1985," in *Globalizing Social Rights: The International Labor Organization and Beyond*, ed. Sandrine Kott and Joëlle Droux (Basingstoke: Palgrave MacMillan, 2013), 293–309.
40. Vincent Gayon, "L'OCDE au travail. Contribution à une sociologie historique de la « coopération économique internationale » sur le chômage et l'emploi," PhD dissertation, Université Paris Dauphine, 2010. See also Vincent Gayon, "Un atelier d'écriture internationale: l'OCDE au travail. Éléments de sociologie de la forme 'rapport'," *Sociologie du Travail* 51, no. 3 (2009): 324–342; Vincent Gayon, "Le crédit vacillant de l'expert.

L'OCDE face au chômage dans les années 1990 et 2000," *Cultures & Conflits*, no. 75 (2009): 53–73.

41. Thomas Hajduk, "A code to bind them all: The multinational dilemma and the endeavour for an international code of conduct," in *Multinationale Unternehmen und Institutionen im Wandel—Herausforderungen für Wirtschaft, Recht und Gesellschaft*, ed. Sandra Brändli, Roman Schister, and Aurelia Tamò (Bern: Stämpfli Verlag, 2013), 311–339; Samuel Beroud and Thomas Hajduk, "OCDE et bonnes pratiques: Une histoire inséparable," in *Les bonnes pratiques des organisations internationales*, ed. A. Klein, C. Laport, and M. Saiget (Paris: Presses de Sciences Po, 2015), 59–75.
42. Matthieu Leimgruber, "Kansas City on Lake Geneva. Business hubs, tax evasion, and international connections around 1960," *Zeitschrift für Unternehmensgeschichte* 60, no. 2 (2015): 123–140; Christophe Farquet and Matthieu Leimgruber, "Catch me if you can! Tax havens, the market for tax evasion and fiscal diplomacy from the League of Nations to the OECD, 1920–1990," working paper, Paul Bairoch Institute of Economic History, University of Geneva, 2015.
43. Carroll and Kellow, *The OECD*. Unfortunately, this book only uses a small subset of select archival files from OECD's highest decision-making body, adopts a strict decadological periodization for all the working areas of the OECD, and relies in large part on OECD inside accounts.
44. Schmelzer, *Hegemony*.
45. Matthias Schmelzer, "The Crisis before the Crisis: The 'problems of Modern Society' and the OECD, 1968–74," *European Review of History* 19, no. 6 (2012): 999–1020; Matthias Schmelzer, "'Born in the Corridors of the OECD': The Forgotten Origins of the Club of Rome, Transnational Networks, and the 1970s in Global History," *Journal of Global History* 12, no. 1 (2017): 26–48.

From the Marshall Plan to Global Governance: Historical Transformations of the OEEC/OECD, 1948 to Present

Matthieu Leimgruber and Matthias Schmelzer

Understanding the OECD's role has long been a controversial and elusive quest. Already in 1964, Secretary-General Thorkil Kristensen complained that not only national delegates in the committees and working groups, but even the bureaucrats working for the OECD in Paris were constantly asking the same questions: "what should the OECD do; what is its domain; what is its raison d'être?"[1] Other questions are equally important: How can the OECD and its mode of functioning be conceptualized? What were its organizational structures and the underlying "anatomy of influence" and how have they evolved over time?[2] How did the OECD manage to survive the major transformations in the global political economy between its foundation and the present? How did the OECD contribute to the production, stabilization, generalization, and legitimation of macroeconomic knowledge, including statistics, models, conceptual frameworks, and policy norms? What was the OECD's relation to professional economics, to

M. Leimgruber (✉)
Department of History, University of Zürich, Rämistrasse 64,
CH-8001 Zurich, Switzerland
e-mail: matthieu.leimgruber@uzh.ch

M. Schmelzer
University of Jena, Humboldtstr. 34, 07743 Jena, Germany
e-mail: m.schmelzer@knoe.org

M. Leimgruber and M. Schmelzer (eds.), *The OECD and the International Political Economy Since 1948*, DOI 10.1007/978-3-319-60243-1_2

member countries, and to other international organizations; was it acting more as an agenda-setter or as a transmission belt of ideas produced elsewhere?[3] What were key developments, continuities, and ruptures?

These questions will be dealt with more comprehensively in the following chapters of this volume and we will not be able to fully answer them in this introductory essay. What we aim to do, however, is to introduce a historical framework of understanding. While the first section presents key OECD modes of governance, the rest of the chapter attempts to give an overview of the Organization's trajectory since 1948. The periodization we propose is linked to the mandates of the successive Secretary-Generals of the OECD, dates that tend to coincide with deeper transformations of the Organization's set-up, tasks, and overall outlook (see Table 1, below p. 26).[4] Even though the OECD was a Cold War institution structurally driven by member country interests and the underlying power structures, the Secretary-Generals (and other powerful officials) exerted a considerable influence on its running and priorities.[5] The conclusion draws together our argument and discusses the OECD as a (geo)political platform, as an expert think tank, and as an identity-generating club.

Ideas, Peers, and Numbers: OECD Modes of Governance

In the classical terminology proposed by Robert W. Cox and Harold K. Jacobson, the OECD can be described both as a "forum organization," providing a framework in which member countries exchanged views, negotiated common initiatives and agreements, and collectively legitimated their policies, and a "service organization," which itself conducted services important to member countries such as the collection, standardization, and dissemination of information and data.[6] In contrast to many international organizations, for the most part the OECD did not rely on legal or financial means to achieve agreements. While these did play a role for the OEEC, in particular in the distribution of Marshall Plan aid and regarding the European Payments Union (EPU) and the European Productivity Agency (EPA), the OECD largely relied on soft power mechanisms. Soft power—getting others to want the outcomes that you want—means that the OECD's way of working aimed at shaping the ideas and preferences of member countries.[7]

Drawing on constructivist, post-structural, and critical theories of international relations and existing political science and sociology studies on the OECD, three mechanisms are particularly important to understand the OECD's role in global governance and to distinguish it from other international organizations: production of policy ideas, policy evaluation, and data generation.[8] First, in its internal reports, the hundreds of annual routine or one-off studies, public statements, and speeches, the OECD produced policy ideas, developed scenarios, set agendas, defined guiding principles and narratives, and framed topics and cause-effect-relationships. By introducing new questions, perspectives, guiding concepts, or policy proposals, OECD officials used the Organization's committee structure, expert conferences, and the Organization's "semi-academic prose" to advance and diffuse their agenda, thus exercising some autonomy from member countries.[9]

Second, the OECD—"an organization of civil servants talking to civil servants"—was engaged in policy evaluation, coordination, and harmonization.[10] Even though financial incentives did play a considerable role in the early years of the OEEC, and some legally binding agreements were adopted (such as the Capital Movements Code), the core instrument of the Organization was the procedure of multilateral surveillance that was developed since the 1950s and became one of the hallmarks of the OECD. This involved processes of "confrontation," "examination," and "peer review." These processes are described in detail in William Gray's chapter in this volume, which analyzes how the performance of a particular member country was scrutinized and monitored by officials, civil servants, and experts from other member countries, leading, in most cases, to the publication of a report that included criticism and policy recommendations after a long process of joint redrafting. While the resultant recommendations did not directly force governments to change their policies, they often strengthened certain factions within national institutions by providing authoritative endorsement to a set of economic policies. Governments could thus use the OECD in the logic of what international relations scholars have described as a two-level game to muster international backing in national controversies. In the words of various sources, the OECD's advice often provided what German economist Alfred Müller-Armack called "effective fire support" for governments in national debates, and the OECD was used by governments as "an independent source against their critics both in and out of Parliament," or, by the US in the early 1960s, as an "ally in its relations with Congress on economic matters."[11] Sometimes, if the OECD worked as a "catalyst of unity" among member countries, it even served, according to contemporary US reports, as a forum to "pre-cook

Table 1 The OEEC/OECD trajectory, 1948–2016

	1948–1961	*1961–1969*	*1969–1984*	*1984–1996*	*1996–2016*	
Secretary-Generals	R. Marjolin (FRA) 1952–1955 R. Sergent (FRA) 1955–1960	Thorkil Kristensen (DK)	Emile van Lennep (NL)	Jean-François Paye (FRA)	Donald J. Johnston (CAN) 1996–2006	José Angel Gurria (MEX) 2006–
Members	*Marshall Plan beneficiaries (and their colonies)* *(N = 18)*[a]	+ *USA, Canada (1961), Japan (1964), Finland (1968), Australia (1971), New Zealand (1973)* *(N = 24)*			+ *Mexico, Czech Republic, Hungary, Korea, Poland (1994–1996), Slovak Republic (2000), Chile, Estonia, Israel, Slovenia, Latvia (2010–2016)* *(N = 35)*	
Perimeter	Western European (including colonies)—Atlantic	Triadic (Atlantic-Pacific)			Global	
Core areas of work	Reconstruction, liberalization of payments and trade, European Productivity Agency (EPA), "economic NATO"	Economic growth, stabilizing Bretton Woods, development aid	Stabilizing liberal capitalism, environment, integration in G7 system	Liberalization, deregulation, Multilateral Agreement on Investment (MAI), adapting to the end of the Cold War, Jobs Study	Managing globalization, financial governance, development, long-term problems	

(continued)

Table 1 (continued)

	1948–1961	*1961–1969*	*1969–1984*	*1984–1996*	*1996–2016*
Economic philosophy	Interventionist, increasingly Keynesian microeconomic	Keynesian consensus, macroeconomic demand side management	First focus on qualitative planning, then increasingly supply-side, microeconomic	Neoliberalism, Washington Consensus	Rethinking of neoliberalism, inclusive globalization
Raison d'être	Reconstruction, European integration, Atlantic cooperation	Economic Cold War, coordinating capitalist rich countries vis-à-vis communist bloc and Global South	Stabilizing economic relations among capitalist countries, rethinking quantitative growth paradigm	Deepening liberalization, managing the transformation of formerly Soviet countries	Stabilizing economic relations among member countries and with BRICS, rethinking the growth paradigm

[a]For a full list of OEEC/OECD members, see Table 1 in the Introduction. Yugoslavia joined as an observer in 1955 then became an associate member of the OECD in 1961. See the chapter by Andrej Markovic and Ivan Obadic in this volume

solutions to be implemented in other international organizations e.g., GATT, UN, IMF."[12] This clearly demonstrates the OECD's geopolitical role, as shown in the chapter by Patricia Hongler in this volume with regard to the OECD's Development Assistance Committee banding together against UNCTAD.

The third governance mechanism, data generation, describes the OECD's capacity to develop and standardize statistical concepts and to assemble large sets of internationally comparable quantitative data and long-term time series. From the beginning, the OECD successfully aimed at building up its "reputation for objectivity and impartiality which elicit increasing confidence in its work," as explained by one of the founding fathers of the Organization.[13] By the early 1970s, the *OECD Economic Surveys* and the *Economic Outlook* were widely regarded "as being the most reliable source of information available anywhere about the economic situation and policy of the country concerned."[14] The production of data in turn proved crucial in shaping the organizational procedures of the OECD as well as in creating its identity. Starting to work on a new area, the OECD regularly synthesized existing academic work and transformed it into a comparative perspective, allowing comparisons between countries and then internationalized existing data over time, and finally used rankings, benchmarking, and indicators to identify "leaders" and "laggards."[15] The publication of OECD rankings was a test of the performance of its member states that often sparked public debates and furthered a policy process of convergence toward what the ranking constructed as best practice.

While these mechanisms—ideas, peers, and data—help us understand the *actual* specificities of OECD work, a closer analysis of the OECD's historical trajectory—the core aim of the following sections and conclusion—reveals *other* important roles and modes of action.

Reconstruction, Liberalization, and Productivity: The OEEC and the Legacy of the Marshall Plan (1948–1961)

Assessments of the OEEC often tend to oscillate between the self-congratulatory perspective of insiders and dismissive scholarly remarks. As reported in 1956 by a US bureaucrat involved in the European Recovery Program (ERP):

> In corridor and dining room conversations during the past eight years among national representatives and Secretariat officials...it has often been boasted that the [OEEC] is the most successful of the many postwar experiments in international organization.[16]

While this view clearly obviated the OEEC's crisis-ridden evolution, historian Alan Milward has described the OEEC contribution as a process of "depoliticization," resulting in nothing more than a mere "forum for registering international agreements made elsewhere, increasingly of a minor kind." Similarly, he characterized the development of the OEEC as a "transition to honest statistical toil."[17] While Milward's perspective might capture the OEEC's legacy as evaluated in light of early American plans for European integration, it ignores crucial soft-power functions that came to characterize OEEC (and then OECD) work. The OEEC was faced with two organizational crises: in the early 1950s, when the Marshall Plan, for which it had been founded, ended; and in the late 1950s, when the OEEC was unable to resolve inner-European trade disputes. Both crises were resolved, and the second led to the re-foundation of the Organization. In this process, it both took on a geopolitical role in the Cold War setting and increasingly focused on the soft-power mechanisms that have become the hallmark of the OECD.[18]

The trajectory of the OEEC was set in the context of postwar reconstruction, the intensification of the Cold War, and diverging conceptions of Western European integration. It began with the Marshall Plan. Because ad-hoc and bilateral US postwar aid had not prevented worsening scarcities of food, housing, raw materials, and fuel, dwindling international liquidity paralyzed trade, and widespread social unrest and strong communist parties swamped many European countries, the US intervened with a more coordinated approach. In his June 1947 speech, Secretary of State George Marshall stated that longer-term US aid in the form of the ERP would be conditional on effective European co-operation in devising a common reconstruction plan.

In July 1947—after it had become clear that the Soviet Union and its satellites could not join this deliberately Western and Cold War program—France and Great Britain invited 16 other Western European countries to a conference that formed the Committee of European Economic Co-operation (CEEC). Although these deliberations were hampered by internal disputes, they led to the foundation of the OEEC in April 1948, with the commanders of the West German occupation zones (West Germany became a full member in 1949), and the US and Canada as observers (both became associated members in 1950). Even though the US was not a member (and only became a member in 1961 when the OEEC was reorganized as the OECD), its influence went far beyond that of many OEEC members, in particular in the early 1950s. The headquarters of the OEEC was set up in Paris as part of a deal between France and Britain, and in 1949 the OEEC moved into the Château de la Muette in the 16th arrondissement.[19]

While US and French authorities attempted to give the new Organization supranational powers, these efforts were successfully obviated by Britain, Sweden, and Switzerland, who promoted the foundation of a merely intergovernmental institution, foreclosing any transfer of sovereignty to the supranational level. As put by Milward, the US initiated the OEEC "as the first stage in the political and economic integration of Western Europe, the embryonic hope for a Western European government."[20] However, the OEEC did not become the executive branch of the United States of Europe. After it was decided that all decisions would have to be taken unanimously, French Planning Commissioner Jean Monnet, and his associates (with the exception of Robert Marjolin, who became Secretary-General of the OEEC) lost interest and pursued integration in the context of the Schuman-Plan.[21] At that time Monnet stated: "But the OEEC's nothing; it's only a watered-down British approach to Europe—talk, consultation, action only by unanimity. That's no way to make Europe."[22]

The Organization's first Secretary-General, Robert Marjolin (1911–1986, OEEC mandate: 1948–1955) was a young French politician and economist who had been involved in Charles de Gaulle's government-in-exile during World War II and closely collaborated with Jean Monnet. Born in a Parisian working class family in 1911, he took evening courses at the Sorbonne and became particularly influenced by two years studying sociology and economics at Yale as a fellow of the Rockefeller Foundation in the 1930s, which turned him from a young socialist into a fervent advocate of capitalist growth, state planning, and economic integration. Even though he was unable to transform the OEEC into the executive of European integration Monnet and he had hoped, Marjolin passionately led the OEEC in its first years and developed new strategic directions, in particular in the area of promoting long-term growth. However, by mid-1953 he grew frustrated with the slow progress toward European unification, came to regard the OEEC as having "outlived its time," and soon left the Château de la Muette to pursue an academic and diplomatic career (notably in the European Commission).[23]

However, in the first years of its existence the OEEC, with its intergovernmental structure, labored to propose a common recovery plan and an agreement on the distribution of US aid.[24] The delegates and experts in the Organization managed to draft yearly plans and to oversee the distribution of ERP funds, but agreement on the allocation of aid could only be reached through arbitration. Furthermore, under US pressure, the OEEC continuously liberalized intra-European trade from 1949 onward.[25] The creation of the European Payments Union (EPU) in September 1950 constituted another prominent achievement. Until its replacement by the European Monetary Agreement in 1958, and despite strains due to large payments imbalances, the EPU helped to rebuild currency convertibility, and thus alleviated the dollar problem by boosting intra-European trade.[26]

By the end of the Marshall Plan, the OEEC had been transformed from a standing political conference with a small staff and an unstable political agenda into an established international bureaucracy with highly formalized operation.[27] Until the mid-1950s, 13 "vertical committees" (coal, electricity, oil, iron and steel, machinery, textiles, chemical products, non-ferrous metals, timber, pulp and paper, food and agriculture, maritime transport, and inland transport) formed the core of the OEEC's economic coordination efforts. Their meetings provided European technicians, civil servants, and many industrialists with opportunities for exchange of views and the harmonization of outlooks and policies.[28] Alongside these vertical committees, several horizontal ones (economic, trade, intra-European payments, overseas territories, and productivity and applied research committee) discussed broader issues of economic cooperation. With the re-foundation of the OECD, the work of the vertical committees was considerably reduced. Apart from Wolfram Kaiser's study of the Steel Committee in this volume, much remains to be done to understand their actual contribution to postwar recovery.[29]

With the phasing out of Marshall Plan aid, the OEEC was losing its original raison d'être: European integration was pursued through competing routes such as the European Coal and Steel Community (ECSC), and, in the wake of the Korean War, several countries, most importantly the US and Britain, shifted their focus to NATO. This triggered an intense debate about the future of the OEEC. Proposals to either use NATO instead of the OEEC as the channel to distribute a blend of economic aid and military assistance, or to amalgamate the OEEC and the Council of Europe, almost dealt a lethal blow to the Organization.[30] A committee of three "wise men" set up to develop an economic strategy for NATO came up with the compromise that the OEEC should take responsibility for economic issues in Western Europe, focusing in particular on tasks of importance for the Atlantic alliance.[31] Decisive was not only the insistence of small countries, which valued the technical work of the OEEC, and of the neutrals, which resisted its militarization, but most importantly the interest of the US, which rejected cooperation with the Europeans on economic issues "as an equal with each of the other fourteen members of NATO or seventeen members of OEEC."[32] As will be discussed below, this stance would change by the end of the 1950s.

This first organizational crisis was resolved not only by turning the OEEC into the "'economic arm' of NATO"—both organizations collaborated very closely—but also by opening up new areas of activity.[33] For example, the OEEC championed the standardization of international economic statistics and became an important site for transatlantic norms production and governance, in particular through the European Productivity Agency (EPA) and by coordinating growth policies. During its existence between 1953 and 1961, the EPA, which worked as a semi-autonomous OEEC body and accounted for 40% of its budget, sent over 3,000 specialists and hundreds of farmers to US factories and farms to spread the "productivity gospel."[34] Furthermore, the OEEC played an important role in colonial affairs—a fact largely ignored in historical scholarship. In the Organization's understanding, the African and Asian colonies of its members were part of the OEEC, and its Overseas Territories Committee coordinated common interests of the European colonial powers, trade issues, and early development aid.[35]

In contrast to the successful work on liberalizing payments and on productivity, the OEEC's diverse membership and mode of governance (decisions by consensus, little legal powers) proved to be ill-suited for the deepening of trade liberalization and in particular the creation of a Western European free trade zone without quotas and tariffs. The OEEC had passed a Liberalization Code in 1952 and continuously worked—rather successfully—through its Trade Liberalization Program on lowering intra-European trade restrictions.[36] Yet, by the mid-1950s, the six members of the ECSC started to push for a customs union and a common market, which raised the threat of a discriminatory bloc within the OEEC.[37]

As a result, from 1956 until its dissolution, the OEEC became entangled in an unsuccessful attempt to form a pan-European free trade area as an alternative to a restrictive customs union, and the standoff between two rival blocs of member countries paralyzed its work. The looming feud between inter-governmentalists and supra-nationalists within the Western European alliance intensified when the ECSC, with tacit US support, established the European Economic Community (EEC) in 1957 with common external tariffs.[38] Incapable of bringing together France and Britain, the OEEC's future was seriously cast into doubt, in particular after "the Seven" (the non-ECSC fraction) started negotiations that led to the creation of the European Free Trade Association (EFTA) in 1960.[39] This antagonism culminated in the hostile break-up of the OEEC's Ministerial meeting in December 1958, which gave a final blow to an organization whose final two years were characterized by the continuous crisis and dissolution of its Secretariat.[40]

René Sergent (1904–1984), who succeeded Robert Marjolin in April 1955 and was Secretary-General throughout the difficult period until the dissolution of the OEEC in September 1960, was another high-ranking French civil servant. Born in a Parisian banking family, he studied at the École Polytechnique and gained extensive experience in the Ministry of Finance, the Allied Control Authority in postwar occupied Germany, and the French embassy in London. Immediately before he became Secretary-General of the OEEC, Sergent was NATO-Assistant Secretary-General (1952–1955), focusing on economic and financial issues. His appointment tightened the many personal and institutional links between the OEEC and NATO, which have been mentioned earlier. It was also an expression of the strengthened tacit alliance between the military and the economic organizations on the Western side of the Cold War conflict. Not only due to the difficulties with resolving the internal disputes about the pan-European free trade area in the late 1950s, but also because of his personal lack of proficiency to effectively steer the OEEC, Sergent's term was widely regarded by member countries as a failure.[41]

Planning, Development, and Cold War Competition: The "Temple of Growth" in Its First Decade (1961–1969)

In sharp contrast to its official historiography, the OEEC was not transformed into the OECD merely because the success of the intra-European trade and payments schemes had made the former Organization superfluous. Rather, after a decade of existence, the OEEC experienced a second existential crisis. As couched in an internal British report, by 1959 the OEEC had become "precarious in the extreme—impossible to kill but very difficult to keep alive."[42] An analysis of this transitional period underscores that continuities in structure, governance mechanisms, and personnel greatly outweighed the substantial changes: the foundation of the OECD constituted more a key "turning point" than a break.[43]

As the OEEC was entangled in its failing attempt to agree on a trade agreement, a new field of transnational governance was increasingly discussed among policy-makers and experts, in particular among US officials, Pentagon experts, and European Commission circles: the need for closer Atlantic cooperation to counter the Soviet economic offensive and to cope with the emergence of the Global South. NATO was unprepared to meet the Soviet offensive on the economic front of the Cold War, in particular in the decolonizing world, and French threats to partly withdraw from NATO disrupted its unity.[44] Further, the rich countries lost their majority in, and thus their ability to dominate, the United Nations around 1960.[45] In this context the idea emerged to transform the OEEC into an Atlantic organization, with the US and Canada as full members, that would focus on two key tasks: coordinating Western responses to the business cycle to boost economic growth, and setting up aid programs to counter communist influence in developing countries and help these countries in their take off toward self-sustained capitalist growth.[46]

Again, the US government was the key driving force behind the foundation of the OECD.[47] In November 1959, the US administration began to consider becoming –alongside Canada, and a few years later Japan– a full member of the OEEC, a fundamental shift from its position during the 1950s, when the US had enjoyed great influence within the OEEC without any of the obligations of full membership. The US estimated that a "revitalized" OEEC could solve two pressing problems: how to increase aid flows from Western European partners and how to prevent an imminent "trade war" between the Six and the Seven. Furthermore, the US aimed at solving severe balance of payments problems related to the functioning of the Bretton Woods system (the US economy had accrued a considerable deficit in the later 1950s), and to strengthen the role of US dollar as the global lead currency by joining the OECD and thus gaining more direct influence over the monetary policies of the larger partner countries.[48] The emergence of international development aid—one of the key activities envisaged for the reorganized OECD—was not only related to Cold War concerns and decolonization, but also had a key function in balancing US deficits though increased foreign aid of surplus countries such as Japan or West Germany.[49] The underlying concern, however, was economic growth. As stated in a memorandum to President Eisenhower:

> If these two vital problems in the field of development and trade are not dealt with through cooperative action, they could lead to a serious decline in the rate of economic growth of the Free World (which must be increased in the face of the Communist threat).[50]

Cold War growth rates were thus at the core of the OECD's (re)foundation.[51] Indeed, in the 1960s, growth became the defining policy goal of the OECD. It was the first aim in its Convention, which prompted countries "to achieve the highest sustainable economic growth," and growth has since then featured prominently at all Ministerial meetings. One could interpret this focus as the "organizational ideology" of the OECD, which has been described by one of its most influential directors as "a kind of temple of growth for industrialized countries—growth for growth's sake was what mattered."[52] At its first Ministerial meeting in 1961, the OECD passed an ambitious growth target for the 1960s—to increase the combined Gross National Product (GNP) of its member countries by 50%.[53] Accordingly, the OECD steered the work of most of its committees toward increasing their specific "contribution" to reaching this growth target.[54] By the mid-1960s, with the subsequent entry of Japan in the Organization, the OECD area garnered around 70% of the world's GDP, a level which represented the apex of its economic predominance (see Fig. 1). With the accession of Finland (1968), Australia (1971) and New Zealand (1973), the OECD community straddled the triadic structure of Western capitalism.

The OEEC had already established itself as an international stronghold of broadly demand-oriented Keynesian policies while at the same time upholding the importance of free trade and price stability. Until the mid-1970s, the OECD further strengthened this outlook and was accordingly known as "the house that Keynes built"—a description that certainly overemphasizes the Keynesian influence.[55] In line with what political scientist John Ruggie described as "embedded liberalism,"

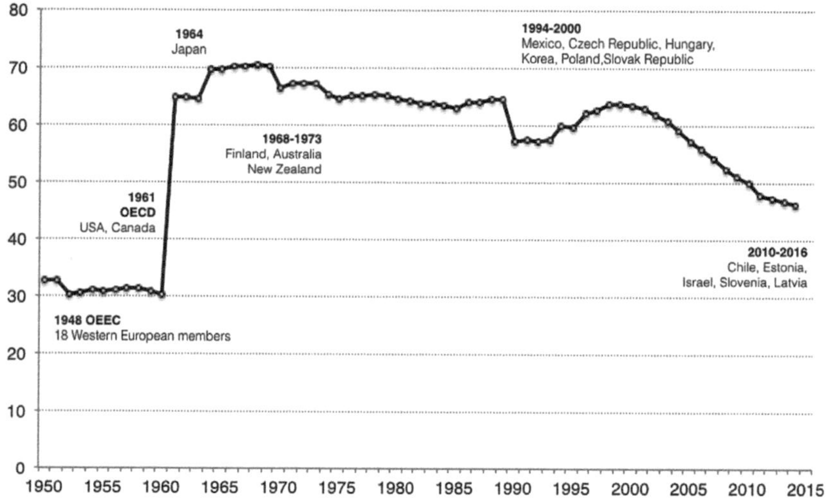

Fig. 1 The OEEC/OEEC countries as a % of world GDP, 1950–2014. *Source* Penn World Table version 9.0, Output-side real GDP at current PPPs (in million 2011 US$)

the OECD "Keynesian consensus" around high growth rates was based on a combination of international competition and free-market policies on the one hand, and Keynesian demand management and economic planning on the other ("Keynes at home, Smith abroad").[56] At an international level, this consensus centered on the notion of "collective demand management for the world economy" and the resulting difficult negotiations about the respective responsibility of creditor and donor countries for the region's balance of payments problems were held largely within the restricted Working Party 3 (WP3) of the EPC, the OECD's "inner sanctum."[57] Next to the management of overall demand and within this broadly Keynesian framework, the OECD also focused on policies aimed specifically at increasing longer-term growth, mainly in the framework of the human capital revolution.[58]

Thorkil Kristensen (1899–1989), the first Secretary-General of the OECD (mandate 1961–1969) quite strongly influenced its outlook. Born in a Danish farming family in 1899, Kristensen was an internationally respected economist and liberal-conservative politician. In his view, the OECD should work as an avant-garde think tank with a "catalytic role," and the Secretariat focused on providing innovative ideas that could be picked up by member countries if they became interested. Accordingly, Kristensen gave considerable autonomy to the various directorates—as stated in an internal British report, running "his office on a shoestring, [and] allowing the various Directors to develop into Robber Barons."[59] Furthermore, in particular during the early 1960s, he regularly isolated himself from administrative routines for several weeks to personally undertake research he deemed important or interesting.[60]

The OECD became an important actor in the emerging international field of development aid. In particular during the 1960s, the OECD was highly influential and at least as important as other international organizations, such as the IBRD/World Bank or the UN Development Program (UNDP). The OECD was instrumental in making development aid a normal function of modern states and it set some of the most influential norms, standards, and benchmarks in the development field, most importantly regarding what counts as public overseas development aid (ODA) and how much aid a modern industrialized country is supposed to give. By constituting itself as a donors' club, the Development Assistance Group (DAG, later DAC) excluded those that were most affected by what it discussed. The participation of recipients or independent experts was never seriously considered, although such proposals came up.[61] When some developing countries approached the Secretary-General for aid, the British delegation made it plain that since "the D.A.C. is…a donors' club [i]t must be for the donors, not the potential recipients to decide whether aid to particular countries should be discussed at all and, if so, which countries should be the subject of discussion."[62] At the same time, DAC members were aware that the new forum looked "very much like a selfish club of the 'haves' from which the 'have nots' were excluded."[63]

Responding to Crises and Stabilizing Intra-capitalist Relations: The OECD During the "Long 1970s" (1969–1984)

In the late 1960s, the OECD became entangled, under the label of the "problems of modern society," in a lively debate about the problems and unwanted side-effects of quantitative growth. The driving force behind this new perspective was a group of scientists and bureaucrats who were either working in the OECD Secretariat or were members of the OECD's Committee for Science Policy. Even though neglected by historical research and in the public memory, this group—concerned about the negative effects of modernization and economic expansion—proved instrumental in launching the Club of Rome. This group introduced the critique of quantitative growth and ecological questions into the epistemic space of the OECD at a very early stage and had a strong influence on the overall outlook of the Organization in the early 1970s.[64] However, the Keynesian and neoclassical economists within the Economics Department fervently opposed this critique, and, after the onset of economic stagflation and the oil crisis in 1973/74, OECD governments realigned the Organization's outlook to the short-term problems of increasing output and reflating the world economy.

In contrast to the research- and think-tank-oriented outlook of Kristensen, the new Secretary-General Emile van Lennep (1915–1996, OECD mandate: 1969–1984) strengthened the OECD's role in policy-making and policy-cooperation, streamlined and restructured the work of the different directorates, and focused the Secretariat on influencing member countries through both its hard and soft power governance mechanisms. Born into a prominent Amsterdam banking family with ties to the royal house, van Lennep was a top-ranking official within the Dutch Ministry of Finance. Before his appointment as Secretary-General, van Lennep had already served in many different functions within the OECD and was one of the most respected and best-connected international experts in the field of monetary policies. His long-term chairmanship of the EPC and its WP3 during the 1960s, a position directly offered to him by President Kennedy, was partly compensation for him not getting elected as Secretary-General in 1961.[65] In the view of a high-ranking OECD director, van Lennep was actually transforming the OECD into "less of a 'think-tank' to which member countries can bring any of their problems and more of an 'action-oriented, policy-making body.'"[66] However, this reorientation brought mixed results. During the collapse of the Bretton Woods system and the economic turmoil and energy shortages of the early 1970s, the OECD on the one hand gained in prominence, as with the "shock of the global" and, as it was dubbed during the 1970s, the related problem of "interdependence," moving international economic questions to the forefront of governmental agendas.[67] This was especially true in the field of environmental policies, as evidenced by the OECD being the first international organization to launch an Environment

Directorate in 1971 (a result of the growth-critical discussion of the "problems of modern society") and in the field of energy policies, as witnessed by the 1974 foundation, under the OECD umbrella, of the International Energy Agency, or North-South relationships, when the OECD was repeatedly used to counter the threat posed by UNCTAD proposals of a New International Economic Order.[68] Yet, with the creation of the G7 in 1975 (France, Japan, the UK, the US, West Germany, Italy, and Canada from 1976 onward), the OECD was relegated to a second tier in the international governance structure. Despite repeated demands, OECD Secretary-General Emile van Lennep was not invited to the G7 meetings. And if the OECD served as a "support infrastructure" for the G7, notably through the expertise and contacts gathered in its Economic Policy Committee, its lack of decision-making power was only more glaring than ever.[69]

Besides the short-lived demoting of the quantitative growth paradigm, the 1970s were also a period of transition for the ideological outlook of the Organization. While the OECD had long been a "bastion of Keynesianism" that was "either ignoring or stoutly opposing monetarist views," from the mid-1970s until the mid-1980s it shifted perspectives and became a strong advocate of supply-side economics and neoliberal policy prescriptions.[70] This transformation is often attributed to an expert group under the chairmanship of US economist Paul W. McCracken, which published a report in 1977. However, as Samuel Beroud underscores in this volume, the influence of this report should not be overemphasized.[71] Nonetheless, within the OECD Secretariat, the McCracken report and related policy debates about how to adjust economies to the ongoing crises sparked a conflict between the Keynesian "macroeconomists," who promoted improved demand management, and the "structuralists," who advocated monetary and wage restraint and supply-side instruments. From the mid-1970s onward, the Organization ceased to recommend fiscal policies aimed at fine-tuning the business cycle and only relied on medium-term macroeconomic goals related to growth, inflation, and employment.[72] In a similar vein, with its *Interfutures* study published in 1979, the OECD presented an official refutation to Club of Rome's *Limits to Growth* by mapping long-term growth paths for sustainably "mastering the probable and managing the unpredictable."[73] Faced with declining growth rates, the OECD started to consider social expenditures as an obstacle to growth, discussed the "welfare state in crisis," and increasingly promoted the privatization of social services. Building on its long-standing work on the *Code for the Liberalization of Capital Movements*, the OECD also emerged as an advocate for the liberalization of capital movements and financial markets.[74] In most of policy areas covered by the Organization, market solutions prevailed.

The transformation from "Keynesian" planning to a "neoliberal" market-oriented policy framework within the OECD was, however, a complicated one and largely dominated by changing member states' interests rather than ideological shifts. As recently shown, various policy proposals generally attributed to these diverging policy schools overlapped and complemented each other during the 1970s, not only within the OECD but more generally in the international policy arena. Within the OECD, structural policies, and particularly "positive adjustment policies," were developed from 1977 onwards by Keynesian economic advisors to President Jimmy Carter and German economists advocating the social market economy approach, and were at first intended as a microeconomic complement to reflationary and interventionist macroeconomic policies. As Samuel Beroud reminds us in his chapter, only later did they become integrated into a "neoliberal" agenda. This question, however, needs to be further studied, as well as its relation to competition among international organizations for "neoclassical" preeminence.[75]

From Warden of Globalization to "Sunset Organization?" The OECD and the End of the Cold War (1984–Present)

The last quarter century of the OECD lies beyond the period that can be analyzed with the help of archival sources. As mentioned in the introduction, it is also the period that has been mostly covered by social science scholarship. We will thus limit ourselves here to point out a few key developments.

The promotion of global liberalization for products, services, investments, and capital became so closely identified with the OECD that in 1991, the new Secretary-General Jean-Claude Paye (born 1934, mandate: 1984–1996), a French economist and diplomat, had to convince its audience that "it would be a shame if the OECD was characterized as an economic success and a social failure."[76] The year 1984 not only marked the coming of a new Secretary-General, but also some fundamental shifts on the level of directors and key OECD personnel and the end of the transition period to supply-side and free market approaches. For example, after a four-year mandate (1979–1983) under Canadian economist Silvia Ostry, the first woman to head an OECD Directorate, the OECD Economics Department was led from 1984 to 1992 by David Henderson, a British economist whose free-market-liberal perspectives clearly contrasted with those of preceding heads of the Department. What is more, van Lennep's Keynesian chief economist and top advisor Stephen Marris left the Château de la Muette in 1983. During the 1980s and 1990s, the OECD played a key role as a promoter of liberal economic reforms in member countries, particularly in the areas of labor policies, public management, deregulation, and privatization.[77]

A thorough survey of OECD reports in that era has shown that by the mid-1980s positions incompatible with neoclassical economics had been ousted from the Secretariat and the Organization's expert advice fully embraced supply-side recipes. The OECD's new blueprint was:

> cut budgets, eliminate labor market rigidities, strengthen competition, free international trade, rationalize production, exploit all new technologies, refrain from demand management, strengthen the personal responsibility of individuals and families and reduce generous social security benefits.[78]

In the 1990s the liberalization of trade, finance, and investment moved center-stage, as did, in the field of environmental policies, the focus on economic instruments and markets for environmental costs. In particular under the new Secretary-General, Canadian market-liberal politician and lawyer Donald Johnston (1996–2006), the OECD became a "champion of more open flows of goods, services, and capital as a vehicle for increasing world economic growth and welfare" and played "a particularly important role...in support of the globalization process" by launching—yet again—an "OECD growth project."[79] One of the key efforts to deepen the globalization of trade, investment, and finance was the so-called Multilateral Agreement on Investment (MAI), which was negotiated within the OECD between 1995 and 1998 but failed due to widespread protests by social movements and civil society groups that spurred what later became known as the anti-globalization movement, which challenged corporate-led liberalization of trade and finances to the detriment of people and the planet.[80]

Both the end of the Cold War and the relative economic sluggishness of OECD members in comparison to the much faster growth rates achieved by non-OECD economies proved highly unsettling. Founded as a Cold War institution with a key role in institutionalizing the hegemony of Western donor countries in North-South relations, the OECD was ill-equipped to face the multipolar world of globalization and the rise of "the Rest." To counter its eclipse as a relevant think tank whose analysis could make universal claims, the OECD admitted trusted "emerging" partners such as Mexico (1994) and South Korea (1996), as well as the most advanced economies in "transition" from planned economy to the free market capitalism such as the Czech and Slovak Republics (respectively in 1995 and 2000), and Hungary and Poland (both in 1996). Informal, and then official, contacts with the USSR and Russia, notably on the topic of development aid, had also begun by the late 1980s.[81]

A second wave of admissions, comprising Chile, Slovenia, Israel, and Estonia, followed in 2010, with Latvia gaining access to the OECD in early 2016. In 2006, former Mexican foreign minister José Angel Gurría (born in 1950) became Secretary-General and the OECD embarked on tightening its relations with key emerging economies (Brazil, China, India, Indonesia, and South Africa) through the so-called "Enhanced Engagement" program. However, faced with the rise of other international fora such as the G20, the influence of the OECD on these countries was rather weak, not least due to the OECD's reputed "Western-ness" and because the OECD had little to offer to these new players on the world markets, which undermined the OECD area's former economic predominance (see Fig. 1). As stated by Judith Clifton and Daniel Diaz-Fuentes: "the organization needs the emerging economies, but do they need the OECD?" The OECD, the quintessential Western international organization, has thus been characterized not without irony by Singaporean diplomat Kishore Mahbubani as a "sunset organization."[82]

Already in the 1990s, the OECD has started to study and discuss inequalities—an issue that had largely been neglected during preceding decades—and this new focus led to a major 2008 report entitled *Growing Unequal* that demonstrated the polarization of income distribution in most OECD countries. In 2009, the OECD Ministerial Council also declared that "'green' and 'growth' can go hand-in-hand" and proclaimed the development of a "Green Growth Strategy in order to achieve economic recovery and environmentally and socially sustainable economic growth" at the same time. Furthermore, building on work from the 1970s, which was taken up again in the 1990s, the OECD further developed social indicators, started to produce its *Society at a Glance* series, and in 2011 finally published a multidimensional and interactive social indicator database, *Your Better Life Index*. The OECD has thus not only opened its membership to newly emerging markets, but has also taken "a more open-minded approach to policy, recognizing there are more ways to economic growth than the 'OECD way.'"[83]

Conclusion

Given this unsettled history packed with fundamental transformations, what could be described as the raison d'être of this elusive organization? On the most general level, the OECD can be characterized as a *warden of liberal capitalism*, a forum and think tank designed for the defense, promotion, and monitoring of capitalist economies and market societies and a place to deal with the internal contradictions of liberal capitalism through specific modes of "cooperation." As the problems and the conceptions of liberal capitalism have changed, the specific functions of the OECD cannot be defined a priori, which contributes to its open-ended status. Three other dimensions are key to understanding the historical trajectory of the OECD.

1) A (geo)political platform and tool: While we argue the OECD was an important geopolitical actor throughout its history, its predecessor—the OEEC—never fulfilled the geopolitical role it was designed for in 1948: to serve as the incubator for the United States of Europe. In this regard, it is interesting that the OEEC/OECD is often strikingly ignored by European studies, which tend to bypass this organization in their accounts of early European integration, and then neglect the contacts and competition between EEC and the OEEC/OECD. Yet it soon took on another related role: up until 1989 (and possibly beyond) the OECD was *the* economic grouping representing the economic interests of the capitalist West. The Organization never openly acknowledged this role as a "warden of the West" and, even though we would argue it is essential to understanding the OECD's history, this role has been overlooked in the existing research. Studies that take into account not only the official publications of the OECD—which display a sanitized language unstained by national interest, let alone Cold War or other antagonisms—but also archival sources, in particular those from national archives of the larger member countries, demonstrate the overarching significance of the Cold War in both the foundation of the OECD and its evolution. The OECD was specifically founded to coordinate the interests of Western capitalist countries vis-à-vis the communist East and—this leads us to the second geopolitical dimension—the decolonizing countries in the Global South.[84]

Many documents from the foundational period are very explicit about the fundamental importance of creating an exclusive forum for development-related issues. At a time when the rich countries were losing their majority at the UN, this was regarded as important not only to advancing a common view on development issues, but also to coordinating Western global relations in a platform that shut out nations from the Global South and the communist rivals, also with regard to broader international fora such as the IBRD/World Bank or the UN.[85] As stated in a 1964 British dispatch, the DAC was

> [an] essential organ in which, untrammeled by hysterical speeches from the Afro-Asian bloc or subversive maneuvers from behind the Iron and Bamboo curtains, the Western Powers can study the real substance of aid problems in all objectivity and think out a coordinated line to take at New York and Geneva.[86]

Finally, throughout its history—but particularly during the 1960s and 1970s—the OECD has been an important meeting place for the small group of its most economically powerful member countries and it actually worked with an informal "two-tier system." [87] During the OEEC period, the Organization's work was particularly dominated by France, Britain, and—even though officially only an associated member—the US. From the 1960s onward, the OECD formalized the exclusion of smaller member countries from some of the key committees (e.g., DAC, WP3) and in particular strengthened informal meetings among the Group of Five (France, Japan, UK, US, West Germany) that fundamentally shaped the Organization's work in its core areas such as economic (international demand management), monetary (balance of payments), and development policies.[88] As a British delegate to the OECD stated in 1974:

> The day-to-day work at Council level is, in practice, organized and controlled by the Ambassadors of the 'major shareholding' countries (United States, Britain, France, Germany, Japan and Canada) who hold frequent unofficial meetings to discuss on-going work.[89]

Whereas up to the mid-1970s these big-power negotiations took place—next to the Group of 10 (G10) and to more closed bilateral channels—within and through the OECD structure, with the foundation of the G7 in 1975, the OECD lost in importance. With the relative demise of OECD member countries related to the rise of the emerging market economies that did not want to join this organization—widely perceived as a Western Club—the geopolitical function of the OECD as a kind of Cold War economic NATO continued to be eroded.

2) An expert think tank and an experts' meeting place: These two functions of the OECD have continuously increased in importance throughout its history—from a minor characteristic in the OEEC to a definitive one after the end of the Cold War. In contrast to many international organizations, the OECD did not for the most part rely on legal or financial means to achieve agreements, but rather on 'soft power' mechanisms. Soft power—getting others to want the outcomes that you want—means that the OECD's way of working aimed at shaping the ideas and preferences of member countries through the production, standardization, diffusion, and legitimation of policy norms and expertise.[90]

One of OECD's key contributions to global governance was the repeated provision of a generally acceptable framing of issues and cause-and-effect relationships, the creation of convincing narratives, and the production of powerful models and metaphors, all of which enabled Western civil servants to perceive social facts and political problems in a convergent way.[91] This process not only took place among members of the international Secretariat—as with most international organizations—but also among the thousands of national delegates that visited the OECD headquarters on a regular basis. As stated by the first Secretary-General of the OECD, Thorkil Kristensen, the OECD's key task was the production of "a common value system at the level of civil servants in the OECD countries that should form the basis for consensually shared definitions of problems and solutions in economic policy making."[92] Part of the production of a "common value system among civil servants"—this rationalization of an international bureaucratic space in a Weberian sense—was a process of socialization that contributed to a culture of shared Western administrative expertise and bureaucratic camaraderie. This process of socialization also encompassed contacts with academics, notably in the field of economics.

Relatedly, the various practices of "cooperation" enshrined in the name of the OECD also contributed to the permeability of national bureaucracies. Soft-power modes of governance such as multilateral surveillance, peer review, and the opening up and collective evaluation of (partly sensible) economic knowledge and economic-policy-making information among bureaucrats helped not only to advance a certain form of transparency among Western industrialized countries, but also in the internationalization of policy makers.

Of particular importance in this regard is the authority of economic expertise. While not many economists were engaged in the early OEEC and its committees—which were largely a meeting place for bureaucrats, politicians, and industrialists—from the 1960s onward economics became the lead discipline within the Organization and the Secretariat began to mainly employ economists. Relatedly, economic approaches increasingly came to expand into and dominate all other policy fields the Organization dealt with—education and environment being interesting examples of this economization process.[93] The Organization's authority in public debates derives to a large degree from the authority of economic expertise, which in the case of the OECD is framed as detached from national interests and thus devoid of a particular economic ideology. And in this regard, the OECD's key task was (and is) to define good economics and the ruling norms of adequate government behavior, not only for its member countries but, increasingly, for the entire globe.

These developments were, however, not unchallenged. The internecine conflicts around quantitative growth and environmental questions between two factions of the Secretariat in the early 1970s or the Organization's shift in economic ideology from a roughly Keynesian framework to a supply-side orientation are two examples of such dynamics.[94]

To fulfill its expert function, the OECD has used various strategies. Based on the three mechanisms outlined in the first section of this chapter, these strategies still need to be studied systematically. Starting from the standardization of national income accounting in the early 1950s, the Organization that had hitherto been known for its "notoriously bad" statistical reputation developed into a hub for the collection, harmonization, and presentation of supposedly neutral and reliable statistics.[95] From the late 1960s onward, the OECD thus strove to become *the* expert on long-term issues so as to anticipate global, interconnected, newly emerging problems.[96] The OECD's publications—ranging from expert reports to regular evaluations of the global economy (its bi-annual *Economic Outlook*) or of member countries' situations (*Country reports*), to its monthly *OECD Observer* magazine—are also an important part of the OECD's self-portrayal as an expert organization.[97]

3) An identity-generating Club of the West: The OECD has been described as a "paradigmatic example of an identity-defining international organization."[98] While some of its founders intended the OEEC to become the nucleus of European integration, the Organization did not fulfill this potentially identity-generating function. However, during the 1950s and in particular from the 1960s onward, it became *the* Organization defining the community of highly "developed" or "advanced" capitalist countries on the "mental maps" of officials, and increasingly the wider public. This also meant that the OECD was founded as an imagined community of "developed" countries that had a common "mission." In the words of Secretary-General Kristensen,

> the industrial countries with market economies have a definite mission in the world during the present phase of history. They have been the forerunners in economic development; and they will remain for a long time the pioneers in a number of fields because their structures are more refined ... They can, therefore, develop certain techniques of economic policy-making that can later be transferred to other parts of the world...that are less highly developed.[99]

The notion of "like-mindedness" was key to all the negotiations about new member countries throughout the OECD's history, in particular in the 1960s and 1970s. When the US proposed that Japan should become a member in 1961, the European countries feared that other countries such as Israel, Tunisia, Yugoslavia, or Argentina would also apply for full membership, which was inconceivable to all concerned.[100] And when New Zealand became the 24th member in 1973, the general view within the OECD was that now "the group of highly industrialized, like-minded countries will be complete."[101] This initial uncertainty was also revealed in the different names that were discussed, such as "Organization for Atlantic Economic Cooperation" or "Atlantic Economic Organization (A.E.O.)." Besides the fact that such "NATO-like" denominations would have upset its neutral members, it was clear to all concerned that the OECD essentially brought together the core countries of "the West."[102] It was founded as the "economic conscience of the free world" that aimed at the "construction of an international economic philosophy" that guarded the principles of liberal capitalism and the interests of this imagined community of countries.[103]

An open question for future research might be how this process of creating the identity of "OECD countries"—which became widely used to denote the rich industrialized nations from Western Europe, North America, and the Pacific (Japan, Australia, and New Zealand, with the

US at the hinge of this trans-oceanic triad)—actually happened, whether it was consciously promoted by the OECD Secretariat, by certain member countries, or whether it was a labeling from those not within this community such as the UNCTAD countries. If we then consider the OECD as a "Rich Man's Club" and a "Donors' Club" (both of course discursively closely related concepts), then the membership of European peripheral countries such as Portugal, Spain, Greece, and Turkey can only be understood as a historical relic from the Marshall Plan era.

Since the demarcation of a community of countries as non-members—or the "other"—is highly important, we can see that with the end of the Cold War and the rise of newly emerging market economies the OECD lost two key identity-defining markers. Since the 1990s, the OECD no longer encompasses *all* the core economies of global capitalism and struggles to find a new identity beyond the Cold War vision of representing rich capitalist countries and the (post)colonial idea of representing the major developed economic powers.[104]

Notes

1. In the early 1960s OECD committees spent 60% of their time discussing operational questions and only 30% on policy discussions. National Archives and Records Administration (NARA), RG 59, Entry 5304, Box 9, Folder 225 Manpower Committee, CES/64.06, Statement by Thorkil Kristensen at the 59th meeting of the Council, 30 January 1964.
2. See the classic study by Robert W. Cox and Harold K. Jacobson, *The Anatomy of Influence: Decision Making in International Organizations* (New Haven: Yale University Press, 1974).
3. Michael Barnett and Martha Finnemore, *Rules for the World: International Organizations in Global Politics* (Ithaca: Cornell University Press, 2004), 33.
4. Secretary-Generals are also used for the periodization by Mahon and McBride. However almost the entire volume focuses on the time after the 1980s. Carroll and Kellow use decades and Clifton and Diaz-Fuentes follow shifts in the political economy (1961–1973–1989–2008). Another periodization might follow major changes in the scope of membership, i.e., 1948–1961–1964–1975–1994. See Rianne Mahon and Stephen McBride, eds., *The OECD and Transnational Governance* (Vancouver: University of British Columbia Press, 2008); Peter Carroll and Aynsley Kellow, eds., *The OECD. A Study of Organisational Adaptation* (Cheltenham: Edward Elgar, 2011); Judith Clifton and

Daniel Díaz-Fuentes, "The OECD and Phases in the International Political Economy, 1961–2011," *Review of International Political Economy* 18, no. 5 (2011): 552–569.

5. See the profiles written for the *Biographical Dictionary of Secretaries-General of International Organizations*, www.ru.nl/fm/iobio: Alix Heiniger, "Robert Marjolin," (2014); Matthias Schmelzer, "Thorkil Kristensen" (2013); Samuel Beroud and Matthieu Leimgruber, "Emile van Lennep" (2017); Aynsley Kellow and Peter Carrol, "Donald Johnston" (2013).
6. Robert W. Cox and Harold K. Jacobson, "The Framework for Inquiry," in *The Anatomy of Influence: Decision Making in International Organizations*, by Robert W. Cox and Jacobson, Harold K. (New Haven: Yale University Press, 1974), 5–6.
7. Joseph S. Nye explains the concept of soft power: "A country may obtain the outcomes it wants in world politics because other countries—admiring its values, emulating its example, aspiring to its level of prosperity and openness—want to follow it. In this sense, it is also important to set the agenda and attract others in world politics, and not only to force them to change by threatening military force or economic sanctions." Joseph S. Nye, *Soft Power: The Means to Success in World Politics* (New York: Public Affairs, 2004), 5.
8. This chapter builds on the existing literature by social scientists mentioned in the introduction. The typology closely resembles that of Woodward, who distinguishes between cognitive, normative, legal, and palliative governance, and that of Mahon and McBride, who distinguish between inquisitive and meditating modes of regulation within the OECD. See Mahon and McBride, *OECD*; Kerstin Martens and Anja P. Jakobi, eds., *Mechanisms of OECD Governance: International Incentives for National Policy Making* (Oxford: Oxford University Press, 2010); Richard Woodward, *The Organisation for Economic Co-Operation and Development (OECD)* (London and New York: Routledge, 2009).
9. The term is borrowed from Martin Marcussen, "The OECD as Ideational Artist and Arbitrator: Reality or Dream?," in *Decision Making Within International Organizations*, eds. Bob Reinalda and Bertjan Verbeek (London and New York: Routledge, 2004), 90–105, here 105.
10. Miriam Camps, *"First World" Relationships: The Role of the OECD* (Paris: Atlantic Institute for International Affairs, 1975), 41; see also Michael Henderson, "The OECD as an Instrument of National Policy," *International Journal* 36, no. 4 (1981): 793–814.
11. Alfred Müller-Armack, *Auf dem Weg nach Europa* (Tübingen: Wunderlich, 1971), 93. The Natioanl Archives (TNA), FCO 69/227, Chadwick to Gallagher, 15 January 1971; TNA, FCO 69/377,

Gallagher to Douglas-Home, 9 August 1973. See also various examples of this in Matthias Schmelzer, *The Hegemony of Growth. The Making and Remaking of the Economic Growth Paradigm and the OECD, 1948-2010* (Cambridge: Cambridge University Press, 2016).

12. NARA, RG 59, Entry 5304, Box 21, Folder Council on Foreign Relations, John C. Renner to Robert Schaetzel, 10 April 1964.
13. Randolph W. Burgess, "Reunion of the Group of Four," *Atlantic Community Quarterly* 9, no. 4 (1971): 441.
14. TNA, FCO 69/227, Chadwick to Gallagher, 15 January 1971.
15. Benoît Godin, *The Making of Science, Technology and Innovation Policy. Conceptual Frameworks as Narratives, 1945–2005* (Montréal: Institut national de la recherche scientifique, 2009), 8–9.
16. Lincoln Gordon, "The Organization for European Economic Cooperation," *International Organization* 10, no. 1 (1956): 1.
17. Alan S. Milward, *The Reconstruction of Western Europe, 1945–1951* (Berkeley and Los Angeles: University of California Press, 1987), 207.
18. See OEEC, *At Work for Europe: An Account of the Activities of the Organisation for European Economic Co-Operation* (Paris: OEEC, 1956).
19. Milward, *Reconstruction*, 71–89, 172. On the sensitive integration of West Germany into the new institution see Werner Bührer, *Westdeutschland in der OEEC: Eingliederung, Krise, Bewährung 1947–1961* (München: Oldenbourg, 1998).
20. Milward, *Reconstruction*, 168, 208. The compromise was that NATO would set up its headquarters in Brussels, and the OEEC in Paris. France would hold the OEEC Secretariat and Britain key OEEC directorates. See also Mark Gilbert, *European Integration: A Concise History* (Lanham: Rowman & Littlefield Publ., 2012), 11–15.
21. Johnny Laursen, "Integration at Cross-Currents. The OEEC and the European Coal and Steel Community, 1952–1956," in *Explorations in OEEC History*, ed. Richard Griffiths (Paris: OECD, 1997), 149–158; Wolfram Kaiser, Brigitte Leucht, and Morten Rasmussen, eds., *The History of the European Union: Origins of a Trans- and Supranational Polity 1950–1972* (London and New York: Routledge, 2009). On Marjolin see Heiniger, "Marjolin."
22. Quoted in George W. Ball, *The Past Has Another Pattern. Memoirs* (New York: Norton, 1982), 81.
23. Quoted from his diary from 16 December 1953, in Robert Marjolin, *Architect of European Unity: Memoirs, 1911-86* (London: Weidenfeld & Nicholson, 1989), 246. On his biography, see Heiniger, "Robert Marjolin."

24. OEEC, *A Decade of Co-Operation. Achievements and Perspectives* (Paris: OEEC, 1958).
25. The arbitrators were a "Committee of Wise Men" (in 1948) and Baron Sncy d'Oppuers, Deputy Chairman of the Council, and Secretary-General Robert Marjolin (in 1949). Wendy Asbeek Brusse, "Liberalising Intra-European Trade," in *Explorations in OEEC History* (Paris: OECD, 1997), 15–33.
26. Monika Dickhaus, "'It Is Only the Provisional That Lasts': The European Payments Union," in *Explorations in OEEC History*, ed. Richard T. Griffiths (Paris: OECD, 1997), 183–200; Milward, *Reconstruction*, 299–334; Jacob J. Kaplan and Günther Schleiminger, *The European Payments Union: Financial Diplomacy in the 1950s* (Oxford: Oxford University Press, 1989); see also Corso Paolo Boccia, "The United States, Convertibility, and the Reform of the European Payments Union in 1954: A View on the Debate in the Eisenhower Administration," in *Explorations in OEEC History*, ed. Richard T. Griffiths (Paris: OECD, 1997), 209–217.
27. Milward, *Reconstruction*, 207.
28. OECD-HA, C(53)324, Activities of the Vertical Committees. Memorandum by the Secretary-General, 19 December 1953.
29. Vertical committees are cursorily mentioned in Griffiths, *Explorations in OEEC History*. See also Ludovic Fulleringer, "Ore, wood and coal. A new look at the OEEC productivity program during the 1950s," paper presented at the conference *Warden of the West. The OECD and the Global Political Economy, 1948 to present*, University of Zürich, 27–29 August 2015.
30. TNA, PREM 8/1434, State Department to Foreign Office, 19 April 1951; FO 371/150087, Foreign Office to Armstrong, 28 April 1951.
31. Helmut R. Hammerich, *Jeder für sich und Amerika gegen alle? Die Lastenteilung der NATO am Beispiel des Temporary Council Committee 1949 bis 1954* (München: Oldenbourg, 2003), 133–160.
32. NARA, RG 469, Entry UD 379, Box 91, Folder OEEC General 1952–1953, John Kenney to William H. Draper, 10 October 1952.
33. NARA, RG 469, Entry UD 379, Box 89, Kay Shorter to John Hulley, 15 April 1953. See also Gérard Bossuat, "The Marshall Plan and European Integration: Limits of an Ambition," in *The Marshall Plan Today: Model and Metaphor*, ed. John Agnew (London and New York: Routledge, 2004), 143f.
34. Bent Boel, *The European Productivity Agency and Transatlantic Relations, 1953–1961* (Copenhagen: Museum Tusculanum Press, 2003); Anthony Carew, *Labour under the Marshall Plan: The Politics of Productivity and the Marketing of Management Science* (Manchester:

Manchester University Press, 1987); Roger Grégoire, "European Productivity Agency," in *At Work for Europe*, ed. OEEC, 5th ed. (Paris: OEEC, 1960), 139–152. See also Dominique Barjot, ed., *Catching up with America. Productivity Mission and the Diffusion of American Economic and Technological Influence after the Second World War* (Paris: Presses de l'Université Paris-Sorbonne, 2002).

35. OEEC, *From Recovery Toward Economic Strength. Sixth Annual Report of the OEEC* (Paris: OEEC, 1955), 157–171; Matthias Schmelzer, "A Club of the Rich to Help the Poor? The OECD, 'Development', and the Hegemony of Donor Countries," in *International Organizations and Development, 1945–1990*, ed. Marc Frey, Sönke Kunkel, and Corinna Unger (Basingstoke: Palgrave Macmillan, 2014), 171–195; Schmelzer, *Hegemony*, chapters 1, 2 and 3; Patricia Hongler, "Die OEEC Und Ihre Unsichtbare Kolonialgeschichte. Lektüre Einer Kakaostudie von 1956," in *Neue Beiträge Zur Wirtschaftsgeschichte*, ed. Thomas David, Tobias Straumann, and Simon Teuscher (Zürich: Chronos, 2015), 235–250.
36. Brusse, "Liberalising Intra-European Trade".
37. TNA, FO 371/72016, Moore on file containing letter of Hall-Patch to FO, 21 July 1951. The entire process is described in Richard T. Griffiths, "'An Act of Creative Leadership': The End of the OEEC and the Birth of the OECD," in *Explorations in OEEC History*, ed. Richard T. Griffiths (Paris: OECD, 1997), 235–240.
38. Emile Benoit, *Europe at Sixes and Sevens: The Common Market, the Free Trade Association, and the United States* (New York: Columbia University Press, 1961); Jeffrey Glen Giauque, *Grand Designs and Visions of Unity: The Atlantic Powers and the Reorganization of Western Europe, 1955–1963* (Chapel Hill: University of North Carolina Press, 2002), 47–76.
39. Richard T. Griffiths, "The Origins of EFTA," in *EFTA 1960–2010: Elements of 50 Years of European History*, ed. Kåre Bryn and Guðmundur Einarsson (Geneva: European Free Trade Association, 2010); Wolfram Kaiser, "Challenge to the Community: The Creation, Crisis and Consolidation of the European Free Trade Association, 1958–1972," *Journal of European Integration History* 3, no. 1 (1997): 7–33.
40. TNA, FO 371/150108, Hankey to Jackling, 12 October 1960. See also Bührer, *Westdeutschland*, 395–416. See also Julie Rausis, "Intégrer le nouvel ordre économique international. La Suisse face à la réforme de l'Organisation européenne de coopération économique (OECE), 1958–1961." Master-Thesis, University of Geneva, Paul Bairoch Institute of Economic History, 2014.

41. In 1960, the British delegate stated plainly: "M. Sergent has not been a success." TNA, FO 371/150075, France to Lee, 22 January 1960. See already the remarks in NARA, RG 469, Entry UD 379, Box 92, Folder OEEC July–December 1954 Urschel to Fitzgerald, 20 December 1954.
42. TNA, T 234/717, Clarke to Makins, 19 November 1959.
43. Griffiths, "Creative Leadership"; Schmelzer, *Hegemony.*
44. Griffiths, "Creative Leadership," 242–244.
45. John Toye and Richard Toye, *The UN and Global Political Economy: Trade, Finance, and Development* (Bloomington: Indiana University Press, 2004).
46. Griffiths, "Creative Leadership," 242. As Randolph Burgess stated, the foundation of "OECD was in part a response" to the debates within NATO to increase economic cooperation. NARA, RG 59, Entry 5304, Box 21, Folder Council on Foreign Relations, Study Group Reports, First Meeting, 13 April 1964.
47. Bundesarchiv Koblenz (BAK), B 102, 139611, Vertretung der Bundesrepublik Deutschland bei der OECD to AA, BMWi and Minister Ludwig Erhard, 12 October 1962; see also TNA, FO 371/134422, Washington to Foreign Office, 9 January 1960; FO 371/134422, M 551/7, letter to Sir Paul Gore-Booth, 4 January 1960.
48. Francis J. Gavin, *Gold, Dollars, and Power: The Politics of International Monetary Relations, 1958–1971* (Chapel Hill: The University of North Carolina Press, 2007); Lucia Coppolaro, "US Policy on European Integration during the GATT Kennedy Round Negotiations (1963–1967): The Last Hurrah of America's Europeanists," *The International History Review* 33, no. 3 (2011): 409–429.
49. Schmelzer, "Club of the Rich".
50. Proposal for U.S. Membership in a Reorganized OEEC, attached to: Memorandum from Secretary of State Herter to President Eisenhower, 24 November 1959, *FRUS 1958–1960, Volume IV,* 58–62.
51. For more on this issue see Schmelzer, *Hegemony.*
52. Alexander King, cited in Robert Shannan Peckham, "Alexander King," *The Independent*, March 26, 2007. On the concept of "organizational ideology" see Cox and Jacobson, "Framework," 22.
53. Matthias Schmelzer, "'Expandiere oder stirb.' Das Wachstumsparadigma, die OECD und die Steigerungslogik wirtschaftlicher Expansion," *Geschichte und Gesellschaft* 41, no. 3 (2015).
54. TNA, T 299/178, Letters to OECD committees, 10 January 1961.
55. Scott Sullivan, *From War to Wealth: Fifty Years of Innovation* (OECD, 1997), 50. See also Michele Fratianni and John C. Pattison, "The Economics of the OECD," *Carnegie-Rochester Conference Series on Public Policy* 4, no. 1 (1976): 75–140; Robert Wolfe, "From

Reconstructing Europe to Constructing Globalization: The OECD in Historical Perspective," in *The OECD and Transnational Governance*, eds. Rianne Mahon and Stephen McBride (Vancouver: University of British Columbia Press, 2008), 35.

56. Stephen Marris, "My History of My Time at the OECD", unpublished record of two seminars given to the OECD Secretariat in June 1983. We would like to thank Dr. Judith Clifton for having shared this document with us. John Gerard Ruggie, "International Regimes, Transactions, and Change: Embedded Liberalism in the Postwar Economic Order," *International Organization* 36, no. 2 (1982): 355.
57. Sullivan, *From War to Wealth*, 62. Even though time and again mentioned in the research of the OECD, we still lack a good account on the history of WP3. See however the chapter by Kazuhiko Yago in this volume, as well as a recent PhD dissertation by Floriane Galeazzi, *La France et la réforme du système monétaire international (1961–1987). Le rôle des experts du Groupe de Travail n°3 de l'OCDE* (Université de Rouen 2015).
58. Schmelzer, *Hegemony*, Chaps. 4 and 5. See also the chapter by Regula Bürgi in this volume.
59. TNA, FCO 55/417, Chadwick to Combs, OECD: Current Round-up, June 15, 1970.
60. Schmelzer, "Thorkil Kristensen." See also Poul Nyboe Andersen, *Thorkil Kristensen. En ener i dansk politik*, Odense: Odense Universitetsforlag, 1994.
61. See for example the proposal by the Belgian delegate to turn the OECD into an organization in which developing countries and donor countries would meet. TNA, CO 852/1922, United Kingdom Note on the 70th Session of the OTC, 5 September 1960.
62. TNA, T 312/860, J.M. Bridgeman, "Future of D.A.C.," 21 September 1964.
63. TNA, FO 371/150075, Holliday, Memorandum: Future of OEEC, 1 January 1960. See also Patricia Hongler's PhD-project at the University of Luzern (Switzerland) entitled "Erzählungen der Dekolonisierung. Berichte aus dem Archiv der OECD."
64. For more on this see Matthias Schmelzer, "'Born in the Corridors of the OECD': The Forgotten Origins of the Club of Rome, Transnational Networks, and the 1970s in Global History," *Journal of Global History* 12, no. 1 (2017): 26–48. On the OEEC and OECD's activities in the key field of science policy see Ludovic Fulleringer's ongoing PhD dissertation at the University of Geneva provisionally entitled "L'OCDE et la genèse internationale des politiques de la science, 1948 à 1979."

65. On van Lennep see Beroud and Leimgruber, "Emile van Lennep." See also Emile Van Lennep, *Working for the World Economy: A Personal History* (Amsterdam: NIBE, 1998).
66. TNA, FCO 55/417, Chadwick to Combs, OECD: Current Round-up, 15 June 1970.
67. Niall Ferguson et al., eds., *The Shock of the Global. The 1970s in Perspective* (Cambridge: Belknap Press, 2010).
68. Richard Scott, *The History of the International Energy Agency: The First Twenty Years* (Paris: International Energy Agency, 1994); Thomas Hajduk, "A code to bind them all: The multinational dilemma and the endeavour for an international code of conduct," in *Multinationale Unternehmen und Institutionen im Wandel-Herausforderungen für Wirtschaft, Recht und Gesellschaft*, ed. Sandra Brändli, Roman Schister, and Aurelia Tamò (Bern: Stämpfli Verlag, 2013), 311–39; Henning Türk, "The Oil Crisis of 1973 as a Challenge to Multilateral Energy Cooperation among Western Industrialized Countries," *Historical Social Research* 39, no. 4 (2014): 209–230.
69. See also Emmanuel Mourlon-Druol, *A Europe Made of Money: The Emergence of the European Monetary System* (Ithaca, NY: Cornell University Press, 2012); Andrew Baker, *The Group of Seven: Finance Ministries, Central Banks and Global Financial Governance* (London and New York: Routledge, 2006); Emmanuel Mourlon-Druol, Emmanuel, & Federico Romero, eds. *International Summitry and Global Governance: the Rise of the G7 and the European Council, 1974–1991* (London: Routledge, 2014).
70. OECD-HA, Folder 239638, Memorandum from J. R. Gass to Angus Maddison, February 4, 1977.
71. Paul W. McCracken, *Toward Full Employment and Price Stability: A Report to the OECD by a Group of Independent Experts* (Paris: OECD, 1977); the classic reference is Robert O. Keohane, "Economics, Inflation, and the Role of the State: Political Implications of the McCracken Report," *World Politics* 31, no. 1 (1978): 108–128; more nuanced: Vincent Gayon, "L'OCDE au travail. Contribution à une sociologie historique de la 'coopération économique internationale' sur le chômage et l'emploi" (Thèse pour l'obtention du doctorat en science politique, Université Paris Dauphine, 2010). For more details on this, see the chapter by Samuel Beroud in this volume, as well as his ongoing PhD dissertation at the University of Geneva entitled "Beyond the Great Depression. The transformation of international economic policies, 1971–1984."
72. J.C.R. Dow, "The Organization of Economic Cooperation and Development," in *The Role of the Economist in Government: An*

International Perspective, ed. Joseph A. Pechman (London: Harvester, 1990), 261; Woodward, *The OECD*, 23–29.

73. OECD, *Interfutures. Facing the Future. Mastering the Probable and Managing the Unpredictable* (Paris: OECD, 1979).
74. OECD-HA, CPE/WP2(80)3, Factor Income Shares and Profit Rates, 25 April 1980; Peter Hill, *Profits and Rates of Return* (Paris: OECD, 1979); Matthieu Leimgruber, "The Embattled Standard-bearer of Social Insurance and Its Challenger: The ILO, the OECD and the 'Crisis of the Welfare State', 1975–1985," in *Globalizing Social Rights: The International Labor Organization and Beyond*, eds. Sandrine Kott and Joëlle Droux (Basingstoke: Palgrave Macmillan, 2013), 293–309; OECD, *The Challenge of Unemployment: A Report to Labour Ministers* (Paris: OECD, 1982); Rawi Abdelal, *Capital Rules: The Construction of Global Finance* (Cambridge: Harvard University Press, 2007).
75. On this see also Jeffrey M. Chwieroth, *Capital Ideas. The IMF and the Rise of Financial Liberalization* (Princeton: Princeton University Press, 2010).
76. Steven Greenhouse, "Making a Difference; The O.E.C.D.'s Polite Pusher", *New York Times*, 9 June 1991, p. F7 (quotation). See also Emile Van Lennep, "The Seventies: A Review—The Eighties: A Preview," *The OECD Observer* 102 (January 1980): 3–8; Woodward, *The OECD*, 29–32; Carroll and Kellow, *OECD*, 80–94. OECD-HA, C (80) 104 (Final), Communiqué, 6 June 1980. Before joining the OECD, Paye was a senior civil servant under Valéry Giscard d'Estaing and a G7 sherpa under François Mitterrand. His candidacy can be interpreted as a compromise choice against the Thatcher-Reagan approach of economic problems.
77. See for example Mahon and McBride, *OECD*; Leslie A. Pal, *Frontiers of Governance: The OECD and Global Public Management Reform* (Basingstoke: Palgrave Macmillan, 2012).
78. OECD-HA, CPE(80)4, Organisation of the Committee's Working Parties, April 29, 1980; Klaus Armingeon, "OECD and National Welfare State Development," in *The OECD and European Welfare States*, ed. Klaus Armingeon and Michelle Beyeler (Cheltenham: Edward Elgar, 2004), 228; see also Leimgruber, "Embattled Standard-Bearer."
79. Donald Johnston in OECD, *OECD Annual Report* (Paris: OECD, 2000), 5; Caroll and Kellow, "Donald Johnston."
80. Andrew Jackson and Matthew Sanger, *Dismantling Democracy: The Multilateral Agreement on Investment (MAI) and Its Impact* (Ottawa: James Lorimer, 1998). On this period see Woodward, *The OECD*, 34–41.

81. William Hynes and Alexandra Trzeciak-Duval, "Instruments of Soft Power. The Donor that Came in From the Cold: OECD-Russian Engagement on Development Cooperation," *International organizations Research Journal* 10, no. 1 (2015): 26–43.
82. Judith Clifton and Daniel Díaz-Fuentes, "The OECD and 'The Rest': Analyzing the Limits of Policy Transfer," *Journal of Comparative Policy Analysis: Research and Practice* 16, no. 3 (2014): 249–265; Schmelzer, "Club of the Rich"; Judith Clifton and Daniel Díaz-Fuentes, "From 'Club of the Rich' to 'Globalisation À La Carte'? Evaluating Reform at the OECD," *Global Policy* 2, no. 3 (October 1, 2011): 310; Kishore Mahbubani, "The OECD: A Classic Sunset Organisation," *Global Policy* 3, no. 1 (2012): 117–118.
83. Ulrich Brand, "Green Economy—the Next Oxymoron? No Lessons Learned from Failures of Implementing Sustainable Development," *GAIA—Ecological Perspectives for Science and Society* 21, no. 1 (2012): 28–32; OECD, *Growing Unequal. Income Distribution and Poverty in OECD Countries* (Paris: OECD, 2008); OECD, *Your Better Life Index* (Paris: OECD, 2011). See also http://www.oecd.org/green-growth and http://www.oecd.org/inclusive-growth; OECD-HA, C/MIN(2009)5/ADD1/FINAL, Meeting of the Council at Ministerial Level, 24–25 June 2009. For an exceptional earlier OECD report on inequality, which made some headlines in the late 1970s, see Malcom Sawyer, *Income Distribution in OECD Countries*, OECD Economic Outlook (Paris: OECD, 1976). The final quotation is from Judith Clifton and Daniel Díaz-Fuentes, "La Nueva Política Económica de la OCDE ante el cambio en la Economía Mundial," 2011, http://mpra.ub.uni-muenchen.de/33043/.
84. Griffiths, "Creative Leadership"; Schmelzer, *Hegemony*, Chap. 4.
85. Schmelzer, *Hegemony*, Chap. 6.
86. TNA, T 312/859, Hankey, "The Future of the OECD," 28 July 1964; see also TNA, FCO 69/227, Britten to Gallagher, Godden, Tickell and Graham, 22 January 1971.
87. TNA, FCO 59/1239, Gallagher to Marshall, 16 December 1974.
88. For more on this see Schmelzer, *Hegemony*.
89. TNA, FCO 59/1239, Gallagher to Marshall, 16 December 1974.
90. Nye, *Soft Power*, 5.
91. On the theory behind such an analysis of economics see Deirdre N. McCloskey, *If You're So Smart: The Narrative of Economic Expertise* (Chicago: University of Chicago Press, 1990); Mary S. Morgan, *The World in the Model: How Economists Work and Think* (Cambridge: Cambridge University Press, 2012).

92. Marcussen, paraphrasing Secretary General Thorkil Kristensen, in: Martin Marcussen, "The OECD in Search of a Role: Playing the Idea Game," 2001, 1. On Kristensen see Schmelzer, "Thorkil Kristensen."
93. For more on this see Schmelzer, *Hegemony*, Chaps. 5 and 8.
94. Schmelzer, "Crisis." This issue needs much further research. Some first ideas can be found in Leimgruber, "Embattled Standard-Bearer"; Schmelzer, *Hegemony*; Samuel Beroud and Matthieu Leimgruber, "A Pilot Fish ahead of the Sharks? The Changing Fortunes of the OECD during the 'Long 1970,'" Paper presented at the Workshop "Crisis, Ideas and Policy Transformation: Experts and Expertise in European International Organizations, 1973–1987", Maastricht University, 2014; Gayon, "L'OCDE au travail." On rise of economics see Marion Fourcade, *Economists and Societies: Discipline and Profession in the United States, Britain, and France, 1890s to 1990s* (Princeton: Princeton University Press, 2009); Alfred W. Coats, ed., *Economists in International Agencies: An Exploratory Study* (New York: Praeger, 1986).
95. TNA, FO 371/72016, Hall-Patch to Makins, 22 November 1948; FO 371/71915, Saunders to Gore-Booth, 31 August 1948. For more on this see Schmelzer, *Hegemony*, Chap. 1; Benoît Godin, *Measurement and Statistics on Science and Technology: 1920 to the Present* (London and New York: Routledge, 2005).
96. OECD, *Interfutures*; Schmelzer, *Hegemony*, Chap. 9; on the context see Jenny Andersson, "The Great Future Debate and the Struggle for the World," *The American Historical Review* 117, no. 5 (December 1, 2012): 1411–1430.
97. Vincent Gayon, "Un atelier d'écriture internationale: l'OCDE au travail. Éléments de sociologie de la forme 'rapport'," *Sociologie du Travail* 51, no. 3 (2009): 324–342.
98. Tony Porter and Michael Webb, "The Role of the OECD in the Orchestration of Global Knowledge Networks," in *The OECD and Transnational Governance*, ed. Rianne Mahon and Stephen McBride (Vancouver: University of British Columbia Press, 2008), 43–59, here 44. For a constructivist discussion of the role of identities in international politics see Alexander Wendt, *Social Theory of International Politics* (Cambridge: Cambridge University Press, 1999).
99. Thorkil Kristensen, "Five Years of OECD," *European Yearbook* 13 (1967): 103f.
100. Yugoslavia was given observer status when the OECD was formed in 1961. For more on this see the chapter by Andrej Markovic and Ivan Obadic in this volume. TNA, PREM 11/4228, Record of a Meeting between Ball and Lord Home, 21 December 1962; FO 371/150108,

Record of a conversation with Kristensen, 18 October 1960; PREM 11/4228, Record of a Meeting between Ball and Lord Home, 21 December 1962; OECD, "Working with Yugoslavia," *The OECD Observer* 3 (March 1963): 12–13.

101. See for example TNA, FCO 69/322, F.G.K. Gallagher, "Some Impressions of OECD," Permanent UK Representative to the OECD at Paris to the Secretary of State for Foreign and Commonwealth Affairs, 24 August 1972.
102. TNA, FO 371/150108, Record of a conversation with Kristensen, 18 October 1960; TNA, FO 371/150087, Ellis-Rees to Foreign Office, 29 March 1960. In April 1960 Soviet Russia expressed its interest in participating in the new economic organization, but the proposal was rejected.
103. NARA, RG 59, Entry 5304, Box 22, Folder OECD Ministerial Meeting 1962, Remarks by Ball, 27 November 1962; Entry A1 5605, Box 12, Folder E 1—EPC, 1967–1971, J.P. Ferriter to Dallas Jones, 2 October 1968.
104. Mahbubani, "The OECD"; Woodward, *The OECD*.

A Short Guide to Historical Archives, Online Resources, and Research Materials on the OEEC/OECD

OECD Library & Archives, Paris, France

www.oecd.org/general/oecdarchives.htm.

The OECD Library & Archives collection dates from 1947. It includes records from the Conference for European Economic Cooperation (CEEC), the OEEC, and the OECD. The collection contains items which document the Organization's work, including agendas and minutes of Council and committee meetings, background documents, technical and working papers, publications, press information, and Secretary-Generals' speeches. Most material is available as microfilm or microfiche. There are also paper-boxes, and some of the newer material since 1990 has been digitalized (see: http://search.oecd.org/officialdocuments/years). The OECD Library & Archives also contains full collections of several key reference books about the OEEC/OECD (see below, key printed and online materials). Unfortunately, a comprehensive finding aid is not yet available on the OECD website. Researchers thus have to rely on the information and guidance of the OECD Library & Archives staff in Paris.

Historical Archives of the European Union, Firenze, Italy

www.eui.eu/Research/HistoricalArchivesOfEU/Index.aspx.

The Historical Archives of the European Union (HAEU) situated at the European University Institute hosts archives of the CEEC and OEEC (1947–1961). Most material is available online at http://archives.eui.eu/en/fonds/173448?item=OEEC. Copies of the documents can also be found at the OECD archive in Paris (as microfilm and microfiche). According to the archive, the HAEU holdings contain: "Mainly official documents of the OEEC describing activities of the various OEEC bodies and committees and working parties, including complete series of Minutes and Working Papers of the Council and Executive Committee. A relevant part of the fonds, arranged in Subject Files concerns the creation of a Free Trade Area." The archive also hosts various holdings on the European Communities and on OEEC-related institutions such as the European Productivity Agency (EPA), European Payments Union (EPU), or the European Nuclear Energy Agency (ENEA).

To supplement these two main archival collections, researchers are highly advised to consult the historical archives of other international organizations, as well as national archives, which often contain copies of OECD documents as well as paper files with much more details on OECD-related work processes, negotiations, or surveys.

Key Published and Online Materials

An annotated bibliography, *The European Reconstruction 1948–1961: A Bibliography on the Marshall Plan and the Organisation for European Economic Co-operation and Development* (Paris: OECD, 1996) is available on the OECD website.

The main OECD Acts, or *Decisions, Recommendations and other Instruments of the OEEC/OECD* (since 1957) are available online at http://webnet.oecd.org/oecdacts/Default.aspx (searchable by type, title, committee, and date). The *Acts* of the OEEC and OECD, which contain further information, are also available in printed form at the OECD Library and Archives. The *Directory of Bodies of the Organization* also contain invaluable information about the committee structure of the Organization and are available in printed form at the OECD Library & Archives.

The *Annual Reports* of the OECD (from 1970 onward) can be found in several libraries, as well as at the OECD Library & Archives. Before 1970, the annual report of the OEEC, and then the OECD, was published as a report to the Council of Europe. Some exemplars are available in printed form, others exist only as typescripts. The *Annuaire européen/European Yearbook*, published since 1953, also contains a regular chronology of OEEC/OECD activities, as well as information on its Secretariat and main publications.

Database of OECD and international tax documents: This joint project of several universities and tax research centers offers a wealth of historic and official documents drafted in preparation not only of the OECD Model Convention of 1963, but also of the older convention drafted under the League of Nations. Online at www.taxtreatieshistory.org

Since 2010, the OECD has also begun to digitalize large quantities of its core publications. These are available on the OECD iLibrary (www.oecd-ilibrary.org). These publications include:

1. The OECD *Economic Outlook* (1967 to present), a bi-annual analysis of the current economic situation of the OECD area.
2. The OECD *Economic Surveys* (1961 to present), which contain periodic reviews of member and non-member economies prepared through a peer review procedure by the Economic and Development Review Committee (EDRC). Currently, member country reviews are generally done on an 18-month cycle, while non-member reviews are done as agreed with the subject country (for more details, see the chapter by William Gray in this volume).
3. The *OECD Observer* (1962 to present), a quarterly magazine presenting concise and up-to-date analysis of world economic and social issues, providing an easy entry-point into current OECD work.

PART I

Being Part of the West

Western European Vs. All-European Cooperation? The OEEC, the European Recovery Program, and the United Nations Economic Commission for Europe (ECE), 1947–1952

Daniel Stinsky

This chapter examines the entangled histories of the OEEC and the UN Economic Commission for Europe (ECE) during the years of the European Recovery Program (ERP). The OEEC and the ECE were intergovernmental organizations founded in 1947/1948 with essentially the same task: to facilitate economic cooperation in Europe. At an OEEC Council meeting in 1948, the British delegate emphasized that OEEC and ECE were "working in a common field and it was important that there should be no overlap…both organisations should be complementary to each other."[1] In practice, however, their relationship was not devoid of antagonism. To the OEEC, the ECE was a competitor, collaborator, sounding board, and alter ego. The continuous self-reinvention so characteristic of the OEEC/OECD was mirrored by the ECE. The key difference between them was their geographical scope. While the ECE as a UN organization covered a wide range of member states,

D. Stinsky (✉)
Maastricht University, 6211 LK Maastricht, Netherlands
e-mail: daniel.stinsky@maastrichtuniversity.nl

M. Leimgruber and M. Schmelzer (eds.), *The OECD and the International Political Economy Since 1948*, DOI 10.1007/978-3-319-60243-1_3

including the Soviet Union and the United States, the OEEC embodied a new conception of "Western Europe" as not only a geopolitical, but also an economic entity. In the ensuing competition between an all-European and a Western European venue for economic cooperation, the OEEC established itself as "Warden of the West"—a platform outside the global UN framework that defined and produced the geographical entity of "Western Europe."

What was the relationship between these two international organizations (IOs), sharing similar tasks and an overlapping membership (see Table 1)? From the very beginning, both organizations were competitors, but also dependent on one another for their success. When the Marshall Plan was first announced, officials at the newly founded ECE expected that they would allocate the ERP money. But once it became clear that the Soviet Union and its satellites would not participate, Western governments instead created the OEEC for this very purpose. To do so, the OEEC's technical committees relied heavily on economic analyses and statistical information issued by the ECE Secretariat. Conversely, the ECE needed the ERP to succeed in order to progress with its own reconstruction agenda. The first ECE Executive Secretary, renowned Swedish economist Gunnar Myrdal, was keenly aware of this complex "community of destiny":

> Right from the start, we in Geneva have been deeply conscious of the community of destiny we share with the ERP. When things go well in Paris, conditions for cooperation in Geneva are also good. When the work in Paris is up to difficulties, the Western countries get sick and tired of international conferences and can, already for political reasons, not allow much progress to be made on an all-European level in Geneva. This is one side of our relationship with OEEC. I am quite conscious of the fact that things can go so "well" in OEEC that there is no space left for us and UN.[2]

While the ECE is still active today, its place in public perception and in historiography is marginal at best.[3] It seems tempting to suggest that Myrdal was right, and that things did go so well in the OEEC and elsewhere that there was, indeed, no space left for the ECE: paralyzed by East-West antagonism, the all-European ECE was outperformed by the Western-centered OEEC and, later on, the European Communities. The standard literature on the history of European integration, while for the most part conscious of the OEEC, rarely mentions the ECE at all.[4] For example, in his seminal work on the reconstruction of Western Europe,

Table 1 The overlapping memberships of the ECE and OEEC/OECD before 1989

Founding members in bold

ECE	*OEEC/OECD*
Albania (1955)	
Austria (1955)	**Austria**
Belgium	**Belgium**
Bulgaria (1955)	
Belorussian SSR	
Canada (1973)	Canada (1961, OECD)
Czechoslovakia	
Cyprus (1960)	
Denmark	**Denmark**
Federal Republic of Germany (1956)	**Federal Republic of Germany**[a]
France	**France**
Finland (1955)	Finland (1969, OECD)
German Democratic Republic (1973)	
Greece	**Greece**
Hungary (1955)	
Iceland	**Iceland**
Ireland (1955)	**Ireland**
Italy (1955)	**Italy**
Luxembourg	**Luxembourg**
Malta (1963)	
Netherlands	**Netherlands**
Norway	**Norway**
Poland	
Portugal (1955)	**Portugal**
Romania (1955)	
Spain (1955)	Spain (1959)
Sweden	**Sweden**
Switzerland (1972)	**Switzerland**
Turkey	**Turkey**
Ukrainian SSR	
United Kingdom	**United Kingdom**
United States	United States (1961, OECD)
USSR	
Yugoslavia	Yugoslavia (observer status)
	Japan (1964, OECD)
	Australia (1971, OECD)
	New Zealand (1973, OECD)

[a]*Note* West Germany (FRG) was originally represented at the OEEC by both the combined American and British occupation zones (the Bizone) and the French occupation zone. The Anglo-American zone of the Free Territory of Trieste was also a participant in the OEEC until it returned to Italian sovereignty

Alan Milward mentions the ECE in the context of the Paris conference, but ignores its active part in European reconstruction.[5] Recent historiography, however, has started to work with ECE sources and acknowledges its role in international cooperation during the Cold War.[6] Historians of technology have further emphasized the ECE's crucial function in what they call the "hidden integration" of Europe via norms and processes of standardization.[7] While the OEEC/OECD turned out to be the more visible and arguably more successful of two elusive organizations, their struggle was not Darwinian: the ECE survived and continues to fill specialized niches of international cooperation.[8]

This chapter argues that the ECE and the OEEC did indeed share a "community of destiny," as Myrdal suggested. While the ECE had only just begun its work when the Marshall Plan was projected, it did provide the machinery and a venue that could have administered the ERP, and was at least considered as a serious option. While the ERP was a caesura, it did not negate earlier efforts at institutionalized rapprochement within the UN framework. The ECE continued to exist in parallel, and provided an alternative to the ongoing bloc formation. Both IOs were designed to be ambitious instruments for the international coordination of general economic policy, but in practice became forums for non-binding agreements on technical and trade-related issues. How these tasks were to be divided between them was a constant bone of contention that could not be adequately resolved, since all coordination had to remain informal. In both cases, the Secretariats became crucial parts of the organizations, issuing statistics and economic analyses.[9] Neither organization became the main vehicle of European integration, but both had a significant, yet unquantifiable, impact on the process. This is true not only concerning their technical work and their contributions to "hidden integration," but also with regard to the political frames they set. While the earliest efforts at economic cooperation in Europe after World War II were strictly within the framework of the UN, the OEEC left this frame and thus paved the way for the purely Western "Europe of the Six." Incidentally, the creation of the European Coal and Steel Community (ECSC) in 1952 repeated the pattern of one group of member states of the existing OEEC forming a new organization outside its framework, just as the OEEC had been a group of countries within the ECE.[10]

Looking at the beginnings of the OEEC through the lens of the ECE thus enables both a comparison and a fundamental reconsideration. In 1947–1948, Western Europe was not so much a given economic entity that could be *re*constructed. Rather, the imagined community of

Western European states had to be actively constructed while the rubble was cleaned up, and the OEEC had no small part in both processes.

The UN and the ERP: From a Global to a Regional Framework

The ideas that shaped both the ECE and the ERP emanated from the same offices of the economic staff headed by US Undersecretary of State William L. Clayton.[11] They were, however, formulated under different circumstances and based on different evaluations of past experiences. The ECE, like the UN in general, was meant to be a continuation of wartime cooperation between the Allies. Its very purpose was to prevent a division of Europe. The decision to give ownership of the ERP to a newly created Western organization marked a shift in American foreign policy, from the global position represented by the UN to a regional approach embodied in the OEEC. When Secretary of State George Marshall proposed American funding for an internationally coordinated reconstruction program, he purposefully did not mention the UN or the ECE.[12] On the day of Marshall's speech, the ECE was just a few weeks old, but it was the only existing body dedicated to general economic cooperation in Europe. Speculation in the press initially saw the ECE as the natural venue for the elaboration of the Marshall Plan. Among and within governments, opinions were divided.[13] State Department officials like Joseph M. Jones "assumed that the ECE would carry the ball." Marshall's speech did not assign any role to the UN, instead leaving the decision to European governments.[14] The British and French were more reluctant to use the all-European platform for the ERP than the State Department, but they did consider the option.[15]

The ECE had replaced inter-Allied humanitarian and emergency organizations active in World War II's final years and immediate aftermath. These organizations were the United Nations Relief and Rehabilitation Administration (UNRRA) and the three so-called "E-Organizations": The European Coal Committee (ECO), the European Central Inland Transport Organization (ECITO), and the Emergency Economic Committee for Europe (EECE). The prevalent idea behind these institutional reforms was to continue inter-Allied cooperation for emergency relief in a permanent form of institutionalized economic cooperation in Europe under UN auspices.[16] Walt Whitman Rostow of the State Department's German-Austrian Affairs Unit drafted the first outline for what would eventually become the ECE.[17] Rostow's draft specifically referred to "the assumption that Europe must one day divide into exclusive eastern and western 'blocs'" and addressed the prevention of such a division.[18] The ECE was thus created as an instrument of preserving the wartime alliance in the face of the emerging Cold War. The ECE was also a continuation of an older form of technical internationalism. Rostow claimed in an interview many years later that he had wanted to "get the old League of Nations building used."[19] Besides being housed in the *Palais des Nations*, the ECE's work shared also practical similarities with the League's technical committees.[20] The organizational set-up and working methods of the ECE reveal a high degree of continuity from the League's technical work, embodying, as historians Wolfram Kaiser and Johan Schot put it, "the technocratic internationalist approach during the Cold War."[21]

The ERP, on the other hand, opened a new chapter in international relations in Europe fundamentally shaped by the Truman doctrine.[22] In Truman's bid to Congress for foreign aid to shore up Greece and Turkey against communist insurgence, the newly founded UN was omitted in favor of a unilateral undertaking. The containment of communist expansion took precedence over rapprochement, and facilitating Western European reconstruction took priority over America's earlier commitment to revive all-European trade. The experience of wartime relief cooperation contributed to this change of mind in the State Department. UNRRA, in particular, became a cautionary tale. It was criticized as overly expensive, inefficient, and granting too little authority to its main financier, the United States. Upon his return from the ECE's first session in spring 1947, Clayton noted that, this time, "we must avoid getting into another UNRRA. *The United States must run this show* [sic]."[23]

Marshall proposed the ERP in a speech at Harvard that took place in between the ECE's first and second sessions.[24] ECE's Executive Secretary Gunnar Myrdal had then already scheduled a tour of European capitals via Paris, London, Stockholm, and Moscow. The American proposition became the main subject of all his conversations with governments. In Paris and London, Myrdal learned of tentative French-British plans to bypass the ECE and to invite only a small number of European countries to discuss the American proposal, including Poland, but not the USSR. Myrdal criticized this approach, believing it would force a split between East and West, "destroy the chances of useful work" in the ECE, and "derogate from standing and value" of the UN. Instead, Myrdal proposed that an "ad hoc European planning committee" should be formed at the upcoming ECE session and "remain in practically permanent session" to supervise the reconstruction plan.[25] This proposed ECE committee was, in effect, a potential alternative to the Committee of European Economic Co-Operation, which was later transformed into the OEEC. At his next stop in Stockholm, Myrdal's proposal received public support from the Swedish Minister of Foreign Affairs Östen Undén. Speaking with Vyacheslav Molotov in Moscow, Myrdal repeated his proposal and warned that a "lack of positive Soviet response to [the] Marshall declaration" would "show green light to advocates of [an] ad hoc West Bloc organization for European reconstruction." In this argument, Molotov allegedly "showed great interest and said it was being carefully studied by his Government."[26] When Molotov left for Paris a few days later, he thus knew that he could attempt to channel the Marshall Plan through Geneva. The alternative to the UN was bloc formation.

Molotov famously left the following meeting with Georges Bidault and Ernest Bevin, taking the delegations of Poland and Czechoslovakia with him.[27] Yet, while the British, French, and Americans had hoped that the Soviet Union would exclude itself from the Marshall Plan, they could hardly have openly rejected a Soviet insistence on funneling the money through the UN. When Molotov's deputy Andrei Vyschinsky attacked the Marshall Plan in the General Assembly as a violation of the UN's principles and "an attempt to split Europe into two camps," he ignored that his government had been offered a potential alternative.[28] Rostow insisted that the choice was, ultimately, Stalin's:

> ...with an unconsolidated Poland, unconsolidated Czechoslovakia, unconsolidated Hungary, what Stalin saw was that if he put this thing in Geneva, and the money was coming out of the United Nations, the pull on Eastern Europe would be too much...there's no doubt in my mind that the Russians had the option open to them, of forcing the Marshall Plan into Geneva...once [Molotov] had left, it was clear that the Marshall Plan would be set up and the ECE would be a separate thing.[29]

Ownership of the ERP by the ECE would have implied that the ERP was labeled as a UN project rather than an American undertaking. It would thus have strengthened the UN and continued the globalist approach to reconstruction, which saw European cooperation as embedded within the UN framework. Moreover, it would have included the possibility for the USSR and Eastern European governments to participate, as recipients and contributors, and with an active part in the distribution process. The decision to forego the UN was an active decision for bloc formation from both sides, and it laid the foundation for the economic consolidation of Western Europe.

Institutional Dualism and Contested Division of Labor

With the creation of the OEEC as a permanent organization to administer the ERP, a Western club emerged within the ECE. The two organizations represented two possible paths for the future: maintaining the possibility for *détente* or exclusive consolidation of the Western bloc. When France and Britain invited 16 countries to the Committee of European Economic Co-Operation' conference in Paris, the delegations of Norway and Sweden objected to a permanent Western organization, arguing that it would further cement the East-West conflict.[30] The Committee's concluding draft report still insisted on the UN as the framework for any long-term economic cooperation in Europe, stating that a new organization "will be of a temporary character and will cease to exist when the special aid necessary for the recovery of Europe comes to an end."[31] Agreement on a permanent OEEC was reached only after a fierce American intervention.[32] The prospect was worrying to Myrdal, who consigned to Undén:

> …my apprehensions are not primarily motivated by a fear that ECE might get a dangerous competitor in a permanent organization to carry out the "Marshall Plan", but rather by the political implications…the establishment of permanent technical committees under the CEEC would mean simply the hardening of the East/West conflict and…a definite closing of the "open door" which exists at the present time in the form of the Economic Commission for Europe.[33]

These fears were mirrored in the British Foreign Office, which conversely regarded the ECE as a threat to the ERP. British diplomats warned their American counterparts about a "risk of ECE being used to sabotage ERP."[34] An internal minute claimed that the "immediate Soviet objective is to prevent the consolidation of Western Europe…. [B]y playing up ECE… they may still hope to create a UNO which will over-shadow the ERP organization."[35] The British attitude toward the ECE turned increasingly hostile over the course of 1948. British diplomats regarded Myrdal's efforts to expand the ECE's activities into the steel sector as dangerous for the nascent OEEC. The Foreign Office even described it as "one of the main preoccupations" of its people in Geneva "to keep the activities of the [ECE] Secretariat within bounds,"[36] leading the director of the ECE's Research and Planning Division, Nicholas Kaldor, to complain that the British government was "sabotaging ECE" in favor of the OEEC.[37]

In contrast, the State Department was determined to keep both IOs running. There were four reasons for continued American support of the ECE while the OEEC began its work. First, withdrawing American backing from the ECE would have had negative repercussions on the entire UN system, especially since the ECE was considered one of the more successful early UN organizations.[38] Second, the ECE could be used to secure raw materials from Eastern Europe that were crucial for Western recovery—especially timber, coal, and foodstuffs. Third, the ECE machinery could relieve the OEEC and allow it to focus on the ERP, without overburdening it with technical problems better left to Geneva. Fourth, in the long run, the ECE could help increase the "economic dependence of Eastern Europe on [the] West," weakening Stalin's grip on the satellites.[39] The US government thus pursued a double strategy: consolidating Western Europe as an economic bloc through the OEEC while keeping the ECE alive to retain a minimum of economic ties across the descending Iron Curtain.

The resulting institutional dualism of the ECE and the OEEC caused a tortuous debate about their division of labor that was never adequately resolved, and led to some intricate maneuvering by the Secretariats and governments. When the OEEC officially entered relations with the ECE in June 1948, both sides said a productive working relationship on the technical level was crucial, but it proved difficult to establish.[40] Worsening East-West tensions brought the ECE into a precarious position, as Eastern governments began to stay away from its technical committees. In September 1948, top officials of both Secretariats met in Geneva, but insisted that no formal relations were established between the organizations, as this would have been opposed by the ECE's Eastern European members.[41] Formal relations were not established on the committee level either, as had previously been done between the ECE and the Food and Agricultural Organization (FAO). The Secretariats suggested instead that governments should send the same delegates to related committee meetings at both IOs, a practice that was largely adopted, but did not solve the coordination problems.[42]

While both sides shied away from open antagonism, the two organizations were clearly competitors. The secretary of the OEEC's electricity committee told a member of the US delegation to the ECE that, ultimately, "either ECE or OEEC will have to be disbanded in favor of the other, depending whether the present political situation with respect to Eastern Europe continues or improves."[43] Both organizations were due for benchmarking around 1951–1952. The ECE was scheduled for review by the United Nations Economic and Social Council after 5 years. If Eastern governments continued to abstain, and Western governments convened exclusively in Paris, there would not be a new mandate. The future of the OEEC after the end of the ERP in the same year was equally uncertain. Without technical committees of its own, it could not steer the ERP efficiently, and might be disbanded or merged with the ECE at the end of the program.[44] It was therefore crucial to both IOs to achieve a clear division of labor without duplication before 1951. Governments and Secretariats drew up plans that should outline areas of responsibility. Averell Harriman, the American official in charge of the Marshall Plan, told the *Times* that "the work of the ECE, which covers the whole of Europe, and that of the OEEC, which is concerned chiefly with Western Europe, were complementary."[45] The negotiations behind the scenes, however, were not that simple, and geographical scope alone did not account for the division of labor between the IOs. By taking over the work of the "E-Organizations," the ECE already controlled highly valuable working structures and expertise, especially in the areas of coal allocation, timber, and inland transport.[46] Parallel structures were nonetheless established at the OEEC. Oil, textiles, and shipping were allocated to Paris, as the ECE was not active in any of those fields. Contestation arose particularly about steel and inland transport.[47] The Secretariats sought to mark the responsibilities by subdividing these topics, leaving questions of a more general concern to the ECE and charging the OEEC with problems directly related to the ERP or American goods.[48] In practice, however, the committees did not adhere to what the Secretariats had agreed on.[49] Western governments began to use the two venues tactically, taking issues to wherever they had the most bargaining value. For example, a Dutch delegate told a member of the ECE Secretariat that even though ECE was better prepared to handle inland transport matters, his government preferred to settle them at the OEEC, where concessions in transport could be used as a bargaining chip in other areas.[50] Such tactical use of the IOs' parallel structures made their division of labor a constant bone of contention.

Although competition continued to mark their relations, the two organizations were also dependent on one another. When government experts in the OEEC's technical committees first took up their work, they relied heavily on studies and statistical material published by the ECE. The ECE Secretariat prided itself with an independent Research Division that published a yearly *Economic Survey of Europe* and a quarterly *Economic Bulletin*. These and other studies were conducted under the sole responsibility of the Executive Secretary and did not need the member states' approval for publication, unlike at the OEEC.[51] The Norwegian OEEC-Council member Arne Skaug told Myrdal confidentially that consensus-based voting on reports prevented the OEEC Secretariat from setting up a similar research apparatus, "which would only be prostituted" and not provide independent analysis.[52] Comparing reports by the ECE and the OEEC, one American reviewer wrote:

> ...whereas the ECE report is mainly the independent expression of the views of the research staff of that organization, the OEEC report required the full agreement...of the various participating governments. This helps to explain...its tendency at times to indulge in platitudes and generalities, and its obvious effort to avoid offending national sensibilities...The ECE study, on the other hand, has no such inhibitions against taking a stand on more controversial matters.[53]

With the commission paralyzed by East-West tension, the research activity of its Secretariat became an important *raison d'être* for the ECE: of 169 staff members in 1954, 63 worked in research.[54] While the OEEC Secretariat employed more than 800 people, the much smaller ECE Secretariat had an edge in research.[55] Experts in the OEEC's committees were keen to make use of this apparatus. When setting up their first annual program, several OEEC committees "invited" the ECE to make specific reports for them.[56] Such direct requests were eventually ruled out by an informal agreement between the Secretariats, but exchange of information remained frequent. Myrdal insisted that as a UN organization, the ECE did not produce anything secret: "Any information at the disposal of the ECE may be supplied to the OEEC."[57] This openness was not reciprocal. To counter Western concerns that sensitive information could be leaked to Eastern governments, the ECE Secretariat had to treat all material they received from Paris as highly confidential. All communication was initially kept at the highest level, and channeled through the respective offices of the OEEC's Secretary-General and the

ECE's Executive Secretary.[58] Secretariat cooperation was still the closest form of coordination between the IOs, although it was consciously kept informal to avoid confrontation with governments. Practical Secretariat cooperation entailed the scheduling of meetings, so that governments would not have to send experts to two meetings simultaneously, and the informal exchange of documents. The Secretariats agreed at their earliest meetings to standardize statistics and the questionnaires they sent to governments.[59] Myrdal urged his Secretariat directors to "adopt a positive and constructive attitude regarding the OEEC"[60] and "to render to the OEEC Secretariat the assistance [ECE] would give to any of its participating governments."[61] Delegates of the Soviet Union and other Eastern governments regularly criticized the ECE Secretariat for its informal connections with the OEEC and other Western organizations, accusing it of maintaining contacts with "organizations…committed to a policy of aggression under United States guidance."[62]

The parallel existence of the ECE and the OEEC thus followed a pattern of competition and interdependence. While the OEEC was ostensibly the more successful organization—with a bigger Secretariat and budget and without the ideological rift of the Cold War running through it—the ECE still filled several important niches, especially with regard to research, the transport and coal sectors, and maintaining a link across the Iron Curtain. When the ERP was nearing its end, blocs were an established reality in international politics. While communist takeovers consolidated Eastern Europe under Soviet hegemony, Western Europe was shored up under the American security umbrella through NATO. Existing economic ties were severed even further. The OEEC was crucial in making Western Europe economically viable, steering traditional trade flows to new outlets within the bloc. Meanwhile, Eastern absenteeism in the technical committees showcased the futility of ECE's all-European setup; geopolitics was driving the consolidation of new, separate economic entities in the East and West.

From the End of the ERP to the Coal and Steel Community

By the beginning of the 1950s, both organizations were experiencing an existential crisis. The ECE's initial core project of preventing or at least cushioning the split of Europe into two camps had failed, and its day-to-day work on technical cooperation had become a Sisyphean task. Fierce ideological disputes and propaganda from both sides dominated the commission sessions for years. Actual results were obtained almost exclusively on the committee level, where Eastern European governments participated only rarely before 1953. The ECE's efforts at East-West trade were made almost impossible by an increasingly discriminatory American trade policy. The United States blacklisted so-called strategic goods from export to the USSR and its satellites and obligated the ERP recipients to do the same.[63] Delegates at the OEEC regarded the American licensing policy as "a business for Geneva," consciously avoiding this difficult and divisive subject.[64] With East-West trade declining further, the ECE's self-proclaimed goal to be a "bridge between East and West" seemed unobtainable for the time being, putting the organization's usefulness into question. At the same time, the OEEC was under pressure by the newly created NATO, a reluctant US Congress, and a resistance by European governments against American demands to "integrate" economically and politically. The OEEC Secretariat was to be downsized considerably, as NATO was about to take over some of its responsibilities.[65] When Congress was about to vote on a prolongation of the ERP, a group of Congressmen visiting Geneva told Myrdal that the ECE and other UN organizations "were carrying out important work on budgets which were drops in the bucket compared with the costs of ERP" and that none of them felt inclined to vote for an extension.[66] In Congress and in published opinion, the pressure on the American leadership increased to demand more from the Europeans. Instead of relying on an indefinite continuation of the ERP, the recipient countries should commit to political and economic integration.

The term "integration" was chosen by the State Department and kept deliberately vague to balance expectations between Congress and European governments. Paul Hoffman, the head of the Economic Cooperation Administration, coined the buzzword in a speech at the OEEC Council in October 1949.[67] Miriam Camps, who coordinated American policy in both the OEEC and the ECE in the State Department, suggested before Hoffman's speech: "Let us use the word 'integration' instead of 'unification,' because unification to the Congress means the United States of Europe, and the Europeans aren't going to do that…'Integration', nobody knows what it means."[68] Following Hoffman's speech, Myrdal criticized the "too big talking" about European integration in his confidential reports to UN Headquarters: European politicians paid lip service to it to please the Americans, but Europe's economies were still bent toward national autarchy.

Even worse, Myrdal continued, grand expectations of European integration were detrimental to the practical work of both the ECE and the OEEC:

> …concrete, hard-won practical accomplishments in the field of European economic cooperation which, measured by any reasonable standard of previous times, are important, get an appearance of being petty and insignificant when measured against the publicised grand expectations of economic 'integration' and the creation of "a single market." This applies to all our work in ECE—road agreements, coal allocation and coal classification, timber market arrangements, etc.—and also to all the work, besides splitting the dollars, which has actually been done in OEEC.[69]

Neither the ECE nor the OEEC became the main instrument of European integration. Both organizations abandoned grand schemes of international economic policy coordination in favor of less politicized, trade- and productivity-related issues. At the OEEC, the trade liberalization program largely replaced aspirations for political integration. This was, as Milward put it, "thought of as a more apolitical route to the same goal, the use of Marshall Aid to force European countries to remove legislative and administrative barriers to trade."[70] At the ECE, Myrdal identified East-West trade as "our responsibility *par préférence.* It cannot be taken over by OEEC."[71] This agenda had little success at first. The ECE survived its benchmarking in 1952 due to its entrenchment in various intergovernmental functions, e.g., coal allocation, the Secretariat's scientific work, and considerable practical accomplishments in inland transport, like the E-road system of European highways or the *Transports Internationaux Routiers* (TIR) convention.[72] When the Six began their comparatively small-scale program of incremental integration with the ECSC in 1952, the ECE and the OEEC had thus each found a different niche.

Following the Korean War and a perceived need to increase military spending, OEEC created a new focus on productivity with the introduction of the European Productivity Agency (EPA), a semi-autonomous organization within the framework of the OEEC in 1952. The purpose of the American-financed EPA was to increase productivity in order to maintain living standards while keeping up with military spending.[73] With the EPA, new OEEC committees on housing and inland transport were created, challenging some of the ECE's core competences.[74] The ECE Secretariat lobbied unsuccessfully against the EPA undertaking any work in these fields, going so far as to threaten governments to close down the inland transport committee if something comparable were to be set up at the EPA.[75] With growing Eastern participation after Stalin's death, the ECE's position was much stronger than before, at a time when the OEEC was still looking for a reorientation after the end of the ERP. The ECE Secretariat declined a proposal by the OEEC's Director of Technical Services to rationalize committee work by abolishing parallel committees. On the contrary, the ECE even expanded into agriculture and industry, areas where its committees had previously been dormant.[76] While the haggling for fields of technical cooperation continued, the principles of Secretariat cooperation were relaxed. The Secretariats agreed to exchange observers to committee meetings, kicking off a lively practice of commuting between Paris and Geneva. The two Secretariats also repeatedly exchanged staff members. Qualified personnel whose contracts ended at the ECE sometimes took up jobs at the OEEC, and vice versa. But both sides stayed guarded: Myrdal, for example, noted on the increasing cooperation between the Secretariats, "[i]t is fine, but we will always have to defend our fortresses."[77] The pattern of institutional dualism established in the beginning—competition and interdependence—thus continued even after the end of the ERP.

While the ECE after Stalin's death and throughout the 1950s made reasonable progress in its trade agenda, particularly in the technical aspects of trade facilitation through transport and infrastructure, the new Western European organizations naturally posed a bigger challenge to the OEEC. The institutional dualism of a Western European vs. an all-European venue was overshadowed by a new antagonism between supranational and intergovernmental approaches. The OEEC had helped to shape Western Europe as an economic entity, an imagined community of countries not just in the minds of geo-strategists, but also of economists and businessmen. The postwar conception of an all-European economic organization embedded in the global UN system that the ECE embodied had been pushed to the sidelines by the Cold War and by the OEEC's relative success. Now, the OEEC found itself being challenged *within* Western Europe. The push for a common market by the six members of the ECSC raised the threat of a discriminatory bloc within the OEEC.[78] The standoff between intergovernmentalists and supranationalists within the OEEC intensified with the establishment of the European Economic Community (EEC) in 1957 and the European Free Trade Association (EFTA) in 1960. Under these circumstances, the dynamic institutional dualism of OEEC and ECE came to an end, at the latest with the re-conception of OEEC as OECD in 1960.[79]

Conclusion

"Institutions, when they are once created, live their own life."[80] For the ECE and the OEEC, this statement from Myrdal's reports to UNHQ is certainly true. Both organizations fell short of becoming what they were intended to be, but nevertheless developed a purpose for their continued existence. The "lives" of the OEEC and the ECE were connected and intertwined from the beginning. They were competitors, not only as venues of diplomacy and technical cooperation, but also as competing conceptions of Europe. While the ECE was in many ways a continuation of the League of Nations' technical work and intended to revive economic activity on an all-European scale, the OEEC helped to constitute "Western Europe" as a new geopolitical and economic unit.

Both IOs had their origins in the US Department of State, but at different points in time and under different policy goals. The ECE was created in 1946–1947 to be a continuation of the wartime alliance. It was meant to help prevent a division of Europe into blocs. With the Truman doctrine, American priorities changed, and the containment of communism took precedence over rapprochement. Yet, the institutions created within the global frame of the UN, including the ECE, continued to exist and offered a potential alternative to bloc formation. When the Marshall Plan was in the making, it was likely that the splitting of the dollars would take place at the ECE. The decision to forego the ECE marked a turn away from the UN and toward regionalism, facilitating bloc formation. This decision was taken by Western governments, but the Soviet side did not attempt to channel ERP funds through Geneva either, even though they had the option. Regionalist motives prevailed on both sides: while Stalin sought to consolidate his control over Eastern Europe, the United States launched the ERP to facilitate Western Europe.

The result was an institutional dualism in the economic sphere: a Western European OEEC and an all-European ECE. Both had similar objectives and an overlapping membership. Their technical work was interconnected. Formal relations could not be established, and the informal agreements between the Secretariats fell short of providing an adequate solution to overlap and duplication. Their different geographical scopes alone were not a sufficient basis for the division of labor. Between 1948 and 1953, Eastern governments hardly participated in ECE's technical committees, rendering the overlap of active membership even more problematic. Important tasks on which other sectors depended, such as the allocation of coal or the coordination of inland transport, had already been taken up by the older ECE when the OEEC began its work. Parallel structures were established nonetheless. Moreover, member governments of both organizations used the two venues tactically, taking issues to wherever they had the most bargaining value. Since formal relations could not be established on the commission level or in the technical committees, the closest form of cooperation between the OEEC and the ECE was between the Secretariats. The two Secretariats agreed on common statistical standards, made use of each other's expertise, and exchanged documents and sometimes personnel. Yet, they were still competitors and eager to defend their organizations' claims on certain areas of technical cooperation. While open competition was avoided, officials in both IOs were aware that too much success at the other venue could mean the end of their own mandate.

Over the course of the 1950s, both organizations turned their focus to trade liberalization, albeit for different reasons. The ECE's original purpose to prevent a division of Europe had lapsed, and the organization tried to reinvent itself as a "bridge between East and West." ECE's Executive Secretary declared increasing East-West trade to be the organization's core project. At the OEEC, trade liberalization seemed like an apolitical route to the goal of European integration after the ERP was running out. Both IOs were created with an ambitious political purpose they did not fulfill, but continued to exist and find useful tasks which changed over the years and were in similar areas: technical cooperation, trade liberalization, economic development, research, and statistics. Neither of the two intergovernmental organizations became the main vehicle of European integration. With the establishment of the purely Western "Europe of the Six," they both moved to the sidelines of ambitions for political integration.

Although the OECD's tasks and relevance today are larger than those of the ECE, they share a long, entangled history of competition and cooperation. The UN initially provided a potential alternative to economic bloc formation. The OEEC left this frame and shaped a *Western* European identity in the economic sphere. Today's OECD is perhaps in some ways more like Myrdal's ECE than its predecessor or today's ECE.

It has become an expert think tank and meeting place for general economic policy, with a strong focus on research and the publication of statistics, and with a geographical scope beyond Western Europe, much like what the ECE was intended to be.

Notes

1. Historical Archives of the European Union, Firenze (hereafter HAEU), C/M(48). Council Minutes of the 36th Meeting, 1 September 1948, 36.
2. United Nations Offices at Geneva Archives (hereafter UNOG), ARR 14/1360, Box 71, Gunnar Myrdal, Two Notes on ERP and East–West Trade, December 1949.
3. Most presentations on the history of the ECE have been written by former Secretariat members, such as Yves Berthelot, ed. *Unity and Diversity in Development Ideas. Perspectives from the UN Regional Commissions*, United Nations Intellectual History Project (Bloomington: Indiana University Press, 2004); Melvin M. Fagen, "Gunnar Myrdal and the Shaping of the United Nations Economic Commission for Europe," *Coexistence* 25 (1988), 427–435; Václav Kostelecký, *The United Nations Economic Commission for Europe: The Beginning of a History* (Göteborg: Graphic Systems, 1989).
4. Wilfried Loth, *Europas Einigung. Eine Unvollendete Geschichte* (Frankfurt and New York: Campus, 2014); Desmond Dinan, *Ever Closer Union. An Introduction to European Integration* (Basingstoke: Palgrave Macmillan, 2010); Gabriele Clemens, Alexander Reinfeldt, and Gerhard Wille, *Geschichte der Europäischen Integration. Ein Lehrbuch* (Paderborn: UTB, 2008).
5. Alan S. Milward, *The Reconstruction of Western Europe, 1945–1951* (Berkeley and Los Angeles, CA: University of California Press, 1984), 61–69.
6. Örjan Appelqvist, "Rediscovering Uncertainty: Early Attempts at a Pan-European Post-War Recovery," *Cold War History* 8, no. 3 (2008), 327–352; Sandrine Kott, "Par-delà la Guerre Froide. Les organisations internationales et les circulations Est-Ouest (1947–1973)," *Vingtième Siècle. Revue d'histoire* 109, no. 1 (2011), 142–154; Vincent Lagendijk, "The Structure of Power: The UNECE and East-West Electricity Connections, 1947–1975," *Comparativ* 24, no. 1 (2014), 50–65.
7. Thomas J. Misa and Johan Schot, "Inventing Europe: Technology and the Hidden Integration of Europe," *History and Technology* 21, no. 1 (2005), 1–19.

8. For an overview of their current activities, visit https://www.unece.org (accessed 4 October 2016).
9. Tom Griffin, "The Relationship of the United Nations Economic Commission for Europe (UN/ECE, Geneva) to the Organization for Economic Cooperation and Development (OECD, Paris) and the Statistical Office of the European Communities (Eurostat, Luxembourg)," *Statistical Journal of the United Nations ECE* 13, no. 1 (1996), 50–65.
10. Johnny Laursen, "Integration at Cross-Currents. The OEEC and the European Coal and Steel Community, 1952–56," in *Explorations in OEEC history*, ed. Richard T. Griffiths (Paris: OECD, 1997), 149–158.
11. Joseph M. Jones, *The Fifteen Weeks (February 21–June 5, 1947)* (New York: Viking Press, 1955), 241.
12. "Annex I: The Marshall Plan Speech. Address by General George C. Marshall, U.S. Secretary of State, Harvard University, 5 June 1947," in *Explorations in OEEC History*, ed. Richard T. Griffiths (Paris: OECD, 1997).
13. Mark Mazower, *No Enchanted Palace. The End of Empire and the Ideological Origins of the United Nations* (Princeton and Oxford: Princeton University Press, 2008), 99.
14. Jones, *The Fifteen Weeks*, 240–256.
15. Sevón, *Visionen om Europa: Svensk neutralitet och Europeisk återuppbyggnad 1945–1948*, Saarijärvi: Gummerus Kirjapaino Oy, 122–128.
16. On relief and reconstruction, see Jessica Reinisch, "Relief in the Aftermath of War," *Journal of Contemporary History* 43, no. 3 (2008), 371–404; "Internationalism in Relief: The Birth (and Death) of UNRRA," *Past and Present*, Supplement 6 (2011), 258–289; Andrew J. Williams, "'Reconstruction' before the Marshall Plan," *Review of International Studies* 31, no. 3 (2005), 541–558.
17. Rostow explains his reasoning behind the creation of the ECE in Walt W. Rostow, "The Economic Commission for Europe," *International Organization* 3, no. 2 (1949), 254–268.
18. UNOG ARR 14/1360, Box 69, Folder "W.W. Rostow," Draft of Proposed U.S. Plan for a European Settlement, Spring 1946.
19. Arbetarrörelsens arkiv och bibliotek, Stockholm (hereafter ARBARK), 3332—Václav Kostelecký (1946–1989): 4/3/7—Övriga handlingar rörande ECE. Transcript: Walt Rostow interviewed by Václav Kostelecký.
20. On the League's economic work, see Patricia Clavin, *Securing the World Economy. The Reinvention of the League of Nations, 1920–1946* (Oxford: Oxford University Press, 2013).

21. Wolfram Kaiser and Johan Schot, *Writing the Rules for Europe. Experts, Cartels and International Organisations* (Basingstoke/New York: Palgrave Macmillan, 2014), 77.
22. Dennis Merrill, "The Truman Doctrine: Containing Communism and Modernity," *Presidential Studies Quarterly* 36, no. 1 (2006), 27–37.
23. Clayton memo, 27 May 1947, in *Foreign Relations of the United States, 1947* (Washington, D.C. 1972), vol. 3, 230–232.
24. This episode is described in detail by Sevón, *Visionen om Europa*, 122–174.
25. Kungliga biblioteket, Stockholm (hereafter KB), Karin Kocks papper, Handlingar rörande Economic Commission for Europe, 1947–1960. Gunnar Myrdal to Trygve Lie, Telegram, Stockholm, 15 June 1947.
26. Ibid.
27. Oscar Sanchez-Sibony, *Red Gobalization. The Political Economy of the Soviet Cold War from Stalin to Krushchev* (Cambridge: Cambridge University Press, 2014), 64–70.
28. Vyshinsky Speech to the United Nations General Assembly, September 1947, in: Jussi Hanhimäki and Odd Arne Westad, eds., *The Cold War. A History in Documents and Eyewitness Accounts* (New York: Oxford University Press, 2003), 126–128.
29. ARBARK: 3332—Václav Kostelecký (1946–1989): 4/3/7—Övriga handlingar rörande ECE. Transcript: Walt Rostow interviewed by Václav Kostelecký.
30. Milward, *The Reconstruction of Western Europe*, 68.
31. UNOG Box 67, Folder I/3/2 ECE and Paris Conference, 1947–1953, Committee of European Economic Cooperation, General Report/Final Draft, n.d.
32. Milward, *The Reconstruction of Western Europe*, 81.
33. KB, Karin Kocks papper, Handlingar rörande Economic Commission for Europe, 1947–1960, Gunnar Myrdal to Östen Undén, 13 January 1948.
34. The National Archives, London (hereafter TNA), FO 371/71802: E.C.E. and C.E.E.C. relations. Brief for Discussion of C.E.E.C.–E.C.E. with the State Department.
35. ARBARK: Václav Kosteleckýs arkiv, 3332-4-2-2 Mars–december 1948, Kostelecký's notes on Foreign Office files, Minute by R.M.A. Hanbury, 20 May 1948.
36. TNA, FO 371/71802: E.C.E. and C.E.E.C. relations, E.R. Warner to Sir John Magowan, 10 March 1948.
37. TNA, FO 371/71802: E.C.E. and C.E.E.C. relations, The Economic Commission for Europe and the Continuing Organisation, 18 April 1948.
38. National Archives and Records Administration, College Park, MD (hereafter NARA): NND959154, US Representative to the Econ.

Commission for Europe, Classified and Unclassified ECE and ECA Files 1947–1951, Box 1, 103.01 ECE—General, Cables, Cable Message, Caffery to Nitze (ECA) and Porter (Geneva), 19 November 1948.

39. NARA: NND959154, US Representative to the Econ. Commission for Europe, Classified and Unclassified ECE and ECA Files 1947–1951, Box 1, 103.01 ECE—General, Cables, Paul Porter US Delegation at ECE, to State Department, 1 November 1948.
40. ARBARK, Vaclav Kostelecky, handlingar lagda enligt arkivplan, 3332-4-1-8: Ekonomiska grupper i Europa (ej FN), Decision of the Council concerning relations between the OEEC and other International Organisations, C/M (48)10 (Final), item 4—Doc, No C(48)28 (Final), 3 June 1948.
41. The relationship between OEEC and the ECE Secretariat was regularly challenged at ECE's Commission sessions. See UNOG Box 67, Folder I/3/2 ECE and Paris Conference, 1947–1953, Untitled Note on ECE and the future Conference of Transport Ministers, 7 October 1953.
42. UNOG Box 67, Folder I/3/2 ECE and Paris Conference, 1947–1953, R. Jeannel to Gunnar Myrdal, Report on trip to Paris to visit OEEC, 30 November 1949.
43. NARA: NND959154, US Representative to the Econ. Commission for Europe, Classified and Unclassified ECE and ECA Files 1947–1951, Box 1, Folder 6: Conversations. Memorandum of Conversation with Mr. Tsirimokos, Secretary of OEEC Electricity Committee, 17 October 1949.
44. TNA. FO 371/71802: E.C.E. and C.E.E.C. relations. The Economic Commission for Europe and the Continuing Organisation, 18 April 1948
45. UNOG Box 67, Folder I/3/2 ECE and Paris Conference, 1947–1953, Newspaper clipping, Mr. Harriman in Geneva. "The Times," 13 February 1950.
46. TNA. FO 371/71802: E.C.E. and C.E.E.C. relations, Brief for Discussion of C.E.E.C.–E.C.E. with the State Department.
47. On steel, see the chapter by Wolfram Kaiser in this volume.
48. UNOG Box 67, Folder I/3/2 ECE and Paris Conference, 1947–1953, Minutes of a Conversation with Monsieur Guéronik, Operational Director of Paris Organization, by Walt W. Rostow [before 22 March 1948].
49. UNOG Box 67, Folder I/3/2 ECE and Paris Conference, 1947–1953, Minutes of an Informal Meeting between members of the OEEC and ECE Secretariats in Geneva, 17/18 September 1948.
50. UNOG Box 67, Folder I/3/2 ECE and Paris Conference, 1947–1953, R. Jeannel to Gunnar Myrdal, OEEC Transport Committee, 30 January 1950.

51. Gunnar Myrdal, "The Research Work of the Secretariat of the Economic Commission for Europe," in *25 Economic Essays in English, German and Scandinavian Languages in Honour of Erik Lindahl*, ed. Ekonomisk tidskrift (Stockholm, 1956), 267–293.
52. UNOG Box 67, Folder I/3/2 ECE and Paris Conference, 1947–1953, Gunnar Myrdal, Memorandum on conversations with Arne Skaug, Norwegian representative to OEEC and member of the Executive Council, in Paris, 6 March 1950.
53. Arthur Bloomfield, "Europe. The Way Ahead," *The American Economic Review* (1954), 194–197.
54. Myrdal, "The Research Work of the Secretariat of the Economic Commission for Europe," 271.
55. On OEEC staff numbers, see Figure S.1 in Matthias Schmelzer, *The Hegemony of Growth. The OECD and the Making of the Economic Growth Paradigm* (Cambridge: Cambridge University Press, 2016), 42.
56. UNOG Box 67, Folder I/3/2 ECE and Paris Conference, 1947–1953, Questions raised by Technical Committees in Connection with O.E.E.C. Annual Programme for 1948/49, undated.
57. UNOG Box 67, Folder I/3/2 ECE and Paris Conference, 1947–1953, Memorandum by the Executive Secretary of the Economic Commission for Europe on General Principles of Relations between the OEEC and the ECE, September 1948.
58. UNOG Box 67, Folder I/3/2 ECE and Paris Conference, 1947–1953. ECE/DD/1, 16 November 1948, the Executive Secretary: Confidential Materials/OEEC Material.
59. UNOG Box 67, Folder I/3/2 ECE and Paris Conference, 1947–1953, Minutes of an Informal Meeting between members of the OEEC and ECE Secretariats, Geneva, 17/18 September 1948.
60. UNOG Box 67, Folder I/3/2 ECE and Paris Conference, 1947–1953, ECE/DD/17, The Executive Secretary to all Division Directors and Members of the Central Office, Relations with the OEEC (Paris Organization).
61. UNOG Box 67, Folder I/3/2 ECE and Paris Conference, 1947–1953, Memorandum by the Executive Secretary of the Economic Commission for Europe on General Principles of Relations between the OEEC and the ECE, September 1948.
62. ARBARK: Gunnar Myrdals Arkiv, Handlingar rörande Gunnar Myrdals verksamhet, Economic Commission for Europe 1947–1957, 405-4-2-7-1, Economic Commission for Europe: Eighth Session, Summary Record of the Thirteenth Meeting held at the Palais des Nations, Geneva, on Wednesday, 11 March 1953. E/ECE/SR.8/13, 27 April 1953.

63. Gunnar Adler-Karlsson, *Western Economic Warfare 1947–1967. A Case Study in Foreign Economic Policy* (Stockholm: Almqvist & Wiksell, 1968); Alan Dobson, *US Economic Statecraft for Survival 1933–1991: Of Embargoes, Strategic Embargoes, and Economic Warfare* (London: Routledge, 2002); Tor Egil Førland, *Cold Economic Warfare: COCOM and the Forging of Strategic Export Controls, 1948–1954* (Dordrecht: Republic of Letters, 2009).
64. UNOG Box 67, Folder I/3/2 ECE and Paris Conference, 1947–1953, Gunnar Myrdal, Memorandum on conversations with Arne Skaug, Norwegian representative to OEEC and member of the Executive Council, in Paris, 6 March 1950.
65. UNOG Box 67, Folder I/3/2 ECE and Paris Conference, 1947–1953, Report on the Informal Meetings between Officials of the OEEC and the ECE Secretariat at the Palais des Nations, 25 and 26 January 1952.
66. UNOG ARR 14/1360, Box 71, Gunnar Myrdal, Two Notes on ERP and East-West Trade, December 1949.
67. Schmelzer, *The Hegemony of Growth*, 121.
68. HAEU: EUI Oral History Collections, Miriam Camps interviewed by F. Duchêne, London, 30 August 1988. http://archives.eui.eu/en/files/transcript/15818?d=inline (accessed 20 July 2016).
69. UNOG ARR 14/1360, Box 71, Gunnar Myrdal, Two Notes on ERP and East-West Trade, December 1949.
70. Milward, *The Reconstruction of Western Europe*, 281.
71. UNOG ARR 14/1360, Box 71, Gunnar Myrdal, Two Notes on ERP and East-West Trade, December 1949.
72. Frank Schipper, "All Roads Lead to Europe: The E-Road Network 1950–1970," in *T2 M Conference, working document* (Paris: Transnational Infrastructures of Europe, 2006); "Changing the Face of Europe: European Road Mobility During the Marshall Plan Years," *The Journal of Transport History* 28, no. 2 (2007) 211–228.
73. Bent Boel, *The European Productivity Agency and Transatlantic Relations, 1953–1961* (Copenhagen: Museum Tusculanum Press, 2003); Schmelzer, *The Hegemony of Growth*, Chap. 2.
74. UNOG Box 67, Folder I/3/2 ECE and Paris Conference, 1947–1953, H.W.A. Waring (Director ECE Industry Division) to E.P. Harten (Director OEEC European Productivity Agency), 6 January 1954.
75. UNOG Box 67, Folder I/3/2 ECE and Paris Conference, 1947–1953, A.F. Ewing to H.W.A. Waring, The OEEC Productivity Agency and Building, 23 December 1953. A.F. Ewing to Gunnar Myrdal, Report on OEEC Productivity and Applied Research Committee meeting, 5 February 1953.

76. UNOG Box 67, Folder I/3/2 ECE and Paris Conference, 1947–1953, A.F. Ewing and Václav Kostelecký to Gunnar Myrdal, Report on visit to Paris, 21 and 22 December 1953, 28 December 1953.
77. UNOG Box 67, Folder I/3/2 ECE and Paris Conference, 1947–1953, Gunnar Myrdal, Memorandum on conversations with Arne Skaug, Norwegian representative to OEEC and member of the Executive Council, in Paris, 6 March 1950.
78. Schmelzer, *The Hegemony of Growth*, 44.
79. Richard T. Griffiths, "'An Act of Creative Leadership': The End of the OEEC and the Birth of the OECD," in *Explorations in OEEC History*, ed. Richard T. Griffiths (Paris: OECD, 1997), 235–256.
80. UNOG Archives ARR 14/1360, Box 71, Gunnar Myrdal, Two Notes on ERP and East–West Trade, December 1949.

A Socialist Developing Country in a Western Capitalist Club: Yugoslavia and the OEEC/OECD, 1955–1980

Andrej Marković and Ivan Obadić

The unique relationship between a socialist country and the OEEC/OECD began in 1955 when Yugoslavia managed to acquire observer status to the OEEC. Yugoslavia's association with the OEEC was a result of the extremely complicated international position in which its regime found itself after the Tito-Stalin split. Until 1948, Yugoslavia had depended almost entirely on economic, military, and technical cooperation with the Soviet Union and its satellites. The country's struggle against Stalin and the detrimental effects of the resulting Eastern Bloc's economic boycott forced Yugoslavia to pivot toward the West. Already since 1949, Yugoslavia had steadily, albeit cautiously, begun to strengthen its economic, political, and cultural ties with the Western powers, capitalizing skilfully on their interest in "keeping Tito afloat."[1] The deepening of these relations opened the question of Yugoslav

A. Marković (✉)
Department of History, University of Zurich, Karl-Schmid-Strasse 4,
8006 Zurich, Switzerland
e-mail: andrej.markovic@hist.uzh.ch

I. Obadić
European University Institute, Villa Salviati, Via Bolognese 156,
50139 Firenze, Italy
e-mail: ivan.obadic@eui.eu

M. Leimgruber and M. Schmelzer (eds.), *The OECD and the International Political Economy Since 1948*, DOI 10.1007/978-3-319-60243-1_4

integration into Western structures. In 1954, with the ever-closer integration of Yugoslavia into the Western alliance through the Balkan Pact and after Belgrade had expressed Yugoslav conditional readiness to associate with the European Defence Community and the Council of Europe, the issue of Belgrade's relationship with the OEEC also became an important foreign policy issue in Yugoslavia.[2]

Despite initial positive reactions to these developments, however, by the mid-1950s, the ideological and political consequences inherent to the country's now more pro-Western policy orientation and the closer integration with the United States (US) and Western European countries started to worry the Yugoslav leadership. In their view, military and economic dependence on the West would, over time, compromise the country's political independence and would undermine its socialist system.[3] Stalin's death and the normalization of relations between Yugoslavia and the Soviet Bloc in 1955 created favourable circumstances for the Belgrade authorities to formulate a policy of non-alignment. While this new foreign policy made closer political and military cooperation with the West less attractive for the Belgrade government, the ambitious modernizing agenda and development plans compelled Yugoslavia to continue and even intensify economic cooperation with the West. Given the centrality of this relationship for the Yugoslav economy and foreign trade, participation in a variety of OEEC/OECD activities (without becoming a full member) played an important role in facilitating partnership with the Western countries in a number of policy areas ranging from trade to education and scientific policy.

Although the history of Yugoslav foreign relations in the Cold War and, in particular, the formulation of the Yugoslav policy of non-alignment has been widely discussed,[4] Yugoslav relations with the OEEC/OECD have been totally neglected. This article, which is based on archival sources from the Yugoslav and Western archives as well as on interviews with formal Yugoslav officials, traces the development of the relationship between Yugoslavia and the OEEC/OECD from its beginnings in the 1950s until 1980.[5] In the first section, which examines Yugoslavia's association with the OEEC, we argue that Belgrade's readiness for cooperation was founded mainly on its concern about deteriorating conditions for trade with Western European countries, especially after the creation of the European Economic Community (EEC) and the European Free Trade Association (EFTA). Secondly, we argue that Western powers, by integrating Yugoslavia into the OEEC, aimed to strengthen its economic ties with the West and support Yugoslavia's independence from the Socialist camp. The second part of the paper explores the Yugoslav-OECD relationship in the 1960s and 1970s. In 1961, the Yugoslav government decided to continue its cooperation with the OECD, focusing on the benefits of technical and scientific cooperation and the exchange of views concerning economic policies with OECD member states. This section critically evaluates the ideological and political differences that either hindered or intensified this cooperation. Finally, it aims at assessing the organizational problems that seriously diminished the advantages of Yugoslav participation in the OECD.

Yugoslavia's Association with the OEEC, 1955–1957

From the early 1950s, Western European countries and the US became by far Belgrade's largest trading and financial partners, accounting for almost two-thirds of foreign trade. Furthermore, Yugoslavia's strategic importance to the Western powers resulted in a massive amount of economic and military assistance provided to the country, in particular until the mid-1950s.[6] Because of this dependence on Western trade, technology, know-how, and financial cooperation, the establishment and development of OEEC policies with the aim of promoting intra-European currency convertibility, trade liberalization and economic productivity had a strong impact on Yugoslav policy circles.

The need for closer cooperation with the OEEC found its origins in the Yugoslav establishment's growing awareness of the shortcomings of bilateral trading agreements with Western European countries. Furthermore, the government was keen to benefit from the trade liberalization and multilateral payments arrangements set up by the OEEC and expected that these would help reduce the existing balance of payments deficit with Western Europe.[7] Already in the mid-1950s, Yugoslav economic policy-makers regarded external economic imbalance as one of their most pressing concerns. The main cause of the endemic balance of trade and payments deficit was the strategy of accelerated economic growth based on import-dependent industrialization of the country.[8] In these circumstances, the authorities assumed that associating with the OEEC would enhance export opportunities to Western markets, as Yugoslavia could participate in the liberalization of the intra-European trade. Furthermore, they believed that the availability of European Payments Union (EPU) credit lines would improve the country's overall financial position.[9] Finally, by taking part in the European Productivity Agency (EPA), Yugoslavia was interested in profiting from Western European experiences to build up a modern, industrialized economy. For these reasons, in December 1954, the Yugoslav government applied for observer status in the OEEC.

The US, British, and French governments strongly supported the Yugoslav application.[10] Their support was based on broader Cold War considerations. Tito's regime constituted a key ideological, strategic, and political asset to counter-balance the Soviet Union: the "Yugoslav Road to Communism" challenged the ideological uniformity of Stalinism and showed that Moscow's claims to ideological supremacy could be questioned; strategically, with the loss of Yugoslavia, the position of the Soviet Bloc in the Balkans and the Eastern Mediterranean was gravely weakened. Finally, Yugoslavia politically served as a constant reminder to the Soviet satellite regimes that it was possible to defect from Moscow and to gain independence. At the same time, the Yugoslav-Soviet rapprochement aroused suspicion in Western policy circles about the country's future foreign policy orientation. The long-term objective of the Western alliance was thus to maintain close Yugoslav economic and political relations with the West to secure its independent and non-aligned position in the Cold War confrontation. The Yugoslav association with the OEEC served this objective.[11] It was for this reason, therefore, that the OEEC Council on 25 February 1955 granted observer status to Yugoslavia.[12]

The association with the OEEC was in accordance with the emerging Yugoslav foreign policy of peaceful coexistence. The Yugoslav government had established three main principles, according to which it evaluated the merits of particular European regional organizations. First, these organizations had to contribute to the constructive development of international relations, particularly in Europe. Second, they had to provide a framework for cooperation with independent European countries. Third, they had to encourage wider European cooperation.[13] Given its delicate position in a Europe divided by the Cold War, Belgrade was undoubtedly eager to promote wider regional economic integration through bilateral relations, the UN Economic Commission for Europe, and appropriate existing regional organizations. The OEEC, as an intergovernmental organization including a large number of European countries, thus corresponded to Yugoslav foreign policy principles.[14]

Ideological differences that Yugoslavia had with the OEEC, although present in certain instances, did not hamper overall cooperation with the organization. Crucial to establishing this relationship were the Yugoslav economic interests, on the one hand, and, on the other, the West's political interest to keep Yugoslavia incorporated within the Western economic system at the moment when a normalization of relations between Yugoslavia and the Soviet Union was underway.

Still, until 1957, Yugoslavia and the OEEC established only limited forms of cooperation. The main initial challenge was to determine the form and parameters of Yugoslav association, since the Yugoslav policy makers dealing with foreign trade disagreed over this issue.[15] The fundamental problem was how to adjust the arsenal of protective foreign trade measures and the foreign exchange system to meet the requirements imposed by the EPU mechanism. However, the debate on cooperation with the OEEC was not only limited to relations with the EPU. There were also contradicting views over participation in the Committee for Agriculture and Food. At a government meeting in June 1956, Svetozar Vukmanović, who was then one of the chief economic policy-makers, strongly objected to participating in this Committee; he argued that the economic benefits of this cooperation were trivial compared to the negative implications for Yugoslavia's international position at the moment when it was attempting to establish closer relations with the Eastern Bloc and with developing countries. Furthermore, Vukmanović stressed that the Western powers would be increasingly opposed to "the socialist elements in our agriculture."[16]

Notwithstanding these internal dissenting opinions within the establishment, Belgrade managed, as a result of its observer status, to secure the transferability of most of its foreign exchange earnings within the OEEC area through bilateral arrangements with OEEC member states. Thus, the major part of Yugoslav funds was transferable even before the introduction of currency convertibility in Western Europe in 1958.[17] Since bilateral export contracts had remained the norm in intra-European trade until then, Yugoslavia favored the continued pursuit of bilateral agreements with Western European countries. Besides securing its trade interests with OEEC countries, in 1957 Yugoslavia also became associated with the EPA. More importantly, the EPA provided an opportunity for the education of Yugoslav experts from federal institutes for planning and trade in Western European countries.[18]

Intensifying Relations with the OEEC, 1957–1961

The year 1957 was in many ways a turning point in the relationship between Yugoslavia and the OEEC. First, from the mid-1950s, the Yugoslav leadership began to formulate policies of economic coexistence. The underlying assumption was that Yugoslavia could maintain the level of trade with its largest trading partners—Western European countries—while increasing its trade with the Eastern Bloc and African and Asian countries.[19] Contrary to these expectations, the relative increase of trade with the Soviet Bloc and developing countries did not substantially lessen the importance of trade with Western Europe for Yugoslavia. Even though Yugoslavia enjoyed political goodwill among developing countries owing to its leading role in the emerging Non-Alignment Movement, Belgrade overestimated its economic and financial capacity to implement the envisioned strategy. At the same time, the second Yugoslav-Soviet confrontation in the late 1950s had an adverse impact on trading relations with the Eastern Bloc.[20]

Yugoslavia's failure to significantly diminish foreign trade dependency on the West coincided with the regionalization of Western European trade. The emergence of the EEC in 1957, soon followed by the British plans for a Free Trade Area and the creation of EFTA in 1959, raised concerns among Yugoslav policy-makers about their future prospects on key foreign markets. Their chief concern was to ensure that the deepening of Western European integration would not hurt Yugoslav trade with Western European countries. This was even more important because, from the mid-1950s onward, Yugoslavia could no longer expect substantial Western financial aid. Instead, the Western powers continued to support Yugoslavia financially through credits. As a result, the deficit of the balance of payments developed into the central problem of Yugoslav economic and foreign trade policy.[21]

In this context, the most important aim of the Belgrade government became ensuring the long-term stability of its trading relations with OEEC countries.[22] Since formal membership in the regional trading blocs was clearly impossible for ideological and political reasons, the government had to find another way of partially integrating into the emerging Western European multilateral trading system. Early responses to the newly fluid and unpredictable situation in Western Europe were cautious.[23] First, Yugoslavia used bilateral contacts and trade discussions to address the impending trade discrimination with Western European countries. Second, policy-makers decided to strengthen multilateral relations with the West through intensifying their cooperation with the OEEC and GATT. Finally, in November 1957, a consensus was reached within the federal establishment that Yugoslavia should find a way of associating itself with the EPU.[24] Although the main question now was not "whether we are going to associate or not (with EPU), but how we are going to achieve this," the debate on the most appropriate model for association continued throughout 1958.[25] However, the replacement of the EPU by the European Monetary Agreement in December 1958 abruptly rendered this discussion void. As Yugoslavia was not a full member of the OEEC and did not have sufficient gold and hard currency reserves, it simply could not participate in such a scheme.[26]

Simultaneously, the government began to review its participation in other vertical (i.e., technical) committees of the OEEC. Most importantly, in January 1958 the decision was reached to ask for associate membership in the Committee for Agriculture and Food.[27] Yugoslav interest in this committee was largely based on concerns about the potentially discriminatory agricultural policy of the EEC, a threat considered all the more severe since the Common Market was the largest outlet for agricultural exports. Policy-makers considered that by participating in the work of the Committee, Yugoslavia would be better informed about the development of Western European agriculture production and markets; that the OEEC could provide material and other help for the development of agriculture in underdeveloped areas of Yugoslavia; and that Yugoslavia could put forward ideas and suggestions regarding particular issues and policies discussed in the Committee.[28] Furthermore, since at that moment the lack of agreement on the future of European integration between OEEC member states had resulted in a critical cleavage, and even the possible economic division of Western Europe, the Yugoslav government wanted to take part in the Committee, as the role that the latter would play in the reorganization of Western European agriculture was not clear.[29]

On the whole, even though Yugoslavia had only observer status in the OEEC, Belgrade's participation went well beyond this. Besides the participation in the Committee for Agriculture and Food and EPA, in 1959 the Yugoslav authorities decided to take part in the activities of the Office of Scientific and Technical Personnel in order to increase the number of scientific and technical experts required to enhance economic growth and productivity of their newly industrializing economy.[30]

Furthermore, Yugoslav officials and experts established relations with the OEEC Committees on Tourism, Energy and Applied Research and the OEEC Economics and Statistics Directorate, and, finally, the Economic Policy Committee.[31] Despite this activity, Yugoslavia received only limited benefits from participation in the OEEC. Partly due to the poor coordination of its activities, but primarily as a result of evolution of the European integration process, it did not manage to open up much needed Western European markets.

The division of Western Europe into two regional trading blocs, along with the revival and strengthening of COMECON in the late 1950s, prompted the government to once again re-evaluate its policy toward European integration. In the early 1960s, a wider debate took place within the Belgrade establishment concerning the country's position in the international economic order. Yugoslav policy-makers and theorists began to recognize the problem of regional integration, alongside the "socialist world market" and the position of the "underdeveloped countries" in the international economy as one of the three main challenges for the world economy. In their view, development and cooperation in the area of trade and international economic relations were instrumental in the struggle of developing nations for their independence.[32] For this reason, they advocated the wide-ranging cooperation of the non-aligned and developing countries on economic issues and an international trading and economic system more beneficial for under-developed nations.[33] Apart from formulating "a long-term strategy for all these countries in order to specify their place in the existing world order," Belgrade's goal was to strengthen its position in international affairs by addressing a wide number of political and economic issues, particularly international trade and financing.[34]

The transformation of the OEEC into the OECD offered an opportunity to the Yugoslav authorities to promote their ideas of international economic order and the integration process. The Yugoslav memorandum to the "Group of Four on Economic Organisation" advocated more integrative global trade regimes, leading toward broader and freer world markets instead of economic isolation and discrimination. Furthermore, it highlighted the need for the organization to focus on the promotion and assistance of the rapid development of "underdeveloped" countries. Assistance was not understood as limited to loans, but also meant creating favorable terms of trade for the developing countries to secure more rapid and stable development. To this end, the memorandum supported the proposal that the new organization should facilitate more liberal trade and payments regimes. In effect, Yugoslavia was arguing for the removal of economic trade barriers imposed by the EEC and EFTA on non-members and, eventually, on their closer cooperation with non-member countries, as this, so the Yugoslav government believed, would contribute to the growth of the world economy.[35]

Across Cold War Divides—Yugoslavia in the OECD, 1961–1980

The founding of the OECD presented new opportunities, but also significant dilemmas to Yugoslav policy-makers. They worried that the OECD, now including the US and Canada, might become an instrument of Western policy toward the developing countries. The organization's principle of unanimity and the participation of several neutral European countries only partially mitigated these concerns.[36] At the first Non-Aligned Movement Summit in Belgrade in 1961, Tito publicly criticized the OECD as yet another bloc-aligned economic organization, the "Atlantic Economic Community," which will have harmful impact on the economic development of developing countries.[37] In the end, economic considerations prevailed, since the collaboration provided Belgrade with better insight into economic and political developments in Western Europe—which accounted for 60% of Yugoslav trade—as well as cooperation in various fields relevant for the country's economic development. More importantly, associate membership was expected to facilitate Yugoslavia's integration in world markets. It also provided Belgrade with an opportunity to emphasize the discrimination the country was facing in trade with Western Europe, above all with the EEC.[38]

The new agreement provided a unique framework for participating in OECD bodies as an observer while enjoying additional rights in specific committees. Being a de facto associated member enabled Belgrade to pursue a wide range of activities within the OECD while avoiding the adverse foreign political implications of a formally closer relationship.[39] In addition, the OECD Secretariat's flexible interpretation of the treaty provisions allowed for enhancing the cooperation.[40] In general, this accommodative policy reflected the ongoing interest of the Western powers in maintaining the country's position outside the socialist camp. Moreover, bringing Yugoslavia into the OECD enabled them to obtain more accurate insight into Yugoslav economy. The relationship also gave rise to hopes of further influencing Belgrade policies.[41] Smaller member states had their own reasons to support Yugoslavia's association with the OECD as well. Neutral states appreciated the widening of the OECD's political profile, while beef-exporting states like Australia and New Zealand found an ally in their fight against the EEC's agricultural protectionism in Yugoslavia, who was a major beef-exporter to Western Europe.[42]

The ideological differences arising from the integration of a socialist country in an organization committed to a Western project of liberal capitalism played an ambivalent role. The French delegation, for example, appreciated the opportunity to gain experience for eventual cooperation with Eastern Bloc countries.[43] As an observing member of COMECON, Yugoslavia was also a valuable interlocutor on issues concerning economic policy deliberations within the Eastern Bloc.[44] Still, the ideological antinomies remained apparent. Belgrade officials perceived the OECD as an organization whose coherence was ensured by the "modern capitalist system" of its otherwise rather diverse member countries.[45] For that reason they were afraid that close cooperation could threaten the socialist order. For example, when the OECD offered to employ a Yugoslav economist, the delegation recommended to carefully vet the political views and reliability of the candidates, as they were aware of their potential return to an influential post in Yugoslavia.[46]

In general, however, the day-to-day relationship was only partially impeded by ideological differences. Western delegates chose to refrain from anti-Communist arguments when peer reviewing the Yugoslav economy and OECD reports did not engage into critical discussions of self-managed socialism.[47] Likewise, Yugoslav officials respected the OECD analytical framework when reviewing other countries. In 1976, when Yugoslav delegates reviewed a member country for the first time, they praised Austria for successfully addressing recessionary tendencies instead of criticizing its capitalist system.[48] The positive evaluation did not simply result from diplomatic restraint or general pragmatism. It also reflected significant Western influence on Yugoslav society. The Federal Planning Institute, which was responsible for participating in the committee that conducted the country reviews, had already sent its economists for further education to Western institutions in the 1950s.[49] The experts' acquaintance with Western economic theories, their participation in Western-dominated academic discourses, and the preference for growth policies which they shared with their Western peers contributed to common understandings and constructive discussions.[50]

Yet, ultimately, such commonalities did not lead to the formation of a "shared identity" with OECD members.[51] It was not simply socialism that differentiated Yugoslavia from the other OECD members. As the OECD played a major role in formulating Western policies toward developing countries, Yugoslavia's insistence on being considered a European developing country and its prominence in international trade and development debates complicated the relationship. Yugoslav delegates were thus excluded from meetings where Western countries negotiated their policies toward the Global South. This was not surprising considering Yugoslavia's repeated advocacy for developing countries' interests in OECD bodies.[52] Belgrade was not overly displeased with these restrictions, considering its wariness of being perceived as associated too closely with a Western-aligned organization.[53] For instance, it declined proposals by OECD officials to take part in development aid programs in East Africa to avoid participation in Western projects.[54] At the same time, Yugoslavia's peculiar position prompted intensified informal relations with the OECD. The government had a substantial interest in the OECD discussions and instructed the delegation to diligently monitor them and to reach out informally to Western counterparts. Because of Yugoslavia's strong influence in the Global South, the Secretariat was also interested in Yugoslav assessment of the North-South debate. During the 1970s, the exchange of views on this issue became one of the main dimensions of the relationship.[55] Yugoslavia's position on global trade and development, which was moderate compared to other influential developing countries, might have helped to secure the necessary trust for establishing these contacts.[56] However, the limits of source material surveyed for this chapter preclude us from analyzing if and how the OECD influenced Yugoslav thinking on viable proposals for a new international economic system. It is evident that the Yugoslav diplomacy appreciated the value of insight knowledge about Western policies for facilitating the formulation of negotiation tactics and as a resource contributing to its influential position in the Global South.[57]

Yugoslavia's relationship with the OECD appears to have been more constrained by organizational and financial problems than ideological or political antagonisms. In addition to the Ministry of Foreign Affairs, which was responsible for the relationship in general, a plethora of state institutions, academic institutes, and economic enterprises participated in the cooperation according to their respective areas of policy responsibility or expertise. Yet, the lack of proper coordinative bodies and the small size of the delegation had a detrimental effect on the cooperation. These administrative problems even resulted in delegates missing committee sessions on issues highly relevant for Yugoslavia, such as agricultural product standards.[58] The dissemination of OECD material was especially impeded, hindering the major objective of benefitting from Western knowledge. Moreover, scarce financial resources curtailed the number of activities Yugoslavia could afford to join.[59] Finally, the collaboration was further complicated by the country's lack of experts. Especially in the 1960s, Belgrade struggled to find specialists sufficiently skilled to benefit fully from courses organized by the OECD and even delegates with the foreign language proficiency needed to participate in proceedings. Thus, the organizational shortcomings were often harder to bridge than the divide between capitalism and self-managed socialism.[60]

While it is well understood that participation in OECD activities is demanding for small and poor countries, these persisting difficulties cast doubt on Belgrade's commitment to the cooperation.[61] Although the government was aware of the problems, appeals to enlarge the Paris delegation and to improve the organization of the cooperation remained largely futile. In 1979, the delegation realized that OECD documents forwarded to various Yugoslav actors did not even reach them.[62] Still, highly regarded aspects of the relationship, such as the OECD technical assistance programs, were apparently adequately organized from the beginning. It would appear that the lack of sufficient attention in other areas of cooperation was to a certain extent the result of comparably smaller interest. After the failure of initial objectives to solve balance of payments deficits by cooperating with the OEEC, Yugoslav policy-makers must have found the potential advantages of the collaboration with the OECD to be rather marginal. Additionally, the OECD occupied a peripheral position in Yugoslav public space. As an illustration, even an economic news publication intended for a Western audience failed to give prominence to this relationship, while much more widely reporting on cooperation with other international economic organizations.[63] With regard to Yugoslavia's position within the OECD, the ideological and political differences, the limitations inherent with observing membership, and the rather inactive delegation placed the country at the organization's margins.[64]

Searching for Tangible Results—Yugoslavia in OECD Committees

The association with the OECD was not only perceived as an opportunity to learn from Western experiences and to take part in confidential discussions. As one Yugoslav delegate noticed: "We did not come here as observers only to observe and study, but to get something done."[65] The immediate context of this comment was an ultimately successful attempt to secure more favorable trade arrangements. Following a Trade Committee's recommendation in 1963, Yugoslavia secured "OEEC liberalization" privileges with most OECD members.[66] The committee's importance to Yugoslavia decreased in the following years, illustrating how Yugoslavia's changing international position impacted its cooperation with the OECD. Namely, after becoming a member of GATT in 1966, and after signing a trade agreement with the EEC in 1970, Yugoslavia attained more effective ways to address the problem of liberalization of Western European trade.[67] Accordingly, Yugoslav delegates only sporadically attended committee proceedings. Moreover, the committee's growing significance for discussing relations with developing countries resulted in restrictions that further narrowed Yugoslav participation.[68] Nonetheless, the Trade Committee kept some of its importance for Belgrade. Like the Economic Policy Committee, it allowed Yugoslav officials to attend discussions between major trading partners and opened up a venue to approach prominent policy-makers. In addition, the delegation benefitted from the Secretariat's willingness to informally share their views on confidential discussions.[69]

The participation in the Economic and Development Review Committee (EDRC) and the Committee for Technical Cooperation (TECO) was regarded as particularly advantageous. The EDRC's peer review process offered Belgrade a chance to praise its economic policies and euphemize their failures. Positive OECD economic reports were important for Yugoslav officials since they perceived them as widely influential with Western policy-makers and business elites. Because Yugoslavia was in constant and dire need of capital imports to support economic development, the government was determined to obtain favorable evaluations in order to enhance their position with Western lenders. Therefore, well-prepared and prominent experts attended the EDRC sessions.[70] Overall, Belgrade was largely satisfied with the resulting country surveys and instructed its diplomats to use them when discussing economic issues.[71]

Other effects of the cooperation are more readily quantifiable. Between 1962 and 1978, Yugoslavia received approximately USD $9.5 million in development aid through TECO. The committee participated in a wide range of projects, mainly by financing foreign experts and scholarships for Yugoslav experts. In general, the projects aimed to produce preparatory study materials for later investments and implementation plans.[72] Administrative and academic institutions as well as companies benefitted from the technical assistance the OECD provided, and particularly valued its sophisticated character. In the 1960s, these projects focused on raising the productivity of the Yugoslav economy, while in the later period they also dealt with other issues ranging from electronic administration to urban management and environmental protection, areas where Yugoslavia had few experience.[73] As the low competitiveness of Yugoslav industry necessitated the import of modern management and production techniques, the productivity issue remained a constant preoccupation of these programs. Accordingly, projects conceived to establish model enterprises in selected branches of the economy were part of the OECD's technical assistance program toward Yugoslavia from 1962 onward.[74]

A 1966 mission concerning management techniques on large state farms illustrates the use of OECD recommendations. The mission report adopted a technocratic approach and urged improvements to the education and wages of agronomist specialists, eschewing to discuss the merits of self-managed socialism.[75] The agronomists were envisioned to collect vast amounts of data, analyzing it and proposing "rational," "most effective" courses of action to the decision-makers in the company; in other words, the management and the workers' councils.[76] In effect, the OECD report argued for reinforcing elite actors' positions, strengthening hierarchies, and developing market-oriented thinking. This advice amounted to disciplining labor, an aim which was an integral part of self-managed socialism from its beginnings.[77] Therefore, the OECD report should not be understood as diluting Yugoslav economic thought with capitalist ideas. On the contrary, the recommendations were in line with Yugoslav market reforms of the 1960s. In fact, some OECD economists even criticized the reforms as being based on an excessive belief in market mechanisms.[78] In any case, the knowledge transfer the organization managed was only a minor part of Yugoslav-Western exchanges, as the

OECD, on the whole, was one of many instruments Yugoslavia used to bridge the divides of the Cold War.[79]

Conclusion

Socialist Yugoslavia's association with the OEEC and later the OECD was fundamentally based on a goal shared by Belgrade and the Western powers: to bolster the country's independence from the Soviet Union. In principle, a socialist developing country and a Western capitalist organization had many opposing interests. Nevertheless, the relationship was advantageous for both sides, if sometimes only in marginal ways. Yugoslavia's initial strategy to seek favorable trade and payment arrangements while abstaining from substantial integration with Western countries was only partially successful. With the establishment of Western regional trading blocs—EEC and EFTA—the cooperation with the OEEC/OECD lost some of its *raison d'être*. Still, the integration of the Yugoslav economy in world markets increased interest in the economic situation and policies of Western countries. The OECD was an obvious place to improve the understanding of these issues. Moreover, integration necessitated the continuing communication with powerful actors in the West and the preparedness to follow their rules. Already being dependent on Western trading partners and lenders, Yugoslavia subjected itself to the OECD's peer review process, hoping for favorable assessments and their beneficial influence on trade and loans conditions. The lack of research on Yugoslav negotiations with Western lenders, however, makes it difficult to assess the ultimate impact of these surveys. Further studies would not only help determine the extent of the cooperation's usefulness but also illuminate how Yugoslavia negotiated the complexities of the system of international economic and financial organizations.

The knowledge accumulated within the OECD was seen as potentially valuable for Yugoslavia's development. Although the organization's capacity to provide development aid was limited, its technical assistance was appreciated for its sophistication. The impact of these projects remains unclear and further research in this regard is needed to better understand not only the OECD's relationship with Yugoslavia, but also the role of the OECD in the circulation of economic knowledge as a whole. Leaving aside these observations, we can conclude that based on the Yugoslav delegation's limited resources, its ongoing organizational problems, and the rather marginal position the Paris organization occupied in Yugoslav foreign policy discourse, that the OECD was of modest importance for Yugoslavia. Cooperation with other international economic organizations established more appropriate ways for Belgrade to advocate trading and economic interests. In addition, the country's general openness, at least compared to other socialist countries, allowed for alternative possibilities to benefit from Western societies' knowledge. For the OECD member states, Yugoslavia's contribution to the organization was equally marginal. Nevertheless, they clearly perceived that fostering this relationship was advantageous. They appreciated bringing Yugoslavia closer to the Western Bloc and gaining additional insight into the Yugoslav economic situation and policies. Furthermore, the debate on development and trade elicited significant mutual interest. The high-ranking representatives of the OECD member states, the Secretariat, and Yugoslav officials found a forum to directly exchange views. If and how they were specifically influencing each other is still unclear and a question worthy to pursuit. Yet, the existence of these contacts invites us to reflect on the OECD not only as an actor standing on the Cold War frontlines but also as a place within whose corridors these frontlines were both drawn and blurred. This relationship was a testament to the pragmatism of Yugoslavia's foreign policy doctrine of peaceful coexistence and Western powers' support for the socialist renegade. However, the case of the OECD's socialist observing member is not a reason to substantially re-characterize the organization. On the contrary, it could only accommodate a socialist society that was in fact economically dependent on the West and fearful of political dominance from the East. As such, Yugoslavia never threatened to seriously challenge from within the OECD's understanding of the world.

Acknowledgements We would like to thank the editors and our fellow conference participants for their comments as well as William Gray for kindly providing us with documents from the US National Archives.

Notes

1. See the aptly named study on US-Yugoslav relations: Lorraine M. Lees, *Keeping Tito Afloat. The United States: Yugoslavia and the Cold War* (University Park, PA: Penn State University Press, 1997).
2. Archives of Yugoslavia, Belgrade (hereafter AJ), The Cabinet of the President Collection (KPR) 837, I-2/2, Turska, 12–18 April 1954; Izvještaj predsednika Republike Josipa Broza Tita o poseti Turskoj

podnet na sednici Saveznog izvršnog veća, 27 April 1954, 12; AJ KPR II-5-c-2/34, Zabeleška o diskusiji kod potpredsednika SIV Kardelja o aktuelnim evropskim problemima, 14 September 1954, 2.

3. Dragan Bogetić, *Jugoslavija i Zapad 1952–1955. Jugoslavensko približavanje NATO-u* (Beograd: Službeni list SRJ, 2000), 175–178.
4. For an overview see: Rinna Kullaa, *Non-Alignment and its Origins in Cold War Europe. Yugoslavia, Finland and the Soviet Challenge* (London-New York: I.B. Tauris, 2012), 5–17.
5. We have decided to limit our research to this period for two reasons. First, archival records for the 1980s are still only partially accessible. Second, 1980 marks a turning point in the history of Yugoslavia. In 1980 the Yugoslav iconic leader Tito died, and soon after the country entered into a long economic and political crisis which profoundly impacted the international positioning of the country.
6. From 1951 until 1955 Yugoslavia received tripartite financial aid from the US, Britain and France. The US financial assistance to Yugoslavia continued after multilateral Western aid ended in 1955 to a much lesser extent. By 1962, Western economic and military aid amounted to USD 1.3 billion. Slobodan Branković, *Impact of Foreign Aid on the Postwar Development of Yugoslavia* (Geneva: UNESCO, 1962), 9.
7. AJ, KPR 837, III-B-2-b, Informacija o stanju i perspektivama u privrednoj politici zapadnih zemalja, 22 May 1953, 4–5; DA MSP RS, PA, f. 67, d. 11, 417758, O problemu ekonomske integracije Zapadne Europe, 1953, 16–17.
8. On the Yugoslav balance of trade and payments disequilibrium, see Oskar Kovač, *Spoljnoekonomska ravnoteža i privredni rast. Problemi i iskustva Jugoslavije* (Beograd: Institut ekonomskih nauka, 1973).
9. Diplomatic Archives of the Ministry of Foreign Affairs of the Republic of Serbia (DA MSP RS), Confidential archives (PA), f-68, d. 6, 424039, Delatnost Evropske platne unije i pitanje naše saradnje, 1956, 13–14, 18–19.
10. The Yugoslav approach to the OEEC was inspired by a joint Committee handling tripartite economic aid to the country: National Archives and Records Administration (NARA), Record Group 59, Subject-Numeric Files 1964–1966, Box 3288 (OECD 6 Yugo), Report of the US OEDC delegation A-57, 30 July 1966, confidential, 3.
11. Lees, *Keeping Tito Afloat*, 81–83, 106, 151–153, 227–236.
12. Historical Archives of the EU, Firenze (hereafter HAEU), OEEC-54, Council Minutes of the 274th Meeting held at Château de la Muette, 25 February 1955, 4–5.
13. DA MSP RS, PA, f-67, d. 8, 422950, Problemi evropske saradnje u novim uslovima, 22 March 1956, 2, 24–25, 28–29.
14. DA MSP RS, PA, f-70, d. 7, 417174, Evropska problematika, 11 January 1954, 2.; PA, f-67, d. 8, 422950, Problemi evropske saradnje u novim

uslovima, 22 March 1956, 5. On the collaboration and competition between the OEEC and the UN ECE, see Daniel Stinsky's chapter in this volume.

15. DA MSP RS, PA, f-75, d. 14, 28900, Problemi deviznog režima u vezi sa saradnjom sa EPU, 1957; PA, f-75, d. 13, 28649, Narodna banka FNRJ: Mogućnosti i posledice našeg pristupanja Evropskoj platnoj uniji, 17 October 1957; PA, f-75, d. 14, 28699, Obaveze zemalja OEEC u oblasti razmene i plaćanja od interesa za našu zemlju u slučaju saradnje sa EPU, 20 December 1957.
16. DA MSP RS, PA, f-67, d. 5, 423251, Zabeleška o užem sastanku Odbora za privredu SIV-a, održanom 2 June 1956, 3–4.
17. DA MSP RS, PA, f-113, d. 8, 417333, Pitanje naše saradnje sa OECD, 30 May 1961, 4; PA, f-93, d. 10, 48496, Savezna spoljnotrgovinska komora: Specijalni bilten br. 6, Evropsko udruženje slobodne trgovine, 20 January 1960, 17.
18. Between 1958 and 1961, Yugoslavia received around USD 2 million from the EPA, DA MSP RS, PA, f-113, d. 8, 417333, Zapisnik sa konferencije održane 23.V. 1961. sa predstavnicima zainteresiranih ustanova po pitanju njihove buduće saradnje sa odgovarajućim organima OECD, 3.
19. DA MSP RS, PA, f-104, d. 3, 43155, Zabeleška o razgovoru Koče Popovića sa George W. Ballom, podsekretarom State Departmenta, 29 May 1962, 4.
20. Svetozar Rajak, *Yugoslavia and the Soviet Union in the Early Cold War 1953–1957* (London: Routledge, 2011), 178–200.
21. AJ, 507, Archive of the Central Committee of the League of Communists of Yugoslavia (hereafter CK SKJ), III/71, Proširena sednica IK CK SKJ, 27 June 1957.
22. Protecting exports to EEC member countries which were Yugoslav largest trading partners was of paramount importance for Yugoslav authorities. Ivan Obadić, "A Troubled relationship: Yugoslavia and the European Economic Community in détente," *European Review of History*, 21: 2 (2014): 331–344.
23. Laurent Warlouzet, "De Gaulle as a Father of Europe: The Unpredictability of the FTA's Failure and the EEC's Success (1956–58)," *Contemporary European History* 20: 4 (2011): 419–420.
24. DA MSP RS, PA; f-76, d. 17, 424354, Beleška sa sastanka Radne grupe održanih 13 i 14 novembra 1957. godine, 1.
25. Slovenian economist Ivo Fabinc made this statement at the meeting in the Foreign Ministry in April 1958. DA MSP RS, PA, f-94, d. 10, 431377, Beleška sa sastanka u DA MSP RS-u održanog 3. aprila 1958. god. po pitanju EPU, 3.

26. DA MSP RS, PA, f-91, d. 17, 44121, Telegram Stalne delegacije Jugoslavije pri OEEC DA MSP RS-u, 9 January 1959, 2–3.
27. DA MSP RS, PA, f-93, d. 6, 42326, Pitanje pristupanja Komitetu za poljoprivredu OECE, 30 January 1958.
28. DA MSP RS, PA, f-93, d. 6, 42325, Zabeleška u pogledu našeg intenzivnijeg učešća u radu Komiteta ministara za poljoprivredu i ishranu OEEC, 17 December 1957, 2–3.
29. DA MSP RS, PA, f-76, d. 18, 425805, Stalna delegacija FNRJ pri OEEC: Uključenje u rad Komiteta ministara za poljoprivredu, 16 December 1957, 7–8.
30. DA MSP RS, PA, f-94, d. 6, 426664, Stalna delegacija FNRJ pri OEEC: Naša saradnja sa Biroom OEEC za naučne i tehničke kadrove (STP), 12 October 1959; PA, f-94, d-2, 49238, II odelenje: Naša saradnja sa OEEC-om, 7 April 1959, 2.
31. DA MSP RS, PA, f-113, d. 8, 417333, Pitanje naše saradnje sa OECD, 30 May 1961, 3.
32. Interview with Janez Stanovnik, director (1958–1962) of the Belgrade Institute of International Politics and Economy, Ljubljana, 21 July 2015. See also: Janez Stanovnik, *Strukturalne promene u svetskoj privredi* (Beograd: Institut za međunarodnu politiku i privredu, 1960), 123, 158–159; Janez Stanovnik, "Društvenoekonomski značaj savremenog procesa regionalne integracije," *Međunarodni problemi*, god. XIII, br. 4 (1961): 136–141; Vladimir Dragomanović, "Teze o problemima ekonomske integracije," *Međunarodni problemi*, god. XIII, br. 4 (1961): 11–12.
33. For example, Belgrade had an important role in organizing the 1962 Cairo Conference on the Problems of Economic Development. Robert B. Rakove, *Kennedy, Johnson and the Nonaligned World* (Cambridge: Cambridge University Press, 2013), 87.
34. Jovan Čavoški, "Between Great Powers and Third World neutralists. Yugoslavia and the Belgrade Conference of the Non-Aligned Movement, 1961," in: *The Non-Aligned Movement and the Cold War: Delhi—Bandung—Belgrade*, ed. Nataša Mišković, Harald Fischer-Tiné and Nada Boskovska (London; New York: Routledge, 2014), 200; *Tito. Govori i članci*, 1961/1962, Volume 17 (Zagreb: Naprijed, 1959–), 79–80.
35. DA MSP RS, PA, f-93, d. 6, 45323, Memorandum za "grupu četvorice," 27 February 1960; DA MSP RS, PA, f-93, d. 7, 45296, Nova ekonomska organizacija OEEC, 23 February 1960; DA MSP RS, PA, f-93, d. 4, 43276, Beleška o integracionim kretanjima u Zapadnoj Europi i neki predlozi za našu aktivnost, 5 February 1960, 12–13.
36. AJ, 130, SIV, 660, 1093, 25, Pitanje naše saradnje sa OECD, 30 May 1961.

37. *Tito. Govori i članci*, 1961/1962, Volume 17 (Zagreb: Naprijed, 1959–), 79–80.
38. DA MSP RS, PA, f-108, d. 11, 410546, DSIP-II odeljenje: Saradnja Jugoslavije sa OECD, 27 March 1963, 1.
39. More specifically, Yugoslavia participated in the Committee for Agriculture, the Fisheries Committee, the Technical Cooperation Committee, the Committee on Science and Technology, the Economic and Development Review Committee, and the Committee for Productivity. The Yugoslavs were also allowed to participate as observers to the OECD Council meetings.
40. DA MSP RS, PA, 1962, f-100, d. 3, 48822, Problemi naše saradnje sa OECD-om, 14 March 1962; AJ, 130, SIV, 133, 24, Predlog akcionog programa, 13 January 1976, 6.
41. See for example NARA Record Group 59, Subject-Numeric Files 1964–1966, Box 3288 (OECD 6 Yugo), Report of the US OECD delegation A-57, 30 July 1966, confidential, 4–5.
42. DA MSP RS, PA, 1963, f-108, d. 11, 410546, Saradnja Jugoslavije sa organizacijom za ekonomsku saradnju i razvoj (OECD), 27 March 1963, 1; AJ, F-130, SIV, 133, 24, Predlog akcionog programa, 13 January 1976, 9.
43. DA MSP RS, PA, 1962, f-101, d. 6, 44126, Telegram Stalnog predstavništva FNRJ pri OECD-u, 17 December 1962.
44. Yugoslavia acquired observer status in the COMECOM in 1964. For an inquiry on COMECON oil policy, see DA MSP RS, PA, 1975, f-162, 410815, Telegram Stalnog predstavništva SFRJ pri OECD-u, 3 March 1975. Conversely, Soviet Bloc states also inquired on developments within the OECD. However, Yugoslav delegates were apparently not instructed to share confidential OECD material with Soviet Bloc states. Most interestingly, USSR and Hungarian inquiries on the OECD's interest for cooperation were recorded in 1961 and 1963 respectively, see DA MSP RS, PA, 1961, f-101, d. 5, 439649, Telegram Stalnog predstavništva FNRJ pri OECD-u, 4 December 1962; as well as DA MSP RS, PA, 1963, f-109, 440446, Pregled kontakata P. Milijevića u mesecu novembru 1963, undated, 2. In 1966 and 1967, the idea to improve cooperation with Eastern Bloc countries circulated within the OECD. Yugoslavia and Austria figured as possible hosts for a potential meeting, DA MSP RS, PA, 1967, f-136, d. 3, 418677, Telegram Stalnog predstavništva SFRJ pri OECD-u, 23 May 1967.
45. DA MSP RS, PA, 1967, f-136, d. 2, 411718, Izveštaj za 1966. godinu, 3, 18 April 1967.
46. DA MSP RS, PA, 1975, f-163, 456426, Telegram Stalnog predstavništva SFRJ pri OECD-u, 21 November 1975.

47. Consider the first peer review as an example, DA MSP RS, PA, 1962, f-101, d. 1, 416535, Beleška o rezultatima postignutim u Ekonomskom komitetu OECD prilikom prve konsultacije Jugoslavije po ekonomskoj situaciji, 17 May 1962. For more information about these country reviews, see in this volume the chapter by William Gray.
48. DA MSP RS, PA, 1975, f-162, 428328, Telegram Stalnog predstavništva SFRJ pri OECD-u, 9 June 1975.
49. AJ, 459, Savezni zavod za društveno planiranje, 431, 1961, Izveštaj o specijalizacijama i službenim putovanjima u inostranstvu. See also Marinko Bošnjak et al., *55 godina planiranja* (Beograd: Savezni zavod za razvoj i ekonomsku politiku, 2000), 24, 71.
50. On Yugoslav economists, see Deborah Milenkovich, *Plan and Market in Yugoslav Economic Thought* (New Haven: Yale University Press, 1971); Johanna Bockmann, *Markets in the Name of Socialism. The Left-Wing Origins of Neoliberalism* (Stanford: Stanford University Press, 2013), 76–104.
51. Porter, Tony, and Webb, Michael: "Role of the OECD in the orchestration of global knowledge networks," in *The OECD and Transnational Government,* ed. Rianne Mahon and Stephen McBride (Vancouver: UBC Press 2008), 43–59.
52. DA MSP RS, PA, 1964, f-149, 416692, Telegram Stalnog predstavništva SFRJ pri OECD-u, 16 April 1973. On the OECD attitude toward the Global South, see Patricia Hongler's contribution in this volume.
53. DA MSP RS, PA, 1962, f-101, d.3, 431218, Uloga i zadaci OECD, 22 September 1962, 5.
54. DA MSP RS, PA, 1964, f-179, 423038, Saradnja Jugoslavije sa Organizacijom za ekonomsku saradnju i razvoj (OECD), 20 September 1964, 2.
55. AJ, 130, SIV, 133, 24, Predlog akcionog programa, 13 January 1976, 12–14. As an example of the Secretariat's willingness to share information on Western policy debates, consider DA MSP RS, PA, 1975, f-162, 410815, Telegram Stalnog predstavništva SFRJ pri OECD-u, 3 March 1975.
56. On Yugoslavia's positions, see Alvin Z. Rubinstein, *Yugoslavia and the Nonaligned World* (Princeton: Princeton University Press, 1970), 167–180.
57. DA MSP RS, PA, 1962, f-100, d. 3, 48822, Problemi naše saradnje sa OECD-om, 14 March 1962; AJ, 130, SIV, 133, 24, Predlog akcionog programa, 13 January 1976, 13–14.
58. DA MSP RS, PA, 1975, f-162, 423910, Neka pitanja u vezi sa učešćem u aktivnostima OECD na planu poljoprivrede i ribarstva, 22 May 1975. The precariously small size of the delegation is best illustrated by their

temporary reliance on the voluntary support a Yugoslav trade chamber delegate to France provided in his leisure time, see DA MSP RS, PA, f-163, 1975, 449762, Korošec to Šnuderl, 14 October 1975.

59. DA MSP RS, PA, 1965, f-143, d. 5, 446459, untitled, 13 December 1965.
60. Consider for example the grievances expressed in DA MSP RS, PA, 1967, f-136, d. 2, 411718, Izveštaj za 1966. godinu, 18 April 1967, 47.
61. Matthias Schmelzer, *The Hegemony of Growth. The OECD and the Making of the Economic Growth Paradigm* (Cambridge: Cambridge University Press, 2016), 61.
62. DA RS MSP, PA, 1979, f-169, 465429, Stalna delegacija-SIP, 17 December 1979.
63. A rare mention of the OECD can be found in "Yugoslavia and the World," *Economic Review* 153 (1973), 2. However, Yugoslav daily press infrequently covered OECD published surveys on Yugoslav topics.
64. Yugoslavia's marginal position was also well understood by the US delegation. See NARA, Record Group 59, Subject-Numeric Files 1964–1966, Box 3288 (OECD 6 Yugo), Report of the US OECD delegation A-57, 30 July 1966, confidential, 5.
65. DA MSP RS, PA, 1962, f-101, 441770, Zabeleška o razgovoru sa G. Keiser-om, 27 November 1962, 2.
66. DA MSP RS, PA, 1963, f-109, 438402, Izveštaj o radu Komiteta za trgovinu OECD, 26 November 1963, 5.
67. Obadić, "A Troubled relationship," 334, 340.
68. DA MSP RS, PA, 1975, f-162, 429951, Izveštaj za 1972. godinu, March 1973, 16–19.
69. On Yugoslav interest in the Economic Policy Committee, see DA MSP RS, PA, 1967, f-136, d. 2, 411718, Izveštaj za 1966. godinu, 18 April 1967, 52. On EDRC country reviews, see also the chapter by William Gray in this volume.
70. DA MSP RS, PA, 1962, f-101, d. 3, 431218, Uloga i zadaci OECD, 22 September 1962, 6. Consider also the impressions of the US delegation, Report of the US OECD delegation A-57, 1. Susan L. Woodward, *Socialist Unemployment. The Political Economy of Yugoslavia, 1945–1990* (Princeton: Princeton University Press, 1995), 226.
71. DA MSP RS, PA, 1962, f-101, d. 1, 41635, Beleška o rezultatima postignutim u Ekonomskom komitetu OECD prilikom konsultacije Jugoslavije po ekonomskoj situaciji, 17 May 1962, 1; PA, 1975, f-162, 432219, pismo SSIP-a, 8 July 1975.
72. DA MSP RS, PA, 1979, f-168, 410995, Informacija o učešću Jugoslavije u delatnostima OECD-a na području tehničke saradnje i pomoći u periodu 1962–1979. god, undated. For an exemplary list of project interests

formulated by Yugoslav actors, see AJ, 130, SIV, 90, Predlog programa korišćenja programa tehničke pomoći koju našoj zemlji pruža organizacija za ekonomsku saradnju I razvoj (OECD) za period od 1973–1975. godine, 15 June 1976.

73. DA MSP RS, PA, 1979, f-168, 410995, Informacija o učešću Jugoslavije u delatnostima OECD-a na području tehničke saradnje i pomoći u periodu 1962–1979. god., undated.
74. DA MSP RS, PA, 1962, f-100, d. 2, 43409, Predlog akcija tehničke pomoći OECD za 1962. godinu, 26 January 1962, 8.
75. OECD, ed., *Economic Management of State Farms in the Kosmet* (Paris: OECD, 1966), 37.
76. OECD, *Economic Management*, 75–80.
77. On this aspect of worker's self-management, consider Woodward, *Socialist Unemployment*, 153–154, and Vladimir Korica-Unkovski, *The Economic Struggle for Power in Tito's Yugoslavia. From World-War II to Non-Alignment* (London: I.B. Tauris, 2016). Contemporaries were well aware of the power relations in self-managed companies. See M. J. Broeckmeyer, ed., *Yugoslav Worker's Self-Management. Proceedings of a Symposium held in Amsterdam 7–9 January 1970* (Dordrecht: D. Reidel, 1970).
78. DA MSP RS, PA, 1965, f-143, d. 4, 437175, Operativno pismo, 14 October 1965, 2.
79. Yugoslavia sent over 17,000 specialists to study abroad between 1953 and 1963 alone. See Miroslav Perišić, *Od Staljina ka Sartru. Formiranje jugoslovenske inteligencije na evropskim univerzitetima 1945–1958* (Belgrade: Institut za noviju istoriju Srbije, 2012), 306.

Shall We or Shall We Not? The Japanese, Australian, and New Zealand Decisions to Apply for Membership in the OECD, 1960–1973

Peter Carroll

While the OECD is a somewhat exclusive organization, this does not mean that non-members have been keen to gain membership. Indeed, two of the states that gained membership in the 1970s, Australia and New Zealand, took over a decade to finally come to a decision to apply for membership. In contrast, Japan, the OECD's first new member after its establishment in 1961, joined in 1964 and might have become a foundation member if there had been greater support for its membership at that time. Australia and New Zealand went through an ad hoc process of slowly increasing their association with the OECD during the 1960s by taking up invitations to attend or work with specific committees or working parties on a largely informal basis, before finally taking up a limited, formal membership in the Development Assistance Committee (Australia, in 1966) and the Agriculture Committee (New Zealand, in 1970), followed by successful applications for full membership in 1971 and 1973, respectively. This slow process of increasing association was

P. Carroll (✉)
University of Tasmania, 2/167a Tranmere Road,
Hobart, TAS 1018, Australia
e-mail: peter.carroll@utas.edu.au

M. Leimgruber and M. Schmelzer (eds.), *The OECD and the International Political Economy Since 1948*, DOI 10.1007/978-3-319-60243-1_5

similar in duration to that of Finland, which had become an observer at several OEEC committees in the 1950s, then a full member of the OECD in 1969.[1]

The broad objective of this chapter is to examine the reasons for the marked variation in enthusiasm for membership in the OECD displayed by Japan, Australia, and New Zealand, the first three states from outside the European and North Atlantic area to gain OECD membership, at a time when the organization had no explicit, formalized accession criteria or accession process. The chapter does not look at the final, formal stage of the accession process in depth—where the applicant government's policies, focused on those relating to trade, are reviewed. It extends the earlier work undertaken by the author in collaboration with Kellow.[2] The approach taken is largely historical, relying on a range of primary and secondary sources.[3]

Access, Influence, Status, and Varying Degrees of Interest in Membership

All three countries had a common motive for seeking membership in the OECD: that of gaining access to, information about, and influence in decision making in what became an increasingly important international body regarding international trade, development assistance, international monetary and financial affairs, and economic growth. However, moving from a general to a more detailed level of analysis, there were also significant differences in their journeys to membership, notably the variation in the initial degree of interest in membership.

While all three were initially uncertain as to what would be the role and functions of the successor to the OEEC, Japan was the more enthusiastic regarding membership, New Zealand less so, with Australia strongly divided over its merits, a division that only slowly declined. Most, but not all, of these differences can be explained by reference to the varying social and economic contexts in which they had arisen. The most obvious lay in membership's value to Japan in further restoring its international status, severely damaged by its defeat in the Second World War.[4] In contrast, neither the Australian nor the New Zealand governments were concerned with status, but were uncertain as to the potential value of membership. It was an uncertainty they shared with the Yugoslavian and Finnish governments, though much of it was brought about by concerns as to the possible reaction of the Soviet Union to their association with the OEEC or OECD.[5] In contrast to Yugoslavia and Finland, there is little or no evidence that OECD members saw much value to be gained by the formal association or membership in Australia and New Zealand in the context of Cold War politics.

In Japan and Australia there was some consideration of working toward full, foundation membership in the OECD in 1960, as the members of the OEEC considered how best to modify the organization. However, there were substantial differences in the degree of external support for such membership from two major powers, the US and the UK. There was consistent and positive support and pressure from the US for Japanese membership, part of its more general concern to integrate Japan both economically and militarily on the Western side in the Cold War.[6] However, it opposed for several years full membership for Australia and New Zealand on the grounds that it would complicate the process of gaining accession for Japan and also encourage undesirable applications from other governments that might reduce the OECD's homogeneity.

The UK initially did not envisage full membership for any of the three countries, as was the case for most of the European states, with the exception of West Germany. Their preference was that the successor to the OEEC should have a membership restricted to European states, the US and Canada, with others being able to participate in the work of specific committees on an ad hoc basis as observers.[7] Hence, the UK initially opposed Japan's full membership, but agreed following intergovernmental discussions and strong US pressure that it could become a member of the Development Assistance Group (DAG, which became the OECD's Development Assistance Committee or DAC, in 1961, hereinafter the DAC), a possibility that had been discussed at a December 1959 summit meeting.[8]

The DAC sprang out of the Eisenhower administration's interest in promoting and coordinating aid to the developing world by Western European states, an interest stimulated largely by the potential threat posed by growing Soviet interests and the increasing aid costs faced by the US. It was an idea promoted by Douglas Dillon, the Undersecretary of State for Economic Affairs, who suggested, initially, that with US and Canadian membership the OEEC could prove a useful vehicle for developing this interest. It was also felt that Japanese membership in the OECD's DAC would be a first step to later, full membership. The American opposition to Australian and New Zealand interest in full membership, even though US officials had initially invited both countries to participate in the DAC, was based on the view that if their application for full membership was supported it would encourage applications from countries such as Israel, Brazil, and Argentina. This potential increase in membership might run the danger of the organization becoming another UN, with too large and too diverse a membership to enable effective decision making. It might also complicate the accession of Japan.[9]

Prime Minister Ikeda's government would have preferred full OECD membership from the outset because, if achieved, membership would have considerable, symbolic importance, especially domestically, further signalling Japan's economic and political revival following defeat in 1945. Ikeda stressed to the Japanese Diet the increasing praise he had received from other nations for Japan's economic revival and democratic system and that OECD membership would further enhance its status and influence.[10] However, membership in the DAC could be presented as a first step toward its full membership, drawing on US support.[11]

Later, in 1962, the US government offered to support Australian and New Zealand attendance as observers at the December DAC meeting.[12] Australia declined the offer as it felt that, as Australia was a net importer of capital to support its own economic development, with little available for investment in developing countries, it would compare poorly with other DAC members as regards the volume of aid. Also, existing Australian aid was provided largely through the Colombo Plan, which had its own consultative and coordinating machinery, so membership in the OECD's DAC with its coordinating role was not felt to be necessary. There were also fears that attendance or membership at the DAC would bring US pressure for an increase in Australian aid. Finally, there was concern regarding the possible, adverse reaction of developing countries at a time when Australia was pursuing a "middle way" in regard to trade and development.[13]

The New Zealand government also declined the US offer to attend the DAC for much the same reasons as Australia, although its preference was for handling its aid interests through the World Bank, in addition to the Colombo Plan, having joined the Bank in 1961.[14] New Zealand's Secretary for the Department of External Affairs (hereinafter DEA), Alister McIntosh, felt that as both Australia and New Zealand had a close interest in having their views taken into account by OECD members, they should consult as closely as possible with the organization. The essential feature of the consultative arrangement would be an informal understanding by both parties that views would be exchanged before approaching the OECD.[15]

Australia's initial caution was further increased by the loud concerns voiced by the Australian Department of Trade, particularly by its Minister John "Black Jack" McEwen and its Secretary John Crawford. They felt that the OECD would have a damaging influence on the pursuit of Australian trading interests at that time. Their concern, combined with the political strength of McEwen, who was also the Deputy Prime Minister and leader of the smaller Australian Country Party, a member of the Liberal-Country coalition government that was in power, was at the core of Australia's early lack of enthusiasm for OECD membership. It led to a division of opinion in the Australian government that was to persist for a decade. At the heart of Secretary Crawford's concerns were what he and other officials perceived as the potential, adverse implications for Australia's interests in trade discussions at the GATT, should OECD members determine prior positions on trade issues in the new OECD. Most importantly, the bulk of the European members of this new organization would be those that had opposed Australia's unsuccessful, but repeated attempts to gain support in the GATT for the liberalization of trade in agricultural products.[16] It is not clear, at least in retrospect, why Crawford or McEwen should be so concerned with the likelihood of the coordination of trade interests within the OECD, as OEEC members had long had a similar opportunity to coordinate those interests at the GATT.

New Zealand's initial position was similar to Australia's, though with the added complication that its officials also needed to be aware of what Australia's position regarding membership might be, as that might have implications for New Zealand's political and economic relations with Australia. In addition, as with Australia, the New Zealand government was concerned that any formal association with the OECD might have an adverse impact on New Zealand's trade relations with developing countries and its "middle way" or "middle zone" policy, especially in GATT and UNCTAD. The New Zealand view (and also Australia's) was that, at the least, GATT's role should not be diminished by the new OECD and that a senior representative from GATT should participate in the discussions designing the organization to protect the interests of its members.[17]

Japanese officials, in contrast, felt that membership would assist its economic growth through enabling greater access to OECD information and expertise. Also, they hoped that OECD membership would provide an additional channel to persuade OECD members to reduce or eliminate their discriminatory trade policies that restricted Japanese exports. Although Japan had gained GATT membership in 1955, nearly half of its members, including the bulk of those who were already members of the

OEEC, had exercised their rights under GATT Article XXXV to refuse it Most Favoured Nation treatment and continued to discriminate against Japanese manufactured imports.[18]

A Rapid Move to Full Membership for Japan but a Slowly Growing, Ad Hoc, and Limited Association with the OECD for Australia and New Zealand: 1961–1966

Japan moved quite rapidly—in a period of only 3 years—from membership in the DAC in 1961, including, from 1962 on, attendance at OECD Council meetings when DAC matters were discussed, to observer at meetings of the OECD's new Development Centre in October 1962, followed by full OECD membership in 1964. In contrast, Australia and New Zealand slowly developed a growing, ad hoc, and limited association with the OECD from 1961–1966. This involved Australia agreeing to attend meetings of a consultative group on Thailand established under OECD auspices to improve coordination of aid to Thailand.[19] In 1962 New Zealand entered into the Gentleman's Agreement on the Export of Whole Milk Powder, negotiated at the OECD.[20] The New Zealand government also accepted a 1962 US invitation to attend DAC meetings as an observer, though Australian authorities decided not to accept a similar offer.[21] Then both Australia and New Zealand accepted an invitation to work with the OECD to discuss and negotiate at UNCTAD I in 1963–1964.[22] This was followed by New Zealand's decision to enter the OECD's Seed Certification Scheme in 1964.[23] In 1966 Australia gained membership in the DAC, entering into a formal association with the OECD for the first time. In addition, both Australia and New Zealand did consider full membership at the level of officials and at Cabinet level on a number of occasions in 1963, 1964, and 1965, but decided not apply.

In the face of persistent US support for full Japanese membership in the OECD and Japan's founding membership in the Group of Ten (G10) in 1962, the opposition of the British Government and other members to Japan's full membership in the OECD ended in late 1962. Also, while Japan had pursued a largely passive, learning role in the DAC, its aid budget was growing, if slowly.[24] In addition, all of the G10 members, with the exception of Japan, were also members of the OECD, where they constituted a restricted membership committee:

Working Party 3. Working Party 3 had been established by the OECD's Economic Policy Committee to consider issues regarding currencies, capital movements, and balance of payments in the more manageable forum of the OECD, and it soon became an influential international actor.[25]

In addition to being influential, Working Party 3 was, unusually for the OECD, initially a committee with restricted membership (much resented by the smaller members of the OECD) very similar to that of the G10, closely linking key actors in the OECD, the International Monetary Fund, and the Bank for International Settlements.[26] The fact that Japan was a member of the G10 but not of the OECD is likely to have encouraged a more positive attitude by Working Party 3 members to its membership in the OECD, so that it could contribute more fully to important discussions in both forums. Hence, after a period of intensive lobbying by Japanese Prime Minister Ikeda Hayato among European leaders in 1962, the US and British governments in November successfully proposed that negotiations for Japanese membership should begin. Japan commenced the accession process early in 1963 and a memorandum of accession was signed in July, leading to membership in 1964.[27]

As well as increasing its status, the Japanese government was keen to be in the "Western" anti-communist camp, as were the Eisenhower and Kennedy administrations. Prime Minister Ikeda Hayato also had increasingly stressed the need to develop strong ties with Europe to accompany Japan's already close relationship with the US.[28] Interestingly, one of the motives underlying the Eisenhower administration's proposal to reorganize the OEEC was to open up the possibilities for full membership in that organization for itself and Canada as well as Japan, though it was well aware of the difficulties it would face in gaining support for Japanese membership.[29] On the domestic front, only the Japanese Socialist Party opposed accession, arguing it was an anti-communist move that would alienate the USSR and China, but there was no other significant public opposition to membership.[30]

The accession of Japan was also something of a challenge for the OECD because its convention, while authorizing new members, did not specify what should be the road to membership. There was no "acquis" or road map to guide the process, and no explicit criteria for accession existed, as has become the norm for OECD practice since 2007.[31] Instead, accession negotiations came to focus on Japan's reservations regarding the OECD's Codes of Liberalization, which are still at the core of the OECD's agreements and related activities. In particular, Japan came under pressure to limit its use of industry policy instruments; for example, its financial support for the shipping industry and restrictions on the use of its foreign capital and foreign currency laws to reject industrial imports and foreign investment. There was particularly strong pressure from OECD members for Japan to reduce its support for the shipping industry and shipbuilding at a time when these sectors were competing increasingly and successfully with European member countries. Japanese negotiators vigorously opposed the latter pressures, pointing out the increasing subsidies offered by European states for their increasingly uncompetitive ship-building companies, to the point that it looked as if accession would be delayed, though the matter was finally resolved.[32]

It was the prospect of Japanese full membership that led the British government in 1963 to inform the Australian and New Zealand governments of this prospect and, importantly, that if they were interested, British diplomats would support their applications for full membership in the OECD. Two factors informed the decision of the British government. The first was its 1961 failure to gain membership in the EEC, leading to an increase in its support for the fledgling OECD and, hence, the attraction of gaining the potential support of two additional members of the Commonwealth in that body. Second, and probably more important, there were fears that there would still be substantial domestic opposition to Japanese membership in the OECD (with wartime memories still strongly held), an opposition that might be lessened if two Commonwealth countries gained membership at the same time as Japan.[33]

Australian and New Zealand officials discussed the British proposal and informally canvassed a number of existing members for their views. While most members were sympathetic, there was continuing opposition from the US for much the same reasons as had been the case in 1960, tempering any increased enthusiasm for membership that had developed.[34] The Australian DEA and especially the Treasury had moved to support full membership in the OECD. They argued that there would be political and economic advantages in Australian membership as it would provide increased access to the members of the OECD Council, the Executive Committee, and other committees that were made up of senior policy makers from Western European, US, and Canadian administrations. In turn, greater access would enable the fuller development of relevant contacts and a greater opportunity for gaining useful information and influence.[35]

The new Australian DEA and Treasury emphasis on the value that membership would bring in regard to access to Western European policy makers had its roots in the first application for EEC membership by the British Government in 1961.[36] As the DEA pointed out, with British membership in the EEC, the Commonwealth was likely to decline in importance and, perhaps, eventually disappear. In addition, there was a rising need to reduce the extent of what was felt to be Australia's increasing diplomatic isolation from North Atlantic and European developments. Also, membership would be useful for promoting Australia's foreign aid and trading interests. The Treasury, irritated by Australia's exclusion from membership in the G10, saw OECD membership as a means of accessing and influencing the G10's key members in international economic and monetary affairs.[37]

The gathering enthusiasm from Treasury and the DEA did not overcome the continuing opposition from Minister McEwen. He pointed out that Australia was in the process of seeking membership in the United Nation's Economic Commission for Asia and the Far East and that an application for OECD membership at the same time might raise suspicions as to Australian motives and the likely strength of its commitments to the Commission by its largely South Asian and East Asian members. Hence, a small, ad hoc Cabinet committee meeting declined the British proposal of support. The committee asserted, not unreasonably, that there was simply not enough time to undertake an appropriate evaluation in the time available, constrained by having to meet a similar timetable as had already been agreed on for the Japanese application. Also, the US Administration had indicated that it would prefer that Australia did not proceed with an application as it might encourage applications from Argentina and Brazil and that, in turn, might complicate its first priority: gaining membership for Japan.[38]

New Zealand's interest in the OECD in 1963–1964 commenced with the British offer to support its application for full membership during the time of Japan's accession process. However, the offer was rejected by Cabinet for much the same reasons as had the Australian Cabinet, plus the additional complication of its continuing view that New Zealand's stance regarding membership should be in line with, if not identical to that of Australia's. While there were differences in departmental views regarding membership, interdepartmental discussions seem not to have been as deeply divided (as was the case in Australia), and there was a feeling that in the long run, full OECD membership would be likely, particularly if the divide between industrialized and developing countries persisted or intensified, making it impossible, or at least very difficult, for New Zealand to continue to pursue its "middle way" stance.[39]

There were changes to both the pattern of support by OECD members for Australian and New Zealand membership and to their views regarding membership in 1964–1966, leading to the Australian decision to apply for membership in the DAC, achieved in 1966, and in the increased engagement of New Zealand in relation to the agricultural activities of the OECD. The rising intensity of departmental support for membership in Australia, notably by the DEA and Treasury, was made clear in their joint September 1965 Cabinet submission. The submission had the "avowed intention" that it should lead to full membership in the OECD and put forward three new arguments to support its case.[40]

The first was that the OECD was undertaking important work on freeing up capital markets, which if successful, would further open Western European markets for Australian borrowers. This was a valuable prospect, given that there were suggestions that the British government was going to restrain its capital outflows to the sterling area, a matter of considerable concern for Australia. The second argument was what Treasury and DEA officials saw as the increasing value of membership in the DAC, which would help "make the Australian aid effort better known." This more positive view sprang from an OECD invitation for Australia and New Zealand to participate in OECD meetings (in DAC and the Trade Committee) regarding the Western Group's position at the UNCTAD meetings.[41] The third argument was that membership in the OECD's Trade Committee would provide Australia with the opportunity to comment on the trade policies of other members and that such membership would not prevent the government from adopting whatever position it thought was appropriate for pursuing Australian interests in other arenas, notably the GATT. This was in marked contrast to the continuing Department of Trade view that, as Australia was a major exporter of primary produce, membership in the OECD's Trade Committee would subject the government to unwelcome influence from the protectionist views of its EEC members. Further, the submission pointed out that the Vernon Committee on Economic Inquiry very recently had recommended the potential value to Australia of trade discussions in the OECD, arguing that this alone warranted Australian membership. Nor would it have escaped the notice of Cabinet members that Sir John Crawford, formerly the Secretary of the Trade Department, had been the vice chair of the Vernon Committee, and now supported OECD membership.

However, in recognizing the strength of the opposition, the Cabinet submission also suggested that if the submission was unsuccessful, then membership in the DAC would be worth seeking as an introductory step toward full membership in the OECD, as had been the case for Japan. The submission was rejected, for much the same general reasons as had been put forward in 1963, combined with McEwen's continuing, if slowly declining, influence (by again arguing strongly against membership) and the continuing, if declining, opposition from US officials. Moreover, at this time Australia and New Zealand were attempting to both gain trade concessions from the US in the context of the Kennedy Round of negotiations, and to work with the US in attempting to reduce EEC trade barriers, so efforts to gain OECD membership in the face of US opposition might endanger progress in both these areas.[42] As a sign of McEwen's declining influence, Cabinet did not entirely accept his views on this occasion, instead agreeing that Australia should seek membership, not of the OECD but of the DAC, overturning its 1960 decision, and that it would leave open "for later consideration" the question of an application for full membership.[43]

The Australian application for membership in the DAC met some initial US resistance. In response to Australian queries as to the reasons for the resistance, it was indicated that its membership would only encourage other, unwelcome requests for membership. US officials also noted that Australia had announced "without forewarning" its intention to give preferences to developing countries at a time when other OECD members of the Western Group were still considering their positions as regards UNCTAD's demand for such preferences.[44] However, after a series of discussions and a strong letter of support from the British government to the US, officials agreed that they would not lobby against Australian membership, though it would make its position of opposition known if asked by other members.[45] Australia's formal application for membership was lodged on 26 November 1965 and agreed to by Council on 15 February 1966.

In 1964, the question of full membership in the OECD was again considered by the New Zealand Officials Committee on Economic and Financial Policy, chaired by the Treasury. However, faced with divisions among its members, it decided to retain the status quo, with representatives of the Treasury and the departments of Agriculture and Customs being in favor of membership, while those of the DEA and Industries and Commerce were opposed, favoring closer relationships with the G77 in UNCTAD.[46] Full membership was again considered by the Officials

Committee in 1965 but the Committee decided not to proceed to the stage of making a submission to Cabinet. Instead, it decided to continue with the government's limited, though increasing, ad hoc association with the OECD, especially as there was still likely to be US opposition to full membership for New Zealand.[47] It was in the context of these discussions in 1963–1965 that most of the reasons put forward in support of New Zealand's eventual decision to apply for full membership in 1972 were identified and evaluated by the Treasury, surfacing repeatedly in later government papers and Cabinet submissions. As such, they warrant a closer examination.

In summary, the reasons were that, first, 90% of New Zealand exports went to OECD members, including Japan, so that membership would be an advantage in gaining greater access to key trade officials, especially those from the EEC, given New Zealand's efforts to gain exemption from the restrictions of the EEC's Common Agriculture Policy should Britain eventually gain membership in the EEC. This was a view given greater weight by New Zealand's (and Australia's) lack of success in the GATT in promoting the liberalization of trade in agricultural products the government strongly desired. Second, officials felt that OECD members would be more likely to help New Zealand when it faced economic difficulties by agreeing, for example, to support its position in the GATT should it propose to raise tariff barriers. Officials noted that this had been the case for Canada, which was assisted in GATT negotiations by earlier discussion in the OECD, following support from its members at the GATT. Officials also felt the membership would enable New Zealand to bring the particular problems of a small economy to the notice of members.

However, New Zealand officials also saw a number of major disadvantages springing from OECD membership. The first was that membership would identify New Zealand with a European group of industrialized countries, which might prejudice its chances of being recognized as a developing country at DAC, the Economic Commission for Asia and the Far East, and UNCTAD discussions, though it was also noted that it was not likely to gain such recognition given its relative wealth compared to other developing countries. However, as this tended already to be the case in practice, this was not a strong argument. The second was that officials expected that over time New Zealand exports to non-OECD countries would increase, especially to Japan and Southeast Asia. This would help reduce New Zealand's reliance on OECD markets, somewhat decreasing the value of membership as a means of gaining access to EEC trade officials in the OECD. Again, given that at this time New Zealand exports to Japan were at a low level, though growing, and that the New Zealand economy would benefit even more from increasing its exports to OECD markets, this was an argument of limited weight.

The third disadvantage was that New Zealand might come under pressure to modify its economic policies if they were to adversely impact other OECD members. While this might have been the case, the very limited economic impact of New Zealand exports on any single OECD member would have been unlikely to stimulate much in the way of such pressure, other than from those with substantial New Zealand dairy imports. The fourth was that neither the OEEC nor the OECD had had any great success in liberalizing trade in agricultural products, a major objective of New Zealand trade policy. However, if New Zealand and Australia were to gain membership then, combined with continuing US influence, greater pressure could be placed on EEC members of the OECD to reduce their agricultural protectionism. A fifth disadvantage was that membership might increase pressure on New Zealand to raise its overseas aid, though, given that it was already a member of the World Bank and other UN agencies, it was regularly subject to such pressure in these forums. Finally, the costs of membership for a small country in terms of both money and human resources would be relatively heavy, requiring an additional three seconded officers at the Paris Embassy, as well as the annual cost of ministerial and officers' visits to Paris.

Despite the divided views of its officials regarding association with the OECD, in 1963 the New Zealand Cabinet, reflecting the overwhelming dominance of agriculture in its economy and exports, approved a recommendation for New Zealand's membership in the Gentleman's Agreement on the Export of Whole Milk Powder, negotiated at the OECD. The agreement was an attempt to manage international trade in whole milk powder by setting minimum prices, and its signatories reported to a subcommittee of the OECD's Agriculture Committee.[48] Similarly, in 1964 the New Zealand Cabinet approved a submission from the Department of Agriculture recommending an application for membership in the OECD's Seed Certification Scheme which was accepted by the OECD in 1966. The submission argued that full membership in the OECD Scheme was necessary as, if Britain joined the EEC, then, without membership New Zealand seed exports would be under threat.

The influential Federated Farmers and the New Zealand Grain, Seed and Produce Merchants' Association strongly advocated membership.

Two further developments further increased the extent of Australian and New Zealand association with the OECD in 1963 and 1964. OECD members agreed in March 1963 that the OECD Secretariat would service the needs of the Western Group (consisting of OECD members, plus Australia, New Zealand, and Finland, known as Annex II or the Western Group) at UNCTAD I in 1964. It was also agreed that New Zealand and Australia should be asked to work closely with them. New Zealand had considerable reservations about the invitation as, for example, it had signed the October 1963 Declaration of the developing countries to the UN General Assembly, and its approach to UNCTAD was based on its established "middle way" stance, designed to enhance its dominant interest in trade in temperate agricultural products. Hence, there was a fear that working with a Western Group serviced by the OECD Secretariat would both damage the credibility of its middle path stance and constrain its freedom of manoeuvre in negotiations. However, both countries agreed to take part in the meetings of the Western Group, though not necessarily to being bound by any agreements reached at its meetings.[49]

New Zealand and Australia also were later invited by OECD Secretary-General Kristensen to attend the 16 July 1964 meetings of the OECD Trade Committee to discuss the largely negative results of UNCTAD I. New Zealand had two concerns regarding the invitation.[50] One was that both New Zealand and Australian trade officials were still reluctant to be associated too closely with the OECD. The second was that given the adverse reaction of the US to the 1963 suggestion of New Zealand and Australian membership in the OECD, New Zealand officials wanted to avoid the embarrassing situation of an objection to its attendance at the Committee being raised.

Nevertheless, the New Zealand Government decided to accept the OECD's invitation, even though it was recognized that New Zealand officials might find themselves in a minority position at the Trade Committee, and there was a continuing desire to preserve their freedom of manoeuvre in regard to UNCTAD. This was because, as noted in an August 1964 Cabinet submission, New Zealand's attempts to maintain its middle path stance at UNCTAD had been unsuccessful (as was Australia's).[51] However, Australia decided not to accept the invitation to attend the Trade Committee meetings, still strongly influenced by the views of Minister McEwen.

In summary, 1962–1966 was a period in which Japan moved swiftly to full OECD membership but, in contrast, Australia and New Zealand only slowly developed a largely ad hoc, limited association with the OECD that culminated in Australia's formal membership in the DAC in 1966. New Zealand's developing association with the OECD was focused primarily on furthering its interests in trade and agriculture, though both countries found the access they gained to discussions at the OECD regarding UNCTAD to be of value.

From a Limited Association to Full Membership, 1966–1973

The limited, partial association with the OECD established in earlier years grew stronger after 1966. In Australia's case, the association was enhanced by its membership in the DAC. DEA official Phillip Flood was appointed as Australia's first representative to DAC. His task was to represent Australia's interests in the DAC and provide more detailed information on the OECD to Canberra, increasingly with a view to supporting moves toward full membership. At least indirectly, New Zealand also benefitted from Australian membership in the DAC, with Australian officials often providing their New Zealand counterparts with information and advice.[52] In 1969 the Australian government moved to apply for full membership, which it achieved in 1971. The New Zealand government moved a little more slowly. Cabinet received a submission recommending membership in the DAC in 1969, but deferred a decision on the recommendation until 1972. In 1970 Cabinet received a submission recommending membership in the Agriculture Committee, which was accepted and achieved later that same year. This was followed by a further, successful Cabinet submission recommending full OECD membership in 1972 that was accepted by the OECD in 1973.

Australia's accession process commenced in mid-1969 with an informal sounding out of the views of OECD members, as well as a detailed examination of the advantages and disadvantages of membership. Opposition from the Department of Trade had dissipated for three main reasons. First was its continuing failure to gain greater support in the GATT from developing countries that would free up trade in agriculture, as highlighted by the failure of the Kennedy Round negotiations. Second, Australian efforts to maintain a middle position stance similar to New Zealand's between the industrialized and developing countries had failed. Both countries were clearly perceived by UNCTAD members as wealthy, if not industrialized, countries, so the risk of offending developing countries by accession to the OECD had disappeared. Moreover, while the US had recognized Australia and New Zealand's "middle position," this had not resulted in any significant concessions for their exports to US markets.[53]

Third, OECD members were increasingly discussing and preparing their positions on key trade issues in its Trade Committee before taking them to the GATT for discussion and negotiation, so that Australian officials did not have the opportunity to engage with them in early discussions at the OECD before any final position was reached.[54] In addition, Philip Flood, when informing the DEA Secretary of the formal invitation to take up OECD membership that had recently been offered to Finland, also noted that after the OECD Council meeting at which the invitation to Finland had been agreed, the Canadian Permanent Representative, a Mr. Short, remarked to him that "Australia will have to hurry up now." Short further stated that some Council members had said Finnish membership would be the last. Flood also noted that the previous week, as a result of dissatisfaction with the somewhat cursory nature of the application process for Finland, the Council's Executive Committee had decided to review and strengthen the requirements for membership. Short also suggested that countries such as Australia should apply sooner rather than later.[55]

Black Jack McEwen remained opposed to membership (in a discussion with Phillip Flood in Paris in 1968, he is reported as stating that "Australia will only join the OECD over my dead body," perhaps irritated by Flood's report regarding Finnish membership).[56] He submitted a separate submission to Cabinet that indicated he would not support membership from the trade point of view, but, rather strangely, that he would not oppose a recommendation for membership.[57] The retirement of long-serving Prime Minister Menzies in 1966 had reduced his support in Cabinet and, while still cautious and constrained, the views of senior officials in his department had changed from opposition to cautious support for Australian membership.

It was expected that there would be at least some opposition from the US to the Australian application for full membership. However, in June

1970, faced with the positive support for Australian membership from all other OECD members, the recent accession of Finland, and Australia's generally respected membership in the DAC, Alexis Johnson, US Acting Under Secretary of State, informed the Australian ambassador that the US would support Australian membership.[58] With American support assured, formal discussions as to the terms and conditions for Australian membership commenced in July 1970 and concluded with the decision to invite the Australian Government to accept membership on 24 May 1971.[59]

In contrast, New Zealand's move to an application for full membership did not take place until 1972, in part because it had informally agreed not to apply until after Australia's application was completed.[60] With the examples of Japanese and Australian membership in the DAC before it, membership in the DAC initially was perceived as a first step to full membership, and in 1969 New Zealand's Acting Minister for the DEA, Jack Marshall, recommended to Cabinet that New Zealand consider applying for membership in the DAC.[61] His submission pointed out that a representative of the Paris Embassy had been attending DAC meetings as an observer since 1962 and that membership would provide useful information and assessments of New Zealand's aid performance. The submission further pointed out that Australian membership in the DAC had not created any difficulties or pressure to increase its aid volumes, and that opinion in the Australian DEA was that membership had increased its experience and knowledge regarding aid management, as well as its international standing. Moreover, Australian officials had expressed the hope that New Zealand would join the DAC. However, the submission noted that no proposal for full OECD membership was "contemplated at present."

The New Zealand Treasury opposed the proposal for DAC membership, rebutting the arguments put forward.[62] In particular, it felt that the submission's claim that membership in the DAC would ensure that New Zealand's aid performance was authoritatively recorded by an international body and brought into "accepted comparative relation" with that of other aid donors should not be accepted. The Treasure paper argued that this would require New Zealand to persuade other DAC members to amend some of the concepts used in quantifying aid flows to more fairly compare New Zealand's aid performance, and that achieving such changes was unlikely. The paper did not identify the concepts in question, nor explain why they showed the volume of New Zealand aid to be low compared to most DAC members. However, the paper then went on to indicate that if the application of the DAC measure of aid flows went public, they would encourage domestic interest groups to put further pressure on the government to increase New Zealand aid by showing the relatively low levels of New Zealand aid, recommending that Cabinet decline the DEA proposal. However, despite the negative Treasury report regarding DAC (though not of full membership in the OECD, which Treasury had supported for some years), Cabinet decided only to defer a decision on the proposal and to reconsider it following a meeting in Paris between the Minister of Overseas Trade Jack Marshall and OECD Secretary-General Kristensen. Their meeting came to focus not on the DAC, but on the possibility of gaining membership in the Agriculture Committee, with which New Zealand had developed a more extensive set of links and which was of greater political and economic interest for New Zealand.

Marshall later recommended successfully that priority should be given to seeking membership in the OECD's Agriculture Committee, building on New Zealand's already well-established association with the OECD in this policy area. He also recommended that membership in the Agriculture Committee should be followed later by an application for membership in the DAC, and that consideration of an application for full membership should be deferred, all of which was agreed by Cabinet between September 1969 and February 1970.[63] Two major reasons were given for delaying an application: its cost and the desire to avoid complicating the Australian application for full membership then in progress.

The application for membership in the Agriculture Committee was successful and, finally, after Sir Keith Holyoake stepped down as Prime Minister and was succeeded by Jack Marshall in February 1972, an ad hoc, interdepartmental committee of Cabinet called the "OECD subgroup" was established to undertake a thorough assessment of the merits of full membership. In June 1972 a detailed submission recommending full membership was put to and endorsed in principle by Cabinet. It argued that if an application was not made at that time, then "the door would be closed," though there was little evidence to support this claim. It also noted that Professor Ralf Dahrendorf, a leading member of the European Commission, suggested to New Zealand officials that membership would enable greater access to, and influence upon, EEC members of the OECD. This was an important factor, given that Britain had managed to gain on New Zealand's behalf (in the Luxembourg agreement) a special arrangement for continuing access for New Zealand's butter, cheese, and lamb to the EEC. Furthermore, the submission argued that Australia, now a member, would offer assistance to New Zealand's application, supplementing the support of the UK, US, and Japan.

With national elections set for 25 November drawing near, in September 1972 Minister Muldoon directed that a report summarizing the major difficulties regarding OECD membership should be put to Cabinet no later than mid-October. This seems to have been an attempt to speed up the accession process to gain electoral support by being able to claim a successful OECD application.[64] However, it soon became clear that it would not be possible to meet this deadline and the Officials Committee agreed that the report would be submitted to the government after the election, which was won by the opposition Labour Party. On 5 March 1973 the Labour Cabinet approved New Zealand's accession to the OECD.[65] In retrospect, it seems unlikely that an earlier submission, as sought by Muldoon, would have made any significant difference to the National Party's electoral results, given that the prospect of OECD membership had attracted little media, parliamentary, or public interest.

Conclusion

As discussed, the reasons for seeking OECD membership by Japan, Australia, and New Zealand had much in common, but also were marked by a range of differences. All three sought access, information, and influence and all three wanted to both protect and advance their economic and political interests by membership in an organization that seemed likely to grow in status and influence. The variations in the time each took to gain full membership—only a few years for Japan and more than a decade for Australia and New Zealand—were caused by several factors. The first was some initial uncertainty as to the new OECD's likely role and influence. The second was the varying support, or opposition, to membership from key, existing members of the OECD, notably the US, but also the UK. The third, for Japan, but not for Australia or New Zealand, was the Japanese government's strong desire to regain Japan's international status, as well as a more influential voice in international economic decision making. The fourth, particularly in Australia's case, was strong and continuing opposition to membership from a powerful Minister and his department. Finally, in New Zealand's case, membership was also further delayed as it decided not to run the risk of complicating the final Australian moves to full membership in 1969–1971 by applying at the same time, as well as by a change in its government in 1972.

In summary, in contrast to Japan's experience, the Australian and New Zealand path to full membership went through an initial and lengthy period of what can be described as a growing, and somewhat ad hoc, association with the OECD, culminating in formal membership in the DAC and the Agriculture Committee, then by full membership in the OECD. In comparison with the earlier accession of Japan and, interestingly, with many of the much later accessions that took place from 1994, the duration of the period leading up to their governments' decisions to seek full membership was far longer. However, it was not unique. Israel, for example, at least informally, expressed an interest in full membership in the OECD in the early 1960s, but did not accede until 2010. Similarly, Estonia and Slovenia, along with several other East European states formerly constrained by their incorporation within the Soviet bloc, expressed an interest in membership in the early 1990s, but were not admitted until 2010, and Latvia not until 2016, with Lithuania still immersed in the accession process in 2016. Also, uniquely in the OECD's experience of accession, while the Russian Federation commenced discussions with a view to membership in 2007, the process was suspended in 2014 and seems unlikely to be resumed for some time. Space does not permit an examination and comparison of the accession experiences of states since the 1990s, especially those that have undergone or are undergoing the formal accession process put in place in 2007, but they are worthy of detailed analyses in the future.

Notes

1. Paavonen, Tapani, "Finland and the question of West European economic integration, 1947–1961," *Scandinavian Economic History Review* 52: 2–3 (2004), 85–109.
2. Carroll, Peter G.H., and Aynsley Kellow, *The OECD A Study of Organizational Adaptation* (Cheltenham: Edward Elgar, 2011).
3. The chapter is based largely on the official Australian (ANA), New Zealand (NZA) and British (TNA) national archives and OECD archives. The author has not yet had the opportunity to gain access to the Japanese Government archives in relation to the OECD.

4. Christine Davis and Meredith Wilf, "Joining the Club: Accession to the GATT/WTO." Paper presented at the Annual Meeting of the American Political Science Association Seattle, Washington September 1, 2011, and Tetsuo Shimomura, *OECD kamei to nihon keizai* (Tokyo: Keizai, 1964), 128
5. Paavonen T, *Finland and the question of West European integration, 1947–1961*, Scandinavian Economic History Review, 52, 85–109. See also in the chapter on Yugoslavia by Marković and Obadić in this volume.
6. "The Sato Visit: Proposed Cabinet-Level Meeting on Economic Problems," 6 January 1965, Document 39. Foreign Relations of the United States (FRUS) 1964–1968, Vol. XXIX, Part 2, Japan.
7. ANA, File A3092, Cabinet Decision 615, 4 February 1960.
8. Kennedy, Charles, "Interview with John W. Tuthill 1987," in *The Association for Diplomatic Studies and Training Foreign Affairs Oral History Project,* transcript of interview with Ambassador John Tuthill. At http://www.loc.gov/collections/foreign-affairs-oral-history/?q=John+W+Tuthill (accessed on 27 July 2015).
9. NZA, File No 15422571, "Brief for discussion with Australian officials," 6 May 1960; ANA, File 1838 724/5 Part 4, "Australian Relationships with the Organization for Economic Cooperation and Development," Cabinet Submission No 1037, 1963.
10. Christine Davis, "More than Just a Rich Country Club: Membership Conditionality and Institutional Reform in the OECD." Paper presented at the SAIS Research Seminar Series in Politics and Political Economy, 2015–2016, Johns Hopkins School of Advanced International Studies, 31. 2016.
11. Allan Rix, *Japan's foreign aid challenge: policy reform and aid leadership* (New York: Routledge, 1993).
12. NZA, File R17247561, "Possible New Zealand Membership in OECD," 26 February 1963.
13. ANA, File 62/992, "OECD—DAC Development Assistance Committee (including Ad Hoc Committee) 1962–1966," 8 May 1962.
14. NZA, File R11197004, "New Zealand Participation in European Working Group on Development Assistance," 3 February 1960.
15. NZA, File R15422571 "Joint Action by Australia and New Zealand on the Proposed Re-organization of the OEEC and Related Matters," 5 April 1960.
16. ANA, File Series 1838, File No 724/4/2 Part 1 Committee on Trade. "Cabinet Decision 615," 4 February 1960, and File A3092, "European Economic Conference Points for Discussion," 20 January 1960.
17. NZA, File R11197004, "European Economic Questions," 7 January 1960.

18. Davis and Wilf, "Joining the Club," 40.
19. ANA, File No. 992/62, A1029, "Development Assistance Committee—Ad Hoc Group on Aid to Thailand," 10 December 1962.
20. NZA, File R6278173, "Proposal for a Gentleman's Agreement Between the Exporting Countries of Whole Milk Powder," 31 January 1963.
21. NZA, File R11197004, "Development Assistance Committee of OECD," 21 November 1962.
22. TNA, File DO 162/82 273341, "Cabinet External Economic Relations Committee—The Future of the OECD Relationship with Australia and New Zealand—Note by the Commonwealth Relations Office," dated 30 September 1964. See also the chapter by Patricia Hongler in this volume.
23. NZA, File R16682044, "Seed Certification: OECD Scheme for Herbage Seed Moving in International Trade," 21 September 1964.
24. Fukushima, Akiko, "Official Development Assistance (ODA) as a Japanese Foreign Policy Tool," in *Japanese Foreign Policy Today*, edited by Takashi Inoguchi and Jain Purnendra, 152–174 (New York: Palgrave, 2000).
25. Jacob Frenkel and Morris Goldstein (eds.), *Functioning of the International Monetary System*, Vol. 1, (Washington, D.C., International Monetary Fund, 1966), 65–69. See also the chapter by Kazuhiko Yago in this volume.
26. Matthias Schmelzer, *The Hegemony of Growth. The OECD and the Making of the Economic Growth Paradigm* (Cambridge: Cambridge University Press), 195.
27. Glenn Hook and Hugo Dobson (eds.), *Global Governance and Japan. The Institutional Architecture* (London: Routledge, 2007), 55–56.
28. Iwanaga, Ken, "Europe in Japan's Foreign Policy," in *The Japanese and Europe: Images and Perceptions*, edited by Bert Edstrom, 208–235 (Richmond: Curzon Press, 2000).
29. C. Douglas Dillon, "Interview with C. Douglas Dillon," *The Foreign Affairs Oral History Collection for Diplomatic Studies and Training*, a transcript of the interview by R.D. Schulzinger, 28 April 1987.
30. Schmelzer, *Hegemony of Growth*, 216.
31. OECD, "A Strategy for Enlargement and Outreach," Report by the Chair of the Heads of Delegation Working Group on the Enlargement Strategy and Outreach, Ambassador Seiichiro Noboru, (Paris: OECD, 2004).
32. Shimomura, OECD kamei, 68.
33. TNA, File DO 162/82 273341. "Cabinet External Economic Relations Committee—The Future of the OECD Relationship with Australia and New Zealand—Note by the Commonwealth Relations Office," 30 September 1963.
34. NZA, File R17247561. "Cable," 26 February 1960.

35. ANA, File A1838-724-4-3 Part 3. "European Economic Relations Integration," 26 February 1963.
36. ANA, File A4940/1, C3368 Part 2. "Bunting to Menzies," 7 July 1961.
37. Mountford, Anthony. "The Historical Development of IMF Governance," IMF Independent Evaluation Office Background Paper BP/08/02, rev. May 2008, 9.
38. ANA, File A1838 724/5 Part 4. "Australian Relationships with the Organization for Economic Cooperation and Development," Cabinet Submission No 1037, Copy No 73, 17 March 1963.
39. NZA, File R16682044. "Proposal for New Zealand Membership in OECD," 12 March 1963.
40. ANA, File Series A1838, File No 724/5 Part 4, "OECD and DAC—Australian Relations With," Cabinet Submission No 1194, 7 September 1965.
41. TNA, File DO 162/82 273341. "Cabinet External Economic Relations Committee—The Future of the OECD Relationship with Australia and New Zealand—Note by the Commonwealth Relations Office," 30 September 1964.
42. Zeiler, Thomas, "Commanding the Middle: The American Agenda at the Kennedy Round," *Australian Economic History Review* 41 (2001): 308–324.
43. ANA, File A1838 724/5 Part 4, "Australian Relationships with the Organization for Economic Cooperation and Development," Cabinet Submission No 1037, Copy No 73, 17 March 1963.
44. ANA, File Series A4311, File No. 147/2, "Report to the Minister for External Affairs by the Inter-departmental Committee to Review Australian External Aid," 25 March 1965.
45. ANA, File Reference A1838 724/5 Part 4, "Cable," 6 November 1965.
46. NZA, File R16682044, "Minutes of a meeting of the Working Party on Economic and Financial Policy," 3 September 1964.
47. NZA, File R16682044, "OECD and New Zealand: Position Paper," 16 July 1965.
48. NZA, File R16682044, "Seed Certification: OECD Scheme for Herbage Seed Moving in International Trade," 21 September 1964.
49. TNA, File DO 162/82 273341, "Cabinet External Economic Relations Committee—The Future of the OECD Relationship with Australia and New Zealand—Note by the Commonwealth Relations Office," 30 September 1963.
50. NZA, File R16682044, "UNCTAD and OECD," 13 July 1964 and "UNCTAD," 14 July 1964. On the OECD and UNCTAD, see also the chapter by Patricia Hongler in this volume.

51. NZA, File R16682044, "Proposal for New Zealand Membership in OECD," 6 August 1964.
52. NZA, File R17247562, "Minutes of a meeting of the Officials Committee on Economic and Financial Policy, held in the 5th floor Boardroom, Treasury," 13 November 1969. At this meeting, the First Assistant Secretary at the Australian DEA, K.C.O. Shann, for example, gave a detailed summary of the Australian position regarding the OECD, including the DAC.
53. Zeiler, Commanding the Middle, 323–324.
54. ANA, File Series A1838-724-4-30 Part 2, "OECD and Australia," 4 July 1969.
55. ANA, File Series A1838 File 724/4/16, "Memo," 23 July 1968.
56. Flood, Phillip. *Dancing with Warriors: A Diplomatic Memoir* (Melbourne: Australian Scholarly Publishing, 2003).
57. ANA, File A1838 724-4-30 Part 4, "Cabinet Minute Decision No 305," 30 April 1970.
58. ANA, File A1838 724-4-30 Part 5, Accession, "OECD," 29 May 1970.
59. ANA, File A1838 724-4-30 Part 5, Accession, "OECD," 7 July 1970.
60. NZA, File R17247562, "Minutes," 13 November 1969.
61. NZA, File R20826193, "Proposed New Zealand Membership in Development Assistance Committee (DAC) Organization for Economic Cooperation and Development (OECD)," 23 September 1969.
62. NZA, File R20826193, "OECD Development Assistance Committee: Proposed New Zealand Membership," undated.
63. NZA, File R20826193, "New Zealand Membership in the Organization for Economic Cooperation and Development," 20 February 1970.
64. NZA, File R17247563, "OECD: New Zealand Membership," 29 September 1972.
65. NZA, File R17247565, "OECD: Application for New Zealand Membership," undated.

The Construction of a Western Voice: OECD and the First UNCTAD of 1964

Patricia Hongler

The OECD and the United Nations Conference on Trade and Development (UNCTAD) can be seen as historical antipodes: while the OECD is known to be a forum for rich countries of the West, UNCTAD has been perceived as an important voice of the poor countries in the Global South.[1] As I intend to show in this chapter, such clear-cut conceptions—although further naturalized through the use of geographical terms—are not self-evident, but rather the result of complex political, economic, and cultural negotiations. They are therefore in need of historical scrutiny.[2] I aim to contribute to this examination by taking a closer look at a defining moment in the relations between the two international organizations: the preparation and review of the first UNCTAD conference from 1964 at the OECD's Development Assistance Committee (DAC).

When the OEEC became the OECD in 1961, a letter was replaced in the organization's name: The "E" for Europe became a "D" for Development. Significantly, this change occurred during the most intensive phase of what has been termed the process of decolonization.[3] In 1960 alone, 7 colonial territories in Africa had gained independence and more were to follow in the years to come. It is in this context that the

P. Hongler (✉)
Department of History, University of Lucerne, Frohburgstrasse 3,
6002 Luzern, Switzerland
e-mail: Patricia.hongler@gmail.com

M. Leimgruber and M. Schmelzer (eds.), *The OECD and the International Political Economy Since 1948*, DOI 10.1007/978-3-319-60243-1_6

establishment of a particular committee for development assistance at the new-founded OECD must be understood. At the DAC, delegates from a select group of OECD member countries met in regular intervals to coordinate and debate their aid policies toward the so-called "developing world." In doing so, they built on previous OEEC discussions on technical assistance and development aid, which had focused on activities in inter-European and colonial settings.[4] The new committee's founding members were exclusively donor states, namely Belgium, Canada, France, Germany, Italy, Japan, the Netherlands, Portugal, the United Kingdom, and the United States, while the countries on the receiving end were excluded.[5] Delegates at the DAC focused on the question of how to increase and improve their governments' aid endeavours and primarily did so through yearly peer-to-peer evaluations, the adoption of common standards and norms, and the publication of reports. Committee meetings at the Château de la Muette in Paris were prepared by an independent Secretariat, followed clear diplomatic rules and rarely had any spectacular or unexpected results.[6]

On 9 July 1964, however, the DAC held an unusual reunion: "Never before has the meeting room been so full—besides the strongly represented delegations—with other interested staff, experts and audience," the Swiss delegate noted in his report.[7] The impressive turnout was due to the fact that this was the earliest debate held at the OECD after the end of the first UNCTAD conference that had taken place in Geneva between 23 March and 16 June 1964. As the meeting minutes of this discussion at OECD indicate, the UNCTAD conference had quite an impact on diplomats from the so-called "Western industrialized countries."[8] The Belgian delegate noted that the scene in Geneva had been "completely dominated by the developing nations," which had tried to revolutionize their relations with the industrialized countries with "myths and buzzwords".[9]

UNCTAD 1964 is considered to be a key moment in the history of international politics and has become synonymous with the Third World's arrival on the scene of international diplomacy.[10] At the Geneva conference, delegates from Africa, Asia, and Latin America formed a strong alliance and tried to fundamentally challenge the architecture of world trade. In contrast to then-dominant Modernization Theory, they refused to see poverty in the Third World as the consequence of underdevelopment that could be remedied by planning and investments. Instead they pointed to the consequences of colonial economic policy.

By referring to respective knowledge claims during the conference, these representatives effectively influenced future ways of thinking and speaking about development in the public and political sphere. UNCTAD 1964 is therefore seen as a decisive chapter in the history of the so-called North-South conflict, which—after further UNCTAD conferences in Delhi (1968) and Santiago de Chile (1972)—culminated in debates at the United Nations about a New International Economic Order in the mid-1970s.[11] However, as I argue in this paper, the 1964 Geneva conference was not only crucial for the constitution of the Third World, but also led to a new conception of "the West." While the developing nations' delegates were able to keep up their unity throughout the conference in a group of first 75 and later 77 countries—the so-called G77—representatives from the Western industrialized countries appeared deeply divided over trade and aid policy.[12] After the conference, this led to a significant process of reorientation, in which OECD took a central stage.

In what follows, I will show how the first UNCTAD from 1964 was perceived in the diplomatic sphere of the OECD and its member countries.[13] In a first step, I will briefly analyze how the representatives of the Western industrialized countries prepared for the conference at the OECD. I will then mainly concentrate on the conference's aftermath and on the importance and meanings that it unfolded.

The Way to the Conference

The decision to hold a United Nations Conference on Trade and Development was taken by the UN Economic and Social Council on 1 August 1962. The UN General Assembly confirmed the decision in December of the same year.[14] This convocation of UNCTAD was made possible by a growing consensus among the UN delegations from Asian, African, and Latin American countries, whose diplomatic alliance went back to earlier international meetings: the Bandung conference in 1955 that had focused on Afro-Asian solidarity and the common fight against (neo-)colonialism; the Belgrade conference in 1961, where the Non-Aligned-Movement had been formed; and finally the conference of Cairo in July 1962, where delegations from Latin America eventually joined the discussion. In this process, the collective designation as "developing countries" became an important point of reference.[15] In light of the growing unity among Third World delegates, resistance by the Western industrialized countries' representatives against a UN Conference on

Trade and Development faded. After the admission of 16 newly independent African nations in 1960, they had lost their majority at the UN General Assembly and could do little to contain increasingly coordinated claims by the "Global South."[16]

Surprisingly, despite this difficult situation at the UN, staff members in the OECD countries' governments stayed relatively calm in the face of UNCTAD. For instance, an internal document of the Swiss Federal Department of Economic Affairs gave quite an optimistic outlook:

> In the beginning, polemic statements and attacks by the developing countries against the Western industrialised countries are to be expected. However, the industrialised countries will aim at curtailing such polemics, particularly in the different Working Parties, in order to examine the problems in a sober and realistic manner.[17]

While the Third World representatives met in regional organizations and commissions in Niamey, Teheran, and Alta Gracia to prepare for UNCTAD, Western preparations were very much confined to national ministries. From late-1963 onward, a certain amount of coordination took place at the OECD but these efforts were overshadowed by internal tensions. According to Guliano Garavini, the fact that a British application for membership in the European Economic Community had been declined 1 year earlier poisoned the atmosphere.[18] In many key areas of trade policy, no agreement could be reached prior to the conference. For instance, the French delegation endorsed regulations for commodity prices, while the British delegation was strongly opposed.[19] Another important topic of disagreement was the question of tariff preferences for developing countries.[20] In general, the willingness for cooperation was very low. For instance, OECD delegates rejected the proposal to inform fellow OECD members on the planned opening statements in which national points of view were to be declared. Even at the OECD's Trade Committee's very last meeting before UNCTAD, national views on which tactic to adopt at the conference strongly diverged. The Swiss meeting minutes actually mentioned a hardening of positions.[21]

Similarly, while the DAC specifically set up an UNCTAD-Working Party, which met three times for preparatory talks, it only reached vague results. They were summarized in a confidential report that was supposed to serve as background material for the conference. However, the Working Party emphasized that the document only reflected the consensus reached and did not contain any binding decisions.[22] The paper reveals to what extent UNCTAD was underestimated at the OECD. It primarily justified why the conference would not be an appropriate place to discuss certain questions of policy, such as the definition of development aid or the significance of overall foreign exchange gaps.[23] Furthermore, the document proposed that DAC members should not only aim at confrontation in Geneva, but also be ready to listen:

> Member governments should express their willingness to listen to preoccupations and problems of the less-developed countries and to associate them fully in the consultative processes which aim at finding solutions.[24]

At a preparatory meeting the French delegate even said that UNCTAD had to be used by the industrialized countries "as a didactic tool to teach the developing countries."[25] In retrospect, this patronizing attitude can clearly be understood as a misinterpretation of the actual situation. As I will show next, it was by no means the delegates from OECD countries who showed initiative at the Geneva conference.

Knowledge as Legitimation and Threat

As Samuel Misteli argues in his historical analysis of UNCTAD, the legitimation of policy positions through economic knowledge was crucial for participants at the conference. Third World representatives based their claims on the works of Argentinian economist Raúl Prebisch, who in 1949 had formulated the argument that large parts of the world were integrated into world trade in disadvantageous ways.[26] According to Prebisch, the world economy was divided between a periphery that produced raw materials and primary products and an industrialized center that benefitted from manufacturing. He argued that the terms of trade for the countries in the periphery would further deteriorate because prices for primary commodities were continuously sinking and the developing countries had to pay more and more to obtain industrial goods. This hypothesis, which was further developed into Dependency Theory in the 1960s, served as an important frame of thought for the developing countries' coalition at UNCTAD.[27]

In light of the 1964 conference, Prebisch, who had been elected UNCTAD's Secretary-General, penned the highly influential paper *Towards a New Trade Policy for Development*. Simply referred to as the

Prebisch Report in many sources, the paper served as a central document of policy debate prior to the conference. Prebisch identified a widening "gap" between developing countries' export revenues and their demand for imports and investments. Furthermore, he judged the growth rate of 5% of GDP for developing countries envisioned by the UN to be totally insufficient. According to his own estimations, economic growth in the "Third World" would lead to a higher demand for imports and therefore to increasing indebtedness. As a countermeasure, Prebisch asked for accelerated industrialization, more financial aid, and—above all—higher prices for raw materials.[28]

This thesis was so virulently discussed among OECD members that it simply came to be dubbed "the Prebisch Gap" or "the Gap"—even in documents in German.[29] Unsurprisingly, most of the DAC delegates considered Prebisch's calculations and forecasts to be wrong. For instance, the French delegate stated "that there were large margins of error in the estimates of all the components of the Gap, and that the size of the Gap was really speculative." The American delegate also stressed the point that in his view "the Gap" was based on political assumptions that did not have to be accepted by the DAC countries.[30] The most frequent criticism, however, concerned the generalizing nature of Prebisch's argument. The thesis formulated inequality on the level of world trade through abstract calculations and took its political strength from its global validity. At the DAC, this global abstraction was criticized to be unscientific. It was claimed, for instance, that every developing country's need for capital should be judged individually.[31] The fact that in this case DAC delegates argued for particularity indicates how uncomfortable the "Gap" thesis was, since under normal circumstances, specific work on an individual country basis was avoided at this committee at all cost.[32]

As the minutes of the first DAC discussion of UNCTAD quoted at the beginning of this paper suggest, the Geneva conference came as a shock to the OECD countries' representatives. The Swiss minutes explained that the delegates at the DAC meeting had only "expressed their personal impressions and views as the conference's wide range of problems had not yet been digested inside their governments and there were no official statements available yet."[33] Around the same time, the American government informed the Swiss embassy in Washington that so far no definitive assessment of the conference existed: "we are still licking our wounds," it declared.[34] Interestingly, it was not individual decisions that troubled officials in the national ministries of OECD countries most. As the political analyses of the conference emphasized, no legal commitments resulted from UNCTAD's final act, even if there were concerns about certain moral obligations.[35] But it was really the general atmosphere at the conference that left a threatening impression. To the Swiss delegation, for instance, the new unity among Third World representatives seemed full of danger for the future. New means of influence seemed to "have put the radical elements into a condition of euphoria."[36] Similarly, the *Frankfurter Allgemeine Zeitung* judged that the developing countries had appeared as a monolithic bloc showing an "aggressive mind-set" and "overreaching self-confidence." The article went on to say that Third World representatives had used their numerical superiority "ruthlessly" and "as in euphoria" in order to vote down the industrialized countries.[37] In what follows, I will analyze how such feelings of threat were dealt with at the OECD and in the ministries of its member states.

Emotional, Unrealistic Others and the White Man's Rationality

The last days of the conference saw a series of official closing statements in which delegates addressed the UNCTAD General Assembly for the last time. Third World representatives like the Ethiopian Minister of Commerce and Industry, Endalkachew Makonnen, praised the conference as "one of the most important events of the post-war era" and described it as a decisive step toward "real" independence for the "victims of Western domination." Syed Amjad Ali, the representative of Pakistan, emphasized the new-found unity between the developing countries "as the outstanding feature of this conference," while Kenyan delegate Julius Gikonyo Kiano declared that now "[t]he day of the black man, the yellow and the brown and any other ex-colonial subject" was finally at hand.[38] Others criticized the developed countries' unwillingness to act and made colonial exploitation responsible for present political and economic problems in the developing world.[39]

Swiss Federal Councillor Hans Schaffner for his part chose to begin with some words of caution that he directed explicitly at the Third World delegates:

> The issues of international trade are sufficiently complex and difficult by themselves so that their solution requires sober and sharp thinking. We must, therefore, not allow our vision to be blurred by emotions.[40]

In future, he said, the developing nations' representatives would have to realize "that one cannot rule the economic reality at will. Nothing can be done in one day...." In his closing statement, Edward Heath, the future British Prime Minister and then Secretary of State for Industry, Trade, and Regional Development, came to a similar conclusion:

> I have been impressed by the way in which the developing countries have discovered a unity of interest which has outweighed the differences between them...This unity has enabled them to put forward their case with greater force. It lays on them all the more responsibility to reconcile their rightful aspirations with a realistic assessment of what is practicable.[41]

Thus, Heath also put the Third World delegates' claims into sharp contrast to a realm of the realistic and the possible. And in the exact same way as Schaffner, he pleaded for a more rational form of collaboration: "Conciliation and the search for an agreed consensus of view may be less dramatic than a majority of a hundred votes but it is more likely to feed the hungry, which is our common task," he explained.

These two closing statements contain the keywords that also shaped Swiss and British analyses of the UNCTAD after the end of the conference. The Third World delegates' attitudes were rejected as theatrical and emotional and their claims were judged to be unrealistic. In particular the method of making decisions per majority vote was criticized as unreasonable.[42] Such descriptions by delegates from OECD countries were set in clear contrast with their self-assessment. They portrayed their own approach in Geneva as having been calm and fact-oriented. For instance, a Swiss analysis stated that all attempts by the industrialized nations at shaping the debates in an objective and realistic manner had failed due to resistance by the developing countries.[43] From this perspective, only the industrialized nations' enduring patience had prevented the conference from failing.[44]

My aim now is not to prove whether these assessments by representatives from OECD countries were true or false and thereby give a definition of what might or might not have been calm, factual, emotional, or irrational behaviour.[45] Rather, I understand these perceptions as a specific way of dealing with the feelings of threat described above. I also see them decisively connected to notions of race and gender that were rooted in the colonial project. Colonial rule had been legitimized through the idea that only the both "white" *and* "male" individual possessed the ability to control his body through his reason. "Female" *and/or* "non-white" subjects were understood to be emotional, irrational, and therefore in need of "white male" control and authority. As Vrushali Patil shows in her analysis of debates held at the UN General Assembly between 1946 and 1960, during the process of decolonization the colonial powers' delegates heavily relied on such notions of "white" and "male" rationality. They imagined their colonial subjects as child-like in order to legitimize their own paternal responsibility as colonial powers.[46] The assessments of UNCTAD 1964 mentioned above give a similar impression. There, the behavior of Third World delegates was pictured as chaotic, hysterical, and emotional and the claims brought forward at the conference were rejected as unrealistic and unscientific. In this way, staff members of OECD countries' delegations and ministries assured themselves of their sovereignty as well as of their natural competence to solve world trade and developing aid issues. What also was invoked in this context is the idea of a common Western responsibility for the rest of the world in the sense of a civilizing mission.[47] Only an increased coordination of Western positions seemed to offer an answer to the "impetuous pressure" exerted by politicians from developing countries.[48] I will further develop this thought in the rest of the chapter.

The Necessity of a Western Voice

As my analysis of OECD discussions about UNCTAD has shown so far, Western preparations for the conference were characterized by conflict rather than by successful cooperation. As to cooperation during the conference, diplomats reached a similar conclusion. The Swiss delegation stated that the industrialized countries were "giving the usual picture of a divided group."[49] After the conference the analysis was even more critical: "Because of lacking preparation and passivity, the Western industrialized states were not able to influence the conference work in their own interest."[50] Another document even stated: "One often had the impression that the West has not yet become fully conscious of the role it has to play here."[51] This last statement is of great significance for my argument.

In the period prior to UNCTAD, the category of "the West" had been of minor importance in OECD discussions about development. At the OEEC's Overseas Territories Committee for instance, "development" had been conceptualized as a hierarchical but mutually beneficial relationship between colonial powers and their colonies. An increase in colonial productivity—especially in Africa—was to enhance general well-being in the territories while at the same time solving one of Europe's most pressing economic problems of the post-war area, namely the dollar gap.[52] Europe and Africa were understood to be a joint economic and imaginary space as well as a potential global force besides the United States and the Soviet Union.[53] Later on, during the establishment of the DAC in the early 1960s, the idea of the West did play a certain role at the OECD, although primarily when opposed to the communist East.[54] In documents written directly before UNCTAD, the category of "the West" was also predominantly perceived in the logic of the Cold War.[55] This changed dramatically in the course of the conference. In various reports, the Swiss delegation expressed its surprise at the subordinate role representatives from the Eastern Bloc were playing in Geneva.[56] It was the confrontation with the developing countries that moved into focus:

> The initiative has clearly passed on to the developing countries who—in the sense of a confrontation between rich and poor—have rendered the conference into an extreme question of prestige. Emotionalism, propagandistic and domestic considerations and the knowledge about the existing disagreements in the industrialised countries' camp have further hardened their position.[57]

According to this report, a certain degree of cooperation between OECD countries was nevertheless attained toward the end of the conference. Swiss delegates now demanded that such cooperation should also be envisioned for the future. Only unity seemed to make it possible to deal with the pressure exerted by Third World politicians.[58]

When looking back at UNCTAD during the DAC meeting in July 1964, Pierre A. Forthomme, who had been the OECD countries' coordinator during the conference, predicted that the developing countries would keep up the pressure on the industrialized countries in the years to follow: "In the face of this, he warned, a passive position by the West would play into the hands of the extremists."[59] As the British minutes indicate, this view got a positive response during the DAC meeting:

> ...there was general recognition that the new found unity of the L.D.C.'s and their voting strength presented the developed countries with an urgent need to close their ranks. The Secretary-General in particular was at pains to stress the necessity for unity.[60]

As OECD Secretary-General Thorkil Kristensen underscored, unity was important to strengthening moderate voices among the developing countries. Such calls for increased Western cooperation can be found in a repetitive and unanimous way throughout the entire minutes of the meeting. The delegates expected that "encounters between the developed and the less developed world" would intensify in the future.[61] Under these conditions, it seemed important to jointly prepare for these challenges at the OECD—or as a telegram by the British Foreign Office put it: "We agree that the West, when confronted with united requests by the developing countries, should speak with one voice."[62] In this common quest for a Western voice, the DAC was supposed to play an important role:

> Most representatives who spoke saw in all this and especially in the united front now presented by the L.D.C.'s compelling reasons for more intensive efforts by D.A.C. members to iron out their differences and to reach common agreed positions. Mark (U.K.) and others also saw a likely need for the D.A.C. to become a Western "briefing Committee" in preparation for future confrontations.[63]

The new focus on Western consensus therefore entailed a re-orientation of the DAC. The committee—which had so far been a place of informal discussion between donor countries—now had to become the forum for solving internal disagreement in the Western camp.

Defining the West

In the face of the new role attributed to the DAC after the 1964 UNCTAD—to serve as the place of Western consultation versus the Global South—the question of membership also gained importance. For instance, during informal meetings, critique on Portugal came up. In a body that understood itself as "the voice of the West," the presence of an economically underdeveloped right-wing dictatorship seemed increasingly anomalous. On the other hand, there were discussions directly after the end of UNCTAD on the question of whether Australia and New Zealand, although not members of the DAC or the OECD, should attend meetings on the consequences of the conference.[64] In fact, together with Finland these non-OECD countries became part of a DAC Working Party on UNCTAD issues.[65]

Apparently, the experiences at the UNCTAD conference made it necessary to negotiate who exactly belonged to "the West" and who did not. In this defining process, the example of Australia is particularly telling. When the Australian government requested official admission to the DAC around 1 year after the Geneva conference, the question proved to be quite controversial. American representatives feared that a positive reply would lead to a "proliferation of OECD and its committees."[66] They stated that "a line had to be drawn somewhere" and that an admission of Australia "would open the way to OECD becoming unw[i.e.]ldy and impossible to work."[67] It seemed necessary to prevent the OECD from losing its "whole character" and becoming a smaller version of the United Nations.[68] This line of argument was not taken well at the Australian Foreign Office:

> ...Australia is the only substantial aid donor not in the D.A.C. It is absurd to keep us, alone, out of this consultative organ, the importance of which in this field is quite clear...Moreover we cannot see at all the relevance of Australian membership of D.A.C. to a "possible" interest by India... or Argentina in O.E.C.D. Both India and Argentina are members of the developing countries' caucus in U.N.C.T.A.D. We do not see how this could be reconciled with membership of O.E.C.D., let alone D.A.C.[69]

In this telegram, the justification for admitting Australia to the circle of aid donor countries and therefore to the DAC, its Western forum of coordination, was directly linked to the conflictive situation at UNCTAD. The Australian government sought to prove its entitlement to DAC membership by providing comparative figures. For instance, it stated that many of the actual DAC members were giving less development aid than Australia. That same telegram also contained a last paragraph that focused on American foreign policy:

> We have noted a disposition in the Administration (especially Rostow) to think in terms of a Northern hemisphere grouping, comprising the developed members of Western alliance, as contrasted with an under-developed Southern hemisphere.[70]

In the view of the Australian Foreign Office, such a division of the world into "North" and "South," where Australia could be excluded due to its geographical position, could under no circumstances be accepted.

In January 1966, the admission of Australia to the DAC was discussed by the heads of OECD delegations together with a Brazilian request for observer status. At this meeting, Secretary-General Kristensen saw the need for giving a basic declaration of the organization's "character." He explained that the OECD was a forum for "a certain type of countries" that he defined as "industrial market economies" or "the Western industrial countries."[71] In a way, the OECD was even a regional organization, Kristensen said, "at least in the negative sense that we don't have membership or committee participation from countries in the three less-developed regions—Latin America, Africa, or Asia." Australian membership therefore seemed unproblematic to him:

> Australia is economically and politically a country of the same type as our Member countries. It is an important donor country. It doesn't belong to any of the three less-developed regions: in fact, it does not really belong to any region at all. It is situated somewhat apart.[72]

It is important to note that Kristensen was only able to give an ex negativo definition of DAC and OECD membership. Besides, he also needed to justify Japan's participation through the reference that the Japanese case was very different from the rest of Asia.[73] Further dissonances, for instance the membership of undemocratically governed countries in Western Europa, namely Spain and Portugal, were ignored. Kristensen's line of argument points to how blurry the situation was in the mid-1960s in respect to geopolitical spheres. Geographical conceptions of a socialist East and a democratic and capitalist West interfered with other conceptions that differentiated between a poor South and a rich North. The example of Australia—which indeed became a member of the DAC in 1966 (see also the chapter by Peter Carroll in this volume)—shows that this paradox could only be solved through a considerable amount of negotiation and the continuous redrawing of boundaries.

The concerns about DAC membership after the end of the 1964 UNCTAD conference can be understood as part of a re-invention of "the West" that took place at the OECD and especially at the DAC. As the above-quoted sources show, this process also entailed drawing a line between "the West" and "the rest of the world." But what exactly did this mean? What about the committee's "character" needed to be safeguarded by impeding the presence of certain countries like Brazil or

Argentina?[74] What was the advantage of preserving an exclusive body where the Western countries could be among themselves? Only a few weeks after the end of the Geneva conference, Lord Robin Hankey, the head of the British OECD delegation, explained the future importance of the DAC as follows:

> The Development Assistance Committee will remain an essential organ in which, untrammelled by hysterical speeches from the Afro-Asian bloc or subversive manoeuvres from behind the Iron and Bamboo curtains, the Western Powers can study the real substance of aid problems in all objectivity and think out a coordinated line to take at New York and Geneva.[75]

Thus, in contrast to UNCTAD or the UN General Assembly, a limitation of DAC membership was primarily supposed to enable an "objective" debate. Only an exclusion of "hysterical" Third World representatives seemed to allow for a calm and substantial discussion of the "real" problems. This idea of a genuinely Western objectivity seems to have been constitutive for a new self-perception that emerged within the OECD in the mid-1960s. As I have noted earlier, the notion of exclusively "white" and "male" rationality was key to the immediate reactions to UNCTAD. Apparently, such ideas also formed the basis for a conception of Western superiority that helped deal with challenges from former colonies in a more general way. This connection is not surprising, since the emergence of objectivity as a concept of empirical, neutral, and apolitical consideration in the mid-19th century was closely interrelated with the history of colonialism and with the definition of human difference.[76] As Lorraine Daston points out, it was the modern idea of scientific authority that created an image of "nature" as an object describable in facts, which again provided the basis for the articulation of racial and sexual difference.[77] The differentiation of scientific knowledge from other forms of knowledge went hand in hand with the production of further dichotomies—for instance between the pure and the impure, the rational and the irrational, the objective and the subjective—and these dichotomies were decisively connected to the on-going knowledge production about race and gender.[78] My point is that for these reasons, the idea of an exclusively "Western objectivity" was particularly effective in a process in which boundaries between former colonial powers and colonies had to be redrawn.

Conclusion

In this chapter I have analyzed how the UNCTAD conference of 1964 was perceived in the OECD's diplomatic sphere. Paradoxically, it was the developing countries' surprisingly organized and coordinated way of dominating the conference that was discarded by delegates from Western industrialized states as being emotional and irrational. The unity established among Third World politicians and their powerful performance provoked a perception of threat, which was answered with recourse to colonial categories. After the end of the conference, notions that saw the "white man" as the only bearer of rationality also formed the implicit basis for a renewed conception of the OECD as the place of calm and factual debate. Notions of "factuality" and "objectivity" that had already fulfilled important functions in OEEC and OECD in previous occasions now attained fresh meaning and importance.[79] Among other things, they allowed for a differentiation between the West and the rest of the world.

This focus on objective work through technical studies and statistical inquiries at the OECD remained crucial for Western self-perception until the mid-1970s.[80] At that point, international high-level summits started to provide alternative options for dealing with the feelings of threat that—for instance during the 1973 Oil Crisis and the subsequent NIEO debates at the UN—continued to dominate OECD countries' relations with the Global South (see the chapter by Samuel Beroud in this volume). As Enrico Böhm argues in his study on the first meetings of the Group of Seven (G7) between 1975 and 1981, leading politicians like German chancellor Helmut Schmidt and French president Valéry Giscard d'Estaing had grown increasingly tired of discussions at international organizations like the OECD, which they dismissed as being too technical, abstract, and ultimately ineffective. In the G7, top-ranking politicians found a new forum for Western cooperation, which emphasized their capacity to deal directly with the "real problems" of North-South relations and the world economy in general. In this context, it was no longer Western objectivity and rationality as embodied by the OECD that stood in the forefront, but Western leaders' ability to act and take responsibility for the well-being of the world.[81] Third World politicians on the other hand, rather than being dismissed as emotional and irrational, were now increasingly criticized for their violations of human rights—an issue that from the mid-1970s onward became a central topic of international North-South debates.[82] The question of how, under these new circumstances, the OECD continued to serve as a forum of Western knowledge production and political consultation toward the Third World could be a fruitful starting point for further research.

Notes

1. This chapter is part of my on-going PhD project on the history of decolonization at OECD. I would like to thank my colleagues at the History Department of the University of Lucerne for their comments on earlier drafts. See for instance Ian Taylor and Karen Smith, *United Nations Conference on Trade and Development*, Global Institutions (Abingdon: Routledge, 2007), 13; Milton J. Esman and Daniel S. Cheever, *The Common Aid Effort. The Development Assistance Activities of the Organization for Economic Co-operation and Development* (Columbus OH: Ohio State University Press, 1967), 28–33.
2. On the historical contingency of spatial constructs and meta-geographical assumptions see Martin W. Lewis and Kären E. Wigen, *The Myth of Continents. A Critique of Metageography* (Berkeley: University of California Press, 1997).
3. On the difficulties of writing a history of decolonization see Frederick Cooper, *Decolonization and African Society. The Labor Question in French and British Africa* (Cambridge: Cambridge University Press, 1996), 6–12.
4. On the roots of the OECD's development concept in OEEC history see Matthias Schmelzer, "A Club of the Rich to Help the Poor? The OECD, 'Development', and the Hegemony of Donor Countries", in *International Organizations and Development, 1945–1990*, ed. Marc Frey, Soenke Kunkel, and Corinna R. Unger (Basingstoke: Palgrave Macmillan, 2014), 171–195.
5. The Commission of the European Economic Community (EEC) was also represented by its own delegation. Before the first UNCTAD conference Norway (1962) and Denmark (1963) joined the committee. More states followed after 1964, see OECD, ed., *DAC in Dates. The History of OECD's Development Assistance Committee* (Paris: OECD, 2006).
6. For the history of the DAC see Schmelzer, "A Club of the Rich to Help the Poor?"
7. Schweizerisches Bundesarchiv (Swiss Federal Archives, Bern, hereafter CH-BAR) E2005A#1978/137#2270*, "Session des DAC vom 9. Juli. Erste Aussprache über die Rückwirkungen der UNCTAD-Konferenz in Genf auf die Tätigkeit des DAC", Swiss Delegation to OECD (R.K. Montandon) to the Foreign Trade Division [*Handelsabteilung*] of

the Federal Department of Economic Affairs (hereafter FDEA), 10 July 1964, 1. All translations from quotes in German and French are my own.

8. For the British meeting minutes see The National Archives (hereafter TNA), Records of the Treasury (T) 317/401, "Significance of UNCTAD as regards Development Assistance", Telegram from UK Delegation to OECD (R. Hankey) to Foreign Office, 11 July 1964.
9. CH-BAR E2005A#1978/137#2270*, "Session des DAC vom 9. Juli. Erste Aussprache über die Rückwirkungen der UNCTAD-Konferenz in Genf auf die Tätigkeit des DAC", Swiss Delegation to OECD (R.K. Montandon) to the Foreign Trade Division of the FDEA 10 July 1964, 2.
10. On the history of the term see B.R. Tomlinson, "What Was the Third World?", *Journal of Contemporary History* 38, no. 2 (2003): 307–321.
11. For the history of UNCTAD see Sönke Kunkel, "Zwischen Globalisierung, Internationalen Organisationen und 'Global Governance'. Eine Kurze Geschichte des Nord-Süd-Konflikts in den 1960er und 1970er Jahren", *Vierteljahrshefte für Geschichte* 4 (2012), 555–577; Samuel Misteli, "Der UNCTAD-Moment. Die Entstehung des Nord-Süd-Konflikts und die Politisierung des Schweizer Entwicklungsdiskurses", in *Handlungsfeld Entwicklung. Schweizer Erwartungen und Erfahrungen in der Geschichte der Entwicklungsarbeit*, ed. Sara Elmer, Konrad Kuhn, and Daniel Speich Chassé, Itinera 35 (Basel: Schwabe, 2014), 185–211.
12. Giuliano Garavini, *After Empires. European Integration, Decolonization, and the Challenge from the Global South, 1957–1985* (Oxford: Oxford University Press, 2012), 36–39.
13. My analysis is based on sources from the British National Archives (TNA), the Swiss Federal Archives (CH-BAR), and on documents from the Zurich-based Archives of Contemporary History (Archiv für Zeitgeschichte, AfZ) that hold the records of Swiss UNCTAD delegate Paul R. Jolles. Jolles was a high-ranking civil servant at the Foreign Trade Division of the FDEA. He led that Division from 1966 to 1984, see Marc Perrenoud, "Jolles, Paul R.", *Historisches Lexikon der Schweiz*, http://www.hls-dhs-dss.ch/textes/d/D14856.php [8 July 2015].
14. General Assembly resolution 1785 (XVII) of 8 December 1962, see http://daccess-dds-ny.un.org/doc/RESOLUTION/GEN/NR0/192/93/IMG/NR019293.pdf?OpenElement [13 April 2015].
15. Marc Williams, *Third World Cooperation. The Group of 77 in UNCTAD* (London: Pinter Publishers, 1991), 31–34; Misteli, "Der UNCTAD-Moment", 191–193.
16. Garavini, *After Empires*, 35–36; Mark Mazower, *No Enchanted Palace. The End of Empire and the Ideological Origins of the United Nations* (Princeton: Princeton University Press, 2009), 185–186.

17. AfZ NL Paul R Jolles/284, "UNO-Konferenz für Handel und Entwicklung; Teilnahme der Schweiz", FDEA (H. Schaffner) to the Federal Council, 25 February 1964, 2.
18. Garavini, *After Empires*, 38; for the declarations by the Organisation of African Unity (OAU), the UN-Economic Commission for Asia and the Far East (ECAFE) and the Inter-American Economic and Social Council (IA-ECOSOC) see Karl P. Sauvant, ed., *The Third World without Superpowers. The Collected Documents of the Group of 77* (Dobbs Ferry NY: Oceana, 1981), vol. 1, 5–18.
19. AfZ NL Paul R Jolles/284, "Conférence des Nations Unies sur le commerce et le développement", Note of the 8th meeting by the OECD Trade Committee on 26–27 February 1964, Foreign Trade Division of the FDEA, 9 March 1964, 5.
20. AfZ NL Paul R Jolles/284, "Probleme der Welthandelskonferenz", 10. Wochenbericht der Schweiz. Delegation, 30 May 1964, 2.
21. AfZ NL Paul R Jolles/284, "Conférence des Nations Unies sur le commerce et le développement", Note of the 8th meeting by the OECD Trade Committee on 26–27 February 1964, Foreign Trade Division of the FDEA, 9 March 1964, 5 and 9.
22. TNA T 317/401, "Report on the Principal Conclusions of the D.A.C. Preparatory Working Party on Aid Issues Likely to Arise at the U.N. Conference on Trade and Development", DAC/PWP/23(Final), 24 March 1964; "DAC Working Party on the United Nations Conference on Trade and Development", Note of the 3rd Meeting on 17–18 March 1964, Treasury (T. Fitzgerald), 19 March 1964.
23. TNA T 317/401, "Report on the Principal Conclusions of the D.A.C. Preparatory Working Party on Aid Issues Likely to Arise at the U.N. Conference on Trade and Development", DAC/PWP/23(Final), 24 March 1964, 7.
24. Ibid., 4.
25. AfZ NL Paul R Jolles/284, "Conférence des Nations Unies sur le commerce et le développement", Note of the 8th meeting by the OECD Trade Committee on 26–27 February 1964, Foreign Trade Division of the FDEA, 9 March 1964, 8.
26. Edgar Dosman, *The Life and Times of Raúl Prebisch* (Montreal: McGill-Queen's University Press, 2008).
27. Misteli, "Der UNCTAD-Moment", 187, 193; Raúl Prebisch, *The Economic Development of Latin America and its Principal Problems* (New York: United Nations, 1950).
28. Raúl Prebisch, "Toward a New Trade Policy for Development", in *Proceedings of UNCTAD*, vol. 2 (New York: UN, 1964), 3–66; Garavini, *After Empires*, 39–40; Williams, *Third World Cooperation*, 43–45.

29. AfZ NL Paul R Jolles/287, "Das politische Ergebnis und die institutionellen Empfehlungen der Welthandelskonferenz", Speech held by Paul R. Jolles at a conference of the Steering Committee (Vorort) of the Swiss Trade and Industry Federation on 6th July 1964, 2.
30. TNA T 317/401, "DAC Working Party on the United Nations Conference on Trade and Development. Note of 2nd Meeting on 27–28 February 1964", Treasury (T. Fitzgerald), 6 March 1964, 1.
31. TNA T 317/401, "Report on the Principal Conclusions of the D.A.C. Preparatory Working Party on Aid Issues Likely to Arise at the U.N. Conference on Trade and Development", DAC/PWP/23(Final), 24 March 1964, 8.
32. Schmelzer, "A Club of the Rich to Help the Poor?", 179.
33. CH-BAR E2005A#1978/137#2270*, "Session des DAC vom 9. Juli. Erste Aussprache über die Rückwirkungen der UNCTAD-Konferenz in Genf auf die Tätigkeit des DAC", Swiss Delegation to OECD (R.K. Montandon) to the Foreign Trade Division of the FDEA, 10 July 1964, 1.
34. AfZ NL Paul R Jolles/288, "Conférence des Nations-Unies sur le commerce et le développement", Swiss Ambassador in Washington to the Foreign Trade Division of the FDEA, July 1964, 1.
35. TNA T 317/401, "The Effects of UNCTAD on the Work of the Development Assistance Committee", Treasury, J. Mark to Milner-Barry, 14 July 1964; AfZ Paul R Jolles/284, "Die Arbeiten der Welthandelskonferenz", Note of a meeting held by the 'Ständige Wirtschaftsdelegation' on 10 June 1964, 1.
36. AfZ NL Paul R Jolles/287, "Das politische Ergebnis und die institutionellen Empfehlungen der Welthandelskonferenz", Speech held by Jolles at a conference of the 'Vorort' on 6 July 1964, 10.
37. Schmitt, Matthias, "Der Kampf um die Weltwirtschaft. Nachbemerkungen zur UN-Welthandelskonferenz", Frankfurter Allgemeine Zeitung 157, 10 July 1964, 25.
38. "Statement by H.E. Lij Endalkachew Makonnen (Ethiopia)", in *Proceedings of UNCTAD, Policy Statements*, vol. 2 (New York: UN, 1964), 491–493; "Statement by H.E. Mr. S. Amjad Ali (Pakistan)", in Ibid., 520; "Statement by H.E. Mr. J. G. Kiano (Kenya)", in Ibid., 508.
39. See for instance "Statement by H.E. Mr. Doudou Thiam (Senegal)", in *Proceedings of UNCTAD, Policy Statements*, vol. 2 (New York, 1964), 526–527; "Statement by the H.E. Mr. A. Romeo Horton (Liberia)", in Ibid., 509–512.
40. AfZ NL Paul R Jolles/284, "Erklärung von Herrn Bundesrat Hans Schaffner an der Plenarsitzung vom 11. Juni 1964", Swiss Delegation to the UNCTAD, 1. Schaffner's speech was held in French. The translation in the official UNCTAD proceedings is slightly different but the content

is the same, see "Statement by Mr. Hans Schaffner (Switzerland)", in *Proceedings of UNCTAD, Policy Statements*, vol. 2 (New York: UN, 1964), 529–531.

41. "Statement by the Rt. Hon. Edward Heath (United Kingdom)", in *Proceedings of UNCTAD, Policy Statements*, vol. 2 (New York: UN, 1964), 539.
42. AfZ NL Paul R Jolles/287, "Das politische Ergebnis und die institutionellen Empfehlungen der Welthandelskonferenz", Speech held by Jolles at a conference of the 'Vorort' on 6 July 1964, 3, 10–11.
43. AfZ NL Paul R Jolles/284, "UNO-Konferenz für Handel und Entwicklung", FDEA (H. Schaffner) to the Federal Council, 11 June 1964, 19–20.
44. AfZ NL Paul R Jolles/287, "Bericht über die Welthandelskonferenz der UNO", Appendix of a meeting minute by the Swiss Chamber of Commerce, 3 July 1964, 31.
45. Emotions have been considered an integral part of any form of (international) politics, see for instance Patrick Bormann, Thomas Freiberger, Judith Michel, "Theoretische Überlegungen zum Thema Angst in den Internationalen Beziehungen", in *Angst in den Internationalen Beziehungen*, eds. Patrick Bormann, Thomas Freiberger, Judith Michel (Göttingen: V&R unipress, 2010), 13–43.
46. Vrushali Patil, *Negotiating Decolonization in the United Nations. Politics of Space, Identity, and International Community* (New York, London: Routledge, 2008).
47. Harald Fischer-Tiné and Michael Mann, eds., *Colonialism as Civilizing Mission. Cultural Ideology in British India* (London: Anthem Press, 2004); Boris Barth and Jürgen Osterhammel, eds., *Zivilisierungsmissionen. Imperiale Weltverbesserung seit dem 18. Jahrhundert* (Konstanz: Universitätsverlag Konstanz, 2005).
48. AfZ NL Paul R Jolles/284, "Eindrücke aus der Schlussphase der Welthandelskonferenz", FDEA, 19 June 1964, 1.
49. Ibid.
50. AfZ NL Paul R Jolles/287, "Das politische Ergebnis und die institutionellen Empfehlungen der Welthandelskonferenz", Speech held by Jolles at a conference of the 'Vorort' on 6 July 1964, 11.
51. AfZ NL Paul R Jolles/284, "Eindrücke aus der Schlussphase der Welthandelskonferenz", FDEA, 19 June 1964, 1.
52. Patricia Hongler, "Die OEEC und ihre unsichtbare Kolonialgeschichte. Lektüre der Kakaostudie von 1956", in *Neue Beiträge zur Wirtschaftsgeschichte*, ed. Thomas David, Tobias Straumann, Simon Teuscher, Schweizerisches Jahrbuch für Wirtschafts- und Sozialgeschichte 30 (Zürich: Chronos, 2015), 235–249.

53. Peo Hansen und Stefan Jonsson, *Eurafrica. The Untold History of European Integration and Colonialism* (London, New York: Bloomsbury, 2014).
54. In general, the organization's allegedly "new" focus on development was presented as a way to prevent the former colonies from joining the communist camp, see Schmelzer, "A Club of the Rich to Help the Poor?", 178.
55. See for instance AfZ NL Paul R Jolles/284, "UNO-Konferenz für Handel und Entwicklung; Teilnahme der Schweiz", FDEA (H. Schaffner) to the Federal Council, 25 February 1964, 1.
56. AfZ NL Paul R Jolles/284, "Eindrücke aus der Schlussphase der Welthandelskonferenz", 19 June 1964, FDEA, 3.
57. AfZ NL Paul R Jolles/284, "UNO-Konferenz für Handel und Entwicklung", FDEA (H. Schaffner) to the Federal Council, 11 June 1964, 4.
58. AfZ NL Paul R Jolles/284, "Eindrücke aus der Schlussphase der Welthandelskonferenz", 19 June 1964, FDEA, 4.
59. TNA T 317/401, "Significance of UNCTAD as regards Development Assistance", Telegram from UK Delegation to OECD (R. Hankey) to Foreign Office, 11 July 1964, 2.
60. Ibid. Today LDCs is used as an abbreviation for "Least Developed Countries." However, in this case it probably referred to "Less Developed Countries."
61. Ibid., 3.
62. TNA T 317/401, Telegram from Foreign Office to Washington, 19 August 1964.
63. TNA T 317/401, "Significance of UNCTAD as regards Development Assistance", Telegram from UK Delegation to OECD (R. Hankey) to Foreign Office, 11 July 1964, 3.
64. Ibid., 6. TNA T 317/401, "The Effects of UNCTAD on the Work of the Development Assistance Committee", Treasury, J. Mark to P.S. Milner-Barry, 14 July 1964, 6. See also the chapter by Peter Carroll in this volume.
65. Schmelzer, "A Club of the Rich to Help the Poor?", 186.
66. TNA, Records of the Foreign Office (FO) 371/183476, UE 1064/129, "D.A.C.", Cablegram from the Australian Embassy in Washington (K. Waller) to the Office of the High Commissioner for Australia in London, 18 November 1965.
67. TNA FO 371/183476, UE 1064/129, "D.A.C.", Cablegram from the Australian Embassy in Washington (K. Waller) to the Office of the High Commissioner for Australia in London, 6 November 1965.
68. Ibid.; TNA FO 371/183476, UE 1064/129, "D.A.C.", Telegram from the Australian Embassy in Washington (K. Waller) to the Office of the High Commissioner for Australia in London, 18 November 1965.
69. TNA FO 371/183476, UE 1064/129, "D.A.C.", Cablegram from the Australian Department of External Affairs to the Australian Embassies

in Washington and Paris and to the Australian High Commission in London, 8 October 1965, 2.

70. Ibid.
71. TNA, Records of the Ministry of Overseas Development (OD) 9/148, "Request by the Brazilian Government to be Represented by an Observer at Meetings of the Development Assistance Committee and the Technical Co-operation Committee. Statement by the Secretary-General at the Meeting of Heads of Delegations on Tuesday, 25th January, 1966", CES 66.07, 27 January 1966, 2.
72. Ibid., 2 and 3.
73. Ibid.
74. On the refusal to admit Argentina with an observer status at the DAC see CH-BAR E2005A#1980/82#1264*, t.831 Band II, OECD CES/67.61, "Demande du gouvernement de la République Argentine à participer en tant qu'observateur aux activités du comité d'aide au développement", Note by the secretariat of the OECD Council, 26 October 1967.
75. TNA T 317/380, "The Future of the O.E.C.D.", UK Delegation to OECD (R. Hankey), 28 July 1964.
76. Nancy Leys Stepan, "Race, Gender, Science and Citizenship", in *Cultures of Empire. A Reader. Colonizers in Britain and the Empire in the Nineteenth and Twentieth Centuries*, ed. Catherine Hall (New York: Routledge, 2000), 61–86.
77. Lorraine Daston, "The Naturalized Female Intellect", *Science in Context* 5 (1992): 209–235.
78. Stepan, "Race, Gender, Science and Citizenship", 68.
79. Hongler, "Die OEEC und ihre unsichtbare Kolonialgeschichte", 241–243.
80. For later UNCTAD conferences see the documents in AfZ NL Paul R Jolles, files 302, 305, 306 and 308–311.
81. Enrico Böhm, *Die Sicherheit des Westens. Entstehung und Funktion der G7-Gipfel (1975–1981)* (München: Oldenbourg Verlag, 2014).
82. See for instance Christopher R.W. Dietrich, "Oil Power and Economic Theologies. The United States and the Third World in the Wake of the Energy Crisis", *Diplomatic History Advance Access*, May 13, 2015, 22–24.

PART II

Managing the Economy

From Post-war Reconstruction to Multi-level Neo-corporatism: The OEEC/OECD and Steel During the Cold War

Wolfram Kaiser

Steel was crucial to (Western) European reconstruction after the Second World War. When the Organization for European Economic Co-operation (OEEC) was founded in 1948, it created an Iron and Steel Committee as one of ten so-called "technical committees." Initially it focused heavily on the reallocation of scrap to increase steel output in Western Europe. Its other reconstruction-related activities included statistical work on production, forecasting steel demand and supply, and the discussion of national investment plans to avoid the misallocation of capital and resulting inefficiencies and overproduction crises within the Western world.

The OEEC also undertook much work that was not closely associated with its primary contemporary role as a kind of international think tank for policy analysis and coordination. Thus, the Steel Committee sought to foster technological innovation and research collaboration among member states and their leading steel research institutes in the 1950s. In the early 1960s, the revamped Organization for Economic Cooperation and Development (OECD) began to address environmental concerns,

W. Kaiser (✉)
School of Social, Historical and Literary Studies, University of Portsmouth, Milldam, Burnaby Road, Portsmouth PO1 3AS, UK
e-mail: wolfram.kaiser@port.ac.uk

M. Leimgruber and M. Schmelzer (eds.), *The OECD and the International Political Economy Since 1948*, DOI 10.1007/978-3-319-60243-1_7

when the steel sector came under increasing political pressure in many member states over its major contribution to air pollution in particular. The OECD maintained its separate Steel Committee until 1970 when steel was temporarily integrated into the Industry Committee, only to become reconstituted in 1978—4 years after the start of a severe steel crisis in the Western world.

This chapter traces the OEEC/OECD's activities in steel from its formation to the late 1980s. At around this time, coinciding with the end of the Cold War, the industry's more fundamental restructuring finally set in. It included transnational mergers, most prominently the formation of Arcelor in 2002 (a merger of Spanish, French, and Luxembourgian firms), before its take-over by the Indian company Mittal Steel in 2007 symbolized the by now marginal role of European and North American steel production and companies in a much more global steel industry. Focusing on the OEEC/OECD and steel can tell us much about the transnational governance of the sector itself. This includes the proximity of the member state representatives to the steel industry, its associations and representatives, the strong influence of domestic political pressures on cooperation and negotiation in the Steel Committee, and the relatively high cohesion of the European Communities (EC)—despite severe internal conflicts—which was fostered by the European Commission's role in coordinating the EC member states and their positions in the OECD.

The steel sector also sheds light on the nature of the OEEC/OECD as a whole, however. This concerns two key points in particular. First, the OEEC/OECD was only one among several international organizations created after 1945 which had different competences, resources, and geographical scope. These "horizontal" organizations covering different policy fields and issues as well as existing and newly founded specialized "technical" organizations were—and still are—engaged in intense cooperation and competition.[1] When Belgium, France, Germany, Italy, Luxembourg, and the Netherlands founded the European Coal and Steel Community (ECSC) in 1951–1952, it crowded out the OEEC to some extent, which had no "supranational" competences and only limited financial resources. Moreover, unlike the United Nations Economic Commission for Europe (UNECE) discussed by Daniel Stinsky in this volume, as a "Western" organization it could not engage in cooperation across the Cold War divide. In light of these limitations in its legal competences, financial resources, and spatial scope, the OEEC/OECD had to be especially flexible in the steel sector in carving out a changing role and identity for itself.[2]

Second, the analysis of OEEC/OECD activities in the sector highlights the extent to which the member states and the Steel Committee remained largely oblivious to the neo-liberal turn in economic thinking and policy-making which set in around the mid-1970s. The sector was marked by a tradition of cartelization and associated close industry relations, widespread state ownership, strong trade unionisation, national patterns of neo-corporatist concertation and negotiation, and high political salience. Policy for the steel sector was neither supply- nor demand-driven. Rather, it was primarily geared toward securing social peace in times of economic crisis. In these circumstances the OECD Steel Committee mainly operated a form of multi-level neo-corporatism. It helped to mediate internationally what were domestically charged mercantilist trade conflicts, especially between the EC, the US, other OECD member states and several third countries with a strong interest in steel. Zooming in on particular sectors or policy concerns like steel thus highlights the OECD's internal fragmentation—something that much complicates answering the puzzle posed by Samuel Beroud's chapter in this volume, whether the OECD was a driver or follower of the "neo-liberal" turn at the turn of the 1980s.

After a brief sketch of the OEEC/OECD's changing institutional set-up for the steel sector within the web of cooperating and competing international organizations, this chapter will develop these larger arguments in three sections. The first discusses the Steel Committee's focus on national investment plans, which highlights the political limits of its early reconstruction-related activities. The second focuses on the expansion of the committee's activities into new areas, especially research collaboration and environmental degradation between the early 1950s and the mid-1960s—something that is at least in part explained by the emergence of the ECSC and its own priorities. The third section explores how the Steel Committee dealt with the fallout from the severe steel crisis after it was reconstituted in 1978. At this point, it began to focus entirely on trade and socio-economic aspects of the crisis—its original starting point when it dealt with reconstruction issues in the first few years after 1948. In steel, the EC and its member states continued to dominate the OECD despite the sector's globalization—this to the extent that in steel, the OECD largely shielded the EC's slow, neo-corporatist restructuring from external challenges instead of playing a larger role as "Warden of the West."

Institutionalizing Work on Steel

When the OEEC started its work in 1948, it created the Iron and Steel Committee as one of initially ten "technical committees" alongside, for example, those for coal, oil, electricity, and inland transport.[3] Their terms of reference were defined by the Executive Committee of the Organization. All of the technical committees had a strong focus on reconstruction-related issues. Thus, in the first instance the Steel Committee concentrated on identifying amounts of scrap available in the member states and the Western occupation zones in Germany and its reallocation across borders to facilitate the more rapid growth of steel output and economic recovery more generally.

The committee's remit was soon expanded, however. Thus, in April 1949 the Executive Committee instructed the Steel Committee to estimate future demand and supply of steel and its use by the steel-processing industries (such as car production and machinery) to ascertain whether the foreseen national investments in the steel sector "during the next two or three critical years…seem justified."[4] At this point, national governments and economic ministries were increasingly concerned about an ongoing enquiry by the UNECE which eventually concluded that the Western European market would be saturated by 1950 and that excessive investment into the expansion of steel plants would lead to overproduction and a steel crisis—a false prediction, as it turned out, not least because of the sharp increase in steel demand as a result of the start of the Korean War in June 1950.

The UNECE's work and the resulting Rollman report show how close the links between various international organizations were in the steel industry.[5] Tony Rollman had represented his native country Luxembourg in the negotiations over the creation of the OECD. He then became the first director of the UNECE Steel Division, where he coordinated the report. Then, in 1951–1952, he participated in the negotiations over the creation of the ECSC, only to become the first director of its Steel Division in 1953. Officials like Rollman with a strong steel industry background and close industry ties greatly facilitated the exchange of information and the transfer of ideas among the different international organizations concerned with steel.

The initiative for the expansion of the Steel Committee's remit in April 1949 came from the member state representatives on the Executive Committee. Frequently, however, experts started new initiatives from the bottom up. They came from universities or research institutes and represented the member states especially at working party level. In their established, technocratic, internationalist mode of working, they identified techno-scientific issues for de-politicized forms of cooperation.[6] One of these issues (discussed below) was the possible collaboration among several member states to facilitate the use of tonnage oxygen and lower quality raw materials for pig iron production.[7]

Throughout the 1950s and the first half of the 1960s, steel remained a core industrial sector with excellent political links. In Western Germany, for example, heavy industry, including steel, largely funded the ruling Christian Democratic Union until it transformed itself into a political party with mass membership.[8] Elsewhere, the close ties between industry and politics intensified as a result of the selective state ownership of failed companies or even, in the case of the United Kingdom, the wholesale nationalization of the entire industry in 1967.[9] Despite the continued expansion of steel output in Western Europe until 1974, smaller crises, usually in the form of falling prices, led to intensified industry cooperation (even in the form of an illegal temporary domestic cartel in the ECSC in 1966[10]) and increased state subsidies. Thus, when the Council of the reformed and enlarged OECD decided on its committee structure for the next 5 years in 1965, it extended the life of the Steel Committee without debate. In contrast to several other sectors there was "unanimous recognition by governments that problems in the iron and steel industry were of importance and did affect government policies and interests."[11]

By 1970, however, the OECD was involved in a wholesale overhaul of its activities in an attempt to reposition itself within the web of Western-dominated international organizations. While cultivating its profile as a Western organization with a primary focus on trade liberalization, the OECD, with its "Problems of Modern Society" agenda, was keen to develop new activities in connected policy fields such as the environment.[12] As there seemed to be no imminent threat to the future of the steel industry, the sector became downgraded in the committee structure and integrated into the general Industry Committee.

The Steel Committee was reconstituted at the end of 1978 in response to the severe steel crisis in Western Europe and North America after 1974. The EC, which had competence for steel after the 1967 institutional merger, began to deal collectively with the steel crisis in 1977–1978. The reconstitution of the OECD Steel Committee responded in part to the evident structural crisis, which also affected the US, and in part to actual or potential trade measures by member states, especially the EC, to reduce imports and stabilize the domestic steel industry—measures that ran counter to the OECD's liberalization credo. Since its reconstitution, the Steel Committee has formed part and parcel of the committee structure of the OECD, which has become more global through the accession of countries with sizeable steel production like South Korea and Mexico, for example, which both joined in 1994.

Economic Reconstruction: Debating and Coordinating Investment

When proposing the Marshall Plan, the US administration initially had high hopes that its security umbrella combined with the offer of its counterpart funds would induce Western European integration, ideally in the form of a common market with federalist features following the US model.[13] However, the French government was reluctant to participate in a large internal market with increased competition for its protected industry, and the British government insisted on intergovernmental institutional structures for the OEEC. In fact, in the late 1940s, few Western European countries were willing to contemplate a radical departure loosely based on the US model.[14] Nevertheless, the virulent conflict between the French and British governments over the "German question" led to the creation of the Council of Europe in 1949.[15] From the French perspective, this initially appeared to promise greater political integration and its remit also included cultural cooperation. As a result, the dreams of American policy-makers and European federalists about the OEEC as a springboard for the creation of a United States of Europe faded and the organization became more clearly limited to economic matters.

Despite their disagreements over the long-term objectives of European integration and the scope of liberalization and economic integration, the OEEC governments agreed to discuss national economic policy-making, including investments in the steel sector. In this field, the OEEC in turn profited from the UNECE's political weakness. There, the Soviet Union was technically unable and politically unwilling to share relevant statistical data. The OEEC discussions about investment plans were not merely window-dressing for the US Congress and the Mutual Security Agency to release the counterpart funds. Instead, the member state governments agreed at the most general level that Western Europe needed to overcome its pre-war economic fragmentation and act more cohesively at a time of rising Cold War tensions.

For a short while after 1948 it seemed as if the OEEC could be able to develop transnational coordination of investments into one of their major activities. The discussions in the Steel Committee about national investment plans soon showed, however, that its "piecemeal approach" to discussing national plans did not work. The committee members were able to discuss the "technical merits" of each plan in isolation.[16] But the committee did not review and evaluate the various national plans in conjunction. As a result, the committee members were never able to debate an OEEC-wide reconstruction and investment strategy for the sector based on up-to-date predictions of production and consumption trends.

The Steel Committee's problems were not limited to the uncoordinated submission of national plans and their evaluation. The committee also had no decision-making powers of any kind. The members represented national governments and had clear instructions to defend "their" national plans. As a result, they did not develop a stronger *esprit de corps*, which could have involved give-and-take by all parties and voluntary compliance with informal behavioral norms as in the inter-war steel cartels.[17] These weaknesses became abundantly clear in the case of a Portuguese submission in August 1949. The Salazar regime had scheduled the construction of a new tin plate factory with a planned annual output of 30,000 tons per annum for welded tube production. All committee members argued that these planned investments were premature before the Douro River could be made navigable, and made no economic sense as long as Portugal had to import practically all raw materials.[18] In the debate in July 1950 about a related Portuguese submission, the committee members found that the plan severely underestimated the production capacity of the proposed plant (if run on three shifts) as well as the cost of producing electronically-welded tubes domestically. Only the Austrian member supported the plan because he was without instructions to oppose it. As usual, the Swiss member abstained due to Switzerland's neutrality.[19]

The Steel Committee critically examined not just the plans of OEEC peripherals like Portugal, but also those of industrialized Western European countries like the Netherlands. The Dutch government wanted to extend the Koninklijke Nederlandse Hoogovens blast furnaces and steel works at IJmuiden. It aimed to increase steel output from 340,000 to 570,000 tons annually through building a slabbing mill, a semi-continuous hot strip mill, and a cold rolling mill to make cold rolled sheets and tin plate. The Dutch member claimed that population growth and the need to increase domestic production and curtail imports to improve the balance of payments situation justified the plan, which had moreover already been scaled down somewhat in response to criticism from abroad. Rejecting the Dutch proposal, he argued, would equate to "discrimination."[20] The British representative argued, however, that in view of the emerging customs union among the three countries, Dutch steel production should be treated in conjunction with that of Luxembourg and Belgium. From this perspective, the Benelux countries together had "rather more" than their "full share…of the total increase in flat product output" when compared to pre-war Western Europe. Agreeing with this point, the Danish and Norwegian members regretted that "it had not been possible to co-ordinate the different projects thoroughly as there had been no opportunity to consider them all at the same time."[21]

Even the most critical discussion of an investment plan had no impact on the decision-making by national governments. Thus, based on the Austrian and Swiss positions, the Portuguese government interpreted the damning criticism of its plans on technical and economic grounds as sufficient international support. In fact, as the Steel Committee concluded in October 1949, the member states treated the submission of a national investment plan as "a formality after the country concerned had made a firm decision to go forward with it." For the committee to work more effectively, it would have been essential, the report argued, to discuss plans at an early drafting stage when they could be adjusted before national governments and parliaments took decisions on them.[22]

Despite the Steel Committee's critical self-evaluation of the futility of its efforts measured in terms of their negligible impact on national policy-making, it took the Executive Committee until 1952 to decide that the Steel Committee's reports should be submitted automatically to the member state and the US Mutual Security Agency when they concerned projects to be co-funded with dollar aid.[23] But this decision, which could have allowed the US agency to withdraw its support and induce national governments to reconsider their plans, came far too late at the end of the 4 years of Marshall Plan aid to have any effect.

Thus, the OEEC quickly reached an impasse with its attempts to foster the coordination of economic policy-making on steel. The member states were determined to prioritize their own national objectives for domestic reconstruction. In many countries, investments in domestic steel production in effect constituted large-scale public works programs with social policy objectives of creating jobs, reducing unemployment, and increasing income and consumption levels—aims that easily outweighed technocratic concerns about the modernization of the entire Western European steel industry and achieving a more rational transnational division of labor. In this sense, the discussions about national investments in the steel industry confirm the prevalent view about the OEEC's domination in its early years by intergovernmental bargaining of interests.[24] In steel, at least, these interests mostly resulted from neo-corporatist domestic policy-making with close concertation among state institutions, the industry, and trade unions.

Policy Diversification: Fostering Research and Environmental Protection

When the ECSC started its work in 1953, moreover, the High Authority under the leadership of Jean Monnet made it crystal-clear in its relations with the OEEC Secretariat that it would take exclusive control of those policy issues for which it had treaty competence.[25] They included, among others, the creation of a customs union among the six founding member states, mergers and acquisitions, state aid, and health and safety in the workplace at steel factories. While the OEEC facilitated the representation (alongside the member states) of the High Authority on its Economic Committee and the Coal and Steel Committees to speak for the newly formed community, the High Authority in turn effectively refused to involve the OEEC Secretariat in its own work in Luxembourg.[26] The OEEC now had to face competition from a new, institutionally-hybrid organization with "supranational" competences and resources of its own. These resources the ECSC could invest to turn Luxembourg, the seat of the High Authority, into a policy-making center not just for the governments of France, Germany, Italy, and the Benelux countries, but also for their steel companies and trade unions which gained formal representation on the ECSC's Consultative Committee. In fact, steel industries from Belgium, France, Germany, and Luxembourg had formed the core of all European and international cartels since the first rails cartel formed in 1884. In 1953, they instantly created an export cartel, which provoked strong conflict with OEEC steel-importing countries like Denmark.[27] Thus, the creation of the ECSC made it even more necessary for the OEEC to diversify its activities and carve out a space for itself in the steel sector after the end of Marshall Plan aid. Two excellent examples of this diversification are research collaboration during the 1950s and work on environmental pollution caused by steel plants in the early 1960s.

Within the OEEC, the British government first suggested a system for disseminating scientific and technical information among the member states, which became operational in 1950. But cooperation should not be limited to information sharing. "The scientific approach," the British government argued, "need not be restricted too narrowly to its application to the immediate physical problems of production." In times of "strictly limited" national resources, "collaboration in the generation and application of new industrial knowledge and 'know-how'" could prove beneficial to all OEEC member states.[28] Following this British initiative, the Council convened Working Party Number 3 on Matters of Co-operation in Scientific and Technical Information. Its terms of reference stipulated that "a very free hand was to be left to the Working Party in the choice of its programme and in the proposals which it might wish to formulate as to its own future within the framework of the Organization."[29] Only 1 year after its creation, in October 1950, the members of Working Party Number 3 proposed in an intermediate report to the Council that their institutional status be upgraded to that of a full OEEC committee. In response the Council created the permanent Committee for Scientific and Technical Matters.[30]

This committee cooperated closely with the existing technical committees, including the Steel Committee, in developing new ideas for research collaboration, bringing together experts in a variety of sub-groups that focused on specific options for such collaboration. One of these groups was the Co-operative Research and Development Group Number 3. It looked into possibilities for collaborative research on the use of tonnage oxygen, or oxygen-enriched air with an oxygen content ranging between 40 and 95% compared to 99.5% in pure oxygen, in the chemical and metallurgical industries. Permitting the use of low-grade fuels and ores in pig iron production substantially lowered the unit costs of such tonnage oxygen, promising efficiency gains for the steel industry.[31]

At their session in April 1950, the tonnage oxygen experts identified the production of pig iron in low-shaft blast furnaces as "a subject particularly well suited for co-operative treatment on an international basis, as it is of wide interest, but difficult and extremely costly."[32] The following month, the tonnage oxygen experts created a new, more specialized panel on low-shaft blast furnaces, held three meetings, and visited existing plants in several member states. By July 1950, the experts were able to confirm that oxygen-fed low-shaft blast furnaces offered "interesting possibilities…for using low grade coal and ores." After all, several continental, Western European, steel-producing countries faced similar problems of energy use and low quality raw materials.[33]

In October 1950, Working Party Number 3 recommended the construction of one low-shaft blast furnace at Ougrée-Marihaye in Belgium and a second at Oberhausen in Germany.[34] Their primary objective would be "perfecting the use of oxygen" in pig iron production "from low-grade or powder ores and ores with high sulphur content, using small brittle coke, coal in the natural state or lignite." Resulting process innovations would make up for the inferiority of the continental European iron ore and brown coal, reduce the need for imports, and make European production more competitive. At this stage, alongside all six ECSC founding member states, Austria, and Greece still expressed an interest in participating in the planned collaboration. Eventually, on 14 February 1951, the Working Party Number 3 submitted a draft agreement to the Council.[35]

Finally, on 2 April 1951, only 1 year after the first session of Working Party Number 3, the OEEC Council took the formal decision to recommend "a programme of research and of trials in the production of pig iron in low-shaft blast furnaces, with the help of appropriate financial, technical and administrative assistance from interested Member countries." The agreement set out the OEEC panel's collaborative research objectives and defined its institutional structure, including qualified majority voting.[36] But although the AIRBO research collaboration had its origins in the OEEC committee structure, it transformed into an ECSC project after it began in 1953. In contrast to the OEEC, the High Authority was not just empowered to promote technical and economic research collaboration, but could also contribute to its cost from the ECSC budget. In the end, the High Authority and later the European Commission were able to claim the continental European AIRBO collaboration for themselves as "one of the most outstanding examples of European collaboration in research."[37] As a result, while the OEEC continued to facilitate research collaboration among its member states during the 1950s, it omitted coal and steel from its agenda in view of the ECSC's strong political and financial pull.

Environmental matters, in contrast, were not on the ECSC's or the EC's list of competences. In fact, the EC became a latecomer to this policy field in the 1970s.[38] Whether in Liège in Belgium or the Ruhr Area in Germany, the inhabitants of urban agglomerations with a high concentration of steel production were well aware of its contribution to air pollution. In one of the first reports by an international organization on air and water pollution initiated by its Chemical Products Committee in 1953, the European Productivity Agency, which operated in the remit of the OEEC, still focused heavily on the chemical industry.[39] Set up to facilitate technology transfer from the US to Western Europe, and to increase productivity levels in the European economy, the European Productivity Agency's two missions in Europe and to North America as well as the subsequent report were dominated by scientists and practitioners from the chemical industry, but they incorporated visits to steel plants.

In a report exclusively devoted to the iron and steel industry and published in 1963, the OECD for the first time analyzed the industry's particular role. It was clearly a "source of pollution" especially due to "the large tonnages and the nature of the raw materials that it uses."[40] The report discussed, in this sequence, the types of pollutants, measurements of pollution, gas cleaning equipment, and types of chimneys, culminating in some general conclusions. It resolved that the industry's emission of particulate matter, or visible dust, "has mainly a nuisance value." The emission of gases concerned, in particular, carbon monoxide, sulphur dioxide, and sulphureted hydrogen. Sulphur dioxide transformed into sulphuric acid mist, or what later became known as acid rain, "as a result of phenomena not yet fully understood," as the report admitted reflecting the state of the art of scientific knowledge at the time.[41] The as yet unknown carcinogenic effects of *fine* particulate matter were not even on the committee's radar at this stage.

Without focusing on the steel sector, another OECD report published in 1964 discussed for the first time methods of measuring air pollution.[42] Compiled for the OECD's Committee for Scientific Research by a Working Party of the Sub-Committee for Co-operative Research set up in January 1957, the report listed and discussed scientific methods for measuring the emission from industrial plants especially of smoke, sulphur dioxide, sulphur trioxide, and hydrocarbons. This report highlighted the persisting scientific and statistical difficulties in measuring different types of air pollution, which complicated attempts to define more precisely the particular role of industries like steel and to develop targeted national, let alone international, strategies for reducing air pollution.

Why then did the OECD member states, the Secretariat, and their scientific and technological experts take up environmental concerns in the early 1960s? The nature of air pollution was obviously transnational. In addition, the OECD could steal a march on the UNECE, which started its work on environmental matters in the mid-1960s, and the EC. Ultimately, however, two other factors help account for the OECD's diversification into environmental matters. To begin with, pollution gained political salience in Northern European and American member states. Alongside chemical plants, steel mills became sites of popular protest against pollution, which in turn induced national legislation to combat it. In an early striking example, the "Great Smog" in London in December 1952 led to 4000 premature deaths and the 1956 British Clean Air Act.[43] In this changing political climate, the steel industry feared the imposition of high additional capital costs for measures to reduce pollution. National ministries and steel companies and their associations saw their OECD cooperation as a suitable strategy to defend the interests of the industry and plead for exemptions.

Thus, the 1963 OECD report claimed that the steel industry had "already spent large sums of money on plant that is very costly to install and operate." If rules became "more exacting," then "the industry's efforts will add to the cost of iron and steel." Moreover, the report argued that any future regulation should not be "inspired by purely abstract concepts based on data that must often be very imprecise" and that it should allow for flexibility, taking into account "local geography and topography, and climate and weather." It should "make allowance for specific cases" and not "apply everywhere and to all emissions irrespective of their nature, type of discharge and their magnitude." Governments should consider the costs involved in possible legislation and support the steel industry financially to combat pollution.[44]

As a second factor accounting for the OECD's activism, the experts in the various technical committees, including the Steel Committee, were keen to use the Organization as a platform to collect and disseminate information about techno-scientific solutions to environmental problems. Knowledge about process technologies had traditionally circulated freely among steel companies. In contrast, pollution control required far more natural science expertise. In the 1960s, such expertise was scarce and not well developed or integrated with the traditional technology- and business-dominated expert culture in the steel sector.

Crucially, the Steel Committee never engaged in serious debate about environmental *policy*. The OECD reports did not seek to identify what later became known as best practice and benchmarking or to recommend legally binding international commitments. The main reason for this lack of environmental *policy* activism is the dominant influence of the steel industry—private and state-owned—on the work of the Steel Committee via government and ministry officials close to the industry. The OECD's work on environmental pollution in the steel sector in the 1960s therefore remained a far cry from the much more ambitious environmental agendas of international organization in the early 1970s. [45]

Crisis Management: Mediating Trade Conflicts

In late 1978, the reconstitution of the Steel Committee reflected a return to the OECD's post-war preoccupations. It turned out that despite its policy expansion to address new challenges in the late 1960s and early 1970s, the Organization continued to stick to its post-war growth paradigm for this sector, as for others.[46] The shift back to a narrower focus in its activities was also in line with the Organization's broader transformation into an international think tank for policy-making which increasingly focused on economic and financial implications. Only now, the Steel Committee had to deal with the fallout from the continuing crisis in the Western steel industry that had started in 1974. It was in this year that steel production in Western Europe fell for the first time. The low industrial growth rates after the 1973 oil crisis reduced demand. Some steel-consuming industries like shipbuilding began to move to Asia in particular, where steel demand and production grew rapidly during industrialization. In addition, steel was increasingly replaced by aluminium and plastics, for example in the production of cars. Instead of another short cyclical crisis initially anticipated by steel producers, governments, and international organizations including the OECD, the sector entered a prolonged structural crisis in the Western world, which lasted well into the 1990s.[47]

As a result, the new committee's remit was clearly delineated to focus exclusively on issues of trade in steel, domestic socio-economic adaptation, and subsidies.[48] At the Council meeting on 6 November 1978, Egon Emmel, the German Permanent Representative to the OECD, stated on behalf of the EC member states that the Steel Committee's reconstitution was "due to exceptional circumstances prevailing in the steel sector." The committee would submit an annual report that illustrated what the member states initially conceived as its "temporary character." Reflecting the strong German preference for reducing state subsidies in other EC countries and accelerating the industry's transformation, Emmel insisted that the OECD's "commitment to expand free world trade and to maintain the free and unimpeded exchange of goods" should not be impaired. As Aldolphe De Baerdemaeker added for the European Commission, "individual measures were not capable of solving the problem on a world scale." Discussions within the OECD could "help to develop a common approach in the search for solutions acceptable to all."[49]

The Steel Committee's Work Programme for 1979 then stipulated that the sector's problems were of a structural nature and "likely to persist for some time." Clearly, the "restructuring and modernization of the industry" posed a long-term challenge.[50] In fact, it quickly became obvious that the crisis would continue and with it the OECD's Steel Committee. At its first meeting on 19 January 1979, Emile van Lennep, the OECD Secretary-General from 1969 to 1984, outlined the sector's problems such as stagnating demand, rising energy prices, the substitution of steel with alternative products, resulting overproduction in Western countries, and sharply rising unemployment following plant closures. The danger was, van Lennep emphasized, that each member state would try to "simply transfer the burden of inevitable adjustments to other countries." Governments, he predicted, would be "under pressure from business and labour to take defensive measures" which in the long run was bad for the global economy.[51]

Anticipating a protracted crisis, the Steel Committee's Work Programme prioritized studying trade flows, supply and demand, specialised steel sub-sectors, and questions of the adaptation of production structures and the retraining of labor. The committee's purely economic focus was also reflected in the set-up of its Secretariat, which was staffed by the OECD. Alongside a Deputy Secretary-General as well as economic and legal advisors, it comprised only officials from the Directorate for Science, Technology, and Industry. Moreover, the Steel Committee consulted regularly with the Business and Industry Advisory Committee (BIAC) and the Trade Union Advisory Committee (TUAC)—both independent organizations of business and labor with a privileged advisory status in the OECD since 1962. Both employers and trade unions were understandably preoccupied with the survival of companies and the retention of jobs in the industry.

The OECD's steel deliberations replicated the tripartite neo-corporatist forms of policy and decision-making for the sector which prevailed at the member state level in different forms, with close consultation among ministries, the (partly state-owned) industry and trade unions.[52] Until the privatization of British Steel in 1988 marked the beginning of more drastic policy measures for the steel sector in Western Europe,[53] this tripartite neo-corporatism was geared toward a slow and heavily managed economic restructuring and minimizing its immediate economic, social, and political impact in times of low growth, rising deficits, and growing unemployment across the Global North.

This neo-corporatism was especially pronounced in the case of the EC and its member states. The EC strongly influenced the Steel Committee's work after 1979. In 1973, it had enlarged to include the United Kingdom as a major steel producer, in addition to Denmark and Ireland as new members. Drawing for the first time on the European Commission's strong formal powers in coal and steel policy, the new Belgian Commissioner for Industry, Etienne Davignon, worked toward a community response to the crisis. From mid-1977 onward, the Commission, in close cooperation with Eurofer, the organization of European steel producers, implemented a policy of mandatory minimum prices, generalized guide prices, and controls on investments. When the market situation deteriorated once more in 1980, the system collapsed. It was replaced with more drastic measures from the second Davignon Plan. This plan included mandatory production quotas for four categories of steel. Even the government in Bonn eventually agreed to this drastic intervention in the market, when German private companies also began to make growing losses. In return, it got the Commission to begin tackling the politically sensitive issue of state aid for steel companies, which it did from 1981 onward.[54]

The EC's "rationalization cartel"[55] was fraught with domestic and international problems. It led to sharp conflicts in Europe after 1980 between the state-owned companies and those in private ownership that received no or limited state aid during the crisis. It also included the threat of anti-dumping measures against third countries to reduce steel imports into the EC, and the negotiation of only apparently voluntary export restraint agreements with countries ranging from Sweden and Austria in Europe to Eastern European countries and Japan and South Korea—agreements that did reduce EC steel imports and mitigated the crisis somewhat. To avoid a direct political clash in the General Agreement on Tariffs and Trade, the EC sought to upload discussion about its highly interventionist and controversial steel policy and the wider crisis into the OECD as a forum for debating policy.[56] Here, the EC's position was especially strong. Alongside the member states, the European Commission represented the EC as a whole ever since it had acquired the status of a "full participant" in the OECD reform of 1961–1962.

Thus, throughout the late 1970s and early 1980s in particular, the European Commission and the EC governments used the multilateral Steel Committee to justify their policies on steel.[57] At the same time, they were able to keep the negotiations about limiting imports into the EC at the bilateral level. Japan, which had joined the OECD in 1964, also preferred the bilateral negotiations. With its similarly close government-industry relations and its comprehensive export subsidy regime, it was not keen to push for liberalization in the steel sector. At the same time, other non-Western steel-producing countries were not (yet) in the OECD. Due to the increasing globalization of the steel sector, the OECD unusually co-opted representatives from four non-OECD countries onto the Steel Committee after 1978, namely Brazil, India, Mexico, and South Korea. This measure was geared toward defusing political tensions over the trade implications of the EC's slow restructuring and continued state subsidies.

The Steel Committee, originally conceived as a temporary measure to create a non-confrontational forum for discussing steel policy issues, continued its work as the Western steel crisis lasted into the 1990s. The sector's accelerating globalization, with Asian crude steel output eventually outpacing the now nearly continent-wide European Union's by roughly eight to one in 2015, guaranteed that the Steel Committee became permanently established in the committee structure of the globalized OECD.[58] At the same time, China as the world's largest steel producer by far, is not a member state, which limits the OECD's scope as a truly global forum for discussing steel issues.

Conclusion

Unlike the ECSC and the EC in the case of the six "core Europe" founding member states and the present-day EU, the OECD had limited direct impact on steel policy or the steel industry in the Western world during the Cold War. It certainly had tangible influence in different ways, but such influence is difficult to measure without tracing it in microscopic empirical studies. Thus, the Steel Committee's collective work to identify and reallocate scrap during 1948–1949 probably helped to increase steel output in Western Europe, accelerating economic reconstruction somewhat. The OECD's attempt to foster research collaboration on steel-related issues in the early 1950s at least led to the major AIRBO project, which was taken over by the ECSC after 1953, however. The Organization's early work on air and water pollution by the steel industry (and other sectors) in the early 1960s may have facilitated the formation of international scientific networks on the intersection between technology and natural sciences. At the same time, it could also have accelerated the formation of transnational industry networks beyond the EC which pleaded for treatment of the energy and capital intensive industry as a special case to be exempted from prospective anti-pollution measures. After 1978, moreover, the reconstituted Steel Committee created a forum for the debate about protectionist measures, their moderation, and eventual reduction—discussions that also involved several non-OECD states and perhaps reinforced the growing perception in the Western world that the steel sector could not forever be exempted from globalization pressures and the new policy agenda of privatization and liberalization as a response to them.

In these and other activities in the steel sector, the OEEC/OECD cooperated and competed with other international organizations. Thus, the OEEC only took over the issue of scrap allocation from the UNECE, which had already started this work, when the Soviet Union refused to share information on scrap available in its eastern German occupation zone.[59] More importantly, from 1953 onward, the OECD had to compete with "core Europe" organizations, beginning with the ECSC, which had strong competences for coal and steel. The ECSC formation reinforced the prevailing continental Western European patterns of cooperation at the company and political levels. Thus, companies from France, Germany, Belgium, and Luxembourg had already founded and dominated the inter-war European and International Steel Cartels and specialized cartel organizations in the sector. Moreover, the High Authority immediately sought to monopolize work for which the ECSC had competences, trying to withdraw such issues from the scope of other international organizations and downgrading them to forums for pure exchange of information between the "supranational" ECSC and its member states, and other member states.

Thus, the emergence of the ECSC as a major player in coal and steel policy helps to explain why the OEEC/OECD temporarily diversified its activities into fields like air pollution, for example, which it did very flexibly. When the Steel Committee was reconstituted in 1978, however, it largely turned precisely into a platform for information exchange and negotiation between the EC and its member states and other OECD and non-OECD states. The OECD now became a forum for policy debate about trade and socio-economic issues in the steel sector, as in other policy fields—a trend that was strongly reinforced when the World Trade Organization was created in 1994 with its own court to decide trade disputes—something that the Steel Committee still dealt with informally for the steel sector during its severe structural crisis in the 1980s.

The case of steel not only sheds light on the OEEC/OECD's cooperation and competition with other international organizations; it also highlights its internal fragmentation and the limits of generalizations about its nature, role, and activities. For a very long time steel had been characterized by limited transnational integration of companies and markets combined with dense European and to some extent, North Atlantic networks and cartel-based cooperation. The policy-making structures in the steel sector were highly neo-corporatist, and they remained so during the 1980s, despite different patterns and interests among countries with nationalized, partly nationalized, and predominantly private companies. The European Commission began to work toward a more European approach to addressing the structural crisis in the steel sector from 1977–1978 onward. In view of the fact that other OECD member states, including the US and Japan in particular, had their own support structures for the steel sector, the Steel Committee never developed into a hot-bed of neo-liberalism, even during the 1980s when the OECD as a whole began acquiring such an identity.[60] Instead, it remained a Western forum for mediating multi-level neo-corporatism for a long time.

Notes

1. See Wolfram Kaiser and Kiran Klaus Patel, "Multiple Connections in European Cooperation: International Organizations, Policy Ideas, Practices and Transfers 1967–1992," *European History Review* 24/3 (2017), 337–357.
2. On institutional adaptation see also Peter Carroll and Aynsley Kellow, *The OECD. A Study in Organisational Adaptation* (Cheltenham: Edward Elgar, 2011).
3. OECD Historical Archives, Paris (hereafter OECD-HA), C (48) 14, Decision of the Council relating to the Constitution of Technical Committees, 11 May 1948.
4. OECD-HA, CE/M (49) 16 (Final), Decision of the Executive Committee concerning Directives to the Iron and Steel Committee, 21 April 1949.
5. UNECE, *European Steel Trends in the Setting of World Markets* (Geneva: UNECE, 1949).
6. On technocratic internationalism and its influence on European integration since the mid-nineteenth century see Wolfram Kaiser and Johan Schot, *Writing the Rules for Europe. Experts, Cartels, and International Organisations* (Basingstoke: Palgrave Macmillan, 2014).
7. OECD-HA, C/WP3 (50) 38, Working Party No. 3 of the Council on Co-operation in Matters of Scientific and Technical Information, Report to the Council, 6 October 1950.
8. Frank Bösch, *Die Adenauer-CDU. Gründung, Aufstieg und Krise einer Erfolgspartei 1945–1969* (Stuttgart: DVA, 2001).
9. Heidrun Abromeit, *An Industry between the State and the Private Sector* (Oxford: Berg, 1986).
10. Charles Barthel, "The 1966 European Steel Cartel and the Collapse of the ECSC High Authority," in *Alan S. Milward and a Century of European Change*, ed. Fernando Guirao, Frances M.B. Lynch and Sigfrido M. Ramírez Pérez (Abingdon: Routledge, 2012), 333–350, here 350.
11. OECD-HA, IS/M (65) 2, 1st Session of the Special Committee for Iron and Steel, 28–30 September 1965, 25 November 1965.
12. Matthias Schmelzer, "The Crisis before the Crisis: The 'Problems of Modern Society' and the OECD, 1968–1974," *European Review of History* 19/6 (2012), 999–1,020. On the environment, see also the chapter by Iris Borowy in this volume.
13. Michael J. Hogan, *The Marshall Plan: America, Britain, and the Reconstruction of Western Europe, 1947–1952* (Cambridge: Cambridge University Press, 1987).

14. Alan S. Milward, *The Reconstruction of Western Europe 1945–1951* (London: Routledge 1984).
15. William I. Hitchcock, *France Restored: Cold War Diplomacy and the Quest for Leadership in Europe, 1944–1954* (Chapel Hill, NC: University of North Carolina Press, 1998); Frances Lynch, *A History of the French Economy: From Vichy to Rome* (London: Routledge, 1997).
16. OECD-HA, IS (49) 21, Iron and Steel Committee, Some Reflections by the Steel Committee on Co-ordination of Investment in the Steel Industry, Report to the Executive Committee and the Council, 7 October 1949.
17. On transnational cooperation in the steel sector in inter-war Europe see Kaiser and Schot, *Writing the Rules for Europe*, Chap. 6.
18. OECD-HA, IS/M (49) 6, Iron and Steel Committee, Minutes of the 55th to the 60th meetings, held at the Château de la Muette on 1–4 August 1949.
19. OECD-HA, IS (50) 8, Iron and Steel Committee, Portuguese Project for the Installation of a Plant for the Production of Electronically Welded Steel Tubing, Memorandum drawn up by the Secretariat on the instructions of the committee, 10 August 1950.
20. OECD-HA, CE (49) 129, Executive Committee, Report by the Iron and Steel Committee on Projects submitted by Belgium, Luxembourg, the Netherlands and Austria for the 1949–1950 Programme. See also OECD-HA, IS/M (49), 6.
21. OECD-HA, CE (49) 129, Executive Committee, Report by the Iron and Steel Committee on Projects submitted by Belgium, Luxembourg, the Netherlands and Austria for the 1949–1950 Programme.
22. OECD-HA, IS (49) 21, Iron and Steel Committee, Some Reflections by the Steel Committee on Co-ordination of Investment in the Steel Industry, Report to the Executive Committee and the Council, 7 October 1949.
23. OECD-HA, CE/M (52) 27 (Final), OEEC Decisions, Resolution of the Executive Committee concerning the Procedure for Investigating Investment Projects in the Iron and Steel Industry, 28 October 1952, 142.
24. See, for example, Richard T. Griffiths (ed.), *Explorations in OEEC History* (Paris: OECD, 1997).
25. On the relationship between the ECSC High Authority and the OEEC see Johnny Laursen, "Integration at cross-currents. The OEEC and the European Coal and Steel Community, 1952–1956," in *Explorations*, ed. Griffiths, 149–158.

26. Historical Archives of the European Union (Florence), CEAB 2/1234, Note pour MM. les membres du Groupe de Travail des Relations Extérieures, 11 January 1956.
27. See Charles Barthel, "De l'Entente belgo-luxembourgeoise à la Convention de Bruxelles," in *L'Europe du patronat. De la guerre froide aux années soixante,* ed. Michel Dumoulin, René Girault, and Gilbert Trausch (Berne: Peter Lang, 1993), 29–62.
28. OECD-HA, CE (49) 84, United Kingdom Memorandum, 28 April 1949.
29. OECD-HA, C (49) 63 (Final).
30. OECD-HA, C/WP3 (50) 38, Working Party No. 3 of the Council on Co-operation in Matters of Scientific and Technical Information, Report to the Council, 6 October 1950.
31. OECD-HA, C/WP3 (51) 6, Note by the Secretariat, 31 January 1951.
32. OECD-HA, C/WP3/CR3 (50) 2, Working Party No. 3 of the Council on Co-operation in Matters of Scientific and Technical Information, Co-operative Research Group No. 3 (Tonnage Oxygen), Minutes of the 1st Session held in the Château de la Muette, 12–13 April 1950.
33. OECD-HA, C/WP3/CR3 (50) 11, Working Party No. 3 of the Council on Co-operation in Matters of Scientific and Technical Information, Group No. 3: Co-operation in Research and Technical Development (Tonnage Oxygen), Minutes of the 2nd session held on 24th and 25th July 1950, at Château de la Muette, 30 December 1950.
34. Ibid.
35. OECD-HA, C/WP3 (51) 6, Note by the Secretariat, 31 January 1951.
36. OECD-HA, C/M (51) 11 (Final), Recommendation of the Council concerning Research on Pig Iron Production in Low-Shaft Blast Furnaces, 2 April, 1951.
37. European Commission, *Steel Research: From the ECSC to the Future* (Brussels: European Commission, no date). See also Pieter Zegers, "Steel Research—Achievements under the ECSC and Future Perspectives," in: *Iron and Steel—Today, Yesterday, and Tomorrow*, vol. 3, ed. Bertil Berg (Stockholm: Jernkontoret, 1997), 145–161.
38. Jan-Henrik Meyer, "Making the Polluter Pay: How the European Communities Established Environmental Protection," in: *International Organisations and Environmental Protection. Conservation and Globalization in the Twentieth Century*, ed. Wolfram Kaiser and Jan-Henrik Meyer (New York: Berghahn, 2017), 182–210.
39. OEEC, *European Productivity Agency, Air and Water Pollution. The Position in Europe and in the United States* (Paris: OEEC, 1957).
40. OECD, *Air Pollution in the Iron and Steel Industry* (Paris: OECD, 1963), 7.
41. Ibid., 49.

42. OECD, *Methods of Measuring Air Pollution, Report of the Working Party on Methods of Measuring Air Pollution and Survey Techniques* (Paris: OECD, 1964).
43. See also in long-term perspective Peter Thorsheim, *Inventing Pollution. Coal, Smoke and Culture in Britain since 1800* (Athens/Ohio: Ohio University Press, 2006).
44. OECD, *Air Pollution*, 91.
45. See also Wolfram Kaiser, "Sometimes it's the Economy, Stupid! International Organizations, Steel and the Environment," in *International Organizations*, ed. Kaiser and Meyer, 153–181. See also the chapter by Iris Borowy in this volume.
46. See in greater detail Matthias Schmelzer, *The Hegemony of Growth. The OECD and the Making of the Economic Growth Paradigm* (Cambridge: Cambridge University Press, 2016); idem., "The growth paradigm: History, hegemony, and the contested making of economic growthmanship," *Ecological Economics* 118 (2015), 262–271.
47. See William Scheuerman, *The Steel Crisis: The Economics and Politics of a Declining Industry* (New York: Praeger, 1986); Yves Mény and Vincent Wright (eds.), *The Politics of Steel: Western Europe and the Steel Industry in the Crisis Years (1974–1984)* (Berlin—New York: Walter de Gruyter, 1987); John P. Hoerr, *And the Wolf Finally Came: The Decline of the American Steel Industry* (Pittsburgh, PA: University of Pittsburgh Press, 1988).
48. OECD-HA, SC (79) 3 (1st Revision), Steel Committee, 14 February 1979.
49. OECD-HA, C/M (78) 19 (Prov.), Paris, 6 November 1978.
50. OECD-HA, SC (78) 1, 24 November 1978.
51. OECD-HA, SC/M (79) 1, Annex 1, Opening Statement by the Secretary General, 19 January 1979.
52. See Yves Mény and Vincent Wright, "State and Steel in Western Europe," in *The Politics of Steel*, ed. Mény and Wright, 1–110.
53. On British Steel in this period, see Heidrun Abromeit, *An Industry between the State and the Private Sector* (Oxford: Berg, 1986).
54. For the EC's steel policy after 1974, see Lukas Tsoukalis and Robert Strauss, "Community Policies on Steel 1974–1982," in: *The Politics of Steel*, ed. Mény and Wright, 186–221; Leboutte, *Histoire économique et sociale de la construction européenne* (Brussels: P.I.E.—Peter Lang, 2008), 477–506.
55. Tsoukalis and Strauss, *Community Policies*, 219.
56. See also OECD-HA, SC/M (79) 2, Annex 1, Statement by Mr. A.W. Wolff on taking the Chair of the Steel Committee, 30 January 1979.

57. See for example OECD-HA, SC/M (81) 2, Steel Committee, Summary Record of the Eleventh Meeting on 14 May 1981.
58. On the globalization of the steel industry, see also Anthony P. D'Costa, *The Global Restructuring of the Steel Industry. Innovations, Institutions, and Industrial Change* (London: Routledge, 1999).
59. See David Wightman, *Economic Co-operation in Europe: A Study of the United Nations Economic Commission for Europe* (London: Stevens & Sons, 1956), 94.
60. On this change in the OECD's identity see also Richard Woodward, *The Organisation for Economic Cooperation and Development* (Abingdon: Routledge, 2009).

A Crisis Manager for the International Monetary and Financial System? The Rise and Fall of the OECD Working Party 3, 1961–1980

Kazuhiko Yago

Throughout postwar history, economic policy makers, economic experts, and international officials were involved in bilateral and multilateral negotiations over the architecture, stability, and reform of the international monetary and financial system, which took place within and were shaped by various forums and institutions. Key among these were not only the Bretton Woods institutions, namely the International Monetary Fund (IMF) and the International Bank for Reconstruction and Development (IBRD, the World Bank), but a host of other less well-known and largely overlapping institutions and informal fora. The Bank for International Settlements (BIS), already set up in 1930, quickly intervened in the banking circle in order to promote the postwar financial system and to maintain its status as an independent institution.[1] The European Payments Union (EPU), founded in 1950 in the framework

K. Yago (✉)
Waseda University, 1-6-1, Nishi-Waseda, Shinjuku-ku,
Tokyo 169-8050, Japan
e-mail: yago@waseda.jp

M. Leimgruber and M. Schmelzer (eds.), *The OECD and the International Political Economy Since 1948*, DOI 10.1007/978-3-319-60243-1_8

of the OEEC, also began to play an important role in the intra-European multilateral exchange arrangement, which differed from the initial Bretton Woods System.[2] The Group of Ten (G10), founded in 1961 as an informal forum of financial agents and central banks of industrialized countries, also served as a platform to discuss an alternative international monetary system to cope with the sterling crisis and then later the dollar crisis.[3] And the IMF's Committee of Twenty (C20), whose membership only partially overlapped with that of the G10, also worked on proposals for a revision of the system to include the developing world.[4]

Among these bodies, the Working Party 3 (WP3) of the OECD's Economic Policy Committee (EPC) is undoubtedly the most enigmatic and is often cited as very influential. Set up in 1961 as a mere technical working group of the OECD's key economic committee, this "Working Party No. 3 on Policies for the Promotion of Better International Payments Equilibrium" soon became an important meeting place to discuss overall strategies for the world economy, starting with the reform of the Bretton Woods system. Chaired at the beginning by Dutch finance official Emile van Lennep (later a Secretary-General of the OECD from 1969 to 1984), the WP3 brought together not only some of the highest level economic officials from the largest OECD member countries, but also representatives from the BIS and the IMF.

Even though often mentioned as highly influential, the WP3 has not received much academic attention so far. Accounts by political scientists Robert Russell and Susan Strange, both published in the 1970s, represented a contemporary view of the WP3. Even though they are not based on archival sources, they do reveal interesting facets of its work and network.[5] Emile van Lennep's memoirs also contain important information from the perspective of a key protagonist of the first decade of activity of the WP3.[6] The WP3 is also discussed in general overviews of the OECD and its history, such as Richard Woodward's synthetic portrait of the OECD trajectory or Peter Caroll and Aynsley Kellow's historical account of OEEC/OECD activities.[7] More recently, historians have started archive-based work on the WP3. Heide-Irene Schmidt has analyzed the WP3 with a focus on Anglo-American relations based on the WP3 archives in the Lyndon B. Johnson Library.[8] Matthias Schmelzer has analyzed the foundational period of the EPC and WP3 with a focus on growth policies.[9] And Floriane Galeazzi has written a doctoral thesis on the WP3 with a focus on French representatives and their role in the WP3.[10]

This chapter analyzes the work of the WP3, focusing on how OECD agents dealt with the crises of the international monetary system in the decade before and after the 1971 collapse of the Bretton Woods monetary system. It appraises not only the rise of the WP3 as a "crisis manager" of the international monetary system, but also describes its fall during the 1970s to the early 1980s. This chapter focuses on three questions.[11] First, what were the strengths and weaknesses of the organizational features of the WP3, and how did the WP3 compare to and interact with other international organizations? While many of the existing studies focus on the individual roles of key participants of the WP3, we shall pay more attention to the organizational background of this working group. Second, when dealing with economic and financial affairs, whose interests did the WP3 represent? Was it in the interest of particularly powerful countries such as the US? Or did the WP3 act as a neutral forum to coordinate several competing interests? Given the strong emphasis on soft power and knowledge in the literature on the OECD, a focus on the WP3 in the period of the collapse of the Bretton Woods system might help rethink the role of economic and national interests within the OECD. And third, how successful was the WP3 in its key task: to regulate the balance of payments of the OECD member countries? How did it deal with the rapid increase of international capital movement in the decades after its creation, and were its policies effective in achieving its set goals?

The chapter starts with an overview of the organizational features of the WP3 and then analyzes these questions by giving a chronological overview of the WP3's history, focusing first on capital movement and balance of payments adjustments from the 1960s to the early 1970s and then on the exchange-rate system and "crisis management" functions of the WP3 from the early 1970s to the 1980s.

The Organizational Features of the WP3: A Soft Core in a Hard Structure

When the OECD was reorganized in the spring of 1961, and in the context of Cold War competition for high growth rates and increasing US balance of payments deficits, the EPC decided on some major institutional changes. Most importantly, the US proposed creating a more restricted forum that would allow for confidential and high-level debates and to institutionalize a "new method" of transnational governance:

"frequent confrontation and consultation on alternative approaches to policies still in the making, as opposed to infrequent and therefore more widely publicized."[12] As Schmelzer has shown, this proposal to discuss "policies still in the making" such as changes in bank rates or exchange parities before important decisions were taken by national governments was a far-reaching suggestion. It amounted to relinquishing sensitive information in key policy areas to experts from other industrialized countries, and was thus regarded by other delegates as provocative and revolutionary, raising many security objections. Nonetheless, with the support of the Secretariat the US managed to convince its peer countries, and the OECD decided to create a new restricted body to discuss the difficult balance of payments situation between the largest deficit and surplus countries.[13] Upon Van Lennep's insistence, the initial membership of the WP3 consisted of the EPU countries, plus the US and Canada. WP3 membership was smaller than the mother organization, the EPC, following the practices of the OEEC to establish restricted spaces within the OECD for high-level negotiations on sensitive policies.[14]

Table 1 lists the members present at the first WP3 meeting held on 18–19 May 1961. Leading politicians and experts in international monetary affairs such as the US Treasury official Robert Roosa, as well as economist James Tobin and German central banker Otmar Emminger, participated in the meeting with important figures in the OECD or the G10 like Italian central banker Rinaldo Ossola and French official Pierre Esteva, each of whom chaired important G10 study groups.[15] Those participating in future meetings were also of importance, often including key persons active in international financial cooperation. After this first meeting, Van Lennep, Emminger, and Valéry Giscard d'Estaing would chair the work of the WP3.

The list of persons present at the first meeting indicates several features of the WP3 and its network. First, as was the case at the G10, the WP3 was primarily composed of representatives of the member countries' treasuries and central banks. After World War II, treasuries' officials gathered at the IMF while the central bankers met at the BIS, and the two groups rarely worked together. The WP3 membership signaled a change of climate in the early 1960s, which brought about a measure of reconciliation between the financial officials and the central bankers. Secondly, the members of the all-male WP3 often held a "deputy" or "sub" rank in relation to Ministers or Governors in their home countries. This organizational position may have restricted their influence, but—as already pointed

Table 1 Founding participants of the WP3 (May 1961)

Emile van Lennep	Chairman (NL)
Robert Roosa	Under Secretary of Treasury for Monetary Affairs (USA)
James Tobin	Council of Economic Advisors (USA)
Ralph Young	Board of Governors of the Federal Reserve System (USA)
Dennis Rickett	H.M. Treasury (UK)
Jack Downie	H.M. Treasury (UK)
Lucius Thompson-McCausland	Bank of England (UK)
Jasper St John Rootham	Bank of England (UK)
Maurice Pérouse	Directeur du Trésor (FRA)
Pierre Esteva	Sous-Directeur des Finances Extérieures (FRA)
Jean-Maxime Lévêque	Conseil National du Crédit (FRA)
Marc Viénot	Fonds de Développement Economique et Social (FRA)
Rolf Gocht	Ministry of Economics (FRG)
Fritz Schiettinger	Ministry of Finances (FRG)
Otmar Emminger	Deutsche Bundesbank (FRG)
Silvano Palumbo	Treasury Department (ITA)
Rinaldo Ossola	Delegate of the Bank of Italy in Paris (ITA)
Carlo Piantoni	Ministry of Budget (ITA)
Mario Cardinali	Ministry of Foreign Trade (ITA)
Suardus Posthuma	Nederlandsche Bank (NL)
Cecil de Strycker	National Bank of Belgium (BEL)
Krister Wickman	Ministry of Finance (SWE)
Gösta Rehn	Ministry of Finance (SWE)
Kurt Hansen	Ministry of Finance (DK)
Alexandre Hay	Swiss National Bank (CH)
Jean Jacques Senglet	Administration Fédérale des Finances (CH)
Henri Bégle	Conseiller d'Ambassade (CH)
Louis Rasminsky	Bank of Canada (CA)
Simon S. Reisman	Ministry of Finance (CA)
OECD Secretariat	
Thorkil Kristensen	Secretary-General (DK)
Jean Cottier	Deputy Secretary-General (FRA)
Gunter Keiser	Director, Trade and Balance of Payments (FRG)
John Fay	Director, Economics and Statistics Directorate (UK)
Angus Maddison	Head, Economics Division (UK)

Source OECD-HA, CPE/WP3(61)5; AEF, B68222 Compte rendu de la 1ère séance du groupe de travail No. 3 du Comité de Politique Economique de l'O.E.C.E. (sic), le 25 mai 1961

out by Russell—it also enabled the participants to speak more bluntly than their bosses.[16] However, as we will see later, the younger officials were not always more clever and future-oriented than their elder ministers.

The membership of the WP3 was soon enlarged to include Japan (which became a member of the OECD in 1964), as well as the IMF and the BIS, a process that was not settled easily and reveals further key features of this body. During the opening session of a WP3 meeting in June 1964, the chairman van Lennep proposed that "Japan, the BIS and the IMF be admitted as new members," insisting that after Japan's entrance "it [would be] made very clear that there were going to be no more increases in membership." To this proposal, Lord Hankey as Chairman of the EPC noted, "the admission of Japan required a decision of the EPC" and, "off the record" he added that "Austria might make some difficulties" if the country was not given a seat on the WP3. Moreover, a Belgian representative replied that "there was undoubtedly some connection between the Working Party 3 and the Group of Ten, and that therefore, the composition of the two groups ought to be the same." With Japan being a member of the G10 and Austria not being a member, this proposal would welcome Japan as a new WP3 member while excluding Austria. After a short exchange of views among the participants, Van Lennep cut short the discussion by stating that the "limit was now reached" and that "Austria should not be given any hope."[17] This underscores some key features of the WP3: limited and restricted membership, its autonomy vis-à-vis the EPC (of which it was formally a working party), and the close connection and overlap between the membership of the WP3 and the G10. The WP3, founded by a formal organizational decision of the OECD and at the same time given its own autonomy, was in fact a "soft" and more informal forum that existed within the "hard" and more formal structure of the EPC and the OECD.[18]

Similarly important were WP3's relations to other international forums and places of coordination. Figure 1, which is based on a schema drawn by a Bank of Japan official, summarizes the relationships between these different international financial forums around 1964. The WP3 was clearly a cornerstone of these relations that connected multilateral surveillance platforms with the OECD.

Coordination was strongest with the G10. The rise of the G10 has been closely related to the 1961 sterling crisis. Starting with the emergency IMF loan, several leading countries including the US, West Germany, and Japan, as well as several institutions, held either official or unofficial meetings. In particular, standing committees at the BIS offered meeting places to discuss the rescue of sterling in relation to gold arrangements and swap facilities.[19] Building on this ad hoc coordination,

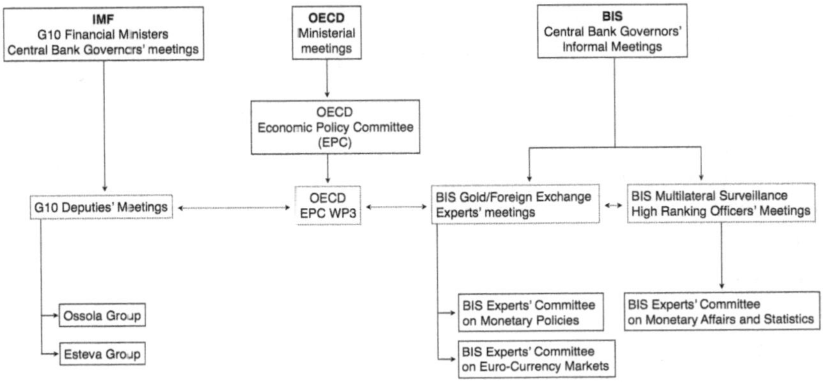

Fig. 1 The network of international financial fora around 1964. *Source* Archives of the Bank of Japan, 075880001, Kawase Seisaku [Foreign Exchange Policy], BIS 39, Getsurei Kaigi [Monthly Meeting], Kokusai Kinnyuu Kankei Shuyou Shokaigi Ichiran [Diagram on Major Meetings regarding International Finance], Gaikokukyoku [Foreign Division], 24 December 1964

the finance ministers and central-bank governors of the ten leading industrialized countries decided to meet several times a year. While the number of participating countries later expanded to 11 with Switzerland also participating, these meetings continued to be known as the G10.[20] Founded as an unofficial IMF forum, the G10 played an important role in rethinking and reforming the Bretton Woods system in the 1960s. Soon after its foundation, the G10 set up a proper working group named the Ossola Group after the name of its chairman, which brought together the "Deputies of the Group of Ten." The task of the Ossola Group was announced in its founding communiqué in October 1963: "to undertake a thorough examination of the outlook for the functioning of the international monetary system and of its probable future needs for liquidity." The Ossola Group gathered together representatives of the IMF, the OECD, and the BIS. The precise agenda of the Group, namely to study the relationship between the process of balance of payments adjustments and the need for international liquidity, was exactly the same as the WP3 work agenda.[21] As mentioned above, Rinaldo Ossola himself was a member of the WP3, again testifying to the close relationship between the WP3, the G10, and the G10 Deputies.

To conclude, the WP3 was in a way the "soft" core of a dense network, built in the "hard" structure of the OECD. In comparison with other institutions and fora, the WP3 was more informal than the IMF and the OECD but still more formal than the entirely unofficial G10 and the surrounding informal groups. As will be shown in the rest of this chapter, this meant that, once a new change occurred in the "softer" networks like the G10, then the structure of the WP3 would be easily influenced; the "hard" framework might endure, but its "soft" core could be replaced.

Capital Flows and Balance of Payments: The Rise of the WP3 as a Planning Outfit, 1961–1971

Since the liberalization of capital flows was one of the three main objectives of the OECD, this issue naturally figured as one of the most important agenda items of the WP3.[22] Discussions on the subject started at the very first WP3 meeting, held in May 1961. During the meeting, chairman van Lennep drew the attention of the participants to the subject of how to avoid the negative effects that capital movement might have on the balance of payments of certain countries after their return to convertibility. The proposal made by van Lennep at this meeting demonstrates the high degree of skepticism against the liberalization of capital movements in this period. In fact, van Lennep enumerated three possible cases: (1) completely deregulating capital movements; (2) policy coordination through the interest rates of large member countries; (3) limiting capital movements through exchange controls, especially for countries with balance of payments deficits.[23] However, soon after its start, the WP3 began to look at the question from a different perspective: instead of worrying about the negative effects of capital movements, the WP3 started to relate the capital movement issue to the openness of the capital market. One typical example can be found in a discussion during the meeting of the WP3 held on 6 November 1962.[24] Just after the session opened, US representative Dewey Daane criticized the OECD Secretariat paper as "disturbing because it failed to correctly present the US' interest in the subject of European capital markets." According to Daane the focus of the paper was "much too narrow." The main point of the American critique was to focus on "the inter-relationship between the development of capital markets and restrictions on capital movement." Daane concluded, criticizing the French and Italian restrictions on capital markets, that "the Working Party No. 3 was perhaps dismissing too lightly the significance of balance of payments in the capital markets-capital controls question." The US representative revealed another interest in lifting capital restrictions: "Increased capital outflows from surplus countries would therefore be needed to compensate for the current account surplus; where controls persisted, they should be removed." As expressed in Daane's comment above, the American interest was to let Europeans open their capital markets to assure the flow of funds from Europe (right after the return to convertibility) to the US (which was beginning to suffer from dollar depreciation and a balance of payments deficit).

Against the American criticism, French delegate Maurice Pérouse objected that "France's attitude toward the question of capital markets and capital movement was not influenced by its balance of payments." After a debate between the US and the continental Europeans, van Lennep summed up the discussion as follows: "the United States was urging greater freedom of capital movement" while "European members, though [they] agreed on this as a matter of principle, thought that the removal of restrictions must come slowly and in conjunction with the closer co-ordination of economic policies to prevent undesirable flows of capital." European interest, as represented above by the French opinion and summed up in the chairman's summary, was to resist the lifting of regulations on capital movements, which was hastened by the US, and to secure the capital market in the context of their economic policy, between "growth" and "inflation."[25] Thus, the key divide during the early stage of the WP3 emerged between the US and continental European countries. In other words, the WP3 quickly became the main platform in which key issues in the international financial system were debated, a development which underscored its rising importance as an international forum.

Who decided the above strategy on the US side? It was the National Advisory Council on International Monetary and Financial Problems (NAC) that gathered the information worldwide and took decisions. During the early 1960s, the NAC was chaired by Robert Roosa of the Treasury Department and was made up of representatives of the Treasury, the Department of State, and the Federal Reserve Bank, as well as the US representatives in international financial organizations. During the NAC meeting held in June 1961, right after the first meeting of the WP3, chairman Roosa referred to the WP3 in relation to the borrowing arrangements in the IMF: "In an unofficial way," he argued, the WP3 "might on occasion provide a diagnosis of problems in leading countries before the point of drawing on the Fund has been reached." He added that "some of these matters might be discussed in Paris in conjunction with the Working Party 3 meetings during the coming week."[26] Roosa and James Tobin being members of the NAC as well as the WP3, the US was aware of the rising influence of the WP3 during its founding period, which occasionally overcame that of the IMF.

Besides the liberalization of capital movements, the WP3 also focused on the adjustment of balance of payments. The issue was first taken up in a discussion on how to elaborate the balance of payments adjustments between the OECD countries as a group with the non-OECD area. According to a 1964 G10 Deputies report, the balance of payments adjustments meant "the smooth functioning of the international monetary system," which "depends on the avoidance of major and persistent imbalances and on the effective use of appropriate policies by national governments to correct any imbalances when they do occur." To settle this process properly, countries should "make use of an appropriate combination" of various measures, including budgetary and fiscal policies, income policies, monetary policies, and other policies.[27] Under the Bretton Woods system, while the exchange rate was fixed by the flexible-peg system, the room for political interference to "adjust" the balance of payments disequilibrium was larger than in later periods. The debate in the WP3, which began in 1964, was focused on the scale and scope of this political interference, including capital market restrictions.

In July 1964, the WP3 adopted a report entitled *Procedure for Study of the Adjustment Process*.[28] The report displayed an optimistic outlook for the international coordination of balance of payments adjustments. During the second half of the 1960s, however, the US balance of payments position had deteriorated radically and experts thought that it would not improve, thus provoking a harsher view of the near future within the WP3. In July 1965, discussing the multilateral surveillance scheme, WP3 Chairman van Lennep proposed to "offer guidance on the presentation of the figures" gathered during the surveillance work, "taking into account both the 'national' and 'global' aspects" of the figures. The proposal was echoed by the other heavyweight of the WP3, German central banker Otmar Emminger, who suggested introducing a "qualitative analysis" of balance of payments.[29] Both van Lennep and Emminger aimed to strengthen the existing procedure in the WP3. The next year, in 1966, these proposals led to the establishment of the "Early Warning System"; the WP3 set up this system "to try and ensure" the adoption of "appropriate policies," as soon as "evidence of an actual or potential imbalance begins to accumulate." Emminger, who reported the outcome of this system in 1967, added that this procedure "was only the initial step towards avoiding and combating an imbalance, and thereby improving the functioning of the adjustment process."[30] Simultaneously, the WP3 focused more and more on the US deficit in the framework of multilateral surveillance.[31] Finally, the WP3 concluded in October 1969 that the US balance of payments prospects for 1970 were "unlikely to bring the basic balance into equilibrium and the deficit might no longer be financed by an inflow of short-term funds."[32] Here again, antagonism between the US and European delegates remained important.

To manage these disequilibria, the WP3 strengthened initial measures to set certain "aims" or "objectives" for the balance of payments of each OECD member country. During its 1969 meeting, the WP3 Secretariat first proposed discussing "interim aims" for the current accounts of member countries.[33] The proposal was then elaborated into the "Medium Term Balance of Payment Aims" covering the period from 1970 to 1975. This medium-term objective, however, was modest, aiming for the balance of payments on "goods, services and private transfers" of OECD member countries to grow from $9.5 billion in 1970 to $15.75–17.75 billion in 1975. This balance represented 0.6% of the OECD gross national product, a level supposed to remain stable in the mid-term.[34] These cautious figures were consistent with the "50% growth target" mainly discussed by the EPC's WP2.[35] In short, the WP3 tried to settle the balance of payments adjustment by using a "yardstick" that was compatible with the OECD growth target.

However, less than a year after this meeting, in July 1970, this fragile consensus was again shaken by a US-European controversy. First, US representatives insisted on their counterproposal, arguing that "subsequent discussion showed that there were doubts about the usefulness of comparing countries' aims when these were fundamentally different."[36] However, it was agreed in the meeting held the next month that "explicit balance of payments aims for the United States" had been put forward for discussion.[37] On the other hand, the G10 Meeting of Ministers and Governors held in September 1971 supported the WP3 decision; the G10 asked the WP3 to assess the "scale of the balance of payments adjustment required for the United States and the implications for other countries." A note prepared by the WP3 Secretariat, following this G10 requirement, emphasized the importance of the target of the "aims" and its consistency among the member countries, stressing that "the Working Party might then take the view that these matters should not be left entirely to market forces, but could appropriately form the subject of a general understanding as to the intention of the United States authorities."[38] The divergence of views on the balance of payments aims, essentially proposed by the Americans, had thus been rejected by the G10, and the aims of the WP3 were supposed to target the US.

The rise of the WP3 was impressive during this phase and it actively managed the balance of payments of a hegemonic country, the US, with its Western partners through the use of "yardsticks." As long as the "adjustment" criteria worked, the majority of the WP3 countries could limit the US appraisal of capital movement, another measure to cope with the balance of payments disequilibria. This strategy of the European member countries, however, would be challenged by developments in the early 1970s. It should also be noted that the rise of the WP3 was backed by the G10; a "soft" WP3 in a "hard" OECD gained support from the "softer" network of the G10.

Coping with the Floating Exchange Rate System: The Fall of the WP3, 1971–1980

The closing of the gold window by the Nixon administration in 1971—often called the Nixon Shock—not only effectively ended the monetary agreement established at the end of World War II in Bretton Woods, but also sent shock waves through the global economy.[39] The first official response of the WP3 to the Nixon statement of 15 August 1971 was expressed in a *press communiqué* of the G10 dated 16 September 1971. In the communiqué, the G10 Ministers and Governors noted that the WP3 would prepare an assessment of "the scale of the balance of payments adjustment required for the United States and the implications for other countries." The situation was exposed in a confidential note by the WP3 Secretariat, dated 4 October 1971. After assessing the present position of the member countries' balance of payments, it aimed "to assess how far the aims of the United States are consistent with those of other countries," to illustrate "the scale of adjustment that might be implied for each of the major countries," and to highlight some points of discussions.[40] From a contemporary point of view, the analyses were rather static and not dynamic. This was partly due to the theoretical level of economics in those days, but mainly due to the fact that WP3 members could not foresee the effects of capital movement in relation to the balance of payments adjustment.

Despite the Nixon Shock, a certain dose of optimism prevailed in the WP3 discussions. For example, in January 1972, in an analysis that compared the new central exchange rates with the parities that had ruled before the shock, the WP3 reported that "the changes in the effective exchange rate for most countries are fairly small."[41] By May 1972, its Secretariat also noted that "the general picture which is emerging seems moderately encouraging."[42] With hindsight, we must regard the WP3's opinion in this period as too optimistic. In this transitional period, however, the OECD Council at the Ministerial level had published an important communiqué on 16 May 1972, just before the WP3 report mentioned above, to be published at the Ministerial Meeting on 24–26 May; the press release emphasized the need "to work for reform of the international monetary system" and confirmed the importance of the role to be played by the OECD and its Working Parties.[43] This declaration was precisely explained in the note circulated at the Ministerial Meeting:

> OECD's work in the field of balance of payments policies, which collectively determine the functioning of the monetary system, has a certain relation to the discussion of changes to the constitution of the system which is proceeding in the International Monetary Fund.[44]

Here in this meeting, the OECD Council stepped forward from the technical discussions over the balance of payments arrangements to designing the international monetary system, in collaboration with the IMF. In other words, it was the Ministerial Council, not the WP3, that prepared the collaboration of the OECD with the other international organizations in the context of international monetary system reform.

From the membership point of view, we can observe in the late 1960s and early 1970s a significant shift of the original WP3 members to the Ministerial Council level: the founding Chairman Emile van Lennep was named Secretary-General of the OECD in 1969, while Otmar Emminger, who had succeeded him, soon left the WP3 to become

President of the Bundesbank. As described by Russell, "the three key chairmanships" of the WP3, the G10 Deputies, and the Monetary Committee of the EEC "were held by just five men between 1960 and 1972," two of which were van Lennep and Emminger.[45] On the other hand, many of the influential WP3 members stayed in the G10 or the G10 Deputies. This shift in personnel propelled WP3 officials to the upper level of the OECD and the G10 network.

The Smithsonian Accord in December 1971 could only keep standing until 1973. The Italian lira and the Japanese yen began to float in February 1973, and other currencies followed, including the pound sterling. The IMF adjustable peg exchange-rate system then collapsed and a floating exchange system was introduced. No one, including the WP3, had ever experienced a floating exchange rate as the main rule in the international monetary system.

Following the suggestion of the Ministerial Council, and facing a floating system, the WP3 gradually widened its notion of the new exchange-rate regime. The change was witnessed over the European exchange-rate arrangements. According to the notion of the WP3 at that time, "the disadvantages of unstable rates would be the greatest between close trading partners, e.g., within Europe." The European skepticism of the floating system was followed by a future-looking view of "a common European float," although "any large movement in the common exchange rate against the rest of the world would heighten tensions resulting from disparities in the positions of countries party to the scheme." On the other hand, the WP3 indicated that "the positive argument for floating is that it would eliminate the conditions which permit the building up of large private speculative positions." The report finally concluded that:

> Floating would not necessarily have to be clean floating [because] there could be a case for financing mobile capital flows [...] even though the exchange rate provided a mechanism which could (at the cost of unwanted rate fluctuations) prevent them.[46]

Furthermore, the WP3 shared information with the C20 on the "experience of countries that maintained fixed margins between their currencies."[47] This collaboration with the C20 on the European "snake" practice would lead to further relationships between the two groups. In fact, on 17 January 1974, the informal WP3 meeting, "which was originally intended to be simply an informal meeting of those Members of the Working Party who were in Rome for the C20 meeting," turned out to be of "great importance," and as a result an official summary was produced.[48] Thus by 1974, the WP3 and C20 had informally been brought together.

To wrap up the case of the exchange-rate system, the first encounter of the WP3 with the new situation in the international exchange-rate system had been arranged by the G10 and the OECD Ministerial Council, not by the WP3 itself. The action taken by the WP3 right after the Nixon Shock was late, that of a follower rather than a forerunner. One can observe here the first sign of the fall of the WP3 as an enlightened crisis manager. Nevertheless, the WP3 rapidly caught up to the change brought about by the Smithsonian Agreement and elaborated its understanding of the "floating system," in collaboration with the C20.[49]

As for the "measures" to be handled by the WP3, the former "aims approach" seemed to be powerless when faced with the high fluctuations of the exchange-rate regime. In fact, as the WP3 Secretariat remarked in July 1972, "there seem[ed] to be little hope of an efficiently-working adjustment process, and little hope of agreeing what would be appropriate for countries to do in given circumstances." Some delegates argued that "the United States [occupied] an unduly privileged position by being able to obtain unlimited finance of deficits, thus escaping the normal disciplines," while others noted that "the United States [could] only accept convertibility and the normal disciplines if it is in a much stronger payments/reserve position." The Secretariat worried that "this conflict of views" may tend to "make the conflict between countries' payments aims even more difficult to resolve than usual."[50]

Despite these misgivings, the WP3 Secretariat maintained its target-setting method. In September 1972, it presented a report entitled *The Possible Use of Balance of Payments Aims as an "Indicator" of the Need for Adjustment*, which proposed using a "mid-term objective" of the current account balance as an indicator for the adjustment, i.e., once the balance of payments of a certain country displayed a margin out of the mid-term trend, then the country would be encouraged to exert corrective measures. Facing this proposal, the member countries "in general criticized this approach to the problem," since the mid-term objective has to be compatible between the countries concerned, not just by a single country adopting the objective. A French delegate, in his note to the Finance Minister, reported the discussion as "long and confusing" and criticized the WP3 report as merely repeating the conclusions already reached in 1966.[51] In addition to the above-mentioned US-European antagonism, further disagreement emerged between the WP3 Secretariat and the rest of the member countries. This divide would encourage the latter to abandon the WP3 and privilege other forums for further discussion, leading to the fall in grace of the WP3.

Although the attitude of the member countries was negative either on the aims or the objectives of the balance of payments, the WP3 Secretariat enforced the proposal. In the next WP3 session, held in late October 1972, the Secretariat presented a note referring to the "philosophies" of the member countries with respect to the use of the balance of payments aims; according to the Secretariat note, "some countries have positive views as to the desired structure of their BP [balance of payments] as being between a current and capital account," while "other countries take the view that controls on capital flows, except possibly as a temporary measure, are undesirable, either they believe them to be harmful or, alternatively, ineffective."[52] After examining the above proposal, the WP3 "agreed to discuss further the possible use of countries' balance of payments aims as 'indicators' of desirable adjustment action," with certain "margins of tolerance," beyond which it could be presumed that a country would wish to take adjustment action."[53] Discussion over the balance of payments "aims," which at first targeted the US deficit, soon changed its focus to the management of every member country's balance, either surplus or deficit, through these "indicators."

During the mid-1970s, the WP3 often referred to "burden" sharing to manage the international monetary system, but they lacked proper thinking regarding an active "yardstick." The WP3 members often exchanged ideas on "the weakness of the dollar," but no one could manage this weakness; the dollar depreciation after the Nixon Shock was far beyond the scope controllable by the balance of payments targets.[54] On the other hand, increasing capital movement including the euro-dollar made the indicators relating to the balance of payments out of date and useless; unlike the Bretton Woods fixed exchange rate system, the correlation between the balance of payments adjustment and capital movement became less coherent.[55]

Faced with the failure of its "yardstick," the WP3 ceased to be the headquarters of crisis management and became a quiet meeting room. By 1976, WP3 discussions became less stimulating than in previous years; country representatives limited themselves to exchanging information on their national economic situations during a round table. A meeting held in February 1976 discussed "factors affecting exchange rates," "the economic situation in Italy," "recent exchange rate experience within the snake," and "international liquidity developments," all the time exchanging views and indicators.[56] During a meeting held in July 1976, "much of the discussion by the Working Party involved a *tour d'horizon* on the prospects for demand, inflation and current balances."[57] At the meeting held in Manila in October 1976, "there was only one item on the agenda, 'Recent trends and prospects.'"[58] The threat of inflation was a common concern, but no concrete political measures were discussed in the WP3. A report presented in September 1980 entitled *Future of the Working Party* symbolized this decline: the members confirmed that "the Working Party was a useful and important committee; it was important that it be attended by senior level people," although the participation of senior and powerful figures had become a rarity by the beginning of the 1980s. The report added that "there had not been agreement on the number of times the Working Group should meet each year and some discussion about whether the half-day meeting at the time of the IMF annual meeting should be maintained," which means that by this period the WP3 had ceased to be a dynamic forum. The important meetings took place within the G10 or within other forums. Finally, the Chairman Emminger "hoped that discussion at the meetings could be a little more blunt."[59]

Conclusion

To understand the rise and fall of the WP3, this concluding section answers the three questions posed in the introduction of this chapter. First, the organizational features: the WP3 was, from its very beginning, a "soft" core, depending on the G10 and other flexible informal networks, but at the same time a working group built in the "hard" structure of the OECD-EPC. This double feature gave the WP3 extraordinary leverage as a crisis manager, dealing with balance of payments adjustments under the fixed exchange rate regime. The organizational feature that brought about the rise of the WP3, however, also prepared its fall once the international monetary conditions changed. With many of its core members moving to other fora, the "soft" core lost its strength and became a silent body of the ever-standing "hard" structure.

Secondly, preferences of the various OECD members were important: while coordinating the balance of payments adjustment, the WP3 as a whole represented the interest of Western continental Europe, to cope with the American deficit. As for capital movement, most Europeans tried to resist the Americans' demand for freer capital movement, and the WP3 became the main forum where the two sides fought against each other. After the Nixon Shock, however, a divergence of opinion emerged between the member countries and the WP3 Secretariat. The WP3, as a consequence, lost its prominence for both sides, the Americans and the Europeans, in the late 1970s.

Finally, the measures: the WP3 was, like other working groups in the OECD, familiar with "yardstick" measures. The WP3 invented several measures, "early warning system," "indicators," "aims," or "prospects" to manage the balance of payments of member countries. It is noteworthy that those measures were highly consistent with the "growth" targets of the OECD. As long as those measures were working, the WP3 could function as a meeting place where members could monitor themselves multilaterally and even criticize a powerful member like the US. The initial impulse often came from the G10, but it was the WP3 that proposed the measures to be implemented. However, once these measures became powerless when faced with the exchange rate regime change in the years after 1971, the WP3 lost its rank, not only within the OECD working groups, but more significantly among other international financial fora, both formal and informal. In the age of the floating exchange rate system, international decision-making took place in even "softer" and more informal networks, and did not follow anymore the "yardstick" measures provided by the WP3.[60]

The OECD's WP3 was one of the important players when it came to managing money and finance in the 1960s and the 1970s, but it was not always the best. It incarnated the emergence and also the decline of "constructivist rationalism," which played a great role in growth politics during that period. During its rise and fall, the WP3 was in fact one key player among many others within a transnational network warding off monetary instability and capitalist crisis threatening the West. But we have to put a small question mark after the label "crisis manager" when describing the WP3.

Notes

1. Kazuhiko Yago, *Financial History of the Bank for International Settlements* (London, New York: Routledge, 2012), 109–129; Gianni Toniolo with the assistance of Piet Clement, *Central Bank Cooperation at the Bank for International Settlements, 1930–1973* (Cambridge: Cambridge University Press. 2005), 283–308.
2. Jacob Kaplan and Günter Schleiminger, *The European Payments Union: Financial Diplomacy in the 1950s* (Oxford: Oxford University Press, 1989), 28–87.
3. J. Keith Horsefield, ed., *The International Monetary Fund, 1945–1965: Twenty Years of International Monetary Cooperation,* vol. 3 (Washington, DC: International Monetary Fund, 1969), 254–255.
4. Masanao Itoh, "Epilogue: How Should We View the Transformation of the IMF? Looking at the Collapse of the Bretton Woods System," in Kazuhiko Yago, Masanao Itoh, and Yoshio Asai, eds., *History of the IMF: Organization, Policy, and Market* (Tokyo, London: Springer, 2015), 317.
5. Robert Russell, "Trans-governmental Interaction in the International Monetary System, 1960–1972," in *International Organization*, 27–34 (1973); Susan Strange, "Multilateral Surveillance," in Andrew Shonfield, Hermia Oliver, and Susan Strange, eds., *International Economic Relations of the Western World, 1959–1971: International Monetary Relations*, vol. 2 (Oxford: Oxford University Press, 1976).
6. Emile van Lennep (with Evert Schoorl), *Working for the World Economy, A Personal History* (Amsterdam: Nederlands Instituut voor het Banken Effectenbedrijf, 1998).
7. Woodward, Richard, *The Organization for Economic Co-operation and Development (OECD)* (London and New York: Routledge, 2009); Peter Caroll and Aynsley Kellow, *The OECD, A Study of Organizational Adaptation* (Cheltenham/Northampton: Edward Elgar, 2011).
8. Heide-Irene Schmidt, "Anglo-American Relations and International Monetary Policy, 1958–1969," in Ursula Lehmkuhl and Gustav Schmidt, eds., *From Enmity to Friendship, Anglo-American Relations in the 19th and 20th Century*, Arbeitskreis Deutsche England Forschung, Band 53 (Augsburg: Wissner Verlag, 2005).
9. Matthias Schmelzer, *The Hegemony of Growth: The OECD and the Making of the Economic Growth Paradigm* (Cambridge: Cambridge University Press, 2016).
10. Floriane Galeazzi, "La France et la réforme du système monétaire international (1961–1987) Le rôle des experts du Groupe de Travail no 3 de l'OCDE," (PhD thesis, l'Université de Rouen, 2015).

11. This chapter partly builds on arguments also made in my earlier paper, "Crisis Management in the International Monetary and Financial System: OECD Working Party 3 (1961–1979)," *Waseda Commercial Review*, 439 (2014).
12. OECD-HA, CPE(61)2, Proposals for a Programme of Economic Policy Co-ordination through the OECD, 6 April 1961, cited in Schmelzer, *The Hegemony of Growth*, 172.
13. Schmelzer, *The Hegemony of Growth*, 173–174.
14. For details on the founding process of the WP3 see also van Lennep, *Working for the World Economy*, 100–105; Carroll and Kellow, *The OECD*, 57–58; Yago, *Financial History of the Bank for International Settlements*, 159–160, 166.
15. Ossola chaired the G10 group studying a new form of reserve assets, while Esteva presided over the G10 group on statistical sources dealing with multilateral surveillance.
16. Russell, "Trans-governmental interaction," 435. Our view coincides with the detailed analysis provided by Russell, however, we also focus on the later period when this structure changed.
17. OECD-HA, Working Party No. 3 of the Economic Policy Committee, Record of the Meeting held on 17 June 1964 at the Château de la Muette, Paris.
18. The terms derive from the organizational approach comparing the "hard law" system and the "soft law" system. Cf. Kenneth Abbott and Duncan Snidal, "Hard and Soft Law in International Governance," in *International Organization*, 54–63 (2000).
19. Catherine Schenk, *The Decline of Sterling: Managing the Retreat of an International Currency, 1945–1992* (Cambridge, New York: Cambridge University Press, 2010), 245–271; Yago, *Financial History of the Bank for International Settlements*, 164–167.
20. Limiting G10 members to the above countries was, according to Erin Jacobsson (daughter and biographer of Per Jacobsson, the Managing Director of the IMF from 1956 to 1963), proposed by Wilfrid Baumgartner, Governor of the Banque de France, at the suggestion of Robert Roosa of the United States. Baumgartner was said to have proposed that G10 membership should consist of "only countries that participated in the financing of British [IMF] withdrawals in July 1961." Erin Jacobsson, *A Life for Sound Money, Per Jacobsson, His Biography* (Oxford: Oxford University Press, 1979), 382. This initial decision seems to have influenced the WP3 membership. Jacobsson points to a memo by Gengo Suzuki, Japanese IMF representative, as a source for this observation.

21. Archives Economiques et Financières, Ministère des Finances, France (hereafter AEF), B69901-1-201, Report by Deputies of the Group of Ten, Annex to Ministerial Statement, July 1964.
22. For a recent synthesis into capital movement in relation to financial history and macroeconomics, see Michael Bordo and Harold James, "Capital Flows and Domestic and International Order: Trilemmas from Macroeconomics to Political Economy and International Relations," *NBER Working Paper*, 21017 (2015).
23. AEF B68222, Le Directeur du Trésor à Monsieur le Ministre des Finances et des Affaires Economiques, Compte rendu de la 1ère séance du groupe de travail No. 3 du Comité de Politique Economique de l'OCDE, le 25 mai 1961.
24. OECD-HA, Record of the meeting of Working Party No. 3 of the Economic Policy Committee held on Monday 5 and Tuesday 6 November 1962. This record seems to have been independently copied and therefore does not have reference number. Another document recording of the same session was made by French representative: AEF B68222, Compte rendu de la 9ème réunion du groupe de travail No. 3 du Comité de Politique Economique de l'OCDE, les 5 et 6 novembre 1962.
25. Galeazzi evaluated the French position before 1964 as a "strategic victory facing the Anglo-Saxon ambitions," (translated from the French) and stressed the change in the French strategy after 1964, inspired by Jacques Rueff and expressed by Charles de Gaulle. Galeazzi, "La France et la réforme du système monétaire internationale," 93–108. From my point of view, however, the French position seemed more defensive when faced with the American demands.
26. National Archives and Records Administration of the United States (NARA), RG56, NAC Minutes, Meeting 61–63, "Proposed Borrowing Arrangements in the International Monetary Fund," 30 June 1961.
27. AEF B69901-1-201, Report by Deputies of the Group of Ten, Annex to Ministerial Statement, July 1964.
28. Bank of Japan Archives, 12929, CPE/WP3(64)22, Annex II, "Procedure for Study of the Adjustment Process."
29. OECD-HA, Working Party No. 3 of the Economic Policy Committee, record of the meeting held at Château de la Muette, Paris, on 6 and 7 July 1965, strictly confidential.
30. OECD-HA, CPE/WP3(67)8, Paris, 20th March 1967, note by Dr. Emminger, "The Implications of an Early Warning System."
31. OECD-HA, CPE/WP3(67)18, Paris, 4 July 1967, Summary Record of Discussion of the 43rd Meeting on 2 June 1967.
32. OECD-HA, CPE/WP3(70)3, Paris, 4 February 1970, Summary Record of Discussion at the 62nd Meeting, 30 and 31 October 1969.

33. OECD-HA, CPE/WP3(69)33, Working Party No. 3 of the Economic Policy Committee, Prospects for Current Balances (Note by the Secretariat), Paris, 29 December 1969.
34. OECD-HA, CPE/WP3(70)7, Working Party No. 3 of the Economic Policy Committee, Medium Term Balance of Payment Aims (Note by the Secretariat), Paris, 7 April 1970.
35. Schmelzer, *The Hegemony of Growth,* 173–188.
36. OECD-HA, CPE/WP3(70)16, Working Party No. 3 of the Economic Policy Committee, Summary Record of Discussion at the 65th Meeting held on 7 July 1970, Paris, 14 September 1970.
37. OECD-HA, CPE/WP3(70)24, Working Party No. 3 of the Economic Policy Committee, Balance of Payments Strategy in the Medium Term, Note by the Secretariat, Paris, 27 November 1970.
38. OECD-HA, CPE/WP3(71)17, Working Party No. 3 of the Economic Policy Committee, The Scale of the United States Adjustment Problem and the Implications for Other Countries, Note by the Secretariat, 4 October 1971.
39. Regarding the Nixon Shock, see Kathryn C. Lavelle, *Legislating International Organization, the US Congress, the IMF, and the World Bank* (New York: Oxford University Press, 2011), 85–92.
40. OECD-HA, CPE/WP3(71)17, "The Scale of the United States Adjustment Problem and the Implications for Other Countries" (Note by the Secretariat), Paris, 4 October 1971.
41. OECD-HA, CPE/WP3(72)1, Working Party No. 3 of the Economic Policy Committee, "Post-realignment Assessment of Current Balance Prospect in 1972," Note by the Secretariat, 18 January 1972.
42. OECD-HA, CPE/WP3(72)8, Working Party No. 3 of the Economic Policy Committee, "Recent Developments in Exchange and Money Markets," Note by the Secretariat, 29 May 1972.
43. OECD-HA, CES/72.47, Council, International Monetary and Trade Issues and the Role of the OECD, Entry in the Council Minutes approved by the Council on 26 May 1972.
44. OECD-HA, C (72) 121 (Final), Council, Documentation for Meeting of Council at Ministerial Level, 24–26 May 1972, Agenda Item 2, International Monetary and Trade Issues and the Role of the OECD, Note by the Secretary-General.
45. The remaining "five men" were Robert Roosa, Rinaldo Ossola, and Bernard Clappier. Russell, "Trans-governmental Interaction in the International Monetary System," 442.
46. OECD-HA, CPE/WP3(73)5, Working Party No. 3 of the Economic Policy Committee, "Prospects after the New Currency Realignment," 19 February 1973.

47. OECD-HA, CPE/WP3(73)11, Working Party No. 3 of the Economic Policy Committee, "Experience with Maintaining Fixed Margins and Multi-Currency Intervention among Certain EEC and Other Countries," Note by the Secretariat, 21 June 1973.
48. OECD-HA, HT.74.14, Informal Meeting of Working Party No. 3 in Rome on 16 January 1974, Brief Summary, 17 January 1974.
49. However, the C20 quickly became powerless. In June 1974, a French C20 representative reported confidentially that "the predominance of the US in the debates was constant," while "the cohesion of the ECC member countries was not satisfying," and "the developing countries provided no useful contribution to the debates." The reporter also referred to other forums like "the meeting of the five" and the G10 which could take over the tasks of the C20. AEF, B62105, Note pour le ministre, Compte rendu de la réunion du Comité des Vingt au niveau ministériel (Washington 12–13 juin 1974), Directeur du Trésor (Jacques de la Rosière), original citation in French.
50. OECD-HA, CPE/WP3(72)14, Working Party No. 3 of the Economic Policy Committee, Payments Aims and Adjustment Policies in Conditions of High Potential Mobility of Capital, Points for First Discussion, Note by the Secretariat, 27 July 1972.
51. AEF B54755, Note pour le Ministre, objet: Réunion du Groupe du Travail No. 3 de l'OCDE les 14 et 15 septembre 1972 (Claude Pierre-Brosolette), le 5 Octobre 1972. Original citation in French.
52. AEF B54755, Working Party No. 3 of the Economic Policy Committee, Balance of Payments Aims: Implied Assumptions regarding Capital Flows (Note by the Secretariat), Paris, 31 October 1972.
53. AEF B54755, Working Party No. 3 of the Economic Policy Committee, The Possible Use of Balance of Payments Aims as an "Indicator" of the Need for Adjustment (Note by the Secretariat), Paris, 2 November 1972.
54. OECD-HA, CPE/WP3(75)3, Working Party No. 3 of the Economic Policy Committee, "Monetary Developments and the Weakness of the Dollar: Main Issues for Discussion," Note by the Secretariat, 24 February 1975; OECD-HA, Summary Record of the Meeting of Working Party No. 3 on 5 March 1975, OECD-HA, CPE/WP3(75)5, Working Party No. 3 of the Economic Policy Committee, "Balance of Payments Aims," Note by the Secretariat, 5 May 1975.
55. On the other topics concerning capital movement and the WP3 such as oil-dollar recycling, see Yago, "Crisis Management in the International Monetary and Financial System," 337–339.
56. OECD-HA, Summary Record of the Meeting of Working Party No. 3 on 16–17 February 1976.

57. OECD-HA, Summary Record of the Meeting of Working Party No. 3 on 19–20 July 1976.
58. OECD-HA, Summary Record by the Secretariat of the discussions at the meeting of Working Party No. 3 in Manila on 7 October 1976 (during the Annual Meeting of the IMF/IBRD).
59. OECD-HA, Summary Record prepared by the Secretariat of the 111th meeting of Working Party No 3 of the Economic Policy Committee held on 2 and 3 July 1980, 12 September 1980.
60. On the emergence of new thinking and measures to deal with the adjustment process from the mid-1970s onward in the OECD, see Samuel Beroud's chapter in this volume.

Peer Pressure in Paris: Country Reviews at the OECD in the 1960s and 1970s

William Glenn Gray

The OECD was a polite club. The governments represented in Paris did not deliberately aim to embarrass one another. Yet the club did have a purpose—to encourage better economic performance on the part of all its members—and it needed some way to gauge how well each member was achieving commonly agreed goals. Neither the Secretary-General nor the Secretariat had the authority to make those judgments in isolation.[1] If the OECD was indeed a "Warden of the West," as this volume discusses, it could only exercise a supervisory role on a peer-to-peer basis.

As a result, peer review played a central role across the organization—building on practices developed under its predecessor, the OEEC.[2] The OECD's Trade Committee staged "confrontations," forcing governments to defend their policies on tariffs and export incentives. The Invisibles Committee pressed member states to justify whatever barriers they erected to the free flow of capital. The Development Assistance Committee (DAC) examined the aid programs of participating countries one by one.[3] Scrutiny was even more intense within the most restrictive coordinating group, Working Party 3 (WP3) of the Economic Policy Committee, as also discussed by Kazuhiko Yago in this volume.

W.G. Gray (✉)
Department of History, Purdue University, IN 47907,
672 Oval Drive, West Lafayette, United States
e-mail: wggray@purdue.edu

M. Leimgruber and M. Schmelzer (eds.), *The OECD and the International Political Economy Since 1948*, DOI 10.1007/978-3-319-60243-1_9

No forum was more emblematic of the peer review principle than the Economic and Development Review Committee (EDRC). During the OECD's early decades, every member had to endure annual economic performance reviews featuring two main components: a closed-door examination and a published survey of the findings. Although the examinations could, at times, be routine and lackluster, the review process was implicitly adversarial. Ministry officials and central bankers faced a battery of questions about their country's policies and prospects. Some acknowledged weakness; others complained that the examiners or the Secretariat were unduly pessimistic. The participants were wrangling over words on a page—yet those words could have political consequences. Whatever cautionary notes appeared in the published OECD surveys could be gleefully exploited by critics of the government under review.

To political scientists, the main scholarly question surrounding peer review is a practical one: did it have a measurable impact on the policy choices of member states? After outlining peer review procedures at the EDRC, the International Monetary Fund (IMF), and the European Union (EU), Armin Schäfer posits that the "inherent voluntarism" of this "soft co-ordination" is "unable to oblige reluctant governments to change their policies."[4] Martin S. Edwards comes to a more generous conclusion after examining 1680 recommendations made to 24 member states in recent EDRC reviews. Edwards' team found that governments implemented OECD recommendations 52% of the time, and that a further 28% were taken under advisement.[5] Unfortunately, a simple before-and-after comparison obscures the problem of causation. Would the policies in question have been adopted anyway? Was the EDRC decisive in each case?

This chapter takes a historical approach to peer review, focusing less on immediate policy results and more on the internal dynamics of the review process. The EDRC offers a unique vantage point during the Cold War years, given its two-stage procedure—first examination, then publication. Other forums for multilateral surveillance, such as the IMF's Article IV consultations, did not generate published reports until the late 1990s.[6] The results of NATO's annual country-by-country defense reviews were too sensitive for public consumption, and the alliance dropped the practice altogether in the 1960s.[7] Even at the OECD, other routine examinations—such as the DAC's annual aid reviews—did not result in published findings. Peer review could, of course, exert genuine pressure even behind closed doors. Yet the stakes at the EDRC were especially high, prompting numerous attempts by member states to 'massage' the numbers or spin the conclusions. How did the EDRC review process maintain its integrity amidst these pressures? More broadly, how did participation in annual reviews reinforce the commitment of OECD members to transparency and accountability?

Official documentation on the EDRC's inner workings is quite sparse. Summary records of all 425 meetings from the years 1961–1980 are available in the OECD archives, yet these documents deliberately omit substantive controversies.[8] Fortunately, well-staffed national delegations in Paris prepared their own confidential accounts of EDRC meetings. This chapter is based mainly on US diplomatic reporting found at the National Archives and Record Administration in College Park, Maryland.[9] To avoid over-reliance on a single national perspective, these American reports are supplemented by German documentation from the Foreign Office and the Ministry for Economic Affairs.[10] Together, the US and German accounts provide a sizeable empirical basis for illuminating the tensions and disputes surrounding the annual reviews.

The first section below highlights the pattern of work at the EDRC. How did the performance of annual reviews enhance the sense of economic interdependence and shared accountability among the member states? The second section discusses how member countries sought to use the published reports to advance their own political objectives. How did the EDRC and the Secretariat manage to preserve the generally sound reputation enjoyed by the annual country surveys? The third section considers efforts by the EDRC to improve its practices. Why did the basic features of the review process remain largely unchanged in the 1960s and 1970s—and in most respects until the present day? Overall, the chapter concludes that the annual review process may have done little to change minds directly, but that the existence of this ongoing pressure was a significant driver of economic transparency within the OECD as a whole.

The Examination Process

Country reviews had already featured prominently in the work of the OECD's predecessor, the OEEC. Indeed, the pace was actually more intensive in the 1950s than in the following decades: major economies were subject to both "periodic" and annual reviews under the OEEC, generating a workload of some 40 examinations per year.[11] The OEEC drew a distinction between high-level policy discussions and the more technical work of the country exams; the former was handled by the Economic Policy Committee (EPC), the latter by the Economic Committee (EC) or its Working Party 13.[12] The OECD retained this dual track, distinguishing between the reconstituted EPC and a new counterpart, the Economic and Development Review Committee (EDRC). The hybrid title of the EDRC reflected two central mandates. Aside from annual economic reviews, the committee was charged with overseeing the development programs of OECD members needing special attention—primarily Greece, Turkey, Spain, Portugal, and Iceland.[13] Within a few years, the review process for those countries was essentially identical with that of all the other members, leaving the EDRC with a somewhat cumbersome and outdated name. (Suggestions for alternative titles were seldom any smoother, however.)[14]

The EDRC's working calendar resembled that of an academic year: the survey cycle began in the fall and continued through to the following summer. The Secretariat prepared advance schedules with 20 or so meetings spaced every few weeks, but some delegations would inevitably ask for postponements. As a result, the EDRC's busiest months were typically June and July as the committee rushed to complete the review cycle. Compared with other major OECD committees, the EDRC could afford to be flexible; its members were attached to national delegations in Paris and could be summoned on short notice. By the standards of international organizations, the EDRC met in continuous session.[15] By way of contrast, the powerful and secretive Working Party 3 (WP3) of the Economic Policy Committee was composed of mid-level officials traveling from their home countries, so it met once a month or less.

Preparations for a given country's review began several months before the date of the examination itself. In the capital of the member state under review, economic and financial officials compiled a "country memorandum" using guidelines issued by the EDRC at the close of the previous review cycle. The Secretariat—specifically, representatives from the Economic Directorate—then embarked on a site visit to the country in question. Conversations with economists and central bankers could provide valuable background information about the sitting government's policy goals and the potential obstacles to sustained growth. Equipped with these fresh impressions, the Secretariat prepared a draft review featuring descriptive elements, growth projections, and policy recommendations. Governments under scrutiny were seldom completely happy with these Secretariat drafts. A typical response was to praise the descriptive portions ("first rate in its analysis of Irish economic situation") while

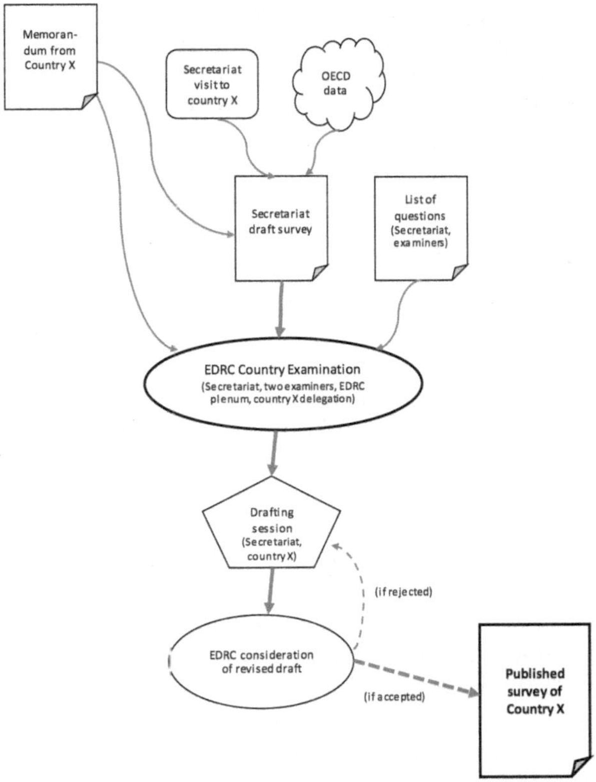

Fig. 1 The OECD review process: the annual examination of country X

questioning the forward projections ("too pessimistic regarding prospects for growth and price performance").[16] However much resistance they provoked, there was no one else to do the work, and drafts from the Economics Directorate furnished the bulk of the prose in the published surveys (Fig. 1).

A second feature of each annual exercise involved designated examiners—two peer countries selected to help guide the conversation on the day of the exam. Working in consultation with the Secretariat, delegates from the examining countries devised a list of questions and passed it around to the EDRC members in advance; these questions provided a sort of agenda for the early hours of the review.[17]

Attendance data suggests that some countries took the role of examiner more seriously than others. Many delegations, including Austria, Belgium, and Japan, simply handed the task over to their usual EDRC representatives. Others, such as West Germany, pulled in an expert or two from their home ministries. On the other extreme, the French delegation sent as many as seven officials into EDRC meetings when it served as examiner; even routine exams often brought in four or five French representatives.[18] The US delegation also prepared its own pointed questions for each review, whether it was a designated examiner or not. Desk officers at the Department of State, the US mission in Paris, and the US embassy in the examined country pored over the Secretariat drafts and passed along their judgments.[19] Whenever possible, US embassies sent reinforcements to Paris to assist in the examinations. As the embassy in Stockholm noted, the OECD's annual reviews of Sweden were proving "invaluable in cementing contacts with influential Swedish decision makers and in gaining additional perspective of viewing Sweden from the outside."[20] In other words, the best way for US embassy personnel in Stockholm to connect with Swedish economic policy makers was to wine and dine them in Paris!

The day of the examination did, in fact, feature a luncheon—in which the country under review hosted the delegations of the two reviewing countries.[21] There was, nonetheless, ample time during morning and afternoon sessions for a probing discussion of economic conditions and policy choices. Central bankers and mid-level officials from the reviewed country delivered an opening rebuttal to the Secretariat draft. They went on to offer prepared responses to the questions submitted in advance by the examiners.[22] Naturally, members of the Secretariat were on hand to defend their draft document. Throughout the 1960s and 1970s, at least one of the leading lights of the Economic Department—Christopher Dow, John Fay, or Kjell Andersen—was usually present, along with the country experts who had prepared the survey.[23]

Exchanges between the examined country and the Secretariat could be testy. In March 1967, the Netherlands review "was particularly lengthy due to the provocative nature of the Secretariat's draft and the defensive and evasive tactics of the Dutch delegation."[24] Tensions between the Secretariat and the German delegations became legendary. In 1973, Bonn's team—led by Hans Tietmeyer, a future Bundesbank president—insisted on removing any talk of an incomes policy from the Secretariat's draft report.[25] The US delegation found Germany's 1975 examination remarkable "for the persistence with which the German delegation sought to evade EDRC questions and give minimum information on policies and prospects."[26] In 1978, the German delegation conveyed a "tidal wave of verbiage which strayed far from the main points, but revealed an underlying unwillingness to engage in any real discussion of German policy."[27]

After the Secretariat and the country under review had spoken, the floor opened for a general discussion led by the peer examiners. The quality of debate ranged from "bland and factual" to "exceptionally enlightening." One enthusiastic envoy characterized the 1964 review of Yugoslavia as "a seven hour seminar in comparative economics."[28] Attendance at the examinations varied considerably, since smaller member states did not have enough personnel to staff every review.[29] Reviews of a large country drew nearly 50 participants; those of small countries might only attract 20. Even so, the examinations were understood as useful opportunities to learn firsthand about other countries' policy choices—and to receive immediate responses to pressing questions. During the 1978 examination of Norway, for example, the Swiss delegate asked whether Norway would align its currency with the new European Monetary System.[30] The question could have been raised through bilateral channels, but the EDRC offered the occasion for up-to-date information about Norwegian views.

The ultimate goal of everyone involved was to reach agreement on a publishable text. This did not typically happen on the day of the examination; at best the conversation produced a baseline consensus about what sorts of changes were needed in the Secretariat's draft. On the day after its exam, while its delegation was still in Paris, the country under review sat down to haggle with the Secretariat over the revised wording. Ideally, this would produce a second draft that could then be circulated for final approval by the EDRC. However, the process of drafting and re-drafting could drag on for weeks. By the time a country survey was released to the press, up to 3 months might have passed since the date of the original examination.

Viewing the process as a whole, the EDRC reviews can be considered a form of accountability theater—a performance with vital significance for the OECD. Countries large and small had to offer up their economic performance and current policies for inspection, thereby acknowledging that decisions made in one economy could have an impact on the overall prosperity of the club. Governments took the outcomes seriously enough to request postponements when they felt unprepared to face their peers. (This happened frequently in the cases of Greece, Turkey, and Italy, the most politically volatile member states.) Tellingly, members of the committee resisted efforts to cancel reviews altogether, as the Secretariat learned in April 1976 when it sought to save personnel resources by foregoing the reviews of Denmark and the United States.[31] The EDRC demanded the same degree of accountability from all members.

As this episode indicates, the EDRC had developed a strong sense of identity bolstered by a tangible *esprit de corps* among the committee members. Most delegations in Paris tasked one or two officials to the EDRC on a semi-permanent basis, so there was considerable overlap in participants from one meeting to the next. When long-serving committee members bid farewell for new assignments, the chair made a point of thanking them for their contributions.[32] Another sort of continuity involved the composition of the national delegations arriving each year for their country's examination day. The same officials—and the same members of the Secretariat—tended to confront one another for several years running. This helps to explain why patterns of behavior at the reviews could play out in a similar way every year for individual member states. As the following section notes, the common purpose on display within the EDRC did not preclude sharp clashes.

The Politics of Peer Review

The sovereign member states of the OECD did not always like being told what to do. Published recommendations from a respected outside authority could generate unwelcome pressure to take actions—or to refrain from actions—contrary to the national government's own preferences. In theory, that was the whole point of peer review; all governments were exposed to one another and vulnerable to the prospect that others would find fault. In practice, the discomfort was greatest for countries facing strong partisan or factional polarization, since the annual country surveys might be parsed for statements criticizing the government line. On the other hand, national governments *also* viewed the published reviews as an opportunity to level external pressure against recalcitrant institutions at home, be it central banks or spendthrift parliaments. The reports might even be wielded as psychological instruments, sending signals to markets about incipient trends. This section explores how these considerations played out in a variety of cases during the 1960s and 1970s, with an eye toward highlighting moments of controversy.

Resistance to EDRC Recommendations

The 1965 review of France brought to light sharp disagreements between French economists and the rest of the EDRC. Since 1963, Finance Minister Valéry Giscard d'Estaing had made "stabilization" the hallmark of his economic program; he had openly tied his political fate to the success of his fight against inflation. Unfortunately for Giscard, his efforts to achieve a balanced budget had contributed to a general economic slowdown—exacerbated by weak growth in Italy and the UK. In its draft survey of the French economy, circulated to the EDRC in late June 1965, the Secretariat insisted that France would need to stimulate consumption to kick-start economic growth.[33] At the EDRC review session on 1 July 1965, the French delegation reacted quite negatively, demanding that the Secretariat's recommendations be expunged from the survey text. They complained that artificial stimulus would destroy budget discipline and nourish inflationary expectations. France was due for a "spontaneous recovery of demand." The other EDRC delegates responded skeptically to the French line. However, as a compromise, they agreed that the government's view should be printed in the final version of the survey. The report would go on to state that if the recovery continued to stall, it might be prudent to engage in stimulus measures.[34]

Upon its release in early August, the 1965 survey received "very heavy coverage" in the French press. *Les Echos*, a financial newspaper, saw the OECD report as a clear rebuke of Giscard's policies—and a friendly nod to the more interventionist preferences of French business and labor circles. *Le Monde* pointed to differences between Giscard and Prime Minister Georges Pompidou, who was thought to favor a more expansionary strategy. Asked point-blank for his thoughts on the EDRC review, Giscard dodged by suggesting that the report was based on older data.[35] His confidence only grew as the French economy did, indeed, register faster growth in the fall of 1965. At the OECD Ministerial Council that November, Giscard boasted that he had been right—and the EDRC wrong—about the proper course for France.[36] He would not crow for long. General Charles de Gaulle won the presidential elections of December 1965, but with a smaller majority than expected. Within weeks, Giscard had lost his post to Michel Debré, known as an advocate of stronger state intervention in the economy.[37] The 1965 EDRC review was not, of its own, a significant factor in Giscard's fall from power. Even so, it is striking how easily a published OECD survey—no matter how carefully worded—could be exploited for the purposes of factional infighting. It also highlights the potential for wide gaps between the perspectives articulated by national delegations at the EDRC, dominated as they were by economic and finance ministry voices, and the priorities of a country's top political leadership. It is little wonder that governments worried about the publication of firm recommendations from the EDRC.

Presumably most member states shared the French desire to avoid negative headlines. In 1963, one Greek delegate petitioned his counterpart in the Secretariat—also a Greek—to avoid formulations in the published survey that would act as "banana peels" for the government to slip on.[38] In the case of West Germany, the aversion to the review process ran much deeper. In part this reflected German suspicions of the OECD Secretariat, which was, they complained, too British and too inclined to favor growth at the expense of stability.[39] By the mid-1970s, German officials were expressing grave doubts about the expertise of their counterparts in Paris. When the Secretariat tried to introduce a section into the 1976 German review concerning medium-term economic projections, Bonn's Ministry for Economic Affairs demanded that the offending paragraphs be buried in an annex—and then invited members of the Secretariat to Bonn for lessons about how investment incentives *really* worked, and how the next year's review should handle medium-term economic developments.[40] Apparently this gesture of deference by the Secretariat did no good. During the 1978 review, German officials "expressed some irritation that the Secretariat should insist on discussing what might be more desirable than current German policy."[41] From the standpoint of the Ministry for Economic Affairs, the best sort of EDRC report was one that exercised "no pressure in the direction of any specific policy measures."[42]

Most member states did not exhibit Germany's pattern of constant clashes with the Secretariat. Strong reactions were not unheard of, though. In March 1975, the Swedish government took issue with the Secretariat's growth projections, and it tried to get the draft survey altered before it was circulated to the EDRC. When that effort failed, Sweden pushed back the EDRC examination date by a month—apparently in the hope that new data would help its case.[43] In 1977, the Canadian government sent back the Secretariat draft in its entirety, arguing that it had misunderstood Canadian policy on several counts. As one official in Ottawa observed, the Secretariat analysts had "gone beyond their competence."[44] Since the vote for publication required unanimity, it was impossible to force unacceptable language upon the country under review. Member states even had the extreme option of blocking publication *after* approval by the EDRC, as Greece did in 1974. This was, to be sure, an unusual circumstance: the caretaker Greek government argued that the fall of the military government in July 1974 had created an entirely new situation.[45]

How did the EDRC manage to publish any surveys at all, given the highly political nature of the review process? As Tony Porter and Michael Webb observe, elementary rules of collegiality prevented member countries from thwarting every last wish of their OECD partners.[46] The combined voices of the Secretariat *and* the overwhelming majority of the EDRC often sufficed to compel the inclusion of mildly worded constructive criticism. More generally, a policy of continued obstruction would, in the end, have derailed the review process—thereby robbing countries with strong opinions, including Germany, from an opportunity to examine and criticize the policies of their neighbors. Meanwhile, as the following section explains, OECD members saw ample positive uses for the reviews.

Affirmative Uses of the OECD Surveys

For smaller member states in particular, the annual reviews represented a welcome occasion for feedback—and a source of fresh policy ideas. At their best, the examinations resembled a technocratic brainstorming session. Where were the bottlenecks in the economy? How could resources be used more efficiently? Would tax breaks or stimulus measures actually achieve the results expected? The delegations from Ireland—led for nearly a decade by Brendan Menton, a skilled and affable finance ministry official—came to the review sessions ready to listen. Even when Menton disagreed with the Secretariat's recommendations, he seldom asked for their removal, since he "preferred that his government receive this spur to early thinking."[47] There may have been a tactical element in these annual Irish displays of agreeableness. Yet it is striking how often Dublin's emissaries expressed satisfaction with the quality of analysis in the Secretariat drafts and avowed their readiness to take the EDRC's suggestions to heart.[48]

At root, the harmonious relationship between Irish officials and the EDRC reflected a sense of shared commitment to the modernization of the Irish economy. As the US embassy in Dublin saw it, OECD documents received a "disproportionate amount of attention in the Irish newspapers," which made them suitable for the Irish government to wield as an "educative devices."[49] In March 1970, at a time when inflation was accelerating rapidly, the EDRC survey was read as a "grim warning" about the trend toward "excessive" wage hikes and "unfettered consumer spending." This verdict bolstered the position of government economists in Dublin vis-à-vis members of the cabinet, who felt pressure from parliament to spend more expansively.[50] Six years later, as tripartite wage negotiations loomed for labor, business, and the government, the Secretariat agreed to time the release of the latest survey to provide maximum benefit to the Dublin authorities.[51]

Icelandic diplomats harbored similar positive views about the annual surveys. As one delegate explained during the 1964 EDRC review, the published reports "played a particularly important role in helping crystallize public opinion in Iceland," lending the government the "support necessary to press needed economic reforms in the face of a strongly ingrained national attitude of protectionism." Government ministers read each report "in its entirety"; business leaders and newspaper editors did so as well. The delegate "expressed his conviction that the EDRC's annual exercise of constructive criticism…has made a notable contribution toward enabling his government to break out of sterile isolation and economic stagnation."[52]

Devious governments found less orthodox uses for the annual reviews. In the summer of 1978, the Greek delegation was unhappy with the Secretariat's draft, which was sharply critical. Rather than endure humiliation at the EDRC, the Greek delegation tried to "short-circuit" criticism by revealing—right in the middle of its examination—that Athens was about to announce a new economic program to fight inflation. Since the Greek delegates "would not provide specifics," the EDRC was "unable to give an opinion on the adequacy of the proposed measures." The examination ended in a farce.[53] The story did not end there, however. The Athens government proceeded to leak the Secretariat's draft survey to convince the home audience that tighter fiscal and monetary measures were needed.[54] Through its clever maneuvering, the Greeks had avoided stern condemnation by the OECD while using the very same document to scare the Greek public.

Aside from political uses, member states sometimes treated the EDRC reviews as an instrument for swaying market expectations. West Germany in particular wanted each published survey to achieve a certain psychological effect. Buoyant numbers during a recession would improve the confidence of the business community. During boom years, such as 1969, German officials wanted to warn the German public about intensifying price pressures.[55] During the 1976 review, the German delegation asked to retain what they viewed as an overly pessimistic statement about the economy's waning competitiveness—in the hope that this passage, when published, might help to ease upward pressure on the Deutsche Mark.[56]

If the Secretariat and the EDRC usually acquiesced to the demands of Germany and other countries under review, this was not necessarily a triumph of "discretion" over "intellectual honesty."[57] The purpose of the published surveys was to convey a compelling picture to business leaders, politicians, and the general public. One way or another, the reviews served to reassure readers about the sophisticated methods of economic forecasting available to the OECD. The image may have been filtered somewhat by the preferences of the governments under review, yet this did not necessarily detract from the larger project of the OECD—the promotion of economic growth. That shared objective provided a common basis for tolerating a certain degree of "retouched" forecasts as well as a judicious number of tangible recommendations.

Reviewing the Reviews

From the earliest years of the OECD, some countries—Germany, predictably, but also Canada—expressed doubts about the utility of the annual reviews.[58] Others thought quite the opposite, proposing that the EDRC be given more authority for policy oversight. There was no systematic process for evaluating peer review at the OECD; but around every other year or so, the member states engaged in discussions about how the yearly exams might be improved. Minor adjustments apparently sufficed, since the review system still in place today closely resembles the model of prior decades.

In the early 1960s, when the EDRC's precise mission was still somewhat in flux, some countries hoped to expand the committee's purview beyond the routine exam cycle. In November 1963, a French diplomat interrupted the examination of West Germany to announce that the Bank of France was raising its central bank rate. Three weeks later, the EDRC devoted an entire session to discussing the economic implications of France's move. Along similar lines, Britain's delegate took the floor in March 1964 to account for a rate hike by the Bank of England.[59]

John Leddy, an ardent trans-Atlanticist heading the US mission, thought the EDRC should encourage a proliferation of comparable ad hoc meetings. "The purpose," he wrote, "would be to develop a tradition of immediate but unhurried review of important changes in economic policy and to keep all governments on notice that they must be prepared to explain and defend their actions before the OECD." Officials at the State Department swiftly reined in Leddy's ambitions, noting that "progress toward more forthright consultations" could only really be expected among that "small circle of policy level individuals who appear regularly at EPC and WP3 meetings."[60] The EDRC was simply too large and disparate to emerge as a locus for policy coordination. That fall, Leddy expressed his vision in more modest terms: the annual reviews, he noted, "provide an unusual opportunity for learning about and influencing policies pursued by other governments."[61]

Reflecting in 1965 on the relative success of the OECD, the US mission continued to stress the value of routine consultation. For one thing, an engagement with the internal affairs of the member states helped to avert the impression that the OECD was "only and exclusively a concealed instrument for opposing the LDC's." The WP3 was especially significant, given its consistent ability to bring together officials "at the highest monetary policy level." Still, the EDRC reports on individual countries had been "helpful in a number of cases in supporting sound economic measures," including "measures taken by Germany to stem the inflow of private capital." Not only Iceland, but also Switzerland, Spain, and Ireland had pointed to EDRC surveys in rallying domestic support for "sound but politically controversial economic projects."[62]

By the late 1960s, the committee was giving some thought to how its work might be streamlined. Examination days were so consumed with data that only two or three delegates contributed actively at some of them. In October 1967, the EDRC reached a consensus that less time should be spent reviewing the recent past, with the thrust of the conversation directed toward "present policies and the appropriateness of those policies." To ensure that discussion honed in on areas of "uncertainty or dispute," the committee chair, the examiners, and the country delegates were to meet in advance to establish where agreement already existed.[63] It is however not clear that this system ever found widespread application. The committee was constantly reaffirming the need to shorten the opening statements by the country under examination.

Over time, more substantive considerations began to drive the conversation about the utility of EDRC reviews. In the fall of 1970, the member states prepared a report reflecting their experiences with the EDRC's recommendations in the area of fiscal policy. The US sounded quite jaded: while still embracing the goal of "stable, adequate, non-inflationary growth," the State Department expressed doubts about the prospects of tailoring fiscal policy or tax measures to fit the "calculated requirements of stabilization policy."[64] This vein of skepticism emerged again during the next sustained discussion about the EDRC system in July 1974. Hadn't the surveys made several erroneous recommendations—telling Japan to pour on the stimulus in 1972, and Italy the same in late 1973? The Swedish delegate agreed, "noting that OECD conclusions for Sweden had been wrong for 4 years running." For the first time, the US team wondered if reviews were really needed on an annual basis. Perhaps they could be saved for moments of particular challenge? Was the EDRC just duplicating work carried out in the EPC, the WP3, the WP4, and the Short-Term Forecasters group?[65]

The Secretariat had ready answers, however, and its vigorous defense of the existing rotation found the sympathy of most other delegations. "One great advantage of annual surveys was the acceptance by governments of the principle of regular reviews," the Secretariat observed. Holding reviews sporadically and episodically would merely invite painstaking negotiations about the timing; and crisis points were not necessarily the best time to pull together expertise from the countries affected.[66] One example had already emerged in July 1974, when the revolutionary government in Portugal asked to have its review pushed forward by 2 months. This was, of course, a mark of faith in the competence of the EDRC; but it meant that the Secretariat had to pull together a hasty report based on outdated 1973 figures. The "review" nevertheless served a purpose in helping the inexperienced coalition in Lisbon anticipate predicaments—and in conveying the views of the left-leaning cabinet about vital topics such as international investment.[67]

In a further review of EDRC procedures held in July 1975, the committee asked for "greater assurance that the conclusions as reflected in the EDRC meeting would not be basically modified in subsequent discussions between the secretariat and the country representatives." If the published surveys flatly contradicted the conclusions reached during the original examination, why should the committee meet at all?

In an attempt to depoliticize the drafting of final conclusions, several delegations urged that the published surveys be considered as "independent views of the OECD Secretariat, and not be confused with official views of the country concerned." The German delegation disputed this theory and insisted that the published reports must represent the collective judgment of the committee. Grudgingly, the US representative acquiesced—under the proviso that "any rough consensus that the EDRC reaches as a technical committee must not be interpreted as reflecting policy views of individual countries represented in the EDRC."[68] To enhance the committee's role in the final edit, the two examining countries were henceforth to be consulted on any substantive changes to the revised surveys.[69]

It was also German delegates who, in 1974, proposed a new type of EDRC session: an interim forecast update to be held a few times each year. Attention at these meetings would center on the "big seven" OECD members—Britain, France, West Germany, Italy, Japan, Canada, and the United States. A year before the G6 (later G7) began meeting for economic summits, the EDRC had already singled out these seven economies as harboring special relevance for the entire OECD membership.[70] These experimental and improvised meetings were held off-the-cuff, with raw, up-to-date forecasts supplied by the Secretariat for the benefit of the EDRC representatives.[71] It was an admission that the OECD had grown large enough in institutional terms that country teams could not easily share enough information across committees. Rather than worrying about a duplication of effort from the short-term forecasters or the various Working Parties, the EDRC preferred to secure direct access to Secretariat views.

A glance at the EDRC's present-day checklist reveals a certain number of institutional innovations since the 1970s. With a substantially larger membership, the pace of reviewing has officially slipped back to once every 2 years. Countries under examination are to circulate a one-page memo highlighting the primary points of disagreement with the Secretariat drafts. Two "examiners" still guide the review, yet their role is less formal now and "more in keeping with the role of lead discussant." Most importantly, the scope for post-hoc revisions has been sharply constrained: the examined country and the Secretariat have a single day—immediately following the review session—to revise the draft in keeping with the results of the review. Final touch-ups are still possible at this point, but "typically, publication occurs within 1 month of the EDRC meeting."[72] Whether or not this streamlined process has enhanced the quality of the reports, it must surely have reduced the rancor sometimes in evidence during the economic doldrums of the 1970s.

Conclusion

Did peer review at the OECD make a difference? The OECD itself claims that it did, and still does, lauding peer pressure as a "means of soft persuasion which can become an important driving force to stimulate the state to change, achieve goals and meet standards."[73] Working in earlier decades, and with a different source base, the present chapter has not concerned itself with the policy impact of EDRC surveys. Regardless of whether or not the published reports actually changed any minds in the national capitals, the process of reviewing was significant in its own right. It reinforced the principle of accountability. It offered fresh outside perspectives. It gave countries a forum for learning about each other's practices—as in 1963, when French and Swedish officials found significant differences in their methods of national planning.[74] More generally, the parade of yearly examinations served as a constant reminder of how decisions in the larger economies affected conditions in all the others. Even if the published surveys were not always models of absolute candor, they found an audience—particularly in the smaller OECD countries, where the Secretariat's expertise (and that of the committee members) was keenly appreciated. Without directly infringing on anyone's sovereignty, the peer review process stimulated a greater understanding of unique and common issues confronting states across the Western community.

As this chapter has shown, a historical, archival-driven view of the EDRC provides a glimpse of the tensions that arose when self-confident officials from the larger nation states confronted the OECD's technocratic expertise. Further study might consider links between the internal evolution of the EDRC and larger shifts in the guiding philosophy of the OECD, i.e., the attempt at medium-term projections in the 1970s, and the turn to structural problems in the 1980s. Did the annual EDRC reports inform other policy work at the OECD, or were they treated mainly as external communications to a wider public? The country surveys were, after all, one of the most visible faces of the OECD. The peer review process at the EDRC combined mechanisms of internal accountability with at least a semblance of outward transparency. This dual function helps to explain why the OECD partners played their assigned roles, however reluctantly, in the accountability theater staged in Paris by the EDRC several times each month.

Notes

1. Richard Woodward, *The Organization for Economic Co-operation and Development* (London: Routledge, 2009), 49–50.
2. Matthias Schmelzer identifies peer pressure as one of the three key mechanisms of the OECD, alongside the "production, legitimation, and diffusion of policy ideas" and the "standardization and generation of comparable and seemingly objective data". Schmelzer, *The Hegemony of Growth: The OECD and the Making of the Economic Growth Paradigm* (Cambridge, 2016), 17.
3. Patricia Hongler and Matthias Schmelzer, "A 'watchdog' watching itself? The historical origins and functioning of the OECD's Aid Review", paper presented at the ENIUGH conference in Paris, 6 September 2014.
4. Armin Schäfer, "A New Form of Governance? Comparing the Open Method of Co-ordination to Multilateral Surveillance by the IMF and the OECD", *Journal of European Public Policy* 13: 1 (2006), 70–88.
5. Martin S. Edwards, "Can economic surveillance make a difference? Insights from the OECD," Global Policy Essay, April 2013; Available at: www.globalpolicyjournal.com (Accessed 14 December 2016).
6. For an outline of the IMF's new transparency procedures, which began in 1997 with the institution of "public information notices", see Martin S. Edwards, Kelsey A. Coolidge, and Daria A. Preston, "Who Reveals? Transparency and the IMF's Article IV Consultations", paper presented to the Workshop on Multimode Governance and Globalization, EUI Global Governance Program, 16–17 December 2011, 8–10; http://wp.peio.me/wp-content/uploads/2014/04/Conf5_Edwards-30.09.11.pdf (Accessed 14 December 2016).
7. Tellingly, one of the most dramatic political scandals in West German history—the *Spiegel* Affair—was touched off by a leaked report indicating that NATO reviewers were dismayed at the poor state of German military readiness. Martin Doerry and Hauke Janssen, eds., *Die SPIEGEL-Affäre. Ein Skandal und seine Folgen* (Munich: Deutsche Verlags-Anstalt, 2013).
8. Most meeting reports are 2–3 pages in length, consisting of a long list of participants followed by a few short paragraphs indicating which country had been reviewed. Meetings from 1961–1974 are available in digital form; those from 1974 onward appear individually on microfiche. Thanks to Sandra Willmott at the OECD's Historical Archives in Paris (OECD-HA) for her assistance in preparing these materials for consultation.

9. Precise archival references to NARA will be provided throughout the notes. For the years 1973–1979, electronic copies of US diplomatic cables are freely available online in a fully searchable digital database.
10. The author thanks Knud Piening at the Political Archive of the Foreign Office in Berlin (PA-AA) and Regina Pawelletz at the Bundesarchiv Koblenz (BArchK); both addressed numerous queries about the remaining extent of German documentation. Unfortunately, many of the files concerning German country reviews prior to 1975 have been destroyed.
11. National Archives and Record Administration—College Park [NARA], Record Group [RG] 59, Central Decimal Files [CDF] 60–63, Box 610 (374.800), USRO-Paris (Nolting) Polto A-35, 14 July 1960. Throughout this text, implied words (an, the, etc.) will be added to cited telegram material to improve readability. Several of the official OEEC country examination reports can be found online at the European University Institute (EUI) Archive; see http://archives.eui.eu/en/fonds/173509?item=OEEC.EC-01 (Accessed 14 December 2016).
12. See remarks by Milton Gilbert of the OEEC Secretariat in conversation with the "Group of Four" charged with studying the organization's reconstitution in NARA CDF 60–63, Box 609, USRO-Paris (Burgess) Polto A-480, 17 February 1960. At the time, the EPC was quite new, having been formed in May 1959 out of Working Party 19 of the OEEC Council. EUI Archive, OEEC files, 259.
13. From the very start, the Secretariat and the committee members had a difficult time defining procedures for the review of development programs. OECD-HA, OCDE_0362, EDR (61) 1, Terms of Reference and Related Acts, 3 October 1961; also EDR (62) 9, "Tasks and Procedures", 19 March 1962.
14. Alternatives suggested by the US included GEC (General Economic Committee), REPAD (Review of Economic Policies and Developments), or REAP (Review of Economic Activities and Policies). OECD-HA, OCDE_365, EDR (67) 24, Note by the US delegation, 4 October 1967.
15. On this point, see NARA, RG 59, Subject-Numeric Files [NARA SNF] 64–66, Box 806 (ECIN 3 OECD), USRO-Paris (Finletter) Cedto 971, 13 March 1964.
16. Review of Ireland as reported in US Paris-OECD (Brown) 6450, 14 March 1974. NARA, Access to Archival Databases [AAD], Electronic Telegrams 1973–1979. All subsequent US telegrams identified only by date can be found in this this extensive, keyword-searchable tool; see http://aad.archives.gov/aad/series-description.jsp?s=4073 (Accessed 14 December 2016).
17. The system was made less onerous, but arguably more effective, by a pattern of pairing the same reviewers with the same subject countries for

several years running. For Dutch efforts to institute an automatic rotation system (opposed by the US) see US Paris-OECD (Turner) 26995, 15 October 1975.

18. Analysis of attendance at EDRC meetings based on minutes (EDR/M) from four intervals: 1964–1965, 1969–1970, 1974–1975, and 1979–1980.
19. See, for example, NARA SNF 64–66, Box 804 (ECIN 3 OECD), DepSta Toced 487, 17 December 1964. Often the Secretariat draft was not ready until a few days before the scheduled EDRC meeting.
20. US Stockholm (Kennedy-Minott) 674, 16 February 1978. This may, of course, have been self-serving on the part of US diplomats looking forward to spending time in Paris.
21. This was not an especially grand affair; the US mission budgeted $400 for its luncheon in 1977. US Paris-OECD (Katz) 37673, 22 December 1976. For a sample schedule of an exam day, see US Paris-OECD (Katz) 15129, 12 June 1975.
22. For example, in 1965, the Secretariat asked to receive questions to be directed to Germany by 8 November for a review scheduled on 23 November. NARA SNF 64–66, Box 713 (E 2-2 Ger W), USRO-Paris (Brown) Cedto 307, 3 November 1965.
23. For a rundown of top Secretariat officials, see Schmelzer, *The Hegemony of Growth*, 72. On the attendance analysis conducted for this chapter, see note 18.
24. NARA SNF 67–69, Box 713 (ECIN 2 OECD), US Paris-OECD (Trezise) Cedto A-409, 23 March 1967.
25. NARA SNF 70–73, Box 745 (E 2-2 Ger W), US Paris-OECD (Brown) 10904, 19 April 1973.
26. US Paris-OECD (Turner) 11608, 7 May 1975. Germany's delegation in Paris acknowledged (with some understatement) that the "lengthy discussions with the Secretariat did not lead to a nearing of positions in all cases". BArchK, B 102/253696, DG Paris-OECD (Funkschmidt), Kurzbericht 188 (draft), 23 May 1975.
27. US Paris-OECD (Salzman) 14194, 3 May 1978.
28. NARA CDF 60–63, Box 615, USRO-Paris (Finletter) W-85, 6 October 1961 (examination of US); NARA SNF 67–69, Box 713 (ECIN 3 OECD), US Paris-OECD Cedto A-368, 23 February 1967 (examination of Ireland); NARA SNF 64–66, Box 805 (ECIN 3 OECD), USRO-Paris (Durbrow) Cedto A-1085, 22 May 1964 (examination of Yugoslavia).
29. Throughout the four periods examined (see note 18), Iceland and Ireland always topped the list of absences. The next three runners-up for most absences varied over time: Canada, Turkey, Austria (1964–1965); Yugoslavia, Portugal, Austria (1969–1970); Portugal, New Zealand, Canada (1974–1975); Turkey, Portugal, New Zealand (1979–1980).

30. PA-AA, B 202/130520, DG Paris-OECD (Brock/Streit), Kurzbericht 247, 3 January 1979.
31. OECD-HA, microfiche, EDR/M(76)6 and 7, 316th and 317th meetings of the EDRC, 1 April and 14 April 1976.
32. According to the minutes of the 212th meeting on 25 June 1971, the lead US representative, Dallas Jones, "stated that he had spent six most interesting years with the Committee" and that "he regretted very much his departure." OECD-HA, OCDE_0366, EDR/M (71) 12.
33. NARA SNF 64–66, Box 804 (ECIN 3 OECD), US Paris-OECD (Brown) Cedto 1373, 25 June 1965.
34. NARA SNF 64–66, Box 712 (E 8 Fr), US Paris-OECD (Brown) Cedto A-19, 8 July 1965.
35. Newspaper articles as summarized in NARA SNF 64–66, ibid., US Paris (Smith) A-342, 12 August 1965.
36. OECD-HA, OCDE_0005, C/M (65) 22 Part I, OECD Ministerial Council, 25 November 1965, 18–20.
37. Eric Roussel, *Georges Pompidou 1911–1974* (Paris: Editions Perrin, 2004), 187–189.
38. NARA SNF 63, Box 3378 (E 2 Greece), US Athens (Blodgett) A-191, 13 August 1963.
39. BArchK, B 102/253696, BMWF/W-I A 2 (Daase), Kurzinformation, 4 August 1972. Scholars tend to confirm this dominance of "British economists espousing Keynesian principles." See, for example, Robert Wolfe, "From Reconstructing Europe to Constructing Globalization: The OECD in Historical Perspective," in Rianne Mahon and Stephen McBride, eds., *The OECD and Transnational Governance* (Vancouver: University of British Columbia Press, 2008), 25–42; here 35. See also Schmelzer, *The Hegemony of Growth*, 72.
40. Extensive documentation in BArchK, B 102/253715. Of special note is a 10-page report prepared by BMWi-I D 3 on 26 July 1976, explaining in pedantic detail the many flawed assumptions in the Secretariat's draft survey.
41. US Paris-OECD (Salzman) 14194, 3 May 1978.
42. BArchK, B 102/253696, BMWi-I A 2 (Daase) to Friderichs, 1 August 1975. A similar phrase appeared in the same unit's summary the following year; see BArchK, B 102/253715, Dick to Friderichs, 14 June 1976.
43. PA-AA, B 202/122473, DG Paris-OECD (Emmel) 206, 13 March 1975.
44. US Ottawa (Enders) 4526, 1 June 1977.
45. US Paris-OECD (Turner) 20352, 27 August 1974.
46. Tony Porter and Michael Webb, "Role of the OECD in the Orchestration of Global Knowledge Networks", in Mahon and McBride, eds., *The OECD and Transnational Governance*, 43–59; here 50–52.

47. NARA SNF 64–66, Box 727 (E 2 Ire), USRO-Paris (Leddy), 19 February 1964.
48. NARA SNF 70–73, Box 754 (E 2-2 Ire), US Paris-OECD (Brown), 9 March 1973; also US Paris-OECD (Brown) 6450, 14 March 1974.
49. NARA SNF 64–66, Box 727 (E 2 Ire), US Dublin (O'Connor) A-422, 9 April 1965.
50. Quotes from an editorial in the *Irish Independent* cited in NARA SNF 70–73, Box 710 (E 3 OECD), US Dublin (Moore) 204, 24 March 1970.
51. US Paris-OECD (Katz) 30243, 13 October 1976.
52. NARA SNF 64–66, Box 805 (ECIN 3 OECD), USRO-Paris (Leddy) Cedto A-285, 29 October 1964.
53. US Paris-OECD (Salzman) 10931, 14 June 1978.
54. US Athens (McCloskey) 5163, 20 June 1978.
55. Admittedly, during the 1969 examination, German officials were merely trying to correct what they saw as an overly optimistic Secretariat draft. NARA SNF 67–69, Box 617 (E 2-2 Ger W), US Paris-OECD (Brown) 4119, 21 March 1969.
56. US Paris-OECD (Turner) 10084, 6 April 1976.
57. For this juxtaposition, reflecting a dilemma felt keenly by the Secretariat at the time, see NARA SNF 67–69, Box 617 (E 2-2 Ger W), US Paris-OECD (Trezise) 3576, 12 March 1969.
58. A German initiative within the Executive Committee—supported by Canada—aimed at abolishing the annual review process and replacing it with quarterly Secretariat reports on the economic situation in the major member countries. OECD-HA, OCDE_0007, CE/M(64)18, ExComm, 81st meeting, 2 July 1964, 3–7.
59. OECD-HA, OCDE_0264, EDR/M(63)20, EDRC, 58th meeting, 4 December 1963; also EDR/M(64)4, EDRC, 64th meeting, 12 March 1964.
60. NARA SNF 64–66, Box 806 (ECIN 3 OECD), USRO-Paris (Leddy) Cedto 911, 29 February 1964; also DepSta (Rusk) Toced 811, 4 March 1964.
61. NARA SNF 64–66, Box 805 (ECIN 3 OECD), USRO-Paris (Leddy) Cedto A-231, 9 October 1964.
62. NARA SNF 64–66, Box 803 (ECIN 3 OECD), USRO-Paris (Brown) Cedto A-40, 14 July 1965, 2 and 5.
63. Quotes from NARA SNF 67–69, Box 686 (E 2), US Paris-OECD Cedto A-441, 9 February 1968. For a five-page list of agreed points, see OECD-HA, OCDE_0264, EDR/M(67)17, EDRC, 136th meeting, 25 October 1967.

64. NARA SNF 70–73, Box 820 (FN 3 OECD), DepSta (Irwin) 161121, 30 September 1970.
65. US Paris-OECD (Katz) 23027, 30 September 1974, summarizing views expressed during the 15 July meeting.
66. Ibid. For a list of procedural points agreed at the follow-up meeting, see OECD-HA, microfiche, EDR/M(74)20, EDRC, 281st meeting, 4 October 1974. Secretariat members present at the 15 July meeting were Atkinson, Andersen, and Gondicas; on 4 October, Andersen and Gondicas.
67. US Paris-OECD (Brown) 16855, 10 July 1974; US Paris-OECD (Turner) 20826, 3 September 1974.
68. US Paris-OECD (Turner) 19104, 23 July 1975. As the US mission observed later, "the EDRC is not a consensus committee in the sense that individual countries can be said to have approved final documents in every detail". There need be no assumption that the US endorsed every sentence in every survey. US Paris-OECD (Katz) 35410, 30 November 1976.
69. OECD-HA, microfiche, EDR/M (75) 16, EDRC, 301st meeting, 7 July 1975.
70. For more on the OECD and the emergence of the G5/G7, see Samuel Beroud's chapter in this volume.
71. For reports of the first several interim forecast meetings, see US Paris-OECD (Turner) 24600, 18 October 1974; US Paris-OECD (Katz) 3728, 12 February 1975; US Paris-OECD (Turner) 26705, 15 October 1975. EDR/M records from 1979–1980 indicate that similar meetings were still being held, typically in September, just as the new review cycle was getting under way.
72. "A Guide to EDRC Meetings for Countries Under Review," https://www.oecd.org/site/ecoedrc/43500738.pdf (Accessed 14 December 2016).
73. http://www.oecd.org/site/peerreview/peerpressurearelatedconcept.htm (Accessed 14 December 2016). See also Fabrizio Pagani, *Peer Review: A Tool for Cooperation and Change* (Paris: OECD, 2003).
74. NARA SNF 63, Box 3412 (ECIN 3 OECD), USRO-Paris (Leddy) Cedto A-485, 13 March 1963.

"Positive Adjustments": The Emergence of Supply-Side Economics in the OECD and G7, 1970–1984

Samuel Beroud

This chapter analyzes the evolution of supply-side economics in the OECD during the 1970s and early 1980s. In particular, it focuses on the development of a broad set of recommendations called "positive adjustment policies" (PAP). These supply-side policies were designed to strengthen the role of the market in OECD economies to facilitate the transformation of economic structures shaken by the economic and energy crises of the 1970s. In a nutshell, PAP advised OECD member countries to refrain from interventionist industrial policies and protectionist measures, to tackle "rigidities" in the labor market, and to encourage the re-training of workers. Such structural changes were seen as a prerequisite to facilitate the transfer of capital and manpower from declining industries toward new economic activities.

Historians of the OECD have generally claimed that the organization underwent a major and sudden shift during these years: championing "Keynesian" demand management until the mid-1970s, the OECD supposedly embraced "neo-liberalism" at the end of the decade. Following Robert Keohane, several authors then identified the call for a more

S. Beroud (✉)
University of Geneva, Bd du Pont-d'Arve 40,
Geneva 1211, Switzerland
e-mail: samuel.beroud@unige.ch

M. Leimgruber and M. Schmelzer (eds.), *The OECD and the International Political Economy Since 1948*, DOI 10.1007/978-3-319-60243-1_10

flexible labor market included in the 1977 McCracken report as a turning point for the economic orientation of the organization.[1] The subsequent development of PAP from late 1977 to 1983 is thus perceived as a clear indicator of how the OECD reoriented its work priorities according to a new orthodoxy.[2] As a result, the OECD is often depicted as a forerunner in the international promotion of neo-liberal economic policies. For instance, in a recent volume on the role of the OECD, Martin Ougaard claimed that "much of the intellectual preparatory work of the 'Reagan-Thatcher revolution' had been done by the OECD."[3] Based on the national archives of four major OECD member states (United States, United Kingdom, France, and Germany) and of the OECD itself, this chapter aims to challenge this interpretation through a proper historization of the development of PAP.

By analyzing the motivation of the key actors who shaped PAP, the context of their emergence, as well as their reception by governments and economists, I argue that PAP should not simply be interpreted as a shift from "Keynesianism" to "neo-liberalism." These concepts—which have no clear definition—do not reflect the complex development of economic recommendations in an international organization such as the OECD. Explanations that focus on ideology as a driving force behind OECD's recommendations neglect both the importance of the economic context and the influence of member states, especially the most powerful of them. This is all the more so that international governance underwent serious transformations during the 1970s. The role of the OECD as a central forum for Western economic cooperation was challenged, in particular by the creation of the Group of Seven (G7), the annual meeting of heads of government, foreign, and finance ministers of the US, West Germany, France, the UK, Italy, Japan, and Canada. To remain a relevant forum and to have its recommendation discussed at the highest level, the OECD was forced to take into account the interests of its most powerful members. This chapter therefore examines how OECD ideas were (or were not) supported and influenced by G7 countries.

In the first section I will show that the argument of a clear-cut ideological shift in the late 1970s is clearly undermined by archival evidence. Indeed, the bulk of ideas developed in both the McCracken report and the PAP program had already been floated as early as 1970 by Secretary-General Emile van Lennep. Yet, at that time member countries refused to implement these OECD recommendations. The second and third sections underscore that liberal supply-side measures and demand-management were not mutually exclusive. On the contrary, they were complementary: the PAP program was developed in 1977 and 1978 to complement the "locomotive theory," a Keynesian strategy designed in 1975 by the OECD to boost world economic growth and overcome stagflation. According to this scheme, major Western economies would have to increase their domestic demand while the PAP would reduce their inflationary effects. In other words, the PAP was initially an attempt to make Keynesian macroeconomic management more effective at the international level, not an attempt to replace it. In the fourth section, I argue that the role assigned to the PAP program changed after the second oil shock. As inflation and problems of balance of payments made macroeconomic reflation impossible in the short term, PAP came to be seen as a prerequisite for future growth. However, as countries were hit by a new economic crisis in the early 1980s, member countries proved to be, once again, reluctant to their implementation. In fact, as the fifth and last section will make clear, the recommendations of the PAP program were only accepted in mid-1983, when the world economy began to recover under US leadership.

The 1970 OECD Report on Inflation: A First (and Failed) Attempt to Reorient Economic Priorities

Most authors claim that the OECD underwent a profound transformation following the 1977 McCracken report and the elaboration of the PAP program.[4] Yet, most of the concepts developed in this context had already been discussed as early as 1970 in an OECD report entitled *Inflation: The Present Problem*.[5] During the 1950s and 1960s, as analyzed at lengths by Matthias Schmelzer, the OECD had principally voiced macroeconomic and microeconomic recommendations to boost quantitative economic growth.[6] Even if the Organization had set in 1970 a 65% growth target for the combined GNP of OECD members for the 1970s, quantitative growth as a paradigm was already being challenged by the late 1960s within the OECD when environmental impacts as well as the overall sustainability of economic growth came to be questioned. Another pressing problem was inflation. From under 2% per annum (OECD average) at the beginning of the 1960s, inflation indeed accelerated throughout the decade and reached 5.8% in 1970.[7] The US, which was conducting a costly war in Vietnam as well as ramping up public expenditures domestically, was criticized by European governments for being responsible for the international diffusion of inflation. Yet, the Europeans were not completely innocent. Echoing the French example of the Grenelle agreements in late May 1968, European governments also accepted significant wage increases and expanded welfare state expenditures. When he arrived at the head of the OECD in 1969, Secretary-General van Lennep was worried that inflation could snowball and jeopardize future economic growth. A former chairman of both the European Monetary Committee as well as the most important committees of the OECD—the Economic Policy Committee (EPC) and its Working Party 3—van Lennep was keen on reinforcing international cooperation to manage the Western economy and presented in late 1970 his strategy for a "concerted attack" against inflation.[8]

Van Lennep's report aimed at implementing a reorientation of both macroeconomic and microeconomic policies to re-balance growth and inflation. In van Lennep's words: "Excess demand should be eliminated and governments should be prepared where necessary, to accept a temporary reduction in the rate of activity until there are signs that better price stability has been achieved."[9] According to the report, microeconomic policies had to serve two different goals: first, the organization listed around 20 measures designed to accentuate the fight against inflation. This included price-income policies, the restriction of subsidies to agriculture and industry, and trade liberalization to increase cheap imports from developing countries. It also encompassed proposals to limit the growth of public expenditures by submitting them to careful "cost-benefit" analyses or by limiting the indexation of social benefits to inflation. The final objective was to limit budget increases as well as to avoid tax increases. Second, the OECD encouraged member countries to implement new structural policies to mitigate public discontent caused by the above-mentioned non-accommodating macroeconomic policies. This included state support to modernize industrial facilities, labor force re-training, and mobility support, as well as specific policies for regions severely hit by de-industrialization. These policies were suggested as a way to "help governments to resist political pressure for too early relaxation of restrictive policies," underscoring that "only the effective introduction of policies for internal adjustment of the structure of industry and employment in advanced countries will permit the acceptance of this international development."[10]

The report was in fact largely drafted by a Keynesian economist, Stephen Marris, who would later act as the main promoter of the PAP program within the OECD. Born in 1930 in the UK, Marris had joined the OECD in 1956 after obtaining a PhD in economics at Cambridge and climbed up through the ranks to become Associated Director of the Economics and Statistics Directorate. In 1969–1970, he had started to work on "structural" economic problems during a short stay at the Brookings Institution—an American think tank dominated by Democrats. Marris later became Special Economic Adviser to Secretary-General van Lennep from 1975 to 1983 and emerged as a central figure in OECD economic committees and initiatives. As we will see below, he was a fervent, and at times passionate, promoter of the "locomotive theory" and monitored the work of the McCracken Commission before taking the lead on "positive adjustments." Marris also represented the OECD in fora such as the Group of Ten, the IMF Interim Committee, the Bellagio Group, and the Group of Thirty. An outspoken detractor of "Reaganomics," he resigned in 1983 after clashes with Martin Feldstein, the chairman of Reagan's Council of Economic Advisers (CEA).[11]

By publishing this report in 1970, Secretary-General van Lennep sought to transform the OECD from a rather academic and theoretical body into a forum that would directly influence economic policy-making of its member countries. Yet, the barrage of opposition that met this inflation strategy proved that this aim was overambitious. Trade unions were especially hostile to van Lennep's recommendations. In major OECD countries, media coverage on the early drafts of the report described it as a threat against full-employment.[12] While member countries rhetorically supported the OECD campaign against inflation, they were not ready to actually follow its recommendations. Paul McCracken, the chairman of Nixon's CEA and van Lennep's successor as chairman of the EPC, repeatedly attempted to convince the Secretary-General to delay the discussion and publication of the report. Such a report, McCracken claimed, required careful political consultation to prevent "fresh proposals too hastily arrived" from raising "false hopes" and creating "friction within countries."[13] Despite revisions in late 1970, the recommendations of the report were largely ignored by member countries and inflation continued to climb during the early 1970s.[14]

When van Lennep publicly criticized the conservative British government's lack of progress in abating inflation, he was summoned to London, blamed, and urged to keep a low profile by Prime Minister Edward Heath.[15] The OECD Secretariat drew painful lessons from this episode and came to admit that "the only useful recommendations

[were] those that governments [were] willing to address to themselves, using the international organization as a screen to pressure domestic public opinion."[16] Therefore, the OECD created new bodies to facilitate consultation with officials from the major member countries. For instance, in the early 1970s, it secretly established an EPC "Bureau," which was attended only by officials of countries that would later form the G7. Van Lennep also regularly organized private dinners with the ambassadors and representatives of the major countries to discuss OECD projects.[17] He also consulted as frequently as possible with the heads of government of these countries to ensure that OECD work was globally in line with their expectations.[18]

The McCracken Report: A Compromise Between "Weak" and "Strong" Countries, 1973–1977

The debate on the macroeconomic objectives of OECD member countries was reopened in the summer of 1973 when West Germany adopted an anti-inflationary line. By October, the issue had become even more pressing as the inflationary and deflationary shockwaves of the first oil shock reached the OECD members. The rising cost of energy pushed inflation to unprecedented peacetime levels, while it depressed the global demand for non-energy goods, thus opening the door to the 1974–1975 recession.

OECD member countries were deeply divided on which issue should be primarily dealt with. On the one hand, the so-called "weak" countries, a term that designated the UK, Italy, and most peripheral OECD countries, claimed that the recessionary impact of the oil shock and the resulting rise in unemployment were the main dangers for the capitalist system. As these countries attempted to buffer the impact of the crisis through accommodating macroeconomic policy, they rapidly faced serious payments and budgetary deficits as well as a spectacular surge of inflation. To redress their balance of payments and indirectly boost their economies, they pressed the so-called "strong" countries to reflate their economy.[19] This second group, which designated West Germany, the US, and Japan, as well as smaller countries such as the Netherlands and Switzerland, championed another strategy. Claiming that the crisis had mainly structural causes on which macroeconomic tools would have a limited impact, this bloc pressed other OECD members to adopt austerity measures to redress their balance of payments. In their view, Western governments had to fight inflation, which was hindering investment, and to implement structural measures to "revitalize the private sector."[20]

As the recession worsened in late 1974, the fear that the world economy could experience a depression grew, especially in Europe. To discuss and prevent such a scenario, a multilateral meeting of the heads of state of the most powerful capitalist countries was organized in November 1975 in Rambouillet near Paris. Initially conceived as a one-shot event, this meeting was repeated the following years and actually developed into the "Summit" of the Group of Seven, a cornerstone of international economic governance.[21] At Rambouillet, one of the major objectives of the European leaders was to secure significant measures from President Gerald Ford to boost the US economy and, indirectly, the world economy. To reduce the pressure on the US and reassure European leaders, Secretary of State Henry Kissinger suggested that the OECD should elaborate a recovery strategy that would lead to "non-inflationary growth."[22] This proposal was taken up and in 1975 the OECD convened a group of international economists led by Paul McCracken with the mandate to find a way to reflate OECD economies and boost investment and employment without fueling inflation.

The McCracken report is frequently depicted in the literature as a main step toward neo-liberalism within the OECD.[23] This overestimates not only the influence of a single report on an international organization but also exaggerates the novelty of its suggestions. As Vincent Gayon's detailed study of the making of this report has underscored, economists from various countries with very different ideological backgrounds wrote the report.[24] The final text was rather a compromise between the positions expressed since 1974 by the weak and the strong countries than a groundbreaking document. The report was in fact more influenced by the political context than by ideological consideration. After the election of Jimmy Carter in November 1976, the US made a u-turn in the domain of economic policy and championed an international economic reflation. The Carter Administration could therefore not accept the anti-inflation orientation of the report previously suggested by the Ford administration. Marris revised the draft in early 1977 to prevent a rejection by the US. Finally delivered in spring 1977, the McCracken report reflected the compromise found at the G7 summit of London in May 1977 between the US and the UK on the one hand, which supported international reflation, and West Germany on the other, which insisted on the dangers of inflation and promoted structural measures. Therefore, member countries did not find the report innovative, even less revolutionary, and it was barely discussed at the OECD ministerial meeting in June 1977.[25]

Regarding macroeconomics, the McCracken report recommended following medium-term objectives rather than short-term fine tuning. It was however not a departure from Keynesian-inspired macroeconomic demand management. The report briefly repeated the strategy developed by the OECD Secretariat in 1975, nicknamed the "locomotive theory."[26] In a nutshell, the OECD stated that strong countries—the "locomotives"—should stimulate their domestic demand to boost the world economy and pull other countries out of the recession, while weak countries should implement tougher anti-inflationary policies to contribute to international price stability. The OECD, however, believed that the stronger countries should act first in order to give some breathing space to the weaker countries. This should help trace a "narrow path" toward international non-inflationary growth.

Most of the McCracken report, however, was devoted to microeconomic issues. More assertively than in the 1970 report on inflation, it called for "a freer play of market forces" and claimed that "to eliminate restriction and rigidity and promote competition and mobility would improve the efficiency of macro-economic policy instruments and make a significant contribution to better price and growth performance."[27] Member countries were encouraged to give priority to competition, claiming that "governments should do all they can to expose the private sector—and, to the extent possible, the public sector—to effective domestic and international competition."[28] Such measures were meant to "facilitate sectoral adjustment in the industrialized countries."[29] Governmental support to certain industries and employment was not excluded as long as it was "confined to circumstances where the pursuit of non-accommodating policies to wind down inflationary expectations leads to a temporarily high rate of unemployment."[30] The report was more explicit regarding the labor market, claiming that the "rigidities" and costs related to the welfare regulations were one of the causes of growing unemployment despite economic recovery.[31]

"Positive Adjustments" and "Concerted Action," 1978–1979

On the basis of the compromise between growth and inflation accepted by the G7 in London, the OECD Secretariat started to develop a new economic strategy entitled "Concerted Action." The locomotive theory was transformed into a more comprehensive approach: surplus countries such as Germany and Japan had to give the initial impulse, but should then be supported by countries in an intermediate economic situation such as France and Canada. The OECD also underscored that weak countries had to adopt urgently more stringent anti-inflationary policies. At the same time, the OECD worked more intensively on accompanying structural policies: the Positive Adjustment Policies (PAP). Coined by OECD economist Stephen Marris, this term aimed at distinguishing policies that would facilitate the adaptation of economic structures through market forces. It was used in contrast to "negative" adjustment measures, a term that embraced most forms of state interventions aiming at preserving existing economic structures such as subsidies or trade restrictions. The progressive implementation of PAP was seen as a necessary complement to the macroeconomic strategy of reflation. PAP had to facilitate private investment and keep under control the inflationary pressure that would result from macroeconomic stimulation by reducing bottlenecks and "rigidities" of domestic economies.[32] In other words, the PAP program was adopted to complement a macroeconomic strategy inspired by Keynesian principles.

It was nevertheless a momentous change. Until this date, the OECD Secretariat had largely focused on macroeconomic strategies to solve the crisis. Protectionist pressures and "structural rigidities" had been considered as the consequences of deficient growth, which could be reversed when economic recovery would be under way. By 1977, the Secretariat had changed its view. Now it argued that even if growth remained low, governments had to actively counterbalance microeconomic rigidities and defeat protectionist trends that the OECD monitored with the greatest concern. Van Lennep expressed to Carter his fear that European societies were becoming "impatient" leading to increasing "demands for faster, more nationalistic, and non-market oriented solutions."[33] The measures adopted so far to prevent protectionism were indeed increasingly undermined. In the spring of 1974, OECD member countries had adopted a Trade Declaration by which they pledged not to use protectionist tools to preserve domestic employment and restore their balance of payments at the expense of their partners. But none had followed the pledge. Besides slow growth, increasing competition from East Asian and Latin American countries was leading to increasing protectionism in Western economies. Japan was also considered by the US and European governments as a source of their industrial problems because of its aggressive export policy and its reluctance to import industrial goods. New forms of trade restrictions to protect domestic markets, such as "voluntary export restraints" and "floor prices," had indeed flourished since the oil shock. Even the US, which usually acted as a vigilant warden of free trade, attempted in 1976 to use the OECD to negotiate an "orderly marketing arrangement" on specialty steel with its partners.[34] Besides trade measures, various microeconomic policies were also used by Western countries to protect and support domestic production.[35] In spring 1977, French President Giscard d'Estaing and Prime Minister Raymond Barre floated the idea of "organized liberalism," a project aimed at restraining industrial competition between industrialized countries and at controlling trade flows with developing countries.[36] By openly questioning free trade, Giscard aimed at slowing down the pace of industrial transformation so as to make it socially and politically more acceptable.[37] The development of PAP must be understood in this context as counter-fire against such protectionism and a reaffirmation of the primacy of the market as the driving economic force for the OECD community. Unsurprisingly, this strategy was supported by the most competitive OECD countries, especially the German and Swiss delegations.[38]

In January 1978, Stephen Marris presented his first thoughts on structural policies to the OECD Executive Committee. He acknowledged that governmental interventions in the economy during the oil shock and the following recession were acceptable. However, because OECD economies had been recovering since late 1975, such interventions had lost their legitimacy. Marris stated that such policies were now "making economies both less productive and more inflation-prone" and increased "the difficulty of getting back onto the path of non-inflationary growth."[39] It was now time to curb this trend and let market forces drive the economic adjustment.

Most major member countries reacted positively to Marris' analysis. Despite some reservations from the its own Department of Labor, the US administration, and in particular the Treasury and the CEA, proved to be the most active supporters of the PAP concept.[40] Facing a growing inflation resulting from its reflationary program of early 1977, the Carter administration was looking for microeconomic measures to combat it. The Carter administration also welcomed OECD efforts that would grant it international legitimacy to resist growing domestic protectionist pressures. Moreover, it was keen to conclude the Tokyo Round of trade negotiations as soon as possible, to reinforce GATT regulations to protect free trade, and it sought to establish a GATT-type agreement on international investments. Furthermore, the US was also preoccupied by interventionist industrial policies such as the Davignon

Plan for European steel, which contradicted these objectives. The work within the OECD had to be the first step for "better international rules or guidelines or to at least exchange views as to what is or is not legitimate in terms of adjustment measures" that could be adopted at the following G7 summit.[41] The German and the Japanese governments also endorsed the concept of "positive adjustment." Whereas their weaker partners and the US were still urging them to reflate according to the locomotive theory, OECD work on PAP gave them the legitimacy to reply that "without a focus on industrial adjustment, the level and structure of production w[ould] be unable to respond to demand."[42] The Germans sought to achieve a trade-off with their major European partners: Germany would reflate its economy, but France and the UK would have to take a more liberal position on trade negotiations at the GATT and to cooperate on PAP. The British remained careful about the PAP. Chancellor of the Exchequer Denis Healey underscored that it was "quite unrealistic to expect any democratically-elected Government to apply this policy in its full rigour."[43] The British could, however, not block the project since it was a condition for additional German reflation measures that they were keen to secure. The French government also finally accepted a "painful discussion" on their trade and structural policies, since this could bring concessions in other fields (such as growth or energy).[44] They refused, however, to subscribe to any project that went beyond a discussion and vetoed the mechanism that the OECD Secretariat proposed to monitor the future implementation of PAP. With the support of key countries, the OECD Council at ministerial level adopted the "concerted action" agenda in June 1978.

Seeking to provide a strong international legitimacy to the PAP, the US endeavored to integrate them to the agenda of the upcoming G7 Summit that had to take place in Bonn in July 1978. The key actor in the transfer of the PAP to the Summit agenda was Charles Schultze, the Chairman of Jimmy Carter's CEA. Schultze, who also chaired the EPC, used the EPC Bureau to transfer elements pertaining to positive adjustments from the OECD to the G7. Like Stephen Marris, Schultze was a resolute Keynesian. Born in 1924, he had graduated from Georgetown University in 1950. After having temporarily worked at the CEA under Truman and Eisenhower, he completed in 1960 his doctorate in economics at the University of Maryland. While working at this University, he was also a senior fellow at the Brookings Institution until his nomination at the head of the CEA in 1977. As a close adviser to the president, Schultze was a major promoter of the "locomotive theory" and "concerted action."[45] Schulze's efforts, supported by the Germans and Japanese, materialized in the final Declaration of the Bonn Summit.[46] The PAP was officially included as a minor component of a broad trade-off between the heads of state that included commitments for domestic reflation, control over inflation, trade liberalization, and energy saving. Such a global package, it was argued, was to overcome the economic malaise in Western countries.

Bolstered by the declarations of the Ministerial Meeting and the G7 Summit, the OECD continued preliminary research on PAP despite French hostility.[47] Encouraged by the reflationary measures taken by its partners after the Bonn Summit, the British government took a more positive stance on PAP. In November 1978, the Treasury noted that "Economic growth and PAP are indivisible. UK's macro-economic policy this year has produced maximum economic growth compatible with objectives for inflation."[48] Interestingly, both business and trade unions' representatives commented positively on PAP work.[49] Initially, Marris sought to establish a "microeconomic committee," but finally set up and chaired a less ambitious "ad hoc" group attended by senior officials.[50] Between October 1978 and March 1979 this group coordinated PAP-related work undertaken by major OECD committees (such as the Industry Committee, the Manpower and Social Affairs Committee, the Committee for Scientific and Technological Policy, the Trade Committee, and the Agriculture Committee). These were tasked with evaluating how domestic policies countries could evolve to reduce economic rigidities. This horizontal work allowed the sharing of information between macroeconomists and civil servants in charge of sectoral policies to "help to create the right climate for positive adjustment both domestically and internationally."[51] This was at least Stephen Marris' objective, who perceived the work on PAP as an "educative process" for national bureaucracies and governments.[52]

The Limited Impact of Positive Adjustment Policies, 1979–1983

The role of PAP changed when OECD economies were hit by the second oil shock. From a supplementary role, where they had to support macroeconomic strategies, structural policies emerged as an autonomous topic. Furthermore, the goal itself of PAP changed. While initially designed to combat inflation in the 1970s, in the early 1980s PAP was promoted as a source of new economic growth. Most countries had reflated their economies according to the package adopted at the G7 Bonn Summit. Additional reflation was impossible in the medium term, as inflation reached 9.2% during the first semester of 1979, 12.3% during the second semester, and peaked at 14.4% in the first semester of 1980.[53] The G7 macroeconomic experts led by Charles Schultze acknowledged in spring 1979 that "the available tools of macroeconomic policy cannot avoid the immediate inflationary and growth-reducing consequences of large and sudden increase in oil prices."[54] Alongside energy-saving policies, microeconomic measures were now perceived as the best way to cope with this new economic and energy crisis. The OECD went even further and stated in its 1979 Economic Outlook that many countries had to "relieve structural constraints before they can move back on to better growth paths and regain high employment."[55]

Positive adjustments came to be seen as a prerequisite for further economic growth. Yet, G7 leaders also knew that the second oil shock brought new economic challenges and that implementing PAP would prove unpopular. As a consequence, while they supported discussion and theoretical work on PAP within the OECD, they simultaneously prevented the creation of implementation mechanisms such as monitoring tools or guidelines.

In early June 1979, the OECD Ministerial Meeting adopted an official program of work on PAP and mandated a working group on positive adjustments to

> keep under review the macro-economic consequences, in particular as regard to employment, productivity, growth and inflation, of measure promoting or hindering necessary structural adjustments in the fields, inter alia, of manpower, social, industrial, scientific, environmental, agricultural, regional, trade and international investment policies.[56]

This Special Group of the EPC replaced the ad hoc group led by Marris. Germany and to a lesser extent the US remained the main supporters of OECD efforts. Although France had abandoned the project of "organized liberalism" and endeavored to liberalize its domestic economy, it remained its main opponent.[57] The French feared in particular that the Americans could use the discussion on PAP to attack the European agricultural policy as well as European attempts to establish state-supported high technology industries at the national and continental level. When it became clear that the creation of the working group could not be stopped, France presented four candidates to chair it. However, other countries understood this sudden interest as an attempt to hinder the working group from within and elected the German candidate, Hans Tietmeyer, as its chair.[58] Born in 1931, Tietmeyer studied economics in the 1950s and received his doctorate from the University of Cologne after a dissertation on Ordoliberalism. In 1962, he joined the Ministry of Economics, where he became Director of the Economic Policy Department in 1973 and led the German Delegation to the OECD's EPC until 1982. Tietmeyer was not a Keynesian but a promoter of "Social Market Economy" with strong ordoliberal credentials.[59] At the EPC, he constantly underscored the structural origins of the 1974–1975 recession—notably the decline in profits of Western companies and the lack of investments—and that the oil price-hike had only worsened an already dire situation. He repeatedly criticized strategies based on expansionary demand management to overcome stagflation, especially the "locomotive theory." He occasionally had heated arguments with Marris and Schultze on macroeconomic issues until early 1978. But the development of the comprehensive "concerted action" brought their positions closer, and all three valued the PAP program as a useful development.

From November 1979 to April 1982 the Special Group of the EPC held nine meetings. The discussions were organized to involve most of the key OECD committees and virtually no activity of the OECD remained unaffected. Although this was not part of the specifications accepted by the Ministerial Council, the US delegation suggested in addition that the working group should peer review the domestic adjustment policies of member countries. This was precisely what the French feared most. The working group accepted this idea on a "voluntary" basis, but this constituted an obvious moral pressure. As a result, the French delegation asked to be among the first countries to be reviewed with the hope that the examination criteria would not be well defined.[60] The peer review was certainly the best way to spread the PAP concept among national administrations: Each country that took part in the peer-review had to submit a report on its adjustment policies in all fields covered by the Special Group, requiring the support of many ministries and national agencies.

In 1982, the final report of the Special Group on PAP was presented to the OECD Ministerial Council, accompanied by several thematic reports. The main report unsurprisingly claimed that market forces had to be the leading force for economic adjustment. The OECD stated that the market economy was "the best mechanism to marshal responses to social, economic and technological change." The report recognized the existence of "market failures." In these cases, the governments had to "remove the cause for failure and enhance the functioning of the competitive system." Contrary to what was claimed as late as 1975, these market failures provided no legitimacy to interventionist structural policies. Industrial policies had to be "temporary" and "integrally linked to action to phase out obsolete capacity and to re-establish financially viable enterprises." In a similar way, regional policies could include "general measures to develop viable industries, through providing infrastructure and fiscal incentives," but should avoid "bailing out enterprises in financial difficulty." More generally the organization recognized the cushioning effect of social and structural policies but finally underscored:

> There is little point in government pursuing non-accommodating demand management to reduce inflation if they at the same time increasingly engage in microeconomic policies that maintain the status quo, i.e. if they undermine the market forces on which the macro-economic policy makers rely to restore the conditions for non-inflationary growth. This may indeed have been one important reason why non-accommodating macro policies have been so slow in achieving their desired results during the latter part of the 1970s.[61]

In little more than a decade, the OECD prescriptions over structural policies had changed dramatically. From a tool that states were encouraged to use to increase economic growth, provide social stability, and cope with the limits of the markets, structural policies now had to be limited to market-friendly measures that facilitate the microeconomic "adjustment," and state interventions were now officially blamed for the poor performance of the capitalist system during the crisis-ridden 1970s. The philosophy of PAP differed, however, clearly from the supply-side policy of Reagan. Indeed, the OECD did not endorse—and in fact criticized—the massive tax cuts that US supply-siders favored.

While the PAP philosophy was broadly diffused within the OECD, its influence on member countries was much less evident. The discussion on PAP within the OECD provided a "de facto policy coordination and cooperation," but no formal mechanism was established to ensure its implementation at the domestic level.[62] The result was far from the "international rules" or practical "guidelines" that the US and the Secretariat initially intended to develop in 1977–1978. However, it was not the French opposition that scaled down the ambition of the PAP agenda. Rather, even governments that had initially supported the development of PAP now sought to preserve their national sovereignty and to keep the pace of economic adjustment under control. The G7 leaders feared that the painful economic situation caused by the second oil shock would impact the political situation and threaten their re-election. Even the Central Intelligence Agency (CIA) was concerned by this question. Assessing the political situation before the G7 Summit in June 1979, the CIA commented that "all governments are determined to retain national control of the positive adjustment process, in part because of the economic, political and social uncertainties surrounding it." The PAP represented a challenge to "the core of national sovereignty, of a government's rights and responsibilities vis-à-vis its citizens."[63] The prospect of a binding OECD mechanism was politically unacceptable. In 1980, Stephen Marris suggested to the EPC Bureau that the G7 Summit to be held in Venice could publicly support the OECD work. He wanted to insert a sentence in the final Declaration that would "make PAP better internationally known as an accepted guideline of the industrial countries."[64] While the representatives of the G7 countries accepted briefing the leaders on PAP discussions, they rejected any reference to PAP as such.[65] Instead, the declaration vaguely acknowledged the need for adjustments in some industrial sectors even if it was "economically and politically difficult in the short term."[66]

From 1980 to 1982, the significance of PAP in G7 debates declined despite the election of Margaret Thatcher and Ronald Reagan, who were sympathetic to this reform agenda. Both the UK and US governments focused primarily on domestic economic issues during the first years in office and their involvement in multilateral discussions was limited. In London, it was agreed to give "some encouragement" to OECD efforts.[67] The US was also positive but its support remained elusive. As late as mid-1982, the US had no clear and comprehensive strategy regarding foreign economic policy.[68] The Administration was absorbed with budget deficit issues and domestic economic reforms. At the same time, France took an even more hostile stance on PAP. With the election of Socialist President François Mitterrand in May 1981, France implemented and championed a diametrically opposed economic policy in which nationalization and state intervention played a key role. In 1981 and 1982, as a severe economic recession was underway, PAP totally disappeared from the G7 agenda. Political leaders remained seriously divided on the cause and the remedies to the crisis. European leaders attacked the unprecedented US interest rates resulting from the monetarist policy of the Federal Reserve as the main problem. Mitterrand promoted a reform of the international monetary system and a revival of the "locomotive theory" to stabilize the world economy. Reagan was unmoved by the criticism of his counterparts. He repeatedly discarded macroeconomic and monetary cooperation claiming that countries should instead "put their houses in order." This non-cooperative stance led to a deterioration of the relation between the US and the OECD Secretariat and diminished the role of the EPC Bureau in the preparatory work of the G7 Summit from 1981 onward. Tensions emerged between key US representatives to the OECD such as economist Martin Feinstein and Stephen Marris, who repeatedly questioned the monetarist approach of the new US administration. Even if the US supported the OECD effort on PAP, it did not perceive the organization as an ally and primarily retained the chairmanship of EPC to prevent OECD criticism of the US macroeconomic policy.[69]

Interestingly, while G7 leaders kept a defensive stance vis-à-vis PAP regarding their own countries, they strongly supported the development of specific international credits designed to accelerate the implementation of structural policies in less developed countries. In September 1979, the World Bank was asked to review its procedure for lending and in May 1980 its Executive Board adopted the creation of a structural adjustment lending program.[70] The IMF was about to follow the same evolution with more stringent conditionality in the early 1980s and the development of credits for structural adjustment in 1985.[71]

Epilogue: The Breakthrough of 1983–1984

Neglected in 1981 and 1982, the question of structural adjustment in Western countries reappeared in the discussions of the 1983 G7 Summit in Williamsburg (US) and became a topic discussed at every summit until 1990.[72] This reappearance and consolidation of the concept can be explained by a conjunction of economic and political factors. After two successive recessions, the US economy started to grow again in late 1982. European leaders remained suspicious about the sustainability of the recovery but softened their criticism of US economic policy and proved more willing to discuss microeconomic issues. The Reagan administration also gained confidence and took a more proactive role in OECD and G7 debates. In the UK, Thatcher was reelected in June 1983 with a clear majority that allowed her to deepen the economic reforms. The US and the UK hosted two consecutive G7 Summits in 1983 and in 1984, which gave them ample opportunity to put structural adjustment on the agenda. At the same time, French opposition weakened. After the Socialist defeat at the local election of March 1983, Mitterrand profoundly reoriented French economic policy toward "rigueur" to combat inflation, balance-of-payments problems, and depreciation of the French Franc. The French socialist approach was no more a credible alternative in international debates.

At the Williamsburg summit in 1983, G7 leaders claimed that they would "promote continued structural adjustment" of their economies. However, the declaration remained vague. The breakthrough came in 1984. The Reagan Administration set as a major objective of its foreign economic policy to get other industrial countries to publicly recognize that interventionist economic policies were a threat to growth and employment over the medium-term.[73] In February 1984, a Ministerial conference entitled "Flexibility and efficiency in the private sector" was held at the OECD. It was a major victory for the US, since "all participants acknowledged the desirability of structural change and saw it as a necessary, even critical precondition for economic growth with expansion of investment and employment."[74] Divisions between member countries were limited to the pace of this change. The US, Germany, the UK, the Netherlands, and Switzerland argued for rapid economic deregulation, while other countries advocated that such measures had to be implemented gradually with the general improvement of economic environment and "education" of public opinion.[75]

This conference paved the way to the adoption of a declaration at the following G7 Summit held in June 1984 in London, which not only recommended tight monetary and macroeconomic policies and budget discipline, but also the liberalization of trade and services as well as the liberalization of capital and labor markets. The idea of macroeconomic cooperation among countries had completely disappeared. The free market was seen as the unique possible source of growth. The G7 designated the OECD as the main body to monitor the evolution of Western economies according to this philosophy.[76] New officials and economists were progressively nominated at key OECD positions and entrusted with this task. Most emblematic were the departure of Stephen Marris and the nomination of David Henderson, a British supply-sider, as chief economist of the OECD in 1984.

Conclusion

When Emile van Lennep left the OECD in September 1984 after three terms as OECD Secretary-General, Ronald Reagan personally thanked him for his efforts to promote the ideas of structural adjustments and his "vigorous and unflagging support for the free-market."[77] By then, the conception of the US administration and the OECD regarding structural policies appeared very similar. This chapter shows, however, that the OECD concept and goal of structural policies underwent complex iterations before taking its final neo-liberal form. Until 1979, the OECD focused primarily on macroeconomic policies to ensure growth and control inflation. Microeconomic measures were designed to complement macroeconomic policies. In the short-lived anti-inflation strategy of 1970, these measures had both to combat inflation and cushion the impact of less expansionary macroeconomic policies. After the first oil shock, they were promoted to prevent inflation that could emerge from the coordinated reflation following the locomotive theory. The mix of moderately expansionary macroeconomic policies and structural reforms was supposed to ensure the non-inflationary growth described by the 1977 McCracken report. With the second oil shock of 1979–1980, microeconomic measures emerged as an autonomous solution that could contribute both to combat inflation and preserve economic growth in this crisis context. This situation proved lasting with the election of Reagan. As the new US administration completely rejected international macroeconomic cooperation to boost the world economy, structural adjustment took on a new role. Microeconomic liberalization measures were now promoted as a source of non-inflationary economic growth, while monetary and macroeconomic policies were to combat inflation. This set of policies, fully accepted by G7 countries in 1984, can be interpreted as the "neo-liberal" approach to economic policy.

With a medium-term perspective on the microeconomic recommendations of the OECD, this article demonstrates that the idea of a clear-cut "neo-liberal" revolution within the organization must be discarded. While it is very tempting to find early signs of an ideological transformation in the McCracken report, this article shows that many ideas of this report had already been floated as early as 1970. Furthermore, it appears that the solution of the McCracken report has very little in common with the G7 strategy of 1984. The neo-liberal era of the OECD started after the retirement of both Stephen Marris in 1983 and Emile van Lennep in 1984, the years when Thatcher and Reagan were reelected.

Notes

1. Robert O. Keohane, Economics, Inflation, and the Role of the State: Political Implications of the McCracken Report Toward Full Employment and Price Stability. *World Politics* 31, no. 1 (1978).
2. Scott Sullivan, *From War to Wealth: Fifty Years of Innovation* (Paris: OECD, 1997), 55; Matthias Schmelzer, *The Hegemony of Growth. The OECD and the Making of the Economic Growth Paradigm*, (Cambridge: Cambridge University Press, 2016), 324–326.
3. Morten Ougaard, "The OECD's Global Role: Agenda-Setting and Policy Diffusion", in *Mechanism of OECD Governance. International Incentives for National Policy-Making*, ed. Kerstin Martens and Anja P. Jakobi (Oxford: Oxford University Press, 2010), 34.
4. Rianne Mahon and Stephen McBride, eds., *The OECD and Transnational Governance* (Vancouver: University of British Columbia Press, 2008), 15–16; Peter Carroll and Aynsley Kellow, *The OECD. A Study of Organisational Adaptation* (Cheltenham: Edward Elgar, 2011), 69; Matthieu Leimgruber, "The Embattled Standard-Bearer of Social Insurance and its Challenger: The ILO, the OECD, and the 'Crisis of the Welfare State', 1975–1985", In *Globalizing Social Rights: The ILO and Beyond*, ed. Sandrine Kott and Joelle Droux (Basingstoke: Palgrave, 2013), 300; Schmelzer, *The Hegemony of Growth*, 322–324.
5. OECD, *Inflation: The Present Problem. Report by the Secretary General* (Paris: OECD, 1970).
6. Schmelzer, *The Hegemony of Growth*, 163–238.
7. OECD, *Economic Outlook*, December 1971, 32.
8. On WP-3 and van Lennep's role, see the chapter by Kazuhiko Yago in this volume.
9. OECD, *Inflation*, 10.
10. Idem., 54.

11. Alfred William Coats, *Economists in International Agencies: An Exploratory Study* (New York: Praeger, 1986); Vincent Gayon, "L'OCDE au Travail. Contribution à une Sociologie Historique de la "Coopération Économique Internationale" sur le Chômage et l'Emploi (1970–2010)", (PhD Thesis, Paris-Dauphine, 2010), 144–147; Stephen Marris, *My history of my time at the OECD. Record of two seminars given by Stephen Marris to the OECD Secretariat on 24th and 30th June, 1983* (typescript). We would like to thank Dr. Judith Clifton, University of Cantabria, for sharing this document with our research group.
12. Emile Van Lennep, *Working for the World Economy. A Personnal History by Emile Van Lennep. Former Secretary-General of the OECD* (Amsterdam: Nederlands Instituut voor het Bank- en Effectenbedrijf, 1998), 244. See for instance, "O.E.C.D. States View: Nations Grapple with Inflation", *New York Times*, 21 November 1970; "L'O.C.D.E. semble mettre en cause la nécessité du plein emploi", *Le Monde*, 16 October 1970; "Inflation/ OECD report. Völlig hilflos", *Der Spiegel*, 30 November 1970.
13. Richard Nixon Presidential Library, White House Central Files: Paul McCracken Files, Box 3, EPC Files 1969–1970, Letter from Paul McCracken to Emile Van Lennep, 24 July 1970.
14. Van Lennep, *Working for the World Economy*, 244.
15. British National Archives (hereafter TNA), PREM15/63, "The Prime Minister's Meeting with Mr Van Lennep. OECD criticism of UK anti-inflationary policies" [no date]; and "Record of the Prime Minister's Meeting with Mr. Van Lennep, Secretary General of the OECD, at 3.30 pm on Wednesday, 11 November 1970".
16. Historical Archives of the OECD (hereafter OECD-HA), Folder 216061, Gérard Eldin" Le renforcement de la coordination des politiques économiques au sein de l'OCDE (Eléments de réflexion sur les propositions belges)", 25 September 1970.
17. Cf. for instance US National Archives (hereafter NARA), Access to Archival Databases (AAD) Electronic Telegrams, 1973–1979, 1974OECDP08574, D740079-0507, OECD Paris [Brown] to State, "Informal Preparations for OECD XCSS Meeting April 23–24", 8 April 1974.
18. Van Lennep, *Working for the World Economy*, 204–212.
19. Archives of the Banque de France (hereafter ABF), Box 1489200206/40, Folder Comité de politique économique, séance: compte-rendu, document de travail, note de la DGE, rapport, communiqué de presse. 1974–1979, Memoradum "CPE 38e séance—16–17 juin 1975. O.C.D.E. Comité de politique économique. 25 juin 1975".
20. Foreign Relations of the United States (hereafter FRUS), 1969–1976, Vol. XXXI Foreign Economic Policy, 1973–1976, doc. 116 "Memorandum

of Conversation: International Economic Summit", 11 November 1975 and doc. 122. "Memorandum of Conversation: Economic Summit", 15 November 1975.

21. On the G7 see Emmanuel Mourlon-Druol and Federico Romero, eds., *International Summitry and Global Governance: The Rise of the G7 and the European Council, 1974–1991* (London: Routledge, 2014); Enrico Böhm, *Die Sicherheit des Westens: Entstehung und Funktion der G7-Gipfel (1975–1981)* (München: Oldenbourg Verlag, 2014); Robert D. Putnam and Nicholas Bayne, *Hanging Together. Cooperation and Conflicts in the Seven-Power Summits*, revised and enlarged edition ed. (London: Sage, 1987).
22. NARA, RG 56, Records relating to the Organization for Economic Cooperation and Development (OECD) 1962–1984, Box 8, Folder OECD Ministerial Meeting (16), "Speech by the Honorable Henry A. Kissinger, Secretary of State before the OECD Ministerial Council. Paris, France, May 28 [1975]".
23. Rianne Mahon and Stephen McBride, eds., *The OECD and Transnational Governance* (Vancouver: University of British Columbia Press, 2008), 15–16; Peter Carroll and Aynsley Kellow, *The OECD. A Study of Organisational Adaptation* (Cheltenham: Edward Elgar, 2011), 69; Leimgruber, "Embattled Standard-Bearer, 300; Schmelzer, *The Hegemony of Growth*, 322–324.
24. On the making of the report, see Gayon, *L'OCDE au Travail*, 127–271.
25. OECD-HA, C/M(77)15, Minutes of the 447th Meeting held at the Château de la Muette, Paris, 23 and 24 June 1977.
26. Rarely used in official documents, this phrase was commonly used in international meetings and in the media. It originated from an EPC discussion in early 1975 during which the Belgian delegation questioned Germany's ability to be the economic "locomotive" of Europe. See ABF, Box 1489200206/40, Folder Comité de politique économique, séance: compte-rendu, document de travail, note de la DGE, rapport, communiqué de presse. 1974–1979, Memoradum "CPE—37e séance 6–7 mars 1975. Comité de Politique Economique. Réunion des 6/7mars 1975. Notes de séance".
27. Paul McCracken et al., *Toward Full Employment and Price Stability* (Paris: OECD, 1977), 28.
28. Ibid., 227.
29. Ibid., 29.
30. Ibid., 205.
31. Ibid., 28.
32. OECD, "Meeting of the Council at Ministerial Level in June 1978, Communiqué", accessed 13 November 2016, http://www.g8.utoronto.ca/OECD/OECD78.htm.

33. NARA AAD, telegram 1977PARIS37917, D780003-0243 from Paris USOECD [Katz] to State, "OECD/XCSS: discussion paper on trade and structural problem (CE/78/1)", 30 December 1977.
34. OECD-HA, C/M(76)5 (Prov), Minutes of the 413th meeting held at the Château de la Muette, Paris, on Wednesday 17 March 1976. See also David John Blair, *Trade Negotiations in the OECD: Structures, Institutions, and States* (London: Kegan Paul International, 1993), 172.
35. Gary Banks and Jan Tumlir, *Economic Policy and the Adjustment Problem*, Thames Essay (London; Brookfield, Vt.: Gower, 1986).
36. French Foreign Affairs Ministry's Archives (hereafter AMAE), 446INVA/1534, Sommet de Londres (7–8 mai 1977), Dossier de Monsieur Henri Froment-Meurice. II—Problèmes du commerce international. Note "Opportunité et contenu possible d'un engagement sur la liberté des échanges" [undated, c.a. spring 1977]. On OECD and steel, see also the chapter by Wolfram Kaiser in this volume.
37. On this concept see Georges Laverdines, "Le libéralisme organisé ou le combat de Jacob", *Pouvoirs, revue française d'études constitutionnelles et politiques*, vol. 9, 1979, 17–26.
38. NARA AAD, telegram 1977PARIS26263, D770327-0385, from Paris USOECD to State: "XCSS 'Bureau' Meeting September 8", 9 September 1977.
39. OECD-HA, CE/M(78)1 Prov. "Executive Committee. Minutes of the 22nd Special Session held at the Château de la Muette, Paris, on Friday, January 13 1978 at 10 a.m. and 3.15 p.m."
40. Jimmy Carter Presidential Library (hereafter JCPL), National Security Affairs, Brzezinski Material 4, Box 13, "Summit Briefing Paper. Economic Policy", 3 July 1978. On these internal disagreements, see JCPL, CEA, Charles L. Schultze Subject Files, Box 50, Folder Meeting of EPC Paris, 5/28/78 [1], Memorandum from Howard D. Samuel for Charles L. Schultze "OECD Ministerial Discussions: The Need for Positive Adjustment Policies", 24 May 1978.
41. JCPL, National Security Advisors, Special Project Files 19, Box 24, Folder 12, Robert Hormats to Cooper "Briefing Memorandum: Summit Thoughts", 28 November 1977.
42. JCPL, National Security Advisors, Special Project Files 19, Box 25, Folder 3, CEA Staff, Draft "Summit Briefing Paper. Positive Adjustment", 23 June 1978.
43. TNA, T385/176, OECD Ministerial Meeting 14–15 June, C(78)94 Final: Concerted Action.
44. French National Archives (ANF), 5 AG 3/893, Conseillers diplomatiques. Conférence économique de Bonn (16–17 juillet 1978), Folder Sommet Economique à Bonn 16/17 juillet 1978, Notes-Messages

concernant la préparation de la rencontre. Bilan: télégramme circulaire du Quai d'Orsay, J.P. Dutet "Sommet économique de Bonn", 2 June 1978.
45. JCPL, Finding Aid "Council of Economic Advisers", 83.
46. See "Declaration", accessed 13 November 2016, http://www.g8.utoronto.ca/summit/1978bonn/communique.html.
47. TNA, FCO59/1536. P.V. Dixon, "OECD—Ad hoc meeting on Positive Adjustment policies 14 and 15 November 1978", 20 November 1978.
48. TNA, T390/671. Letter from R.A.B. Parsons to Dixon, "OECD—Positive Adjustment Policies. Ad hoc group meeting. November 14/15", 10 November 1978.
49. TNA, FCO59/1536. Letter from R. H. Baker to P. V. Dixon "Positive Adjustment", 16 October 1978.
50. TNA, T364/159, Note for the record "Visit from Mr. Marris", by N. R. Sallnow-Smith, 12 January 1979.
51. TNA, FCO59/1642, Letter from P. V. Dixon to D. Gore-Booth "Positive Adjustment", 11 June 1979.
52. TNA, T364/159. Note for the record "Visit from M. Marris", by N. R. Sallnow-Smith, 12 January 1979.
53. OECD, *Economic Outlook*, July 1981, Table H11, Consumer Prices (annual rates).
54. ANF, 5 AG 3/895, Charles Schultze, "Memorandum for the Summit Preparatory Group. Oil Prices and Economic Policy", 15 June 1979.
55. OECD, *Economic Outlook*, July 1979, 12.
56. OECD-HA, C(79)93 Final "Council. Resolution of the Council establishing a Special Programme of Work for the Organisation on Positive Adjustment Polices. (Adopted by the Council at its 494th Meeting on 7th June, 1979)." For the quote, see OECD-HA, CPE/PAP(79)1, "Draft programme of work for the new special group on positive adjustment policies", 7 November 1979.
57. OECD-HA, SNM(79)89, Stephen Marris to Secretary-General, "Memorandum. The next steps on PAP", 12 April 1979. Annex. Contacts on PAP with Member governments. JCPL, CEA, George C. Eads' OECD Files, Box 278, Folder Positive Adjustment Meeting 11/79 [1], Memorandum from George Eads for Charlie Schultze "French Opposition to PAP", 23 March 1979; JCPL, CEA, Box 8, Folder 6, CIA, National Foreign Assessment Center "Positive Adjustment Policies in the Big Six", 14 June 1979.
58. TNA, T390/670, Letter from A.F. Maddocks to P.V. Dixon [HM Treasury], "Special Group on Positive Adjustment", 24 September 1979.
59. For a biography, see "Tietmeyer, Hans" in Munzinger Online/Personen – Internationales Biographisches Archiv, accessed 19 January 2017, http://www.munzinger.de/document/00000016856.

60. AMAE, 446INVA/1536, Folder Préparation de Venise. Réunion Washington 21.12.79, Jean-Yves Haberer "Note pour le Ministre Compte-rendu de la première réunion du groupe ajustement positifs de l'OCDE", 27 November 1979; TNA, T390/673, Letter from R.H. Baker to Peter Dixon "Positive Adjustment", 23 June 1980. On the OECD peer review process, see the chapter by William Gray in this volume.
61. Quotations from OECD, *Positive Adjustment Policies: Managing Structural Change* (Paris: OECD, 1983).
62. JCPL, CEA, Box 8, Folder 6, CIA. National Foreign Assessment Center "Positive Adjustment Policies in the Big Six", 14 June 1979.
63. Ibid.
64. JCPL, CEA, Charles L. Schultze Subject Files, Box 90, Folder Venice World Economic Summit, Stephen Marris "Comment on Draft PA Pledge", 3 March 1980.
65. TNA, T390/672, Letter from P.V. Dixon to C.B. Benjamin, "OECD—Special Group on Positive Adjustment Policies", 3 April 1980; JCPL, CEA, Charles L. Schultze Subject Files, Box 91, Folder Venice World Economic Summit 1980 [2], Letter from Charlie Schultze to Members of the Summit Preparatory Group, 8 April 1980.
66. "Declaration. Inflation", accessed 13 November 2016, http://www.g8.utoronto.ca/summit/1980venice/communique/inflation.html.
67. TNA, FCO59/1642, Letter from P.V. Dixon to D. Gore-Booth "Positive Adjustment", 11 June 1979.
68. Ronald Reagan Presidential Library (hereafter RRPL), Bailey, Norman: Files, Box 9, Folder Versailles Summit [1982] (2 of 10), "Is US Foreign Policy bold enough?" [no date].
69. RRPL, Feldstein, Martin: Files, Box OA 9812, Folder OECD/Economic Policy Committee (EPC) September 1982–December 1982, "Meeting with OECD Secretary General Emile Van Lennep" [no name, undated].
70. JCPL, CEA, Charles L. Schultze Briefing Book Files, Box 123, Folder "IBRD/IMF General Issues 1980 [1] "Background Paper on Structural Adjustment Lending", 10 September 1980.
71. RRPL, WHORM: Subject Files. International Organizations; IT044 IMF; Murray L. Weidenbaum, "Memorandum for the President. International Monetary Fund/World Bank Meetings", 17 September 1981; Margaret Garritsen De Vries, *The IMF in a Changing World, 1945–1985* (Washington, D.C.: International Monetary Fund, 1986), 165.
72. See the G7 Summit declarations, accessed 13 November 2016, http://www.g8.utoronto.ca/summit/index.htm.
73. RRPL, Poole, William: Files, OA10700, Folder OECD Positive Adjustment Policies, Chris Cannon to Bill Poole "Treasury Comments: OECD Meeting on Positive Adjustment" [no date].

74. RRPL, Poole, William: Files, OA10700, Folder OECD Positive Adjustment Policies, Telegram from AmEmbassy Paris to Secstate WashDC "Ministerial conference on longer-term performance of OECD economies February 13–14: Flexibility and efficiency in the private sector", telno 06987, 18 February 1984.
75. RRPL, Poole, William: Files, OA10700, Folder OECD Positive Adjustment Policies, Telegram from AmEmbassy Paris to Secstate WashDC "Ministerial conference on longer-term performance of OECD economies February 13–14: Flexibility and efficiency in the private sector", telno 06987, 18 February 1984.
76. See "The London economic Declaration", G7 Summit, 9 June 1984, accessed 13 November 2016, http://www.g8.utoronto.ca/summit/1984london/communique.html.
77. RRPL, WHORM: Subject Files. International Organizations; IT071 OECD; Letter from Ronald Reagan to Emile Van Lennep, 7 September 1984.

PART III

Coping with Socio-ecological Challenges

The Narrowing-Down of the OEEC/ OECD Migration Functions, 1947–1986

Emmanuel Comte and Simone Paoli

This chapter shows how member states gradually defined the functions of the OEEC, later the OECD, in the field of migration policies, from its inception in 1947 until the mid-1980s, when those functions were finally stabilized. When the Organization was created, it was supposed to be influential in migration politics in Western Europe. The functions of an international organization might vary and range toward an increasing role to govern international relations. With *information* functions, an organization is mainly in charge of studies in order to advise member states implementing national policies.[1] With *coordination* functions, the organization serves as a forum to specify member states' respective national actions so as to reduce friction between those actions, using binding norms (*strong coordination*) or not (*weak coordination*).[2]

Emmanuel Comte is primarily responsible for the introduction and the first part while Simone Paoli is primarily responsible for the second part and the conclusion.

E. Comte (✉)
Department of History, University of California, 3229 Dwinnelle Hall, Berkeley 94720, United States
e-mail: emmanuel.comte@icloud.com

S. Paoli
University of Padova, Via Del Santo, 77-35123 Padua, Italy
e-mail: simone.paoli@unipd.it

M. Leimgruber and M. Schmelzer (eds.), *The OECD and the International Political Economy Since 1948*, DOI 10.1007/978-3-319-60243-1_11

When an organization assumes *cooperation* functions, member states use the organization to carry out joint actions in that domain, which implies devolving responsibility for the management of those joint actions to one or several international institutions. Finally, when member states give an organization *integration* functions, the complete management of a defined domain of their relations is transferred to the organization and no longer pertains to the level of national policy.[3]

This chapter shows that member states initially expected the OEEC to perform functions at the level of *cooperation*, or even *integration* in migration policies, but that over time it came to assume functions at the level of *coordination*, and more and more at the strict level of *information*. To analyze the underlying reasons for these shifts, we scrutinize the debates within the Organization and pay particular attention to the strategies and preferences of the most important states in the Western European migration system. These included the United States, one of the main actors within the Organization in general, but also major Western European immigration states, namely France, Britain, and West Germany. Diplomats and experts represented those national governments in the OEEC/OECD. We also scrutinize the role of the OECD Secretariat in developing *information* functions in the 1970s and 1980s.

This chapter is based on documents held in the archives of the OECD in Paris, in particular those of the Manpower Committee. In addition, we have used targeted documents from French, German, Italian, and US archives to complete our sources about OEEC negotiations. The first part of this chapter is devoted to the early years of the Cold War, from 1947 to the aftermath of the re-foundation of the OECD in 1961. The second part analyzes the period starting with the restrictive shift in national migration policies in Western Europe in the late 1960s up to the mid-1980s.

Facilitating Migration in Western Europe in the Early Cold War, 1947 to Mid-1960s

When founding the OEEC to administer Marshall Plan aid, member states agreed on broad ambitions to solve disturbing migratory tensions in the Cold War context. Unemployment in West Germany and Italy in the late 1940s threatened political stability and favored Communist parties, which endangered the cohesion of Western Europe. Facilitating migration movements between member countries could reduce unemployment and contribute to the containment of Soviet influence.

Moreover, regular flows of migrants continued to arrive in Western countries from Central and Eastern Europe.[4] The countries of first arrival of those migrants, namely West Germany, Austria, Italy, and Greece, were already affected by internal labor tensions and threatened to close their borders to those Eastern migrants without broader cooperation at the West European level to manage and absorb those flows. In that context, Cold War interests encouraged cooperation in the field of migration policies in Western Europe.

The weight of the United States in Western Europe in those years implied that Cold War interests defined the priorities of the newly founded OEEC. The US government was regularly pushing for developing more cooperative migratory arrangements between OEEC member states. As early as summer 1947, US Under- Secretary of State for Economic Affairs William L. Clayton invited French Foreign Minister Georges Bidault to promote a European customs union, whose definition was then as large as involving migratory issues.[5] Around 1949–1950, increasing unemployment in West Germany in the face of continued immigration from Eastern Europe created a worrying situation for the US government and threatened to destabilize a strategic country in the Western alliance. The US government was therefore eager to use the OEEC framework to develop migration opportunities in Western Europe for Germans. US leaders also considered high unemployment in Italy as a threat to Western unity and a waste of productive resources. After the outbreak of the Korean War, NATO member states gathered in Lisbon in February 1952 for a special summit to discuss deeper cooperation. In the wake of the summit, US Special Representative in Europe for Economic Affairs Paul R. Porter wrote to the Chairman of the OEEC Council, Dutch Foreign Minister Dirk Stikker: An "area which we feel needs more attention and renewed effort is the whole question of utilization of European manpower.... An attack needs to be made on the obstacles to labor mobility, particularly as they impede essential production."[6]

Cold War interests and US pressure translated into broad ambitions to develop an open migration regime through the OEEC. France, eager to benefit from US payments, defended new migration arrangements among member states already at the foundational conference in Paris in July 1947. Addressing the Committee of European Economic Cooperation, French representative Hervé Alphand promoted "a freer movement of persons between the various European countries."[7]

The French delegation was responsible for the creation of a special expert committee in charge of evaluating the needs and availabilities in manpower of participating countries and deciding about transfers of workers between these countries.[8] The Convention of European Economic Cooperation, signed on 16 April 1948 and instituting the OEEC, stipulated in Article 8 that OEEC member states would "take the necessary measures to facilitate the movement of workers and to ensure their settlement" and would "co-operate in the progressive reduction of obstacles to the free movement of persons."[9] On this legal basis, in March 1952, following the aforementioned US impulsion, the OEEC Ministerial Council founded a working party to liberalize manpower migration. The working party was in charge of ensuring that "maximum possible progress" was achieved in abolishing "restrictive regulations, formalities and other barriers to free movement of workers between member countries."[10] At the OEEC's foundation, member states envisioned thus a deepening process of integration, with binding regulations to remove national restrictive practices. However, several factors caused those ambitions to fail.

The first and most important factor was that Western Europe's labor markets were highly unbalanced, with the overall supply of labor exceeding demand. Several member countries were either poor or affected by high unemployment. Italy, Greece, Turkey, Spain, and Portugal faced both problems. High unemployment was also rampant in Ireland, Austria, and West Germany. For example, unemployment in West Germany increased throughout 1949 and affected 1.8 million people in the first months of 1950.[11] France, Belgium, Switzerland, Britain, and Sweden were immigration countries among the OEEC, but their labor demand fluctuated in the five years following the creation of the Organization and was low in most years.[12]

The migration pressure within the OEEC was therefore high, which created the prospect of painful adjustments for national workers in immigration countries in the event of liberalization. In the context of the Korean War and US requests, the British representative within the Executive Committee of the OEEC, Edmund Hall Patch, considered in May 1951 that there were no needs for more manpower within Britain. On the contrary, he said, manpower availability was superior to needs.[13] In July 1952, Giovanni Malagodi, an Italian delegate to the OEEC, reported to Italian Foreign Minister Alcide De Gasperi about an informal conversation he had with an unnamed delegate of an immigration country, who feared that any "breaking of the dam" would open the way to a "flood" of Italian workers.[14] The lack of a labor demand in immigration countries commensurate to the labor supply in emigration countries hindered a successful deal between the two groups of member countries.

Furthermore, the external migratory pressure that Western Europe was facing impaired new migration arrangements. In January 1951, the West German government counted on its territory almost 9.5 million migrants from Eastern Europe, mostly German expellees. They were responsible for acute tensions on the German labor market. In border Länder, where those Eastern immigrants had arrived, the unemployment rate was higher than in the rest of the country, reaching 23% in Schleswig-Holstein and around 14% in Niedersachsen and Bayern as early as October 1949.[15] At the end of July 1950, the West German government informed British, French, and US governments that "1.3 million people" were in West Germany "available for emigration" further west.[16] To achieve this, Otto Rieck, a director in the West German ministry for the Marshall Plan, considered during a West German inter-ministerial meeting in January 1950 that "the free movement of workers was indispensable within Europe."[17] In early spring 1952, the West German representative in the OEEC Manpower Committee continued to stress that the population problem, resulting from the continuous influx of migrants from Eastern Europe, had reached extreme severity.[18]

Already in January 1948, a conference organized by the Manpower Committee of the Committee of European Economic Cooperation concluded that resolving the problem of surplus manpower was impossible in the European framework and that overseas emigration was necessary.[19] The Belgian and British governments also made clear in December 1950 and January 1951 that the solution had to be found in overseas emigration.[20]

Given that the OEEC included almost all Western European countries, and given both the internal and external migratory pressures affecting that regional group, the OEEC was not appropriate for more open migration arrangements. In addition, this organization was ill-suited for cooperation regarding overseas emigration. Already in December 1949, Philip W. Bonsal, on behalf of the Office of the Special Representative in Europe of the Economic Cooperation Administration (ECA), recognized in a letter to OEEC Secretary-General Robert Marjolin that an overseas emigration program was necessary. However, the letter continued, the Organization lacked both weight and experience in this domain, and given that it did not include overseas immigration countries, the OEEC would need to transfer funding for such a program to the International Labor Organization (ILO). Thus, in July 1950 and June 1951 the OEEC Council decided to transfer ECA funds to the ILO.[21] This program included missions to study emigration opportunities in Italy, Germany, and Austria, and immigration opportunities in Latin America.[22]

When the US Congress recognized that broader cooperation including emigrants' transportation was necessary, again the OEEC lacked the administration and was not in a position to benefit from American financial aid. In the fall of 1951, the US Congress voted a credit of 10 million dollars to transport emigrants from Western Europe. To achieve this, an international conference in Brussels in November 1951 set up a new organization, which later became the Intergovernmental Committee for European Migration.[23]

After those failures, member states redefined the role of the OEEC in the field of migration policies to implement the objectives that the 1948 Convention had provided for. First, the Organization served as a forum for the weak coordination of short-term visa practices in Western Europe. In the early 1950s, most OEEC member states continued to require a visa from German nationals to prevent tensions associated with German immigration. A June 1948 report within the French Ministry of the Interior underlined that the liberalization of the circulation of persons between France and Germany could create tensions, "especially… in the departments of Alsace and Lorraine, and in particular Moselle."[24] The resentment against German occupation and, more generally, the willingness to avoid the immigration of former Nazis supported those practices. They affected the migratory and commercial flows between West Germany and the rest of Western Europe. Within the OEEC Manpower Committee in February 1950, the West German delegation wished that "only those who are recognized as really dangerous would be excluded from immigration and not anymore entire groups without individual checks."[25] Discussing these issues within the Organization created pressure on immigration member states to generalize to all OEEC countries the special arrangements they had concluded with just a few of them. In February 1953, the OEEC Ministerial Council recommended the removal of systematic visa requirements for German nationals. In the following months, most OEEC member states abolished such a requirement.[26] The Organization thus played a role in accompanying the spectacular growth of tourist flows within Western Europe, which increased from 25 million to around 290 million people between 1950 and 1980 and accounted then for half of the global tourist flow.[27]

Nevertheless, German requests for passports were less successful, showing that this mere forum of coordination did not infringe on the autonomy of immigration states. West Germany favored abolishing passport requirements to travel between OEEC member countries. By contrast, within the OEEC Tourism Committee, British and French representatives declared that passports remained useful tools to control immigration. The date of entry in the territory was written on passports, which prevented tourists from overstaying the legal 3-month period.[28] In April 1956, those representatives also made clear that the special arrangements their governments had with some other OEEC governments regarding the abolition of passports were not likely to be extended to all OEEC countries. The reason was, as the French representative put it, "the necessity to maintain a control of labor immigration" in relation with "a certain number of European countries."[29] In the end, negotiations thus failed because of the economic heterogeneity that existed among member countries, creating a vast emigration potential in some of them.

Second, OEEC member states agreed to coordinate their foreign labor recruitment procedures. The Italian government unsuccessfully tried to use the OEEC as a framework to obtain the abolition of labor immigration controls. A 1952 Italian plan submitted to the OEEC envisioned the abolition of work permits for OEEC nationals. This plan was inacceptable for British and French representatives, given the large labor surplus existing within the OEEC.[30] The main decision adopted within the OEEC to facilitate the movement of workers as per Article 8 of the 1948 Convention was the October 1953 Council decision governing the employment of nationals of member countries.[31] This decision did not abolish work permits or other types of devices intended to control and limit immigration, but only specified the process through which states could use those instruments. In particular, the main point of the decision was that work permits should be granted to nationals of other member states when national candidates could not be found one month after the release of a job offer.

This instrument was legally binding and thus amounted to *strong coordination*. However, a more detailed analysis reveals various loopholes and limits. Member states maintained the option to extend the one-month period to two months. France, the main immigration country within the OEEC at the time, used this option to find jobs for unemployed Algerian workers.[32] Even in 1956, France, Austria, and Denmark were still using the two-months limit. Moreover, this act amounted to a codification of practices that most member states already applied. Sweden, another important immigration country within the OEEC, "already applied most of the principles present in the Council resolution."[33] Indeed, it was rarely in national economic interest to prevent immigrant workers from taking up job offers when no national candidate had applied during more than one month.

The third field of action for the OEEC pertained to weak coordination efforts to host migrants from Eastern Europe. At the time in Western Europe, there was a continuous inflow of migrants from Communist countries in Eastern Europe. They arrived mainly in West Germany, but also in Austria, Italy, the Netherlands, and Greece. In March 1954, the OEEC Council extended the 1953 decision to those migrants.[34] But, again, wide divergences existed among member states. In the late 1950s, France was worried that it could not expel those refugees from Eastern Europe who had arrived on its territory after transiting within Western countries closer to Eastern Europe because their right of return to those countries of first arrival had elapsed. As a condition to accept more refugees, France wanted an extension of their right of return in the country of their first arrival, while countries of first arrival, mainly West Germany, wanted precisely the opposite, so that once refugees had left their territories, they could not come back.[35] Therefore, Western European states had to solve a coordination problem to ensure that refugees move further west.

In October 1958, the OEEC Council finally agreed on a non-binding recommendation for a two-year right of return for refugees in the country of their first arrival.[36] The West German government made clear that it would not take action against German Länder that would limit the right of return of refugees to less than two years.[37] Similarly, in contact with the UN High Commissioner for Refugees, the OEEC Council recommended in May 1960 that visas be delivered without costs to refugees and that the length of validity of their work permits should not be lower than one year in principle. However, during the session when the Council adopted this recommendation, British representative Stewart Crawford reserved the position of his government regarding visas, since a number of provisions of the recommendation did not match "completely" current British practices.[38]

More generally, the competition of the new European Economic Community (EEC) created by the March 1957 Rome Treaty heavily affected the OEEC's role in migration policies. Thanks to its more homogeneous membership, the EEC became the main forum for strong coordination and cooperation about manpower migration in Western Europe in the following years.[39] The transformation of the OEEC into the OECD in 1961 did not change much in the field of migration policies. The 1953 decision remained in force. All the acts of the OEEC related to migration were unified in one single act, but without, in the words of the Manpower Committee, "bringing any changes to the substance of the earlier acts."[40] And the new member states—the United States and Canada, and then Japan from 1964 onward—did not participate in the 1953 decision.[41]

The functions that the OEEC/OECD developed in the field of migration policies until the early 1960s were therefore those of a weak coordination forum on issues that mattered to Western interests. But the economic heterogeneity among member countries and the resulting conflict between emigration and immigration countries prevented this forum from enacting binding provisions. To monitor the various OECD recommendations for migration policies, the OECD Secretariat started preparing several reports on the recruitment practices of member states, which, in the absence of binding commitments, had primarily an informative value.[42] In the following years, the functions of the Organization evolved thus mainly in the direction of information. As discussed in the next section, migration policies in Western Europe changed deeply from the mid-1960s onward, with increased migration pressure and more restrictive immigration policies, subjecting the relationships between emigration and immigration countries within the Organization to even greater tension.

Mitigating Restrictive National Migration Policies, Mid-1960s to 1987

The second stage in the definition of the functions of the Organization took place in the wake of the shift toward more restrictive migration policies in Western Europe in the late 1960s and early 1970s. In this new context, the political equilibrium previously reached within the OECD between emigration and immigration countries persisted, but the information function of the Organization was expanded to orient national migration policies toward economic growth in Western Europe and the new member countries.

Between 1968 and 1969, as demonstrated by the annual reports on the application of the 1953 decision drafted by the Manpower and Social Affairs Committee (MSAC), both Switzerland and Belgium inaugurated policies aimed at containing the immigration of foreign workers and, in the following years, similar developments took place in the Netherlands, Denmark, West Germany, and France.[43] The Council of Europe and the EEC noticed this new trend at a very early stage.[44] The European Commission, in particular, drew up a comparative study on the immigration policies of EEC members in 1970, which began to draw attention to the emerging change in attitudes toward third-country migrants in Western Europe.[45]

The OECD, however, was the first international organization that investigated the reasons for this change and that inferred a political motive, rather than an economic one, behind the adoption of restrictive policies. Between 1968 and 1970, the economies of all the Northern European members of the OECD were booming, which brought an increased demand for foreign labor. This did not mean, however, that there was an accompanying relaxation of controls; "in fact, there has been the same tendency, and in some places a greater tendency, to impose a degree of order on migration movements."[46] The MSAC reported that member states, when restricting immigration, emphasized the supposed need to guarantee migrant workers' security of employment and housing, plus social protection. Moreover, the Committee highlighted changes in public attitudes: "With an increase in the number of immigrants, there is reason to fear them being more and more unfavorably viewed by the home population and in particular by the less well-educated actors at the lower end of the social scale."[47] Growing migration flows from Africa and Asia, which occurred throughout the 1960s, also stimulated the rise in anti-immigrant sentiment in former colonial countries.[48]

After the early restrictive migration policies adopted in the late 1960s, all immigration countries in Western Europe unilaterally decided to interrupt further foreign labor inflows during the economic crisis of the 1970s.[49] This strategy dealt a shattering blow to Mediterranean emigration countries. The immediate effect of border closure was to redistribute the burden of unemployment to those countries least able to cope with the problem; this had potential implications not only for the social cohesion but also for the political stability of the countries involved. In the longer term, in addition, border closure might mean a severe reduction in remittances to emigration countries; an ultimate decline in remittances, in turn, could lead to a further deterioration in already serious balance of payments difficulties and lower the already uncertain development prospects of most Mediterranean countries.[50]

On the basis of the debates in the MSAC, and particularly of those held by its Working Party on Migration (WPM), the Secretariat of the OECD realized that a renewal of the migration strategy of the Organization was imperative. Secretary-General Emile van Lennep took the lead and played an active role in shaping this process. Bearing in mind the failed attempt of the 1950s to consider the Organization as a normative framework able to enact binding legal stipulations, the Secretariat favored setting out only general principles for migration policy. Moreover, the Secretariat assumed that the conceptual apparatus of those responsible for decision-making in this highly sensitive area was not always appropriate and that the instruments at the disposal of governments to approach the problems that faced them were not always adequate. There was the need, consequently, to provide member countries with accurate statistics and information, and with up-to-date tools and concepts. This new awareness led the Secretariat to propose three kinds of action.[51]

The first action entailed the provision of information not only to discern in a timely manner any change in both facts and policies, but also to distribute this information as quickly as possible to interested parties. To this end, the Continuous Reporting System on Migration (SOPEMI) was established in 1973 at the request of the WPM. The extent of SOPEMI's mission caused at first tensions, notably between British representatives which thought that SOPEMI should restrict itself to the provision of data and French delegates which held that it should also analyze and interpret these data.[52] Yet, by the mid-1970s, SOPEMI was fully on stream and generally considered a precious instrument for dealing with migration matters. The core of its work was implemented by a group of national experts, the so-called "correspondents," who prepared annual reports on the migration situation in their respective countries, a summary of which was published annually.[53]

The second action dealt with thematic examinations. The Secretariat aimed at constructing a more coherent body of doctrine, designing a conceptual framework to facilitate decision-making at government policy level and identifying recommendations and principles for international action and coordination. Unsurprisingly, national delegates in the MSAC disagreed over the study priorities. While representatives from emigration countries put special emphasis on the integration of return migrants, those from immigration countries focused on foreign investments as an alternative to migratory movements.[54]

The Secretariat suggested thirdly the formulation of coordination principles to harmonize national policies. Predictably, this proposal gave rise to much dispute. Representatives from emigration countries, including Italy, Greece, Spain, Portugal, Turkey, and Yugoslavia, plus an immigration country, Denmark, required binding principles.[55] As argued by the Danish delegate, in fact, "if the countries concerned were allowed to choose 'à la carte' the principles which suited them, the guiding principles…would not have any great impact on member countries' policies in this field."[56] On the other hand, representatives from immigration countries, apart from Denmark, opposed the adoption of binding principles in order to maintain full sovereignty over migration policies. Representatives from emigration countries, including Turkey, Portugal, and Yugoslavia, also hinted at a financial contribution from immigration countries to accompany and, to a certain extent, compensate for restrictive policies. However, representatives from immigration countries, especially Germany, made it adamantly clear that "activities in this area should not lead to a request for additional resources."[57]

The debate in the OECD culminated in 1975 with the publication of *The OECD and International Migration*, a report based on work undertaken by the MSAC's Working Party on Migration and published under the responsibility of Secretary-General van Lennep. The study analyzed the role of the Organization in the migration sector from the initial emphasis on the removal of barriers to free movement of workers to the contemporary preoccupations with coordinated policies between immigration and emigration countries. The report stressed in particular that the Euro-Mediterranean region was becoming increasingly interdependent because of migration. Accordingly, if receiving countries in Western Europe wanted to restrict immigration to preserve internal cohesion and stability, they had no alternative but to promote economic cooperation aimed at raising the standard of living in Southern countries. At the same time, if sending countries in the Mediterranean wished to mitigate the negative repercussions of restrictive policies, they had every interest in adopting a conciliatory attitude rather than impeding emigration or exploiting nationalist ideologies.

The OECD, the report claimed, could make a valuable contribution to the search for "new solutions to a problem which reformulates the whole question of development and cooperation between OECD countries."[58] In particular, due to its mission, experience, and membership, the Organization might provide a suitable forum to discuss and adopt guiding principles for facilitating the orientation of national policies and their coordination at international level. The report also condemned the unilateral and short-term approach to migration policies recently taken in receiving countries and advocated cooperation between immigration and emigration countries.

Emboldened by these conclusions, representatives from emigration countries used the meeting of the MSAC at ministerial level that took place in Paris in March 1976 to advocate a fairer redistribution of the cost of restrictive policies. In response to these demands, ministers concluded the meeting by calling for intensified cooperation between immigration and emigration countries to share more equitably the burden of adjustment.[59]

Shortly afterward, the Secretariat further showed its interest in this issue by commissioning four studies on migration, which were published between 1977 and 1979. Although they did not make a great impact on the OECD, not least because of opposition from immigration countries, these studies signaled the Secretariat's intention to strengthen the role of the Organization in this field and to use it to enhance coordination and cooperation between immigration and emigration countries.[60]

The first study, written by the French economists François Bourguignon, Georges Gallais-Hamonno, and Bernard Fernet was entitled *International Labor Migrations and Economic Choices. The European Case.* It discussed, without giving a definite answer, whether there existed alternatives to manpower migration and to what extent it was in the interests of sending and receiving countries to support such alternatives.[61] The second study, *Return Migration and Reintegration Services*, prepared by Dutch economist Rien van Gendt in consultation with Spanish expert Garcia Passigli, aimed at helping emigration countries develop a comprehensive approach to the reintegration of return migrants into their respective socio-economic systems.[62] The third study, *The Migratory Chain*, was drawn up with the collaboration of the Director of the Immigration Policy Division of the Swedish Ministry of

Labor, Jonas Widgren. It analyzed the extent to which the migration and manpower policies of immigration countries could be better related to measures for employment creation and regional development in emigration countries. According to the report, the organization of the migratory chain meant to try to arrange the various stages of the complex process of migration to increase the range of choice open to the workers and the countries involved. This, of course, implied cooperation between immigration and emigration countries.[63]

The fourth study, *Migration, Growth and Development*, was the most ambitious and contentious one developed by the OECD in that period. The research was a consequence of a request from Portuguese and Turkish delegates at the aforementioned 1976 meeting of the MSAC at ministerial level. Following that meeting, Secretary-General van Lennep invited a group of independent experts "to study the problems of employment and manpower in a long-term perspective and to work out a development strategy in a context of migration problems."[64] This group, chaired by the prominent American economic historian Charles Poor Kindleberger, displayed an almost perfect balance between immigration and emigration countries. Politically, however, they were overwhelmingly liberal.[65] After a year and a half of meetings with administrators, planners, as well as employers', employees', and migrants' representatives in France, West Germany, Portugal, and Turkey and further of analysis of reports submitted by officials from Greece and Yugoslavia, the Kindleberger Group presented a report that was widely discussed in both the Council and the MSAC.

The 1979 report was resolute in recommending that the OECD should provide machinery for consultation between immigration and emigration countries. In the short term, this system should enable these two groups of countries to embark on bilateral consultations to avoid unilateral actions. In the medium term, it should promote agreements, going beyond the traditional "manpower agreements," to coordinate policies and to better organize the international utilization of manpower. In the longer term, finally, it should encourage the development of programs so that policies leading to the termination of migration flows were tied to employment creation in emigration countries; this, of course, implied an intensification of economic cooperation with the objective of a development strategy in favor of poorer countries.

This approach was naturally welcomed by the governments of emigration countries and met with skepticism in those of receiving countries.

Immigration states were not ready to let the OECD play an incisive role in this policy area. Nor were they willing to spend significant resources to help emigration countries manage the negative repercussions of restrictive policies. Regarding this, the MSAC delegate for Britain was quick in highlighting that "as this was the report of Professor Kindleberger, all the points could not necessarily be expected to be acceptable to all member countries. [After all], the Report was [only] a contribution to the subject."[66]

Due to opposition from immigration countries' representatives, the Kindleberger study did not exert a strong influence; despite high hopes, its most innovative proposals were quickly dismissed on political and financial grounds. In the same period, further disagreements emerged over the specific issue of the return and reintegration of migrant workers. During the 1976 meeting of the MSAC at ministerial level, which also led to the Kindleberger report, the Greek Minister of Labor, Konstantinos Laskaris, proposed a system to facilitate such return migration flows through an OECD Special Fund. While representatives from all emigration countries supported that proposal, delegates from immigration countries, especially the Netherlands, Austria, Switzerland, and West Germany, rejected it. During two years of fruitless discussions, the immigration bloc remained unwilling to pay for policies that exclusively benefited sending countries and argued against any active role of the OECD in this delicate policy area. As emphasized by the Swiss representative in the MSAC, "multilateralism should be completely excluded and national autonomy must not be hindered by the proposed machinery."[67] As a consequence of this strong opposition, the Greek proposal came to nothing: all the work and discussions resulted in the preparation of a Model Machinery, a detailed project plan which remained a paper exercise.[68] The failure of the Greek proposal was crucial in undermining Southern members' trust in the potential of the OECD to coordinate migration policies. Meanwhile, the Mediterranean enlargement of the European Community, combined with the increasing part played by the EEC in the migration field, further contributed to the marginalization of the OECD.[69]

The MSAC continued to discuss the matter, promote studies, facilitate exchanges of experiences and opinions, and develop the SOPEMI's activities. However, the Secretariat and the MSAC, in particular representatives from emigration countries, were constrained to abandon the ambitions developed during the 1970s. In addition, in the late 1970s and early 1980s the MSAC gradually shifted its emphasis from emigration countries' priorities to issues that were important to immigration countries, including concerns about illegal immigration and flows of asylum seekers.[70] This shift was spurred by an increase in migration and refugee pressure and a parallel politicization of these issues in Western European countries, in particular in France and West Germany.[71] This evolution, along with the restrictive and unilateral approach that immigration countries continued to follow, increasingly embittered the governments of the emigration countries within the OECD, Greece, Turkey, Portugal, and Yugoslavia in particular.[72]

To give new impetus to a multilateral approach to migration politics and revitalize the role of the OECD in this field, representatives from emigration countries within the WPM proposed in mid-1983 convening a conference on international migration under the aegis of the OECD.[73] That proposal immediately met with resistance in the delegations of immigration countries. Delegates from Austria, Switzerland, the Netherlands, Great Britain, and West Germany, in particular, "were much more cautious in their approach to the idea, given the abundance of international conferences recently on the subject."[74] They accepted the idea only when they succeeded in forcing their priorities onto the agenda, ruling out policy conclusions and having participants speak only as experts, whatever their level of representation decided upon by countries when forming their delegations to the conference.[75]

The meeting, which was entitled *The Future of Migration* and took place in Paris in May 1986, was nevertheless important because "[subsequent OECD] work on migration followed up on [its] results."[76] The conference, in particular, underscored governments' growing concern about illegal immigration and the difficulty of containing such movements; on the other hand, it highlighted the negative consequences that strict controls by certain countries might have for others equipped with fewer controls or whose attitudes were more liberal. Moreover, the conference emphasized that entry controls and the coordinated fight against illegal immigration should be accompanied by improvements in international trade relations, by the revival of development policies, by the reorganization of labor markets, and by the restructuring of economic and demographic dynamics in emigration regions.[77] The conference, however, confirmed for good the status of the OECD as a forum for debate and exchange of information, rather than as a medium for initiatives of strong coordination.[78]

Conclusion

When the OEEC was established in 1948, it was expected to play a major role in the multilateral liberalization of the circulation of the European workforce. This was especially important for the United States, preoccupied with the social tensions associated with Eastern immigration in West Germany and with manpower surplus in the least developed members on the periphery of Western Europe. These tensions could politically destabilize those countries and jeopardize their participation in the Western camp in the context of the Cold War. As we have shown, however, heterogeneity among OEEC members undermined the Organization's position. Because of the divergence of interests between immigration and emigration countries, combined with the formation of a more economically homogeneous regional organization allowing the free movement of workers, namely the European Community, the Organization found itself in the 1960s assuming migration functions only at the level of weak coordination and information.

The shift from liberal to restrictive migration policies in Western Europe in the late 1960s and early 1970s appeared to open a window of opportunity for the OECD. Turkey, Portugal, and Greece, which as emigration countries were faced with the negative repercussions of restrictive policies adopted by immigration countries, tried to develop cooperation to redistribute these costs. The Secretariat and a group of experts close to the OECD supported this strategy. By defending the interests of Southern European countries, the Secretariat then acted as a facilitator for the continued cohesion of the West. This attempt, however, met with opposition from immigration countries. Again, the heterogeneity among member countries, namely the opposition between immigration and emigration countries, prevented the adoption of binding norms and the commitment of financial resources. In addition to disagreements within its heterogeneous membership, the OECD also suffered competition again from the European Community.

But in the field of information provision—in order to promote migration policies conducive to economic growth—the Organization's role became more important. The OECD, in particular, became prominent in providing trustworthy data, statistics, and arguments, which generally stressed the need to adopt a long-term approach to migration policies and emphasized the potential of well-regulated migration flows.

Notes

1. On questions of information in international relations see Rita Cruise O'Brien and G.K. Helleiner, "The Political Economy of Information in a Changing International Economic Order," *International Organization* 34/4 (1980): 445–470; James D. Morrow, "Modeling the Forms of International Cooperation: Distribution Versus Information," *International Organization* 48/3 (1994): 387–423.
2. Arthur A. Stein, "Coordination and Collaboration: Regimes in an Anarchic World," International Organization 36/2 (1982): 299–324.
3. Donald J. Puchala, "International Transactions and Regional Integration," *International Organization* 36/2.
4. Kim Salomon, *Refugees in the Cold War. Toward a New International Refugee Regime in the Early Postwar Era* (Lund: Lund University Press, 1991).
5. Vincent Auriol and Pierre Nora, *Journal du septennat, 1947–1954*, vol. 1, 1947 (Paris: Armand Colin, 1970), 391.
6. *Foreign Relations of the United States*, Dwight D. Eisenhower, 1952–1954, 7 March 1952, vol. VI, 10.
7. OECD Historical Archives, Paris (hereafter OECD-HA), Committee of European Economic Cooperation (CEEC), Box 366, Folder 3, CEEC/63, Statement by Mr. Alphand, 15 September 1947.
8. OECD-HA, CEEC, Box 366, Folder 4, Minutes of the Executive Committee, 31 July 1947; Folder 1, Minutes of the session of Committee of Cooperation, 1 August 1947.
9. OECD-HA, Convention for European Economic Co-operation, Final Act of the Second Session of the Committee of European Economic Co-operation, 16 April 1948.
10. Federico Romero, *Emigrazione E Integrazione Europea, 1945–1973*, Studi Di Storia (Roma: Edizioni Lavoro, 1991), 51.
11. Auswärtiges Amt, Politisches Archiv, Berlin (AAPA), Bundesrepublik Deutschland, Politische Abteilung B10: 412-00: 2365, Office of Administration, Frankfurt A/M, for the US High Commission for Germany, Unemployment in Western Germany. A Graphic Study, January 1950, 7 and 45.
12. OECD-HA, MO(49)14, Annex, Note by the Secretariat, Request of foreign workers included in the Recovery Program, 8 February 1949.
13. OECD-HA, CE/M(51)016, Minutes of the session of the Executive Committee, 3 May 1951.
14. Archivio Storico del Ministero degli Affari Esteri, Rome, AP, Italia 1951–1957, box 167, folder OECE, Malagodi to De Gasperi, 28 July 1952. In: Pier Luigi Ballini and Antonio Varsori, *L' Italia E L' Europa: 1947–1979*, 2 vols. (Soveria Mannelli: Rubbettino, 2004), vol. 1, 169.

15. AAPA, B10: 412-00: 2365, Office of Administration, Frankfurt A/M, for the US High Commission for Germany, Unemployment in Western Germany. A Graphic Study, January 1950, 7 and 45.
16. AAPA, B10: 412-00 1877, Letter of the German Delegation to the Conference of Experts on emigration issues in Paris, 28 July 1950.
17. AAPA, B10: 412-00 1877, Minutes of the meeting concerning emigration in the Ministry of the Interior, Bonn, 14 January 1950.
18. OECD-HA, C(52)127, Report of the Manpower Committee to the Council, 9 May 1952. In February 1951, the Greek government also reported that they favored the emigration of 40,000 refugees, who were held responsible for an increase in the unemployment rate.
19. Historical Archives of the European Union, Florence, ECSC High Authority, CEAB, 11, 392, Note of the Working Group for the Application of Article 69, about international action to promote intra-European movement of labor, October 1953, 68.
20. OECD-HA, C(51)175, Annex B, Report of the Secretary-General of the Council of Europe to the Committee of Ministers on the refugee problem, 17 May 1951.
21. OECD-HA, CE(50)003, Letter from the Office of the Special Representative, 28 December 1949; C(52)002, Note by the Secretary of the Council, 16 January 1952.
22. OECD-HA, MO(51)13, Annex, Estimated expenditures under the special fund for migration, 16 April 1951.
23. OECD-HA, MT/M(51)7, Minutes of the meeting of the Maritime Transport Committee, 23 October 1951; C(51)344, Letter from the Permanent Representative of Belgium, Comte de Meeus, to the OEEC Secretary General, Robert Marjolin, 21 November 1951.
24. Archives nationales, Paris, Ministère de l'Intérieur, F7 16066, Sous-direction des étrangers to Affaires étrangères, 1 June 1948.
25. AAPA, B10: 412-00 1877, Proposal on emigration by the German delegation to the Manpower Committee, 3, 15 February 1950.
26. OECD-HA, C(53)064, Council Recommendation concerning the exemption of entry visas for nationals of member countries, 23 February 1953. See also C(54)318, Report of the Tourism Committee on visas and passports, 4 December 1954.
27. Alan S. Milward, George Brennan, and Federico Romero, *The European Rescue of the Nation-State* (Berkeley: University of California Press, 1992), 13.
28. OECD-HA, TOU(55)7, Report of the Tourism Committee Working Group on visas and passports, 7 May 1955.
29. OECD-HA, TOU(56)5, Report of the Tourism Committee Working Group on visas and passports, Annex I, 14 May 1956, 15.

30. OECD-HA, MO(53)25, Report of the Working Group on the Liberalization of labor movements, 26 June 1953.
31. OECD-HA, C(53)251(Final), 30 October 1953.
32. OECD-HA, MO(54)2, Annex I, Letter from the Head of the French Delegation to the OEEC to the OEEC Secretary General, 14 January 1954.
33. OECD-HA, MO(57)17, Report of the Working Group on the Liberalization of labor movements. For the example of Sweden, see OECD-HA, MO(54)21/12, Report of Sweden on the implementation of the Council Decision, 24 September 1954.
34. OECD-HA, C/M(54)007, Minutes of the session of the Council, 5 March 1954.
35. OECD-HA, MO/M(57)4, Minutes of the session of the Manpower Committee, 9–11 December 1957.
36. OECD-HA, C (58) 196 (Final), Council recommendation on the regulations and administrative practices governing the movement and employment of refugees, 3 October 1958.
37. OECD-HA, MO(61)1, Annex II, Survey on the implementation of the Recommendation concerning the right of return of refugees, 10 January 1961.
38. OECD-HA, C (60) 65 (Final), Council Recommendation on the administrative regulations and practices governing the movement and employment of refugees, 6 May 1960; C/M(60)12, Minutes of the session of the Council, 6 May 1960, 14.
39. Emmanuel Comte, "La rupture de 1955 dans la formation du régime européen de migrations," *Relations internationales* 166 (2016): 137–158.
40. OECD-HA, OECD/P(61)34, Report of the Manpower Committee to the Preparatory Committee on the Consolidation of the Recommendations for the introduction and employment of foreign labor, 7 July 1961.
41. Ibid.
42. OECD-HA, MO(60)17, Report of the Working Group on the Liberalization of labor movements on the implementation in 1959 of the Council Decision, 8 August 1960.
43. OECD-HA, MO(70)6/19, Manpower and Social Affairs Committee (MSAC), Application in 1969 of the Council Decision governing the employment of nationals of member countries. Reply to questionnaire: Switzerland, Paris, 29 July 1970; MO(70)6/03, MSAC, Application during 1969 of the Council Decision governing the employment of nationals of member countries. Reply to questionnaire: Belgium, Paris, 1 September 1971. See also: MS/M/402/375, Working Group on Migration (WGM), Application in 1969 and 1970 of the Council Decision governing the employment of nationals of member countries, 30 August 1971.

44. Marcel Berlinghoff, *Das Ende der "Gastarbeit": Europäische Anwerbesstopps 1970–1974* (Paderborn: Schöningh, 2013). See also: Idem, "Der europäisierte Anwerbestopp," in *Das "Gastarbeiter"-System. Arbeitsmigration und ihre Folgen in der Bundesrepublik Deutschland und Westeuropa*, ed. Jochen Oltmer, Axel Kreienbrink, Carlos Sanz Díaz (München, Oldenbourg, 2012), 149–164.
45. Archives Diplomatiques de Nantes (ADN), 2876, Etude comparative des politiques migratoires des Etats membres de la C.E.E à l'égard des pays tiers, Bruxelles, June 1971.
46. OECD-HA, MS/M/402/375, WGM, Application in 1969 and 1970 of the Council Decision governing the employment of nationals of member countries, 30 August 1971.
47. OECD-HA, MSACF, MO(71)15, MSAC, Application in 1969 and 1970 of the Council Decision governing the employment of nationals of member countries, 2 November 1971.
48. James Hollifield, *L'immigration et l'État-Nation à la recherche d'un modèle national* (Paris: L'Harmattan, 1997).
49. Emek Uçarer, Donald Puchala, *Immigration into Western societies: problems and policies* (London: Pinter, 1997); Didier Bigo, Elspeth Guild, *Controlling Frontiers. Free Movement Into and Within Europe* (Aldershot: Ashgate, 2005); Andrew Geddes, *Immigration and European integration: beyond fortress Europe* (Manchester: Manchester University Press, 2008).
50. Sarah Collinson, *Europe and international migration* (London: Pinter Publishers for Royal Institute of International Affairs, 1994); Giuliano Garavini, *After Empires: European Integration, Decolonization, and the Challenge from the Global South 1957–1986* (Oxford: Oxford University Press, 2012).
51. OECD-HA, SME/MI(74)2, Working Party on Migration (WPM), Future orientation of OECD activity in the field of international migration (Note by the Secretariat), Paris, 10 December 1974.
52. OECD-HA, MSACF, MO(75)1, MSAC, Report of the Working Party on Migration on the Future Orientation of OECD Activity in the Field of International Migration, Paris, 21 February 1975.
53. John Salt, "The SOPEMI Experience: Genesis, Aims and Achievements," *International Migration Review* 4 (1987): 1067–1073.
54. OECD-HA, MSACF, MO(75)1, MSAC, Report of the Working Party on Migration on the Future Orientation of OECD Activity in the Field of International Migration, Paris, 21 February 1975.
55. Although Yugoslavia had a mere observer status, it played a very active role in the discussions on migration issues. See Bob Reinalda, *Routledge History of International Organisations. From 1815 to the Present Day* (New York: Routledge, 2009), 578. See also the article by Andrej Markovic and Ivan Obadic in this volume.

56. OECD-HA, CE/M(75)9, Executive Committee, Summary Record of the 390th Meeting held at the Château de la Muette, Paris, on Tuesday, 8 July 1975, Paris, 3 October 1975.
57. Ibid., See also: OECD-HA, C/M(75)23, Council, Minutes of the 398th Meeting held at the Château de la Muette, Paris, on Thursday 10 July 1975, Paris, 16 July 1975.
58. OECD, *The OECD and International Migration* (Paris: OECD, 1975), 41.
59. OECD, *Meeting of the Council at Ministerial Level: Final Communiqué* (Paris: OECD, 1976).
60. Peter Carroll, Aynsley Kellow, *The OECD. A Study of Organisational Adaptation* (Cheltenham: Edward Elgar, 2011), 65–79.
61. François Bourguignon, Georges Gallais-Hamonno, Bernard Fernet, *International Labour Migrations and Economic Choices. The European Case* (Paris: OECD, 1977).
62. Rien van Gendt, Garcia Passigli, *Return Migration and Reintegration Services* (Paris: OECD, 1977).
63. Jonas Widgren, *The Migratory Chain* (Paris: OECD, 1978).
64. Charles Kindleberger, Necat Erder, Ross Fakiolas, René Frey, Giorgio Fuà, Harald Gerfin, Bernard Kayser, Américo Henrique Rodrigues Ramos dos Santos, *Migration, Growth and Development* (Paris: OECD, 1979). Erder was a Turkish civil servant in the International Bank for Reconstruction and Development, Fakiolas, a senior official in the Greek Centre for Economic Development and Planning, Kayser was a French geographer and sociologist. The remaining four were economists originating from Italy (Fuà), Portugal (dos Santos), Switzerland (Frey) and Germany (Gerfin).
65. Charles Kindleberger, *The Life of an Economist. An Autobiography* (Cambridge, Basil Blackwell, 1991), 121–127.
66. OECD-HA, MAS/M(78)2, MSAC, Summary Record of the 48th Session held at the Château de la Muette, Paris, 17–19 May 1978, Paris, 13 September 1978.
67. OECD-HA, MAS/M(78)1, MSAC, Summary Record of the 47th Session held at the Château de la Muette, Paris, 13–15 March 1978, Paris, 13 April 1978.
68. OECD-HA, MAS(80)11, MSAC, Report to the Council of the Working Party on Migration, Paris, 4 April 1980.
69. Jörg Monar, "The Dynamics of Justice and Home Affairs: Laboratories, Driving Factors and Costs," *Journal of Common Market Studies* 4 (2001): 747–764. See also Janna Teltemann, "The Activities of the OECD in International Migration: How to Become a Relevant Actor in an Emerging Policy Field," in *Mechanisms of OECD Governance. International Incentives for National Policy-Making?* ed. Kerstin Martens and Anja Jakobi (Oxford: Oxford University Press, 2010), 241–259.

70. OECD-HA, MAS(82)8, MSAC, Draft programme of work for 1983, Paris, 07/05/1982; OECD-HA, MAS(83)3, MSAC, Draft programme of work for 1984, Paris, 6 April 1983.
71. Tim Bale, *Immigration and Integration Policy in Europe: Why Politics—and the Centre-Right—Matter* (New York: Routledge, 2009).
72. OECD-HA, MAS/M(82)1, MSAC, Summary Record of the 57th Session held at the Château de la Muette, Paris, 1–2 June 1982, Paris, 20 July 1982.
73. OECD-HA, MAS/WP2/M(83)1, WPM, Summary Record of the 6th Meeting held on 7 and 8 July 1983, Paris, 24 October 1983.
74. OECD-HA, MAS/M(83)2, MSAC, Summary Record of the 60th Session held at the Château de la Muette, Paris, from 14–16 December 1983, Paris, 24 February 1984.
75. OECD-HA, MAS/WP2(84)10, WPM, Possible Conference on "The Future of Migration," Paris, 4 May 1984; OECD-HA, MAS/WP2/M(84)1, WPM, Summary Record of the 7th Meeting held on 23 and 25 May 1984, Paris, 24 August 1984; OECD-HA, MAS/WP2/M(84)2, WPM, Summary Record of the 8th Meeting held on 10 and 11 December 1984, Paris, 27 February 1985; OECD-HA, MAS/M(84)2, MSAC, Summary Record of the 62nd Session held at the Château de la Muette, Paris, 12–14 December 1984, Paris, 21 January 1985.
76. OECD-HA, MAS(86)11, MSAC, Draft Program of Work for 1987, Paris, 3 June 1986.
77. OECD-HA, MAS/(86)8, MSAC, Progress Report on Activities, Paris, 10 June 1986.
78. Reginald Appleyard, "The Future of Migration," *International Migration Review* 1 (1987): 128–154.

Engineering the Free World: The Emergence of the OECD as an Actor in Education Policy, 1957–1972

Regula Bürgi

The O.E.E.C. should always bear in mind that it is an economic organisation and should confine its activities to those which have economic implications. It should avoid turning itself into an institute of pedagogics or of [sic] taking on activities which are best left to the various scientific institutions.
Dana Wilgress, 1960

This warning from Dana Wilgress, Canadian representative to the OEEC, comes from a report on cooperation in scientific and technological research, which Wilgress was commissioned to write by OEEC Secretary-General René Sergent.[1] Considering the developments and formations of the OEEC's successor, the OECD, this particular warning was ignored completely: the organization established a Centre for Educational Research and Innovation (CERI) in 1968, closely followed by an Education Committee in 1970, and has since become a key player in the field of education policy.

R. Bürgi (✉)
FHNW School of Education, Obere Sternengasse 7,
4502 Solothurn, Switzerland
e-mail: regula.buergi@fhnw.ch

M. Leimgruber and M. Schmelzer (eds.), *The OECD and the International Political Economy Since 1948*, DOI 10.1007/978-3-319-60243-1_12

This chapter analyzes the process of institutionalization, completed in less than a decade after Wilgress's warning. I argue that several networks, characterized by technocratic "styles of reasoning,"[2] considered the OEEC, and especially the OECD, as an ideal platform to develop education policies and the corresponding national structures intended to create a specific kind of people—in fact, to engineer the so-called free world. The governing and controlling medium on which these networks relied was a goal-oriented science, and here the US played a crucial catalytic and shaping role on both the governmental and the private level.

To flesh out these developments, I seek to decipher the styles of reasoning and networks, while also identifying key governing and disseminating mechanisms. I also compare and reflect on developments in the OECD and its international counterparts, namely the UN Educational, Science and Cultural Organization (UNESCO), the Council of Europe, and the European Economic Community (EEC). My analysis draws on a heterogeneous range of sources consisting of documents produced by relevant OECD bodies, on sources from other international organizations, non-governmental institutions (such as the Ford Foundation), and key individuals. The period of investigation extends from the OEEC's first attempts to grapple with education policy, in 1957, to 1972, when almost all OECD member states contributed to the funding of CERI.

Through the institutionalization of this educational research center, the OECD created—in contrast to university-based expertise called in on an ad hoc basis—a new form of institutionalized and thus professionalized educational expertise that was anchored in the international level, oscillating between research and policy. This type of expertise rose to prominence, in fact becoming omnipresent, in the 1990s, when CERI first developed the internationally comparable indicators collated in *Education at a Glance*, before going on—unprompted by its member countries—to produce the famous Programme for International Student Assessment (PISA) surveys. While these processes became increasingly salient after 1989 we cannot interpret them merely from a post-Cold War perspective—a bias often found in recent research.[3] As we shall see in what follows, the crucial structural preconditions for these later evolutions were forged during rather than after the Cold War.

My argument proceeds in four stages. I begin by highlighting how—within the context of the Cold War scientific and technological race—the OEEC was used to create a strengthened and enlarged scientific and technical elite in its European member states. In the second section

I outline that the newly founded OECD orientation toward economic growth fostered a shift from science education to education as a means of generating and guaranteeing a plentiful supply of human capital. Third, I underscore how the failure of these attempts at governance culminated in the institutionalization of an educational committee and research body to secure the development of people needed for *the* modern society. In the fourth and final section, I point to the OECD's role as engineer of the West, its governing instruments, and the recurrent mechanisms that shaped and facilitated the processes of institutionalization.

A Scientific and Technical Elite for Progress

In 1958, 10 years after its establishment, the OEEC set up a Committee for Scientific and Technical Personnel (CSTP). This committee became a key interface for science and education, securing these issues a permanent place on the agenda of the hitherto mainly economic OEEC and later OECD. Founded immediately after the Sputnik shock, the CSTP was undergirded by the universalistic notion that all societies in the modern world are essentially science-based, that their problems could be solved by science regardless of context, and that scientific developments would ultimately determine who would "win" the Cold War.[4] Europe, which was classified as technologically and scientifically backward, had to face these facts, it was argued.[5]

One of the key initiators and later head of the CSTP was Scottish chemist Alexander King, a technocrat *par excellence*. According to Norwegian economist Kjell Eide, a permanent expert at CSTP, King:

> was a natural scientist who had played a major role in the British war effort, and through that he had become convinced of the ability of applied and goal oriented research to transform modern society. He belonged to a circle who saw scientists as the key political actors in the future society, and he wanted the OEEC to promote science and technology, not least through an increased supply of experts in these fields.[6]

This account is consonant with the portrait Alexander King included in his autobiography, which depicts him examining the globe through a lens and bears the caption "monarch of all he surveys."[7] King worked in the British Central Scientific Office in Washington DC during the Second World War and, as a scientific advisor, he was responsible for

British relations with US bodies engaged in war research. As a result he was in close contact with the so-called US "defense intellectuals."[8] After the War—not least in order to ensure their own survival—these intellectuals began to apply war planning methods to civilian social policy fields (such as education policy), carving out institutional platforms and forums in think tanks such as RAND to influence or even formulate policy through goal-oriented science (above all systems analysis).[9]

Like his US colleagues, after the Second World War, King—now back in the UK—was involved in attempts to introduce war planning techniques to the British civil service. But his efforts came to nothing.[10] Following this setback he seemed to have found a suitable platform in the OEEC to strengthen the sciences while also promoting them as providers of policy advice. The OEEC, which emerged out of the Marshall Plan, enjoyed considerable advantages over UNESCO, where King also served as an expert in the 1950s, or the Council of Europe.[11] While UNESCO with its large membership was caught in the crossfire of the Cold War and was therefore permanently underfunded, the Council of Europe was hamstrung by the conflict between the UK and the Scandinavian countries on the one side and particularly France and Belgium on the other; the latter fraction was pressing for the creation of a supranational framework, resulting in the establishment of the EEC in 1958.[12]

Initially, the OEEC too balked at efforts to establish a committee on science and technology questions. The French delegate seemed particularly aghast at the idea, as it would involve "academics in the serious business of politics." After a French veto, the OEEC Council limited itself to appointing a Working Party on Scientific and Technical Information. The disappointment felt over this modest step was, as King put it in retrospect, "somewhat tempered by gastronomic excellence and calmed by good wine," but "later, over a final cognac," he and his colleagues decided to extend the working party's mandate to include *research* as an essential element in its work.[13] This strategy appears to have been successful. King was elected chairman of the working party and in 1953—when Marshall Plan funding dried up—it was expanded into the European Productivity Agency (EPA), which received financial support from the US to the tune of a further 100 million dollars. Eventually, the EPA represented around 40% of OEEC's budget.[14]

The OEEC's Manpower Committee subsequently carried out comprehensive comparative studies on the demand and supply of scientific and technical personnel. Despite deficient comparative statistical data, noted by the authors themselves, these reports caused widespread concern about Western Europe's lack of scientists and engineers, triggering the establishment of a working party "on scientific and highly qualified technical manpower" in 1957.[15] This group, which was appointed before Russia's Sputnik satellite had been launched into orbit, came to the same conclusion as the studies that triggered its creation. The group voted to establish a CSTP, whose necessity was explained to the OEEC Council as follows:

> If countries are to reap the benefits of technical progress, there must be general appreciation of the influence of science in modern life, and an adequate supply of trained people fully employed to support rapid progress.[16]

The working group was a success and in May 1958, six months after it had submitted its findings, the OEEC Council created the CSTP with Alexander King as its head. The institutionalization of the CSTP became possible against the background of—as Alexander King called it—a "productivity saga," namely, more science meant better technology and thus the better economic productivity. This trinity was complemented by a fourth element: education, more precisely science education.[17] Accordingly, the CSTP focused primarily on curriculum development for natural science and mathematics subjects, wrote country reports on the lack of scientific and technical personnel, and sought to improve science-based educational governance through educational forecasts. These forecasts remained open with respect to their goals; they were centered on extrapolative, descriptive data that identified educational needs in light of calculations of increasing economic production.[18] Dana Wilgress, quoted at the beginning of this article, upbraided the Europeans for being overly concerned with their uniqueness and for favoring the liberal arts over science: "In particular they [Europeans] are reluctant to adapt their educational systems to the needs of science and technology."[19] He was unequivocal, however, in stating that the OEEC should not concern itself with education as a whole, but merely with drawing up policies to enlarge and foster a natural scientific and technical elite in Europe.

The establishment of the CSTP was fast-tracked by the US, which had been unnerved by the Soviet Union's Sputnik launch, with the Defense Department promising to cover half its budget (half a million dollars). At the third CSTP meeting, the American delegate revealed the intentions underlying this funding, emphasizing that the US was supporting the CSTP chiefly in the hope that the European members "would become increasingly aware of how their own interests coincided with the general objectives of the programme and would increase their support for achieving those objectives."[20] In short, the US government hoped that the European countries would cover two-thirds of the CSTP's funding within 2 or 3 years. The US did in fact reduce its contribution by the 1960s and some European countries were willing to fill the gap.[21]

Natural scientists, engineers, and delegates from education policy institutions sat on the CSTP governing board. Alexander King, who, as he remarked in his autobiography, had very little experience with education policy, recruited a former colleague from the British Ministry of Production, social scientist Ronald Gass, to help him. The latter had worked for the Royal Air Force during the Second World War and was subsequently involved mainly in behavioral studies and the human factor in the production process; like King, he had no experience in education policy.[22] Colleagues and OECD experts perceived Gass and King as "empire builders" who aimed to influence events and people in a top-down, controlling way. The duo not only helped shape the OEEC, but continued their collaboration for more than a decade in the OECD. While King rose to become director of the OECD's newly founded Directorate for Scientific Affairs, Gass headed the CSTP program: "He [Gass] and King were both extremely controversial, some liked them, some hated them, but all took notice of them."[23]

Human Capital for Development and Growth

The transition from OEEC to OECD in 1961 and the latter's emphasis on growth and development also affected the CSTP, which had broadened its focus on a scientific and technical elite to education as a whole to bolster human capital, which the Committee began stylizing as a key contribution to growth.

The OECD's preamble states that the organization's aim is not just growth but the highest sustainable economic growth for the free world, which was perceived to be "threatened" by the Soviet Bloc and the emerging Global South. Shortly after the OECD was founded, the first Ministerial Council adopted the goal to increase the combined GDP of all member states by 50% within a decade. This set a benchmark according to which member states' policies could be measured and compared.

Uncertainty regarding the causes of rapid economic growth gave all OECD committees the opportunity to present their own concerns as growth inducing and thus to elevate their position within the organization—and the CSTP was no exception to this trend.[24]

According to King, in the early days of the CSTP it was "dangerous" to talk of a broad approach to education. The OECD's adoption of economic growth as its ultimate goal eliminated this danger. The new paradigm was used to argue that it was the CSTP's "duty" to investigate education's role in economic growth in a general sense.[25] But this view was not shared by all CSTP delegates. The US representative, for example, remarked that the Committee should do its utmost to avoid focusing on education "as a whole" and should try to provide solutions rather than identify problems.[26] But these objections did nothing to halt the process the CSTP Secretariat had set in motion in the late 1950s. By 1959, the Secretariat was warning delegates that expansion and growth rather than recovery were the organization's lodestones and that the CSTP too must take its lead from them and integrate more economic experts: "OEEC cannot, and should not, attempt to play the role of a body whose representatives are limited to scientific or educational matters."[27] A corresponding program, entitled "Economic Growth and Investment in Education," was soon issued by the CSTP Secretariat; though it sparked some criticisms, it was approved by a majority of delegates. The program description emphasized that "Europe will be required to make a major effort during the next decade if it is to preserve its competitive position on world markets and raise its living standards." This would require research on the hitherto neglected field of "investment in men." [28]

Subsequently, the Secretariat in cooperation with the Ford Foundation—which was also closely involved in recruiting committee staff—began establishing a Study Group in the Economics of Education. This group, which consisted of experts from a limited number of "Northern" OECD countries—France, US, Sweden, Denmark, Germany, and the UK—was responsible for writing the background reports for the OECD conference, entitled "Economic Growth and Investment in Education," which was held in October 1961 in Washington DC and was perceived as ground-breaking by key staff members.[29] In contrast to earlier descriptive CSTP forecasts of a more open nature, the most significant background report on Europe, entitled "Targets for Education in Europe in 1970," stressed clear educational targets for the next decade. In line with the arguments originally put forward to justify the establishment of the CSTP, this report emphasized that science, or rather scientific research, was the key to the progress of society. But it went further than most early CSTP documents: progress was not viewed solely as emanating from a scientific elite but also from the education of society as a whole: "More people are needed to master the problems of modern technology, not only at the top but all the way down the line."[30]

In much the same vein as the background report, Philip Hall Coombs, US Assistant Secretary of State for Education and Cultural Affairs and conference host, emphasized that only countries that understood how to develop their "human resources" would win "the prize of progress." This, he asserted, had been demonstrated by the Soviet Union, but in contrast to the Soviet form of planning, the Western development of human resources would enable citizens to maintain and enhance their freedom.[31] Before his appointment to the US State Department, Coombs had worked at the Ford Foundation, where he was responsible for its educational activities and was thus already in contact with the OEEC.[32] At the OECD conference in Washington, Coombs approached UNESCO and OECD representatives, urging them to jointly found an international institute of educational planning and research. As he recalled, "[w]e readily agreed that while effective educational planning was undoubtedly needed, the real problem was that few if any people knew how to do it, at least in the OECD countries (with the partial exception of France)."[33]

Both institutions subsequently took action, though not as a direct response to Coombs's request and not through the joint approach he had envisaged.[34] In 1963, with financial support from the Ford Foundation, UNESCO founded an International Institute for Educational Planning (IIEP) and appointed Coombs its first director. The IIEP, which had a particular focus on developing countries, was granted a semi-autonomous status by UNESCO. The latter fast-tracked its establishment to steal a march on the OECD—laying bare the significance of interorganizational rivalry.[35] While the OECD did not set up its own educational research institute yet, it established a comprehensive educational planning project entitled "Programme on Educational Investment and Planning in Relation to Economic Growth" (EIP) right after the 1961 Conference. This was met with great interest and even enthusiasm among CSTP delegates: their initial reticence having vanished entirely, they called for the integration of economists in the Committee's work:

> Several Delegates thought that the terms of reference should not be confined to scientific and technical personnel trained in the exact sciences but should empower the Committee to extend its action to other categories and especially to economists and statisticians specializing in problems of educational development.[36]

The assumption was that societies develop through specific "stages," rendering them amenable to scientific planning, management, and control. The universalism envisaged by scientists who had shaped the early CSTP thus underwent a fundamental change. While the scientists tended to work on the assumption of an open form of development, the economists began to set specific goals (such as the background report for the Washington conference).[37]

The EIP was intended to calculate or plan—on the macro-level of structural planning—appropriate long-term educational goals for the industrialized OECD member states. A bespoke planning project (Mediterranean Regional Project; MRP) was launched to meet the needs of six Southern European countries (Greece, Italy, Yugoslavia, Portugal, Spain, and Turkey) in the early 1960s, though this was fused with the EIP in the mid-1960s. The long-term educational goals of the EIP were based, among other things, on the OECD's newly issued 50% growth target or output.[38] In particular, the EIP aimed at encouraging the development of national planning "machineries" or supporting them, where they existed at all. The members of the national planning teams, some of whom had been trained by the OECD, provided the organization with the channels and data that allowed it to undertake comparative studies.[39] The orientation toward a common goal made member states' education policies amenable to economic planning, measurable, and comparable. In this process the formerly descriptive country reports were transformed into normative national exams. While the experts recruited to this end continued to act in an individual capacity, a renewed effort was made "to be more explicitly concerned with problems of policy" rather than producing mere descriptions of structures and initiatives.[40]

In addition to the EIP, the OECD Council concurrently extended the life of the Study Group in the Economics of Education, which was intended to serve as "a scientific basis" for EIP's activities.[41] But the problems involved in integrating an academic body into an international governmental organization soon became glaringly apparent. First, at CSTP meetings delegates constantly demanded to be more involved in the selection of experts. Second, the experts were criticized for taking an overly theoretical approach rather than providing practical guides to policy.[42] Some of those attending Study Group meetings did in fact question the fundamental assumption that education contributed to economic growth. During the group's second meeting, for example, Thomas Balogh from the University of Oxford asserted: "To assume that some simple sort of (and only numerically different) quantitative relationship holds between education and economic progress in all countries is to fly in the face of all historical evidence."[43] The CSTP Secretariat's light-handed response to these criticisms was neatly captured in a lecture for prospective educational planners during which British economist John Vaizey, a permanent expert on the committee, though acknowledging the uncertainty of human capital theory, declared that:

> Nevertheless, I must confess that more education of a sterile "cultural" kind seems to me to be not only uneconomic but unwholesome…A truly cultivated man must surely be well-read, musical, a good linguist, a good conversationalist, have good taste in food, women and the theatre, and be reasonably fit. A man like Mr. Kennedy, for example. But that just shows how hard it is to be civilized unless you are rich.[44]

Vaizey's argument proved more successful than the above-mentioned scientific reservations: the Secretariat opted to cease the "sterile discussion of the limitations of the residual factor approach, the differential earning approach and so on" in support of a practical approach to planning.[45] In consequence, the Study Group was wound up in 1964 while the associated form of policy implementation, namely educational planning, flourished. Among other things, this was evident in the fact that the Standing Conference of European Ministers of Education urged the OECD to produce a handbook on educational planning.[46] While the conference actually convened under the auspices of the Council of Europe, which had its own documentation center, the education ministers presented their concerns to the OECD. In contrast to the Council of Europe, the OECD had no parliamentary substructure that might have resisted such attempts at statistical standardization and centralization by calling to mind the diversity of European states and European educational systems. Consequently, when the CSTP mandate was renewed in 1964, educational planning was integrated into the committee's work as a core activity. While the delegates agreed to study education as a whole on a macro-level rather than solely from the perspective of scientific and technical personnel, they wished to preserve national sovereignty over the qualitative aspects of educational policy and fended off attempts to transform the CSTP into an education committee.[47] However, as we will see in the next section, this defense of the national diversity of the European educational systems soon faded.

The Right Kind of People for *the* Modern Society

In the early 1960s, very few OECD member states had their own planning agencies. A decade later, virtually all of them did, even those with no ministry of education as such. Despite the fact that such a development could be considered a success of EIP activities, planning was beset by crisis from the mid-1960s onward. Problems included flawed plans (which failed to include change) and the tendency of politicians and administrators to ignore them, while key proponents of human capital theory failed to back up its claims with evidence.[48] In this section, I argue that this inability of the OECD to govern and control the educational systems of member countries—especially at a time when the West was challenged not just by the Eastern Bloc, but also, as was increasingly apparent, by the emerging developing countries—strengthened and encouraged attempts to propagate a new cultural understanding of *the* modern society.[49] It also fostered efforts to utilize new methods of comprehensive educational planning or total *systems* planning. By controlling output and intervening in the qualitative aspects of education, these approaches were intended to remedy the failure to produce the specific kind of people needed for modern society. It was against this background that the OECD Council launched in 1968 the CERI.

The difficulties of human capital theory were increasingly evident from the mid-1960s onward. It is illustrated by an internal note composed by IIEP's director Philip Hall Coombs for the attention of his colleagues. The head of the institute, who had been in office for about four years and was one of the pioneers of human capital theory, asked his colleagues about education's contribution to economic growth:

> What can we say here—apart from repeating theoretical propositions? Do we by now have any hard evidence?...One can defend this argument with a theoretical model, if one makes the right assumption. But, in practice, is there good reason to think that much of education's money and manpower would in fact, if released, be so spent as to accelerate development?[50]

The same problems that Coombs was setting out to his colleagues were troubling the OECD as well. The report to a small-scale conference held in 1966, which was considered a follow-up to the 1961 Washington event, stated: "There is perhaps a need to define a culture suitable for our own time which would certainly not coincide with the 'classical humanities.'"[51] In other words, in order to provide human capital theory with hard evidence education must be geared less toward tradition and more toward a *socio-economic* amalgam of technological modernity because, according to the CSTP Secretariat, it was no longer truly possible to distinguish between economic and social goals.[52]

Education's functional orientation toward "the world of tomorrow" was to be guaranteed by "new" forms of planning—after all, the "old" methods had failed.[53] The CSTP Secretariat had its planning agenda reviewed in the mid-1960s. Right from the outset, however, the authors of the review were given to understand that their report ought to come to positive conclusions—certainly, it was acknowledged, there were "logical" difficulties with respect to estimating education's contribution to economic growth, but the report had to avoid engaging in "sterile discussion." In brief, it was argued, there had been enough theory and discussion of principles; what was needed now was advice on "practical action."[54] In almost self-accusatory fashion, the planners subsequently contended that planning had hitherto failed to consider qualitative aspects, the inner workings of the system, and the fields of administration and implementation. Interpreted from the perspective of the member states, however, these were precisely those areas they either had not ceded to the international organization or over which this one had no power of governance, implementation, and monitoring due to its dearth of legislative and executive instruments and lack of financial incentives. OECD planners thus capitalized on their own failure by using comprehensive planning to penetrate the spheres of policy-making, administration, and the qualitative aspects of education—extending all the way to curricula and teaching—and integrating them into the organization's agenda, activities, and studies.

The CSTP found suitable methods in the form of total, goal- or output-oriented systems planning, which they began piloting in 1966 and which was intended to result in an improved understanding of "and therefore increased control over, the [educational] system as a whole."[55] Systems analysis had been forged chiefly in the 1950s by the RAND think tank, providing it—and all institutions (such as foundations) that lacked means of input governance (such as legislative instruments, control of teacher education, or curriculum development)—with a potent form of political influence. Sponsored by the Ford Foundation, and under the leadership of Philip Hall Coombs, RAND researchers applied systems analysis to the field of education in the late 1950s.[56] In light of the dearth of hard evidence, Coombs began to stylize this method with its output-orientation as the ultimate panacea. At a conference in Williamsburg "on the world educational crisis" in 1967, which created quite a stir, he emphasized that educational processes could only be organized in a "relevant, efficient and effective" way with the help of systems analysis.[57] In his monograph on educational planning, Coombs declared that only comprehensive planning could guarantee the "right kind of education," namely one that generated "'development-minded' people."[58] So the crisis did not prompt planners to question human capital theory itself; instead, it led to a tendency to describe education as dysfunctional. This malfunctioning could be eliminated—the CSTP, explicitly referring to the RAND study, also believed—if one conceptualized and investigated education as an educational *system*. This meant transferring the methods used for economic development on a quantitative macro-level to educational development on a qualitative micro-level.

In parallel, the OECD Secretariat took steps to create a research institution appropriate to comprehensive, systemic planning—the CERI. The OECD's Deputy Secretary-General Michael Harris had been in contact with the Ford Foundation since 1964 in order to organize an informal conference in England, in 1966, on the premises of the Ditchley Foundation, with the aim of hammering out the details of an educational research center. Conference participants included specialists in systems analysis and representatives from the quartet of core OECD countries (UK, France, Germany, the US) as well as planning pioneer Sweden.[59] Next to the economic experts who had shaped education policies in the early 1960s, sociologists dominated the conference. Since the CSTP's early days the latter had tried to instrumentalize the committee and the human capital "boom" by arguing that an economic focus on education was key to achieving the social goal of "equality of educational opportunity."[60] Conference participants acted not as country representatives but in their personal capacity as experts. A number of those attending, particularly the British and French representatives, were interested in establishing the center chiefly as a form of "effective fire support"[61]—to break down national resistance to reforms or acquire funds for reform projects that they had been denied on the national level.[62]

The center, it was asserted, would help achieve a better understanding of how the education system as a whole functioned. The economic interests at play were apparent, among other things, in the proposal by the British delegate (as it was reported by a staff member of the Ford Foundation) that CERI should include only economically strong countries. Countries such as Greece, Spain, and Portugal "which had little or nothing to offer in the way of capability for educational research or for effective launching of educational innovation" should be excluded.[63] Looking back, Ian Cox of the Royal Dutch Shell Foundation, that became a second sponsor of CERI next to the Ford Foundation, described the project in blunt terms:

> [The] CERI was created because King [who headed the Directorate for Scientific Affairs] and others recognized that the educational system produced the people needed to carry out technological and scientific development and that the educational system needed substantial revision if the *right kind* of people were to be produced. The idea was to make CERI the operational arm of OECD in bringing about the necessary changes.[64]

The Ford Foundation envisaged CERI as a "sister institute" to the IIEP, which it also funded, a sister responsible for the "developed" part of the world.[65] The Ford Foundation characterized the European education system as particularly incapable of keeping pace with modern society and thus saw it as vital that it be organized more effectively.[66] Experts at the foundation saw two key advantages in the patronage of the OECD. First, they knew about the resentment typically felt by national governments when it came to the establishment of new international bodies; by integrating CERI within the well-established framework of the OECD the institutionalization would be less visible and, as it was assumed, cause less resistance. Second,

> it became apparent to them [the Ford Foundation] that the reason why OECD had such a notable record of success and achievement in educational fields was in part due to its governmental nature; the fact that once an experiment was carried out and policy conclusions were deduced from the experiment, there was machinery in the various Governments to do something about it....[67]

Both the Council of Europe and the EEC might have provided these structures, but once again the OECD proved to have specific advantages: as mentioned above, the Council of Europe was impeded by its parliamentary structure and within the EEC education policy remained a touchy subject because of the organization's supranational dispositions.[68]

Sociologist Albert Henry Halsey, who organized the 1966 conference and was involved in financial negotiations with the Ford Foundation, underscored how little CSTP delegates were integrated into preliminary moves to establish CERI: "We [A.H. Halsey and the Secretary-General of the OECD] set off overnight from Paris, landed at Kennedy airport, drove into New York, extracted a promise of a million dollars...and took off again from Kennedy that afternoon." This, he stated, was exemplary of the "buccaneering atmosphere" he experienced during his many years of consultancy at the OECD.[69]

The Ford Foundation presented the OECD with the prospect of one million dollars for a two-year pilot period. Deputy Secretary-General Harris then advocated the establishment of CERI in the OECD Council, stating that education accounted for the greatest expenditure after defense in most member states, and means had therefore to be found to assess the "efficiency" and "productivity" of education systems.[70] However, this attempt to establish an educational research center met with considerable resistance. Certain country delegates noted, for example, that educational goals varied from country to country and that such an institute would distort the organization's key objectives.[71] There was particular resistance to the Ford Foundation's suggestion and expectation that the center should be semiautonomous. This meant that the governing board would be composed not of country representatives, but of select experts, and that not all member states would be represented. Despite this looming loss of control, no country wished to lose the funding of the Ford Foundation and the Council finally agreed to establish a semiautonomous center for a two-year pilot period—on the condition of voluntary membership.[72]

CERI's key concern during these two years was comprehensive educational planning, in other words: *educational management*. For instances, CERI was

> training people in the new skills required to plan, administer and control rapidly-changing educational systems. The "managerial revolution" which has had profound influence on industry, administration and the armed forces is only now beginning to influence the world of education, an yet the tasks of educational management and change are as technically complex and politically more sensitive than those of industry, for example.[73]

The center was founded "at the most opportune time" both in terms of the OECD's internal dynamics and the sweeping political and social developments occurring in the wider world. The latter were particularly evident in Europe's willingness to step up cross-border cooperation. One of the key motivations here was the renewed concern over Europe's backwardness in relation to the US, while President de Gaulle's resignation also removed an obstacle to cooperation.[74] At the same time, individual states were facing pressure from the 1968 student movements, which catapulted education policy onto national as well as international policy agenda. The CERI was thus in a strong position to present itself as *the* international lifeline to the national governments. The CERI's Secretariat was in contact with the "revolutionaries" and arranged even a meeting with some of the student leaders and the Secretary-General of the OECD. In this challenging context, even the supranational EEC could take on an active role in the field of education, drawing on the advice of numerous OECD experts.[75]

Not only did CERI benefit from the abovementioned social and economic developments, but from the fact that from the mid-1960s onward the purely quantitative pursuit of growth was increasingly challenged because it generally meant disregarding the social and environmental consequences of technological innovations.[76] Attempts to respond to this problem within the OECD reached their apex when Secretary-General Thorkil Kristensen presented before the Ministerial Council a paper entitled "Problems of the Modern Society" in 1969. Focusing on the negative by-products of technology, Kristensen underscored that education was key to dealing with these problems and made the case for CERI's work to continue.[77] This discourse seems to have been a watershed, opening up OECD policies to diverse qualitative aspects and social fields such as the environment, health, and, of course, promoting the official institutionalization of an educational body. Characteristically, Alexander King, the "monarch of all he surveys," was at the forefront of the movement to incorporate qualitative aspects into planning and thus into OECD policies. His deputy Ronald Gass was quick to emphasize that education "fitted quite naturally into the new orientations of the Organisation's work."[78]

In 1970 the formerly critical OECD Council voted to renew CERI's mandate despite the absence of any new funding commitment from the Ford Foundation. The latter's disengagement was due to what it saw as the OECD's failure to uphold the center's autonomy. First, Ronald Gass managed to keep his position in the CSTP while also taking on a new role as director of CERI, despite the Ford Foundation's preference for an external director. Second, the member states accepted the center's continued existence, and thus consented to fund it, only if they gained greater control over it. This resulted in the semi-politicization of the governing board, previously composed of a small panel of experts, as each member state could now send its own expert, who, however, was not considered to act as country representative.

This did not eliminate all opposition, with the British delegate to the CSTP warning the committee that since member states' educational goals differed, an international research center was of questionable value. His colleagues, however, informed him that "modern society" was marked by an increasing convergence of goals. The French delegate stated that:

> The choice of objectives depended to a large degree on the system of values accepted by society. It was with these values in mind that the Minister of National Education had at the Versailles Conference envisaged a 'new European standard of culture.[79]

In the same vein, the OECD Council not only agreed to renew CERI's mandate but also to transform the CSTP into an Education Committee. As a consequence, CERI and the Education Committee became virtually indistinguishable in their personnel, programs, and methods. In fact, as Kjell Eide, head of the OECD educational planning program, revealed in retrospect: while no one could clearly identify the boundary between the two bodies, this meant they were getting twice the financial resources.[80]

Both bodies subsequently devoted themselves to developing a comprehensive, systemic form of management for the education system:

> Whereas educational planning of the 1960s has been "quantitative"; reactive; and partial in its approach, educational planning for the 1970s should become programmatic (as opposed to reactive); and comprehensive.[81]

Planning, which was supposed "to transform education into a truly effective instrument of social and economic progress," could no longer merely respond to existing policies but must instead design such policies from the bottom up with the help of a goal-oriented science.[82] This downgraded the political sphere to a more or less executive role. In order to monitor implementation, a mechanism was found that is neatly captured in the key term "result-oriented."[83] Both CERI and the Education Committee drew up policies detailing how member states' "administrative machineries" must be adapted in order to carry out continuous "assessment of goal structures"[84] and report the findings to the OECD—a form of educational monitoring and output governance *avant la lettre*. Here the two bodies could fall back on structures already established by the EIP.

Subsequently, and in line with the imperatives of socio-economic modernity, human capital theory was amalgamated with the discourse of "equality of educational opportunity," culminating in the notion of "equality of achievement."[85] In this shift from input to output, equality was no longer defined as a status, but could supposedly be produced through a process—namely the *right kind* of education. So the goal of the OECD educational bodies was not international exchange and cooperation. Instead, with the help of a goal- or output-oriented science, education was to serve the needs of a *single* system of modern society (supposedly without alternative)—and the emphasis was thus on homogenization and standardization. The OECD bodies were now embracing the ambitious objective of "educating the whole man," which resulted in what we might call "ontological engineering"—covering everything from health to leisure time and culminating in the lofty goal of "fate control."[86]

Engineer of the West

The OECD's attempts to adapt Europe to technological, science-based, socio-economic modernity—as outlined in this chapter—are indicative of the organization's "identity-shaping" tendencies.[87] The OECD sought actively—by means of education—to engineer the West as a community. To this end the OECD, which had virtually no legislative or financial powers at its disposal, increasingly turned to an instrument typical of foundations (like the Ford Foundation) or think tanks (such as RAND) in order to compensate for its missing capacity for input governance—namely science and an orientation toward output.[88] In the shape of systems analysis, these institutions professionalized a scientific, goal- or output-oriented form of governance. But in contrast to RAND or the Ford Foundation, connected to governments by purely informal channels, the OECD's links with governments were an intrinsic part of its character, making it more powerful than these bodies.

The OECD's resulting hybridity, oscillating between professional think tank and international governmental organization, has not only contributed to its elusive character but also appears to be a hallmark of its success. Its focus on goals, standards, and output, which chiefly arose due to its powerlessness, allowed the organization to professionalize a form of soft-law governance. This could evolve virtually unnoticed while national governments kept a hawk-like gaze fixed on the EEC, with its explicitly supranational aspirations and while the Council of Europe was monitored and controlled by its affiliated parliament.

Because CERI was granted semi-autonomous status, it could benefit from the OECD's established channels of cooperation and information with national governments but was mostly spared inhibitive processes of political negotiation. CERI's formal independence, moreover, created an air of scientific objectivity that was reinforced by the figures- and numbers-focused presentation of its findings.[89] Here we see the politicization of science, which entailed the depoliticization of negotiation processes or—calling to mind the portrait of Alexander King in his autobiography—the establishment of a "monarchy of evidence."

In this chapter I have argued that the OECD's education policies and institutional processes were the product of a number of experts, or rather, of technocratic networks. At the same time, however, the organization positioned itself as an "actor in its own right,"[90] eager to perpetuate itself—as evident above all in the establishment of CERI. The CSTP's official channels were usually activated only once ideas had already gained traction through unofficial channels, and these generally excluded the Southern European member states. All the key bodies, from the EPA through the CSTP to the CERI, were initially financed with American money (either from the government or the Ford Foundation), with responsibility passing to the member states after about two years, when national "machineries" had been built up.

More research is needed on these structural if not existential interdependencies between the national and international bureaucracies and on the interplay between them. When the golden era of planning was over, the CERI continued to exist and most national planning bodies also endured. But we should not conceive of these relations between the national and international level in dichotomous fashion; instead we should understand and investigate them as networks. These networks seem likely to illuminate how, beginning in the 1990s, the OECD could attain such a pronounced role as the expert in education, with countries across the world awaiting the publication of the PISA reports with bated breath and allowing this organization to determine their educational success or failure. Future studies might also show how the Western European welfare states came to increasingly embrace output governance and thus utilize an instrument that, given their capabilities to control inputs, they had no fundamental need to embrace.

Notes

1. Dana Wilgress, *Co-operation in the Field of Scientific and Technical Research: Report* (Paris: OEEC, 1960), 18.
2. Ian Hacking, "Style for Historians and Philosophers," *Studies in History and Philosophy of Science* 23, No. 1 (1992): 1–20.
3. See for example Kerstin Martens, "How to Become an Influential Actor—The 'Comparative Turn' in OECD Education Policy," in *New Arenas of Education Governance: The Impact of International Organizations and Markets on Educational Policy Making*, ed. K. Martens et al. (Basingstoke: Palgrave Macmillan, 2007), 40–56; Enno Aljets, *Der Aufstieg der Empirischen Bildungsforschung: Ein Beitrag zur institutionalistischen Wissenschaftssoziologie* (Wiesbaden: Springer VS, 2015); Fazal Rizvi & Bob Lingard, *Globalizing Education Policy* (New York: Routledge, 2010).
4. Regula Bürgi, *Die OECD und die Bildungsplanung der freien Welt. Denkstile und Netzwerke einer internationalen Bildungsexpertise* (Opladen: Barbara Budrich, 2017), 51–80.
5. OEEC, *The Problem of Scientific and Technical Manpower in Western Europe, Canada and the United States* (Paris: OEEC, 1957); OECD Historical Archives (hereafter OECD-HA), C(58)52, Report to the Council of Working Party No. 25 on Scientific And Highly Qualified Technical Manpower, 7 February 1958.
6. Kjell Eide, *30 Years of Educational Collaboration in the OECD* (Paris: UNESCO, 1990), 8.

7. Alexander King, *Let the Cat Turn Round. One Man's Traverse of the Twentieth Century* (London: CPTM, 2006), 378.
8. Bernd Greiner, "Macht und Geist im Kalten Krieg. Bilanz und Ausblick," in *Macht und Geist im Kalten Krieg*, ed. B. Greiner et al. (Hamburg: Hamburger Edition, HIS, 2011), 9.
9. Philip Rocco, "Wissensproduktion in der RAND Corporation," in *Macht und Geist im Kalten Krieg*, ed. B. Greiner et al. (Hamburg: Hamburger Edition, HIS, 2011), 301–320; Regula Bürgi, "Systemic Management of Schools. The OECD's Professionalization and Dissemination of Output Governance in the 1960s," *Paedagogica Historica* 52, No. 4 (2016): 3–6; John L. Rudolph, *Scientists in the Classroom. The Cold War Reconstruction of American Science Education* (New York: Palgrave Macmillan, 2002), 57.
10. King, *Let the Cat*, 182–195.
11. UNESCO Historical Archives (UNESDOC), UNESCO/NS/W/10, Science and Government, A Report by Dr. Alexander King, 10 May 1950.
12. Klaus Brummer, *Der Europarat: Eine Einführung* (Wiesbaden: VS Verlag für Sozialwissenschaften Springer, 2008), 21–24.
13. King, *Let the Cat*, 194.
14. George S. Papadopoulos, *Die Entwicklung des Bildungswesens von 1960 bis 1990. Der Beitrag der OECD* (Frankfurt am Main: Peter Lang, 1996), 25; Bent Boel, *The European Productivity Agency and Transatlantic Relations, 1953–1961* (Copenhagen: Museum Tusculanum Press/University of Copenhagen, 2003), 9.
15. OEEC, *Problem of Scientific and Technical Manpower.*
16. OECD-HA, C(58)52, Report to the Council of Working Party No. 25 on Scientific And Highly Qualified Technical Manpower, 7 February 1958, 12.
17. King, *Let the Cat*, 182.
18. Bürgi, *OECD und die Bildungsplanung*, 68–73.
19. Wilgress, *Co-operation in the Field*, 4–5.
20. OECD-HA, STP/GC/M(58)3, Record of the 3rd Session (3–4 December 1958), 31 December 1958, 7.
21. OECD-HA, STP/GC/M(60)3, Record of the 11th Session (25–26 October 1960), 19 December 1960, 5.
22. King, *Let the Cat*, 264; Eide, *30 Years*, 9.
23. Rockefeller Archive Center (RAC), Catalogued Reports, No. 2537, Centre for Educational Research and Innovation. A Retrospective Review of a Ford Foundation Grant, 15 March 1976, 2, 33 and 28 (quotation).
24. Matthias Schmelzer, *The Hegemony of Growth. The Making and Remaking of the Economic Growth Paradigm and the OECD, 1948–1974* (Cambridge: Cambridge University Press, 2016), 34–53 and 189–214.
25. King, *Let the Cat*, 272.

26. OECD-HA, STP/M(61)1, Record of the 1st Session (19–21 June 1961), 29 September 1961, 17.
27. OECD-HA, STP/GC(59)22, Policy Considerations to Be Taken into Account in the Preparation of the Third Annual Programme, 21 May 1959, 2.
28. OECD-HA, GC(59)59, Economic Growth and Investment in Education, 28 October 1959, 7–8.
29. OECD, *Policy Conference on Economic Growth and Investment in Education*, Washington 16–20 October 1961 (Paris: OECD, 1962). Eide, *30 Years*, 12. King, *Let the Cat*, 273–274. Papadopoulos, *Entwicklung des Bildungswesens*, 43–47.
30. Ingvar Svennilson, Friedrich Edding & Lionel Elvin, "Targets for Education in Europe in 1970," in OECD, *Policy Conference*, 15.
31. Ibid., 5.
32. Bürgi, "Systemic Management," 5.
33. Philip Coombs, *Recalling the Origins of Unesco's International Institute for Educational Planning* (1992), 2. http://www.unesco.org/iiep/PDF/IIEPOrigins.pdf [03.01.2017].
34. Bürgi, *OECD und die Bildungsplanung*, 85–101.
35. IIEP Historical Archives (IIEP-HA), Unclassified, Guy Benveniste, Creation of the International Institute for Educational Planning (Unesco). A Personal Account, 2007.
36. OECD-HA, STP/M(61)2, Record of the 2nd Session (6–8 November, 1961), 29 December 1961.
37. OECD, *The Residual Factor and Economic Growth* (Paris: OECD, 1964), 181.
38. For MRP see esp. Daniel Tröhler, "Standardisierung nationaler Bildungspolitiken: Die Erschaffung internationaler Experten, Planern und Statistikern in der Frühphase der OECD," *International Journal for the Historiography of Education* 3, No. 1 (2013): 60–77; OECD-HA, CSTP, STP(62)1, Pilot Studies on Long Term Needs for Educational Resources in Advanced Countries, 4 January 1962.
39. OECD-HA, STP(62)19, Programme on Educational Investment and Planning in Relation to Economic Growth, 25 May 1962, 10–14, 14 (quotation); Eide, *30 Years*, 14–16.
40. OECD-HA, STP(62)36, Country Reviews, 13 September 1962, 2.
41. Herbert S. Parnes & OECD, *Planning Education for Economic and Social Development, Lectures Presented at the Training Course for Human Resource Strategist. Organised by the Directorate for Scientific Affairs at the Villa Falconieri, Frascati, Italy, 3–28 September 1962* (Paris: OECD, 1963), 256.
42. Töhler, "Standardisierung nationaler," 60–77; OECD, *Residual Factor*, 56.

43. Ibid., 181.
44. Parnes & OECD, *Planning Education*, 42.
45. OECD-HA, STP(64)38, Educational Investment Planning (The Need for a Critical Review of Problems and Methods), 28 August 1964, 3.
46. Europarat, *Resolution on Planning and Investment in Education, No. 2* (Europarat: 1964). http://www.coe.int/t/dg4/education/Source/MED25/4_MED_London_April1964.pdf [03.01.2017].
47. Bürgi, *OECD und die Bildungsplanung*, 98–101.
48. Gareth L. Williams, "Educational Policies, Plans and Forecasts During the Nineteen-Sixties and Seventies," in *The Development of Educational Planning, ed. OECD* (Paris: OECD, 1972), 12.
49. On development aid see the chapter by Patricia Hongler in this volume.
50. IIEP-HA, IIEP/S14/1, IIEP director (Philip Coombs) to IIEP staff members, Confidential—Internal Working Paper, 11 May 1967, 12.
51. OECD-HA, STP/67(1), Inter-Governmental Conference on the Education and Utilization of Highly Qualified Personnel, 30 January 1967, 8.
52. OECD-HA, STP/M(65)3, Record of the 11th Session (10–12 March, 1965), 5 May 1965, 17.
53. OECD, *Curriculum Improvement and Educational Development. Modernizing our Schools* (Paris: OECD, 1966), 32.
54. OECD-HA, STP(64)38, Educational Investment Planning, The Need for a Critical Review of Problems and Methods, 28 August 1964, 3.
55. OECD-HA, STP(67)6, Programme of Work for 1968, 5 June 1967, 11.
56. Philip Rocco, "Wissensproduktion," 308–309; Bürgi, "Systemic Management," 3–6.
57. Philip H. Coombs, *The World Educational Crisis* (New York: Oxford University Press, 1968), 9.
58. Philip H. Coombs, *What is Educational Planning?* (Paris: UNESCO/IIEP, 1970), 42.
59. RAC, Reel 1486, Proposal for a Centre for Educational Innovation, Second draft, 15 April 1966.
60. OECD, *Ability and Educational Opportunity* (Paris: OECD, 1961), 45.
61. See Mathias Schmelzer and Matthieu Leimgruber's overview of the OECD's history in this volume.
62. Bürgi, *OECD und die Bildungsplanung*, 159–170.
63. RAC, Reel 1486, OECD Discussions, 8 December 1966, 2.
64. RAC, Catalogued Reports, No. 2537, Centre for Educational Research and Innovation. A Retrospective Review of a Ford Foundation Grant, 15 March 1976, 14 (my emphasis).
65. RAC, Reel 1485, Establishment of a Center for Educational Innovation and Research (Report), 1 April 1968, 3.

66. RAC, Office Files, Frank Bowles, Series 2, Correspondence Files, Box 3, Folder 57, Memorandum. Re: OECD Project, 2 January 1968, 2.
67. OECD-HA, CES/67.42, Programme of Cooperation in Educational Research and Innovation Support Offered by the Ford Foundation, Statement by Mr. Harris at the Meeting of the Executive Committee (12 July 1967), 18 July 1967, 2 (quotation) and 4.
68. European Commission, *The History of European Cooperation in Education and Training. Europe in the Making—an Example* (Luxembourg: European Communities, 2006), 45.
69. Albert Henry Halsey, *No Discouragement: An Autobiography* (Basingstoke: Macmillan), 63.
70. OECD-HA, CE/M(67)16, Executive Committee, Summary Record—Meeting (11–12 July, 1967), 4 October 1967, 53.
71. OECD-HA, C(67)88, Programme of Co-operation in Educational Research and Innovation: Support Offered by the Ford Foundation, Note by the Secretary of the Council, 16 August 1967.
72. OECD-HA, CES/67.39, Programme of Co-operation in Educational Research and Innovation Support Offered by the Ford Foundation, 6 July 1967; OECD-HA, C(70)111, Review of the Work of the Organization in the Field of Education, 23 June 1970. OECD-HA, C/M(70)21, Council Minutes, 226th Meeting, 22 July 1970.
73. OECD-HA, CERI/68.8, Draft Programme of Work for 1969, 23 August 1968, 16.
74. OECD-HA, CERI/GB/M/68.1, Summary Record of the 1st meeting, 24–25 June 1968, 2 (quotation). See the classical contemporary account in Jean-Jacques Servan-Schreiber, *The American Challenge* (New York: Atheneum, 1968).
75. Eide, *30 Years*, 32; Bürgi, *OECD und die Bildungsplanung*, 156–159.
76. On the OECD's work on the environment, see the chapter by Iris Borowy in this volume.
77. Matthias Schmelzer, "The Crisis before the Crisis: The 'Problems of Modern Society' and the OECD, 1968–1974," *European Review of History* 19, No. 6 (2012): 999–1020; OECD-HA, STP(69)6, Progress report on Activities in the Committee's Programme, 24 March 1969, 2.
78. OECD-HA, CERI/CD/M(71)1, Record of the first Session (12–13 July 1971), 17 August 1971, 5.
79. OECD-HA, STP/M(69)2, Record of the 24th Session (19–21 November 1969), 4 March 1970, 14–18.
80. Eide, *30 years*, 31.
81. OECD, *Educational Policies for the 1970's*, Conference on Policies for Educational Growth, Paris, 3–5 June, 1970 (Paris: OECD, 1970), 111.
82. Ibid., 62.

83. Eide, *30 years*, 34.
84. OECD-HA, STP(70)32, General Lines of the Proposed Programme of Work for 1971, 1 July 1970, 2.
85. OECD, *Educational Policies*, 35.
86. OECD-HA, DAS/EID/71.62, Working Group of the Education Committee on Educational Statistics and Indicators, 11 October 1971, v.
87. See the historical overview by Matthieu Leimgruber and Matthias Schmelzer in this volume.
88. See Barbara Howe, "The Emergence of Scientific Philanthropy, 1900–1920: Origins, Issues, and Outcomes," in *Philanthropy and Cultural Imperialism: The Foundations at Home and Abroad*, ed. Robert F. Arnove (Boston, Mass: G.K. Hall, 1980), 25–54.
89. See Theodore M. Porter, *Trust in Numbers: The Pursuit of Objectivity in Science and Public Life* (Princeton, N.J: Princeton University Press, 1995).
90. Michael N. Barnett & Martha Finnemore, *Rules for the World: International Organizations in Global Politics* (Ithaca, N.Y.: Cornell University Press, 2004), 12.

Negotiating Environment: The Making of the OECD Environment Committee and the Polluter Pays Principle, 1968–1972

Iris Borowy

In 1970, the OECD created an Environment Committee, making it the first international organization to establish a permanent committee specifically dedicated to environmental issues. Two years later, on the eve of the Stockholm Conference on the Human Environment, it released *Guiding Principles Concerning the International Economic Aspects of Environmental Policies.* As its most prominent element, this text included the first formulation of the so-called Polluter Pays Principle (PPP), which subsequently became a significant element in international environmental debates.[1] Activities during the short time in between determined not only what shape environmental activities at the OECD would take but, by extension, how these decisions would position the OECD vis-à-vis other international organizations (IOs) engaged in environmental issues and how the OECD would influence international environmental debates. This chapter analyzes how, between 1969 and 1972, the OECD went from being an organization with only marginal interest in environmental topics, via one aiming at becoming the central reference institution for environmental concerns, understood in broad social terms, to

I. Borowy (✉)
College of Liberal Arts, Shanghai University, 99 Shangda Road,
Shanghai 200444, China
e-mail: irisborowy@shu.edu.cn

M. Leimgruber and M. Schmelzer (eds.), *The OECD and the International Political Economy Since 1948*, DOI 10.1007/978-3-319-60243-1_13

one among several organizations with an environmental program, albeit one of considerable international influence in the key sector of its organizational competence.

Accounts of the OECD environmental program have so far focused on its significance for the OECD as an institution, and offered various interpretations. Bill Long, head of the OECD Environment Directorate from 1987 to 1997, unsurprisingly, paints a positive picture of these events, listing the PPP as one of several achievements in international environmental work and as part of the OECD's successful efforts to integrate environmental considerations into economic thinking.[2] In a more critical vein, economist/political scientist Steven Bernstein has depicted the OECD environmental program as a moving force behind the emergence of "liberal environmentalism," a format that reflected a Western, market-oriented economic agenda.[3] Similarly, Matthias Schmelzer, focusing on the OECD as a motor of the postwar economic growth paradigm, has analyzed its environmental activities as part of the refashioning of growth politics in the 1970s.[4] Looking at the subsequent decade, I have interpreted the OECD environmental program as both an input into and a pivotal Western reaction to the concept of sustainable development.[5] Views differ regarding the impact of the OECD in the field. While Long, Bernstein, and Schmelzer have highlighted the institutional identity of the OECD, thus suggesting that it could and did establish its economic and ideological agenda on the international scene, Per-Olof Busch and Markku Lehtonen have depicted a comparatively powerless agency without any enforcement capabilities, which resorted to various strategies to impact opinions or even to be heard beyond a small group of economic and environmental experts.[6] Indeed, the oft-contradictory nature of early OECD environmental activities offers room for different interpretations. One explanation may lie in the somewhat hasty circumstances in which the PPP program was conceived and the compressed time frame in which crucial decisions about the future of environmental work in IOs were made. The stage was set between the late 1960s, when a burgeoning environmental movement in many OECD countries placed the environment onto the national and international agenda, and 1972, when the Stockholm Conference created the UN Environment Programme. In between, all agencies with ambitions in the field maneuvered to find a place for their specific program while defining what it should be.

To different degrees, this situation affected numerous IOs, which, in one way or another, addressed environmental aspects of various issues, ranging from health (WHO), to agriculture (FAO), climate (World Meteorological Organization), and development (UNDP).[7] Given the tense relation between environment and economy, where it was unclear if or to what extent economic achievement was compatible with environmental stability, it was the economic organizations that faced the potentially most challenging questions. They also found themselves in most direct competition. For the OECD, this translated to implicit rivalry with the United Nations Economic Commission for Europe (UNECE or ECE). This competition, as analyzed by Daniel Stinsky in this volume, added to their traditionally edgy relationship. The creation of the OEEC for the implementation of the Marshall Plan had marginalized the ECE from this key event in postwar European economic development, its central field of responsibility.[8] This background strengthened the overall OECD position, particularly providing the reliable support of Western member states. However, the ECE had an obvious advantage in issues like transboundary air and water pollution, which crossed the lines between East and West. For both organizations, the environment, as a new field of work, offered the opportunity to enrich their organizational profile and consolidate their international position. The situation became even more complicated when NATO created an additional commission in charge of environmental affairs.

This competition for organizational pre-eminence was influenced by the upheavals of the late 1960s, which challenged key tenets of the traditional socio-economic order, ranging from gender relations to economic goals. These debates included and went beyond the question of economic growth. For some years, before the oil crises and emerging neoliberalism cut short such discussions, decisions about where the ongoing development should lead to and what type of society it entailed were questioned more profoundly than either before or for years afterwards, and environmental concerns provided an opportunity either to fuel or to channel these considerations.[9]

These conditions formed the background for vehement debates at the OECD. This chapter chronicles this development within the context of the organization itself as well as in connection to other international institutions.

The Origins of Environmental Work at the OECD

The OEEC, predecessor of the OECD, first addressed environmental topics through its Committee for Applied Research, established in 1957. Designed to address various technical issues that were challenging for member states, the Committee initiated several small studies on industrial water and air pollution. After 1961, its successor body, the Committee for Scientific Research (CSR), continued these activities, adding studies on noise and pesticides. In 1966, the CSR was renamed Committee for Research Cooperation, gaining higher though still quite modest status, and was endowed with some limited human and financial resources. Its purpose was to provide guidance for governmental policy and investment decisions, and its selection criteria for topics of work reflected the overall function of the OECD: issues the OECD worked on had to be important regarding national economic or social goals; they had to be relevant to many member countries, their solution supposedly required further cooperation in the future and had to be compatible with the economic interests of those concerned; research should provide tangible help to decision makers; and experience gained in one country should provide help to others.[10] It was a utilitarian approach in line with the general expectations that international organizations should provide knowledge and service in fields that were difficult or impossible to manage nationally. Pollution was relevant as a problematic side effect of economic activities, perceived as a technical problem requiring technical solutions.

These activities were coordinated by the Directorate for Scientific Affairs, and in particular by a new Science Policy and an Environmental Research Division. This Division was organized in several advisory and study groups, addressing, respectively, water research, auto exhaust and sulfur products, pesticides and innovation, urban management, as well as pesticides in the environment. By 1968, staff and funding devoted to these issues had more than quadrupled.[11] In 1970, the structure of the organization's environment-related work was once more reorganized, and the following five sectoral working groups were attached to the Committee for Research Co-operation:

- Water Management Research Group
- Air Management Research Group
- Study Group on the Unintended Occurrence of Pesticides
- Consultative Group for Transportation Research
- Study Group on Innovation in Urban Management.[12]

In practical terms, these working groups addressed topics ranging from the eutrophication of lakes and reservoirs to the biodegradability of synthetic detergents, increasing emissions of sulphur compounds, and the decline of wildlife diversity in forests and rivers due to pesticides. In addition, the OECD worked alongside the European Nuclear Energy Agency (a semi-autonomous OECD institution) on radioactive pollution and radiation protection norms.[13] None of these activities questioned the existing economic system or the principle that it entailed some degree of environmental degradation. Environmental concerns appeared as technical rather than social issues. Pollution was considered a price that had to be paid for economic prosperity, but some effort was necessary to keep this price under control. Governments were prepared to provide some money for this purpose and hoped that IOs would make this process more efficient.

Similar efforts were taking place at the ECE. Here, studies were initiated in the 1950s by the inland shipping and the coal industries, concerned that their real or perceived environmental impact would place them at a disadvantage compared to train transportation and oil. In 1967, the ECE added a broader perspective. In phrases that anticipated OECD discussions two years later, it declared that the time had come to reconsider the environmental consequences of recent increases in per capita income and to "adopt comprehensive, systematic and long-term policies related to environmental problems as a whole."[14]

Meanwhile, initiatives at the UN introduced a North-South dimension into the discussions. The 1968 *Intergovernmental Conference of Experts on the Scientific Basis for the Rational Use and Conservation of the Resources of the Biosphere*, jointly organized by UNESCO and the International Union for Conservation of Nature, referred to the specific challenges of developing countries before stating unequivocally that the environment was being degraded at an accelerating rate and recommending the establishment of an "international and interdisciplinary programme on the rational utilization and conservation of the resources of the biosphere" under the auspices of UNESCO.[15] During the following years, preparations for a *United Nations Conference on Human Development* got bogged down in a tense controversy between governments of high-income countries in the North and low-income countries in the global South about the extent of environmental degradation and related responsibilities and consequences.[16] This tension partially obstructed and delayed the forming of an umbrella environmental organization at the UN level.[17]

The need for some coordination was not far-fetched. In 1970, an OECD report listed no fewer than 19 IOs engaged in environmental matters, addressing various types of pollution and/or underlying products or processes such as pesticides, transportation, industrial production, or nuclear energy.[18] Increasingly, environment turned into a must-have topic for IOs, and this proliferation created rivalry between them, as their administrations competed for limited national funding, experts, and attention. In addition, the prospect of a future central coordinating agency, which would reduce the status of the other institutions to second-grade importance, increased the potential advantage of a strong position in this field to influence or—potentially—to become this institution. This situation inevitably upgraded the position of the environment within the OECD.

These considerations gained a new dimension in February 1969, when OECD Secretary-General Thorkil Kristensen presented a note to the OECD Ministerial Council entitled *Problems of a Modern Society.* Citing various manifestations of social and environmental problems the paper described a widespread feeling in OECD countries that rapid economic growth, though a coveted goal of economic development, was not without problems in that it raised a series of new questions.[19] Suddenly, environmental issues appeared not as technical problems but as components of larger social challenges.

The idea was copied swiftly. In April, US President Nixon attended a Ministerial Session of the NATO Council and urged NATO to foster exchanges of views between member states regarding ways to improve their environments. He accompanied his initiative with substantial pressure on allies to support this new NATO program. In July, the NATO Council created an open-ended Preparatory Committee to explore terms of reference and methods of work of a "proposed Committee on the Challenges of Modern Society."[20] The idea of establishing a new committee in a field that was already relatively crowded was not overly popular among other member governments. But the full weight of the US administration was difficult to resist, and during the following months the *Committee on the Challenges of Modern Society* (CCMS) got underway.[21] Inexorably, gaining control over the environmental agenda became a question of organizational prestige and of preventing rival organizations in the East-West and/or the North-South divide such as NATO, ECE, or the UN from appropriating the topic. For the OECD to retain a leading position in the field, it required further activities which would take social as well as technical aspects into account.

The Creation of the OECD Environment Committee

These activities were driven by Kristensen's successor, Secretary-General Emile van Lennep. In September 1969, he summed up the promises and challenges of the current socio-economic situation in a 30-page position paper: the unprecedented economic growth of the 1960s, expected to continue in the 1970s, had led to rising living standards as well as extensive problems of environmental destruction and social fragmentation, which alienated some citizens, especially young people.[22] Van Lennep's suggestion that the OECD should address these issues was welcomed by most members of the OECD Council in January 1970, who were ready to take a new look at the desired form of economic growth, though not the principle as such.[23] The topic had the potential for a radical reconsideration of a growth-centered economy, and part of the related thinking branched out into the Club of Rome, which developed with the active cooperation of OECD personnel and eventually gave rise to the famous MIT study on the Limits to Growth.[24] Meanwhile, discussion within the OECD quickly focused on environmental topics as foremost challenges. However, this shift demanded decisions on which topics should or should not be included in such considerations, in which manner, and for what purpose.

These questions were discussed at the OECD Executive Committee in February 1970, when the ambivalent character of the issue became amply clear. Experts and national delegates differed not only in their understanding of what exactly they were discussing, but also on what level of abstraction and for what purpose these discussions should take place. Deputy Secretary-General Gérard Eldin, who chaired the meeting, and the US delegate felt that nothing more than some modifications of the existing activities of the Committee for Research Cooperation was necessary. By contrast, Alexander King, head of the Directorate for Scientific Affairs and a key protagonist in the *Problems of Modern Society* debate, pointed out the inadequacy of this committee, which had hardly engaged in research but had focused instead on the management of technology regarding water, urban development, and transport, only part of which had environmental repercussions. Delegates generally disagreed on whether environmental issues should be viewed as a component of larger socio-economic questions mentioned in the *Problems of Modern Society* or as independent topics requiring technological solutions. Meanwhile, other delegates recognized the potential for the creation of a permanent new structure, and several declared that, as an economic organization, the OECD was best suited to deal with problems of the environment and should, in fact, become the central coordinating organization for these issues.[25]

Given the cacophony of budding international environmental bodies, the idea of establishing the OECD as the center of international environmental work was not unrealistic, and it offered the promise of shaping the global agenda according to the interests and perspectives of high-income OECD member countries. Potentially, the OECD could thus become a "Warden for the West" in international environmental debates. The overall feeling among delegates at the meeting just described wavered between pride of being the organization which, because of its specific competence, ought to oversee environmental issues, and uncertainty about which issues should be addressed and in which way.

This ambivalence surfaced again shortly afterward during the first meeting of the new "Preparatory Committee on the Activities of the OECD on Environmental Problems Related to Economic Growth," which had been created in parallel to similar NATO structures. Debates revealed a shared conviction that the OECD was particularly well situated to study economic aspects of environmental problems since it was a homogeneous body of industrialized countries where environmental problems were acute, and it could rely both on its experience in economic studies and on the support of a well-established Secretariat. But divisions remained on whether OECD studies should retain a strictly economic focus or also integrate social aspects. Officially the question was left open, but the choice of selection criteria for topics revealed that delegates were most interested in issues of tangible policy relevance: the urgency of a problem for several countries, the magnitude of foreseeable economic consequences, and the need for government action. Other aspects referred to repercussions for the OECD, notably the relevance of the issue for cooperation between OECD member states, pre-existing work at the OECD, and its absence in other IOs, as well as the capacity of the OECD to effectively address the issue and to link it to its overall work on economic growth. Nevertheless, the conceptualization of relevant topics was left undecided: should issues be defined according to external manifestations (notably of pollution), to their origins (such as industry or transport), to their effects (on the economy, on health, etc.) or to possible strategies (such as standards, charges, etc.)?[26]

Van Lennep confirmed the institutional frame of this initiative, while at the same time insisting on a broad understanding of the topic.

Commission members should keep in mind that work on environmental questions should be related to the general functions of the OECD, i.e., to support member states, individually and collectively, in their socio-economic development. Emphasizing the complexity of the issue, he called for a multi-disciplinary approach and recommended the creation of a "Committee for Environment Policy" consisting of top officials working in the environmental field in their countries, in order to supervise and coordinate the work of sectoral groups. This structure would thereby give a new title to groups already in existence, i.e., in charge of analysis, assistance in international standardization, and cost-benefit estimates, while new specific issues, such as fuel combustion, street noise, solid waste disposal, or thermal pollution could be addressed via ad hoc problem groups.[27] Van Lennep's attitude was in line with his general efforts to increase the coherence of OECD activities as well as its relevance to governmental decision-making.[28] But his focus on building on existing structures may also have reflected the need for speedy results to withstand pressure from other institutions. Thus, ECE Executive Secretary Janez Stanovnik was likewise eager to turn his organization into the center of international environmental policy-making.[29] By late March, a British government official commented that the OECD, the ECE, and the NATO were "tripping over themselves to get into the environmental bandwagon."[30] The need for some coordination seemed obvious, but the British idea that the OECD "should be responsible for coordinating Western policies on the environment, after which suitable issues could be discussed by E.C.E," found little support among other countries, especially in NATO circles.[31] The sheer number of OECD members made it difficult to agree on a single format.

Meanwhile, discussions at the OECD Preparatory Committee dragged on. In April 1970, the majority of committee members argued that the OECD should not mainly aim at theoretical studies but at tangible results for international cooperation, particularly regarding cost-benefit analyses of different policy options and uniform standards to prevent trade distortions. But in a larger sense, efforts should also be directed at a systemic prevention of environmental degradation, i.e., at questions of how to achieve harmonious development policies and of what to do when no such development was forthcoming.[32] During the Ministerial Council Meeting in May 1970, this dichotomy was conceptualized as a micro- versus a macroeconomic approach. The former entailed a continuation of the work of the Committee of Research Cooperation with increased attention to economic and social implications, while the latter meant including broad question regarding the allocation of resources and of overall costs and benefits. The balance shifted to a micro-approach when van Lennep made clear that large macroeconomic questions would be addressed separately in different groups discussing the issue of long-term growth.[33] On this basis, the Council formally established the Environment Committee in July 1970, effectively limiting its approach to the environment as a component of socio-economic development in a primarily technical sense, excluding larger political or structural questions. The Commission held its inaugural meeting in November, headed by its first chairman, US Deputy Assistant Secretary of State for Environmental and Population Affairs, Christian Herter. A supporting Environment Directorate in the Secretariat was established in early 1971, receiving 19 staff members from the Scientific Affairs Directorate, which was discontinued, 3 from other directorates and 15 new positions. It began its work with a modest budget of 4.4 million French Francs, to be shared among a Direction and Control Central Analysis Unit, a Natural Resources Division, and an Urban Division.[34]

Despite Herter's assurances of cooperation with the ECE, the establishment of this commission, supported and funded by states which were also ECE members, was a clear victory of the OECD over the ECE, and Stanovnik could not help showing his bitterness in a fruitless and somewhat embarrassing attempt to prevent a resolution that committed the ECE to avoid duplication with environmental programs of other IOs.[35] But it was only a partial victory. In April 1970, US diplomat George Kennan had proposed in a *Foreign Affairs* article to situate a new environmental organization outside the UN. But when this suggestion was met with vehement protests from developing countries, it became clear that such a body would have to be placed within the UN system to find global acceptance. In view of the all-encompassing character of the environment, which made its various facets relevant to different contexts, the UN body was organized as a "program" rather than a specialized agency, encouraging a continuation of work in existing IOs along sectoral lines.[36] Thus, the OECD would not become *the* special agency in charge of environment, but it could strengthen its position by contributing in ways that underscored its specific competence in this field.

The Sub-Committee of Economic Experts

Initially most OECD environmental activities simply continued prior work, as the five sectoral groups continued with few changes. The Water and Air Management Research Groups dropped "research" from their names and turned into "sector groups," the group on "unintended occurrence of pesticides" broadened to address "chemicals," whereas groups on transportation research and on innovation management fused into an Urban Sector Group. These topics largely carried on the conventional technical approach. The one program which was specific to the OECD and which reflected the strand of addressing larger societal debates evolved into a Sub-Committee of Economic Experts, newly created in early 1971. Its establishment may have been spurred by the lack of enthusiasm for cooperation among established OECD economists.[37] But it was also in line with the search for a specific OECD approach to environmental questions, reflecting its idiosyncratic mixture of a commitment to economic orthodoxy and doubts about the direction of the resulting socio-economic development. This ambivalent and partially contradictory approach shaped the ensuing debates.

Divisions became rapidly apparent between, on the one hand, macroeconomic and technical, microeconomic perspectives; and on the other hand, between the Sub-committee, whose members were delegates of national governments, and the Secretariat, whose staff consisted of highly-qualified experts, predominantly economists, often with notable academic backgrounds.[38] Naturally, their interests differed: while Secretariat staff tended to be interested in questions of principle and in-depth analysis, delegates were interested in short-term applicability. In slightly simplistic terms one may argue that the Secretariat experts wished to know which policies could be effective in serving long-term goals, while delegates wished to know which policies produced a sufficiently positive cost-benefit balance to be acceptable to governments and electorates.

During 1971, the Sub-Committee sought to balance these two antagonistic approaches. First, it took up discussions with the Central Analysis and Evaluation Unit regarding international aspects of environmental policies, stressing the need to produce tangible results through cooperation with ad hoc groups. Second, it commissioned studies on two questions of principle: the cost allocation of environmental policies and the impact of environmental policies on international trade.[39]

The problem, repeatedly explained, analyzed, and considered at length, was quite simple: any measure designed to internalize environmental costs into product prices, such as legal standards or specific pollution taxes, would increase prices for the most environmentally friendly supplier and thereby provide an unfair market advantage for the polluters. What is more, measures purportedly taken to protect against such unfair advantages, such as regulations or import charges, might conceal arbitrary standards or unfair trade barriers, thereby similarly distorting market mechanisms.[40]

In principle, the solution seemed simple. Already at the first meeting of the Sub-Committee, all delegates agreed that "the polluter should be the payer."[41] But in practice, as governments had to reconcile environmental with other, sometimes contradictory objectives, this principle was easily compromised. Besides, delegates disagreed on the degree to which environmental policies should or should not directly be part of foreign trade policy and to what degree environmental standards should be harmonized, thereby moving beyond national sovereign control.[42] In search of counsel, the Sub-Committee delegates asked the Secretariat to provide papers to serve as a basis for further discussions.

The so-called Polluter Pays Principle was no new invention. The idea of demanding redress from a perpetrator may be as old as antiquity, and the principle of holding the producer of environmental destruction responsible already existed in the nineteenth century, though it had routinely been contested and rarely implemented.[43] During the second half of 1971, the Secretariat provided several papers, whose analyses made clear why such an implementation was difficult. An analysis by University of Maryland professor John Cumberland pointed out some practical challenges: competitive pressure provided a powerful temptation for countries as well as producers to reduce pollution costs by emitting waste across national boundaries, and the differences in environmental, economic, social, and political circumstances between countries made a consensus on environmental standards difficult, anyway. Views differed not only about the specific numeric standards but also on what such standards should even apply to: to the amount of waste or emission released in total or per (time) unit, to the concentration of a pollutant in a medium, or to its degree of danger to environmental or human health?[44] In a second paper, University of Columbia professor A.D. Scott Treating argued that the entire discussion risked missing the point. Rather than focusing on trade, Treating called for more research attention to the broader and more urgent problem of controlling reservoirs of pollution like water basins (rivers, lakes, coastlines, oceans) or "airsheds," which all countries used as free resources. He proposed establishing international "basin agencies" in charge of collecting data and organizing the protection of specific basins against excess pollution. Treating realized that this scheme opened a host of problems, of which the delineation of a "basin" was just the beginning. As a partial remedy, he suggested cultivating the concept of "common goods" to manage the shared use of space for pollution.[45]

A third paper, written by the Secretariat, was hardly more reassuring. It warned that some countries might see an advantage in becoming "pollution havens," comparable to existing "tax havens." In addition, the text warned that developing countries might be discouraged from setting up basic—often highly polluting—forms of industry if faced with stringent international environmental standards. Besides, conservationist countries could also suffer domestic trade distortions when protecting one sector of their domestic industry from unfair advantages from more polluting foreign competitors. Highly polluting industries (iron and steel, paper, chemical industry) tended to affect many economic sectors, many of which would be exposed to foreign competition without benefitting from protective measures.[46]

By late 1971, further studies by the Secretariat tied considerations of the PPP to a more fundamental critique of the market economy, which had been developed within other parts of the OECD:

> It is already common knowledge that economics, the science of managing scarce resources so as to maximise human welfare, is still far from embracing all the factors which contribute to human welfare. Among these factors the provision of a healthy and balanced environment has been widely neglected, mainly because market mechanisms are not capable of taking account of them.[47]

More specifically, the text explained that present economics provided a flawed picture of reality by counting only the positive results of economic activity, like products or services, while ignoring the negative results, such as waste and pollution, as "externalities." Even more radically, it questioned central tenets of economic theory, arguing that there was little reason to assume that the economic optimum, generally perceived as a Pareto optimum, would coincide with an ecological optimum. Though in principle the PPP was to be welcomed as an effort to redress the imperfections of markets by internalizing externalities, in practice its implementation entailed serious difficulties. Using the examples of vehicle pollution and noise, the text listed unsolved questions. Who should be defined as the "polluter": the producer, the designer, the fuel supplier, the urban planner, the mass of users or specific users who, because of their behavior, produced pollution to an above-average degree? Should the identification of "polluters" consider or ignore questions of income, power, and access to alternatives? Since pollution typically occurred in complex systems, determining one "producer" bore little relation to reality. And which measures should reasonably be used to make polluters "pay"? Should that be charges proportional to the nuisance? Or perhaps flat rate charges, which would privilege large-scale polluters and provide little incentive to reduce pollution? How would measures affect social equity, given that price increases and charges would disproportionately affect the lower classes and/or those with few alternatives (e.g., in the case of cars, areas without public transport). How could measures deal with possible pay-offs between different forms of pollution, i.e., noise and exhaust fumes? And would this pollution-centered approach make economists and planners lose sight of the larger picture of traffic, of which noise and air pollution were only a few of several problems, thus preventing them from thinking of integrated solutions to transportation?[48] Clearly, taking the PPP seriously entailed a fundamental reconsideration of the Western economic system.

However, these analyses had little impact on the work of the Sub-Committee. Instead, discussions focused on accounts of PPP practices in member countries. Here, the PPP was perceived not as a cause for systemic reconsideration but as a means to re-conceptualize ongoing economic developments. Often, delegations provided simple descriptions of existing environmental regulations, freely labeling them as manifestations of a "polluter pays" principle without engaging in serious considerations about who those "polluters" were and how they got to pay for what type of pollution. A collection of case studies on France, Germany, and Japan showed that authorities used a combination of charges and regulations, often without clear outcomes, of which costs were carried by producers or consumers or – through modernization subsidies and remaining non-regulated areas – by citizens and tax payers.[49] A similar picture emerged from a collection of information on restrictions of the PPP in national policies. Reasons to exempt individual corporations or entire economic sectors from being held accountable for the pollution they produced revealed that governments were generally not ready to engage in serious conflicts about the concept: reports cited lack of acceptance of payment, especially when existing environmental standards had been honored (an inadvertent admission that existing standards were insufficient to internalize costs) or in cases where costs were considered "not reasonable" or where nobody in particular could reasonably claim compensation. Within this watered down understanding of the term, most delegates felt that the PPP was well accepted and widely implemented in their countries. If difficulties were mentioned at all, they were usually considered solvable or solved by market mechanisms.[50] This attitude openly contradicted the studies on the PPP prepared or commissioned by the Secretariat.

Given a choice of either following the line of the studies of principle and initiating a discussion on how economic systems would have to change to satisfy serious PPP requirements or of following the line of the national contributions and find a way of adapting the concept to existing policies, the Sub-Committee chose the latter. In a summary report to the Environment Committee, complications of the concept due to regional differences in costs and standards or to difficulties of identifying the "polluter," "pollution" or "costs" were simply defined away. Rather than being considered difficulties, they were conceptualized as signs of freedom and diversity: each country should define for itself what were appropriate environmental costs according to the "standards of pollution control appropriate to its circumstances," and identifying the "polluter" was declared unnecessary since "the operation of market forces" would distribute costs to different economic actors involved. In fact, the document took a black-box approach to national economies. The "chosen instrument of pollution abatement" should be applied where it was "most effective and most efficient" and then, instead of looking at the immediate impact, it would be necessary to observe the "final incidence of a particular pollution reduction instrument." Exemptions from the PPP might be justified if the PPP was likely to exacerbate other local area problems, but they should be temporary and should not offset, in the long term, the effects of internalizing external environmental costs.[51] It was left unclear how, without looking at internal market mechanisms, it would be possible to decide which instruments were most effective and efficient.

The more demanding Secretariat papers, cited above, hardly seem to have affected subsequent discussions at the Sub-Committee, except for a brief remark, in December 1971, that the Sub-Committee considered them "useful and interesting as preliminary papers, but…did not agree with all the analysis in them."[52] Clearly, delegates wished to limit discussions to those elements that promised quick solutions with minimal disruption of already existing structures. Thus, a lengthy discussion of the PPP concluded that apart from short-term adjustment problems there was no reason to expect a "fundamental choice to be made between jobs and pollution abatement."[53] Similarly, a survey of existing pollution control measures in member countries concluded that, apart from exceptional cases, pollution control costs would "not have a substantial impact on a nation's ability to satisfy the other needs of its economy or society." However, in a revealing proviso, the study also explained the essentially political character of these findings:

> These conclusions are valid only as long as the present political preferences do not substantially change. If more ambitious objectives were set for pollution control and environmental policies in general, or if some other reasons were to cause a considerable increase in pollution control costs, the above conclusions would need to be revised.[54]

Overall, governmental fears regarding domestic political and economic difficulties were certainly the main reason why discussions on the PPP remained on a superficial level in 1972, but institutional considerations may also have played a role. The UN's Stockholm Conference was scheduled to take place in June, and a contribution reflecting specific OECD competency was called for. By March, the plan was to provide a declaration on guiding principles of environmentally relevant economic policies, including the PPP as a central point.[55] Protracted, divisive discussions, questioning basic tenets of Western economic belief systems, would hardly have been conducive to a strong presentation of OECD environmental recommendations.

In May 1972, the OECD Council issued *Guiding Principles Concerning the International Economic Aspects of Environmental Policies*, which it recommended to member countries to observe. The PPP was listed prominently as the first principle with five out of fifteen paragraphs. As its underlying rationale it explained that environmental resources were limited and public measures were necessary to internalize the costs of this deterioration to reflect this scarcity, so that market agents could act accordingly and pollution would be reduced. Thus, the PPP was a means to bring about rational use of scarce environmental resources and to avoid international trade distortions.[56] It was a good explanation of the principle that appeared plausible as long as no questions regarding its implementation were asked. Above all, it was a declaration that was acceptable to OECD member countries and that established the OECD both as a major player among environmental IOs and as an organization that went beyond pollution control on the basis of technical case studies and put forward globally relevant economic environmental policy principles.

Undoubtedly, the PPP ascertained the use of market mechanisms for environmental purposes, making it a contribution to the rise of "liberal environmentalism."[57] But the picture is more complex. As shown, loyalty to the market in the OECD Secretariat was less than complete and the existing loyalty was not the main reason for limited commitment to environmental protection. The main impediment to a more far-reaching transformation in the interest of preventing environmental degradation was the unwillingness of national governments to consider changes that would come with high economic and political costs. While the Secretariat staff involved in early environmental work was willing to go far in reflecting on the repercussions of the PPP, including questioning central elements of market economics, such considerations were far removed from the world of policy-makers who faced voters, lobbies, and constituents, all of whom were likely to prefer lip service to a principle to a change that would profoundly affect their businesses and lives. This unwillingness to engage in painful changes did not stem from a strong commitment to market mechanisms, as demonstrated by the ready acceptance of exceptions to a market principle. Rather, a true distribution of pollution to all polluters would not only have been impossibly complicated, it would have alienated far too many people to be politically feasible. In this sense, the frank studies by the Secretariat may have deterred Sub-Committee delegates from even trying to devise a more honest version of the PPP.

Aftermath

Since 1972, the OECD has expanded its environmental program, becoming active in a wide range of sectors. Among others, the impacts of energy production and consumption, transportation, biodiversity, and especially hazardous waste and chemicals, which got its own committee, have received priority attention.[58] OECD work has also provided essential behind the scenes work for important international agreements in the environmental field, such as the 1979 Convention on Transboundary Air Pollution, prepared by the Long-range Transboundary Air Pollution Project,[59] or the Basel Convention, prepared by the Waste Management Policy Group.[60] Similarly, work of the OECD Environmental Directorate provided an important input into the Brundtland Commission and its conceptualization of sustainable development.[61] In this sense, the PPP provided the ground for profiling the OECD as an agency generating rules and agreements with a potentially global reach. In addition, the OECD became an important source of widely accepted environmental data, such as the 1979 *State of the Environment in OECD Member Countries*, the only international survey of this sort at the time.[62] In subsequent years, the organization was an important actor in international monitoring and negotiations regarding risks emanating from chemicals.[63] Clearly, the OECD has been successful in establishing itself as a major environmental IO. In the process, it strengthened the dominant Western approach to environmental consideration, one that did take serious efforts to mitigate environmental degradation while safeguarding basic tenets of a market economy.

Meanwhile, the PPP gained a life of its own. From the 1970s onward, it featured prominently in the budding environmental program of the European Community and was adopted in a long list of international conventions and protocols.[64] By the 2000s, the PPP was considered a "normative doctrine of environmental law" which had come to guide a substantial part of environmental policy.[65] At the OECD, ironically, the Secretariat retained its critical view. In 1987, it discussed the toothless character of the PPP, which excluded any type of provisions for compensation, national resource management, or distributional justice, and was designed as a purely domestic measure incurring minimal costs. Far from preventing market distortions, internationally, power asymmetries prevented shifting costs of environmental degradation to consumers, turning the PPP to dead letter.[66] This analysis continues to be accurate. Until today, there is no effective instrument for international application, and even nationally, polluters have never been obliged to pay the full costs of pollution. Regulations or charges put into place have never been sufficient to cover expenses resulting from environmental degradation, since their full extent, while remaining difficult to quantify, would be high enough to drive many companies bankrupt.[67]. Thus, the PPP has been effective in establishing a strong position of the OECD within international environmental governance, and in a weak version it has been widely adopted into inter-governmental agreements; but its effect on global pollution has probably been limited—as originally predicted and observed by the OECD Secretariat.

Conclusions

In several ways, the establishment of the OECD Environment Committee and the PPP played important roles in redefining the organization in the 1970s: it positioned the OECD within the dynamics of international environmentalism, it strengthened its standing within the struggle for positions within the field of IOs, and it helped shape the identity of the OECD within a changing world. At a time of rising environmental concerns among OECD countries, the organization responded with expanding earlier technical activities and tapped into rising, albeit diffuse, doubts regarding the existing, growth-oriented economic system and its propensity to degrade the physical basis of (economic) life. These early debates made sense for an IO whose focus was on international economy, but they were insufficient to distinguish the OECD from similar activities in other IOs, notably NATO and the ECE, and to establish the OECD as an authority in international environmental governance. The PPP, though not invented by the OECD, lent itself to becoming an early trademark achievement and served to define its profile both within the organization and to the outside: it was readily acceptable to all member states, it was reconcilable with the lukewarm national environmental policies already in place, and it could be molded into an official declaration in time for the 1972 Stockholm Conference. However, adopting the PPP as an OECD guideline was only possible by glossing over substantial differences of approach embraced within the OECD. The main differences were between a macro approach, which questioned the broader implications of a principle that seriously aimed at distributing the costs of pollution according to responsibility (favored by the Secretariat), and a micro approach, which constructed a large range of environmental policies as serving the goal of producing "correct" prices, often in a non-reflected manner. These differences tied into an underlying conflict between two concepts of what the purpose of an environmental program at the OECD should be: to provide in-depth scientific studies and debates about questions of substance and long-term relevance, or to aid with immediate policy challenges, applicable through national legislature and international agreement.

In 1972, under the prodding of Secretary-General van Lennep, the delegates of member countries clearly decided this question in favor of the latter, and the OECD Secretariat could do little but comply. However, the PPP and the OECD's role in it established the precedent of declaring a principle whose policy potential went far beyond its limited interpretation and which continues to influence legal debates today. It also established the role of the OECD as a forum for preparations of international guidelines or agreements on a wide range of issues of environmental concern. Thus, in the long run, the principle of creating the PPP may have been more significant than its contents.

Notes

1. Jan-Henrik Meyer, "Making the Polluter Pay: How the European Communities Established Environmental Protection," in *International Organizations and Environmental Policies,* ed. Wolfram Kaiser und Jan-Henrik Meyer (New York: Berghahn Books, forthcoming, 2016).
2. Bill Long, *International Environmental Issues and the OECD 1950–2000. An Historical Perspective* (Paris: OECD, 2000), 39.
3. Steven Bernstein, "Liberal Environmentalism and Global Environmental Governance," *Global Environmental Politics* 2: 3 (2002), 1–17; Steven Bernstein, *The Compromise of Liberal Environmentalism* (New York: Columbia University Press, 2001).
4. Matthias Schmelzer, *The Hegemony of Growth. The making and remaking of the economic growth paradigm and the OECD, 1948–2010* (Cambridge: Cambridge University Press, 2016).
5. Iris Borowy, "(Re-)Thinking Environment and Economy: The OECD and Sustainable Development," in *International Organizations and Environmental Policies,* ed. Wolfram Kaiser und Jan-Henrik Meyer (New York: Berghahn Books, 2016), 211–240.
6. Per-Olof Busch, "The OECD Environment Directorate. The Art of Persuasion and its Limitations," Working Paper 20, *The Gobal Governance Project*, 2006, http://www.glogov.org/images/doc/wp20.pdf, (accessed 26 June 2014); Markku Lehtonen, "Environmental Policy Integration through the OECD Peer Reviews: Integrating Economy to the Environment or Environment to the Economy," 2004, Berlin, http://userpage.fu-berlin.de/ffu/akumwelt/bc2004/download/lehtonen_f.pdf (accessed 29 March 2016).
7. Maria Ivanova, "Designing the United Nations Environment Programme: a story of compromise and confrontation," *International Environmental Agreements* 7 (2007), 337–361, 345; Jan-Henrik Meyer, "Appropriating the Environment. How the European Institutions received the novel idea

of the environment and made it their own," KFG Working Paper Series, No. 31, September 2011, Kolleg-Forscher-Gruppe "The Transformative Power of Europe," Freie Universität Berlin www.transformeurope.eu.

8. Robert Wolfe, "From Reconstructing Europe to Constructing Globalization. The OECD in Historical Perspective," in *The OECD and Transnational Governance*, Rianne Mahon and Stephen McBride, eds., (Vancouver: UBC Press, 2008), 25–42.
9. Gary Haw and Alistair Paul, *Environmentalism since 1945* (London: Routledge, 2012).
10. OECD Historical Archive (OECD-HA), 4 March 1970, ENV(70)4, Present Status of Work of the Committee for Research Cooperation and other OECD Bodies Relating to the Environment, 28–31.
11. Long, *International Environmental Issues*, 30–31.
12. OECD-HA, ENV (70)9, Note by the Secretary General in preparation for the second meeting of the Committee, 15 April 1970, 4.
13. OECD-HA, CE/M(70)2 (Prov.), Executive Committee, Summary record of the 228 Meeting held 27–28 January 1970, 17 February 1970; ENV (70)4, Present Status of Work of the Committee for Research Cooperation and other OECD Bodies Relating to the Environment, 4 March 1970; Long, *International Environmental Issues*, 29.
14. The National Archives Kew (hereafter TNA), Records of the Foreign and Commonwealth Office and predecessors (FCO) 55–423, ENV/PG/13, UNECE, Report of the Second Meeting of the Preparatory Group for the Meeting of Governmental Experts on Problems Relating to Environment, 20 March 1970, Annex II, Note by the Preparatory Group of Experts.
15. Intergovernmental Conference of Experts on the Scientific Basis for the Rational Use and Conservation of the Resources of the Biosphere, Final Report, Paris, 4–13 September 1968, http://unesdoc.unesco.org/images/0001/000172/017269EB.pdf (accessed 20 March 2016, quote §128).
16. Iris Borowy, *Defining Sustainable Development for Our Common Future* (Milton Park: Routledge, 2014), 30–33.
17. UNGA 2398 (XXIII), 3 December 1968, http://www.un.org/en/ga/search/view_doc.asp?symbol=a/res/2398%28XXIII%29 (accessed 20 March 2016).
18. OECD-HA, ENV(70)3, Ad Hoc Preparatory Committee on the Activities of the Organisation on Environmental Problems Relating to Growth, 27 February 1970.
19. OECD-HA, C(69)168, Problems of Modern Society. Note by the Secretary General, 12 December 1969.
20. NATO archives (hereafter NATOA), C-M (70) 19 (Final), Progress Report by the Chairman of the Committee on the Challenges of Modern Society, 15 May 1970.

21. For background see Jacob Darwin Hamblin, "Environmentalism for the Atlantic Alliance: NATO's Experiment with the 'Challenges of Modern Society'," *Environmental History* 15: 1 (2010), 54–75; Evanthis Hatzivassiliou, "Nixon's Coup: Establishing the NATO Committee on the Challenges of Modern Society, 1969–1970," *The International History Review* 38: 1 (2016): 88–108; Thorsten Schulz, "Transatlantic Environmental Security in the 1970s? NATO's 'Third Dimension' as an Early Environmental and Human Security Approach," *Historical Social Research* 35: 4 (2010), 309–328.
22. OECD-HA, C/M(70)1 (Prov.) (1st Revision), Problems of Modern Society. Note by the Secretary-General, C(69)123, 18 September 1969.
23. OECD-HA, C/M (70)2 (1st Rev.), Minutes of Council Meeting, 13 Jan 1970, and C(70)12, 16 Jan 1970, Council. Minutes, 20 Jan 1970.
24. Matthias Schmelzer, "The Crisis before the Crisis: The 'Problems of Modern Society' and the OECD, 1968–1974," *European Review of History* 19: 6 (2012), 999–1020; Matthias Schmelzer, "'Born in the corridors of the OECD': the forgotten origins of the Club of Rome, transnational networks, and the 1970s in global history," *Journal of Global History* 12: 1 (2017), 26–48.
25. OECD-HA, CE/M(70)2 (Prov.), Executive Committee, Summary record of the 228th Meeting held 27–28 January 1970, 17 February 1970.
26. OECD-HA, ENV(70)5, Ad Hoc Preparatory Committee on the Activities of the Organisation on Environmental Problems Related to Economic Growth. Annotated Agenda, 26 February 1970.
27. OECD-HA, ENV(70)9, Note by the Secretary General, 15 April 1970, 5.
28. Schmelzer, *Hegemony*, 61.
29. TNA, FCO 55–422, UKDel NATO to Foreign an Commonwealth Office, 9 April 1970.
30. TNA, FCO 55–422, Science and Technology Department, untitled document, 31 March 1970.
31. TNA, FCO 55–422, Summary Record of a Meeting Wednesday, 1 April 1970.
32. OECD-HA, ENV(70)11, Ad hoc preparatory committee on the activities of the OECD related to economic growth. Overall conclusions, 4 April 1970 [corrected: 30 April 1970].
33. OECD-HA, C/M(70)13 (Prov.), Council, Minutes of the 218th Meeting held on 12 May 1970, 16 June 1970.
34. Long, *International Environmental Issues*, 34–38.
35. TNA, FCO 55–424, Johnson, UK Mission, to Wheeler, 8 December 1970.
36. Ivanova, Designing UNEP, 347–349.
37. Schmelzer, "Crisis before the Crisis," Long, *International Environmental Issues*, 41–42.

38. Schmelzer, *Hegemony*, 65.
39. OECD-HA, AEU/ENV/71, Environmental Committee, Sub-Committee of Economic Experts (EC, SEE), Draft report on the Sub-Committee's activities in 1971 and outlook for 1972, 14 December 1971, 16.
40. OECD-HA, AEU/ENV/71.2, Comments by the Swedish delegation on ENV(71)4, 14 June 1971; AEU/ENV/71.4, Allocation of Pollution Control Costs. Statement by the US delegation, 19 May 1971.
41. OECD-HA, AEU/ENV/71.5, Record of the first Meeting held on 15–16 June 1971, 21 July 1971.
42. OECD-HA, AEU/ENV/71.5, Record of the first Meeting held on 15–16 June 1971, 21 July 1971.
43. Meyer, "Making the Polluter Pay."
44. OECD-HA, AEU/ENV/71.7, John Cumberland, The Role of Uniform Standards in International Environmental Management, 26 August 1971.
45. OECD-HA, AEU/ENV/71.8, A.D. Scott, The Economics of International Transmission of Pollution, 26 August 1971.
46. OECD-HA, AEU/ENV/71.6, The Impact of Environmental Measures on International Trade: Some Policy Issues, 26 August 1971.
47. OECD-HA, AEU/ENV/71.14, Note by the Secretariat, The "Polluter-Pays" Principle and Vehicle Pollution and Noise Control, 10 November 1971, 4.
48. OECD-HA, AEU/ENV/71.14, Note by the Secretariat, The "Polluter-Pays" Principle and Vehicle Pollution and Noise Control, 10 November 1971. For a discussion of these arguments, see Schmelzer, *Hegemony of Growth*, 245–266.
49. OECD-HA, AEU/ENV(71)13, Note by the Secretariat, Allocation of Environmental Costs—Case Studies, 29 October 1971.
50. OECD-HA, AEU/ENV/71.17, Swedish Statement on Exceptions to the "Polluter Pays" Principle, 22 November 1971; AEU/ENV/71.18, United States Statement on Exceptions to the" Polluter Pays" Principle, 25 November 1971; AEU/ENV/71.21, Danish Statement on Exception to the "Polluter Pays" Principle, 8 December 1971; AEU/ENV/71.20, Netherlands Statement on Exceptions to the "Polluter Pays" Principle, 30 November 1971; AEU/ENV/71.22, Norwegian Statement on Exceptions to the "Polluter Pays" Principle, 8 December 1971; AEU/ENV/71.23, United Kingdom Statement on Exceptions to the "Polluter Pays" Principle, 8 December 1971.
51. OECD-HA, AEU/ENV/71.27, Exception to the "Polluter Pays Principle," 29 December 1971.
52. OECD-HA, AEU/ENV/M/72.3, Record of the 3rd Meeting held on 16–17 December 1971, 3 February 1972.

53. OECD-HA, AEU/ENV/72.2, Wilfried Beckerman, The Polluter Must Pay Principle: Interpretation and Principles of Application, 3 March 1972, 33.
54. OECD-HA, AEU/ENV/72.4, Collection and Analysis of Pollution Control Data, 24 March 1972, 12.
55. OECD-HA, Report of the Environmental Committee. No. 91, 23 March 1972, Folder 161714.
56. OECD, C(72)128, Recommendation of the Council on Guiding Principles, 26 May 1972—available on http://acts.oecd.org, (accessed 3 August 2015).
57. See Bernstein, *Liberal environmentalism.*
58. Busch, "The OECD Environment Directorate," 1.
59. Rachel Rothschild, "Burning Rain: The Long-range Transboundary Air Pollution Project," in *Toxic Airs: Chemical and Environmental Histories of the Atmosphere*, James Rodger Fleming and Ann Johnson, eds. (Pittsburgh: University of Pittsburgh Press, 2014), 181–207.
60. Jonathan Krueger, *International Trade and the Basel Convention* (London: Earthscan, 1999), 22–25.
61. Bernstein, *Liberal environmentalism*, 212–216; Borowy, *Defining*, 39–40, 49–50.
62. OECD, *The State of the Environment in OECD Countries* (Paris: OECD, 1979).
63. Iris Borowy, "Endocrine Disruptors: an Evolving Health Concern in International Organizations," *Hygiea Internationalis* 13: 2 (2016), 135–161.
64. Meyer, "Making the Polluter Pay"; Kenneth Ruffing, "The Role of the Organization for Economic Cooperation and Development in Environmental Policy Making," *Review of Environmental Economics and Policy* 4: 2 (2010), 199–220, 205; Petra Lindhout and Berthy van den Broek, „The Polluter Pays Principle: Guidelines for Cost Recovery and Burden Sharing in the Case Law of the European Court of Justice," *Utrecht Law Review* 10: 2 (2014), 46–59.
65. Jonathan Nash, "Too much market? Conflict between tradable pollution allowances and the polluter pays principle," *Harvard Law Review* 24 (2000), 465–535, 465.
66. OECD-HA, WCED Report Subjects Calling for Examination and/or Action in OECD, undated, Folder 161714.
67. Sharon Beder, *Environmental Principles and Policies* (London: Earthscan, 2006), 32–46, 192–198.

Gendering Development: The OECD's Development Assistance Committee, 1981–2000

Rianne Mahon

Introduction

Development has been part of the OECD's mandate from the start. As "Warden of the West," the OECD's mission was to coordinate its members' responses not only to the economic challenge posed by the Soviet Union, but also to demands from the decolonising South. By the time of the OECD's foundation in 1961, the rich Northern countries had already lost their majority in the United Nations (UN) and with the foundation of UNCTAD, the need for a common position vis-à-vis the South had become pressing.[1] The OECD's Development Assistance committee (DAC) provided a forum that would enable its members to forge a common position vis-à-vis the South. As Schmelzer argues, "the raison d'être of DAC was… the creation of an exclusive forum for the rich Western countries, in which they could advance a common view of the global development problem and could, undisturbed by nations from the Global South, coordinate their development work, also with regard to broader international fora such as the International Bank for Reconstruction and Development or the United

R. Mahon (✉)
Balsillie School of International Affairs and Department of Political Science,
Wilfrid Laurier University, 75 University Avenue West,
Waterloo, ON N2L 3C5, Canada
e-mail: prmahon@rogers.com

M. Leimgruber and M. Schmelzer (eds.), *The OECD and the International Political Economy Since 1948*, DOI 10.1007/978-3-319-60243-1_14

Nations."[2] The first UN Conference on Women, followed by the launching of the UN Decade for Women (1976–1985), brought the gender dimension of these challenges to the fore.

At the 1975 UN Conference on Women, Western officials' efforts to focus on equal opportunity clashed with the Soviet emphasis on world peace and disarmament and Southern demand for a New International Economic Order and the dismantling of apartheid.[3] This chapter examines the OECD's response on this new front through the creation of the Expert Group on Women in Development. Based on original sources, it focuses on the two decades from the Group's formation in 1981 to the end of the century, as this was the period when the DAC, along with the World Bank and the International Monetary Fund, was most influential in the field of international development.[4] The chapter does not attempt to assess the Group's ability to alter donor country policies at headquarters, although there is evidence of this, much less to consider the impact on recipients.[5] Rather it argues that "aid femocrats"—feminists staffing the newly created Women in Development units within donor agencies—seized the opening of these challenges to the OECD's role as "Warden of the West" to establish their own space within the DAC.[6] They used this space with effect to push for the gendering of development assistance and, in the 1990s, to join the forces contesting the premises of the Washington Consensus.[7]

The DAC Within the OECD

Development was already on the agenda of the OECD's predecessor, the OEEC, around the time the first bilateral aid units began to be established in the 1950s.[8] At this juncture, it focused on coordinating aid among the European colonial powers, developing comparative financial statistics, including Western countries' financial contributions to the South, and assisting its own underdeveloped member countries in Southern Europe. On the eve of the OECD's foundation, a Development Assistance Group was created, becoming the DAC in 1961. DAC's creation was not uncontroversial within the new organisation, drawing protests from the Southern European countries, who sought to defend their favored status, and from neutral Switzerland and Sweden, concerned about the link it implied between aid and the Cold War.[9] It also drew the ire of the South, which preferred a global aid agency under UN, hence majority, control.[10] Indeed, according to

Toye, the creation of the DAC helped spark the formation of the Group of 77 "as a counterweight to the newly formed OECD, which represented the common interests of the advanced industrial countries."[11] DAC, however, not only survived, but enjoyed preeminent status within the development field during the 1960s, a status it would subsequently share with the World Bank and the IMF.

In many respects, the DAC functions in a similar way to other OECD committees. It presides over numerous subsidiary bodies over which it exercises control through annual discussions of work programs at the Senior and High Level meetings and the approval of committee mandates and key policy documents. It has developed sophisticated statistical surveillance capacities and concepts that lie behind these such as the definition of "official development assistance" (ODA), adopted in 1972. DAC uses peer reviews (the "DAC exam") to examine each member's performance.

DAC also produces important reflective pieces that establish new organisational discourses. In the 1960s, its development discourse centered on Rostow's five-stage model of development, replaced in the 1970s by the notion of basic needs in recognition that growth in itself was insufficient to deliver a desirable distribution of its benefits.[12] In the 1980s, a decade dominated by structural adjustment, DAC offered a space to contest the premises of the Washington Consensus, as countries with neo-liberal governments such as the US under Ronald Reagan and the UK under Margaret Thatcher faced opposition from those concerned about the social costs of structural adjustment.[13] DAC's various working parties also provided a haven for "guerilla bureaucrats" who rejected the neo-liberal stance taken by their own governments.[14]

Within the OECD, and to this day, DAC has a special status relative to other directorates and their associated committees. It is the only committee with a full-time chair who is not under the Secretary-General's supervision, and it is one of the few committees with restricted membership. Among its members, the US, from which its chair has typically been drawn, clearly holds a preeminent position. Nevertheless, "the fact that the US is represented by USAID (and not by the US State Department) has an extremely important impact on the positions taken by the US and hence on the positions taken by the DAC as a whole."[15] In the early years, the United Kingdom, France, and Germany also wielded considerable influence. Nevertheless "good citizens" like the Nordic countries have also established a strong standing within DAC.

Carving Out a Space for Gender, 1979–1989

For much of its first decade of its existence, women remained largely invisible to the OECD, including DAC. This would begin to change in the 1970s when the first UN conference on women, followed by the declaration of the UN Decade for Women, helped to put gender firmly on the international agenda. On the eve of the first UN conference, the Working Party on the Role of Women in the Economy, on which officials from the newly-minted status of women machineries would come to dominate, was established within the Directorate for Manpower, Social Affairs and Education.[16] The ability of aid femocrats similarly to carve out a space within the DAC, however, needs to be located in relation to the particular challenges that surfaced in the development field in the 1970s and 1980s. To be sure, the importance of addressing women's role in development had been raised in Sweden as well as in Kenya and other parts of the South in the 1960s. It was the UN Council for the Status of Women (CSW), however, that lay behind the 1970 UN General Assembly resolution encouraging "the full integration of women into the total development effort."[17] That same year Esther Boserup's influential *Women's Role in Development* was published, giving birth to the concept of women in development (WID). These developments helped set the stage for the first UN conference on women, which took place in Mexico City in 1975.

The first UN conference on women was marked by sharp East-West and North-South divisions.[18] The tensions expressed in Mexico reflected the broader clash between the Group of 77, which was pushing for a New International Economic Order, and donor agencies. The issues of South Africa and Palestine also proved divisive—to an extent that countries like Canada and the US ultimately opposed the resulting Declaration of Mexico City. DAC's willingness to accept the establishment of the Expert Group on Women in Development thus reflected its recognition of the need for a forum to develop a common Western front in this arena too.

This is not to say that WID would have entered DAC's agenda without the concerted efforts of an emerging cadre of aid femocrats in key countries. Women's importance to development had begun to filter into the Scandinavian countries in the 1960s and the movement to set up WID units within donor agencies gained impetus from the successes of American feminists who, in 1973, secured the passage of the Perry Amendment requiring women to be "integrated into all the new basic needs programs detailed in the foreign assistance bill."[19] The WID movement gained added momentum following the Mexican conference such that, by the late 1970s, "European donor nations along with Canada and Australia had also established WID offices."[20] Arvonne Fraser, head of USAID's WID unit under Carter, notes that it was the then-US representative to the DAC, Lloyd Jonnes, who championed the first (informal) WID meeting at DAC headquarters on the eve of the next UN conference in Copenhagen in 1979.[21]

The group used the time to forge a common DAC position in advance of the Copenhagen UN conference for women. As Fraser explains:

> Our DAC/WID members were all on their countries' delegation to the Copenhagen conference and the preparatory meetings preceding it. Working with UN allies, we inserted language in almost every section of the Program of Action that explained, amplified or instructed governments about the goals of the WID movement…Inserting this and much more language in the documents could not have been done without our DAC/WID network…[22]

Following Copenhagen, the group moved to consolidate its status within DAC, initially named the DAC Corresponding Group on WID. After considerable lobbying on the part of the Group and its allies, it became the Expert Group on WID in 1984 and remained so until 1998 when it was renamed the Working Party on Gender Equality. Although the US had provided the initial impetus for its formation, the election of Ronald Reagan, which marked the US government's official conversion to neo-liberal reforms including the Washington Consensus, meant that the US representative ceded leadership to other donors that had a strong WID profile.[23] As Jaquette and Staudt note:

> [I]n this changed environment, the WID Office in USAID took a much lower profile…Leadership on WID issues began to shift to other institutions, including Canadian and Northern European bilateral aid agencies, UN agencies, private foundations and NGOS.[24]

The European Commission also remained an active member while the World Bank and IMF enjoyed observer status from the outset. At this juncture, the Group did not have formal links with the UN agencies or women's organisations

The Group immediately set to work on finding ways to influence DAC's key instruments—the collection of statistics for the Creditor Reporting System on Aid Activities that had been established in the 1960s, the annual country reports to the DAC, and the DAC Exam. The latter was a particularly important objective. As the Dutch representative noted:

> We saw the DAC exam as an important instrument to help integrate women into the development policies of the member states. To that end we worked toward the inclusion of questions related to women in the exam. In addition, we argued for the use of sex-segregated data in the statistics used by DAC. Subsequently, to put more pressure on the member states, the DAC/WID group formulated a document titled *Guiding Principles to Aid Agencies for Supporting the Role of WID*...officially adopted at the DAC High Level meeting in November 1983. Through these principles, Member states committed themselves to formulate a mandate, policy and plans of action for WID; establish a structure for the systematic implementation of policy; and elaborate policy in all phases of the project cycle.[25]

The Guiding Principles officially committed DAC members to provide information on action to include women in development in their annual memorandum to the DAC and to incorporate this as an item to be included in the DAC exam.[26] The document underlined the importance of consulting women in developing countries and argued for measures to improve women's access to productive resources such as land titles, credit, and training. The Guiding Principles also referred to the importance of women's contribution in the areas of nutrition, hygiene, family planning, and disease prevention.[27] In other words, it reflected an ambiguous position between WID's emphasis on women's productive roles and the more traditional view of women's appropriate role as one focused on the sphere of reproduction.

By the third UN conference in Nairobi in 1985, the WID approach the Group had adopted was coming under criticism from feminist development economists like Lourdes Benería and Gita Sen who argued that women's subordination in the productive sphere was linked to their reproductive roles.[28] On the eve of the conference, a new Southern feminist organisation, Development Alternative with Women for a New Era (DAWN), was formed, which similarly highlighted the contribution of colonialism and neo-colonialism to underdevelopment and challenged neo-liberal structural adjustment policies.[29] As Peggy Antrobus, a Caribbean feminist and participant in the UN conferences and a founding member of DAWN, put it:

> We questioned the mainstream concept of development and introduced a broader framework of analysis that acknowledged the structural and political barriers to women's participation as well as the extent to which economic development, far from excluding women, actually benefits from them when women's time, labor and sexuality are exploited.[30]

In the North, this critique was developed by feminist development scholars like Maxine Molyneux, Ruth Pearson, Diane Elson, and Carolyn Moser. Their ideas, brought together in the concept "gender and development" (GAD), would begin to influence the OECD Group's thinking in the wake of the third UN Conference where representatives of OECD countries were able to reach an accord with those from the South.[31]

Following the Nairobi conference, the Group commissioned a report by Ria Brouwers, *Follow-up on the "Nairobi Forward Looking Strategy for the Advancement of Women" in the Development Policy of DAC Members*, which picked up a number of important themes from GAD. Thus, it highlighted the importance of structural changes and critiqued the macroeconomic policies associated with structural adjustment programs. Recognizing the limits to gender equality posed by women's traditional reproductive roles, it called for greater sharing of domestic responsibilities between men and women within the household and the provision of childcare programs. It also took up the contentious issue of women's right to have control over their own bodies, including their reproductive rights.

This document was the first to articulate criticism of neo-liberal structural adjustment as well as other critical insights associated with the GAD approach within the DAC. At the same time, the report continued to reflect on the methodological nationalism that runs through donor views of development in that it did not pick up on DAWN's critique of the way past and present North-South relations serve to perpetuate underdevelopment. Nonetheless, it was considered too radical for some representatives, leading the Group to decide not to release the report.[32] Many of its ideas would, however, resurface in the 1989 Revised Guiding Principles.

Following Nairobi, the Group renewed its efforts to influence DAC procedures. It got the DAC to recommend that the category gender should become a part of the peer review process. Although participation was voluntary, Canada, Denmark, Germany, the Netherlands, Norway, Sweden, the UK, the US, and the European Commission agreed to do so.[33] The Group also drew on each other's national networks to get the DAC Exam reviewers to ask "difficult questions," as British representative Rosalind Eyben has noted.[34] The Bureau chair also got the support of US, Canadian, Danish, French. and Norwegian representatives to the Appraisals Committee for her proposal to insert women into the important economic section of the DAC Principles for Project Appraisal.[35]

The review of DAC's Principles for Project Appraisal was seen as critical to making gender visible through sex-disaggregated statistics and the inclusion of the latter in DAC's much-vaunted Creditor Reporting system. Coming to an agreement on how to track WID presence in donor projects, however, proved difficult. Already in 1984 the Group had asked DAC to require sex-disaggregated statistics on project commitments and technical cooperation (TC-1). DAC agreed to this in principle but referred the matter to the Working Party on Statistical Problems, which felt that further experiments were needed. Canada, Norway, and Switzerland agreed to work on this, along with the Australians, the Dutch, and the French.[36] This sub-group went on to suggest a distinction between "gender integrated" and "women specific" projects, with the former embodying more of a GAD-inspired relational approach while the latter reflected WID's emphasis on women per se. In doing so, however, it was conscious that such measures would be insufficient in the absence of an attempt to identify barriers to women's participation and design measures to overcome them.[37]

Although the Working Party on Statistical Problems approved the new measure in 1987, an assessment conducted several years later made two things clear. First, only a few projects actually qualified as either WID-specific or WID-integrated. Second, aid femocrats were encountering resistance at home.[38] As we shall see, it would take more than a decade to overcome such resistance sufficiently in the majority of DAC members.

The Group also set about revising the Guiding Principles in light of lessons learned from the Nairobi Conference. The new guidelines reflected a move away from WID's narrower focus on women's productive role in favor of GAD's more critical perspective. Evoking the commitment by DAC and many recipient countries to the promotion of gender equality, the new version, approved in 1989, highlighted women's dual roles in production and reproduction, such that their ongoing responsibility for the latter hindered their ability to contribute equally to the former.[39] Accordingly, the new Guidelines argued for "access to improved child care facilities as well as those supportive of their care roles such as health care, water supply and waste disposal facilities, public transport and electricity."[40] In the productive sphere, the document highlighted women's economic contribution through informal and formal sector activities and argued for education and training programs so that women would not be restricted to traditional female occupations.

Cognizant of the resistance met by the Brouwers report, the Group sought to make the case for the new approach by representing women as useful to development in the way this was being construed by DAC members at the time. Thus women were represented as playing a critical role in *project sustainability*; as having a strong interest in protecting the *environment*; and as acting as *shock absorbers* in the face of the disruptions caused by structural adjustment.[41] This way of framing the argument addressed DAC's ongoing concern with "effective assistance" as well as its then-current interest in the environment. Of particular importance, however, was the third image, which was designed to resonate with broader debates within DAC about neo-liberal structural adjustment, in light of UNICEF's effective campaign to promote "adjustment with a human face."[42]

Launched in 1985, UNICEF's campaign, which emphasized the adverse impact of structural adjustment on children and women, helped to open up space for critical reflection on the Washington Consensus. The DAC was well aware of the growing backlash against the World Bank's structural adjustment policies. Although the US continued to push for market-led growth, the skeptics within DAC, concerned about the social costs of adjustment, argued for participatory development.[43] Within DAC, the compromise took the form of a new organizational discourse focused on "broad based growth and participatory development," a position that accepted the need for structural adjustment while allowing room for modifications.

The 1989 Guiding Principles made use of this opening. Thus, women were presented as ready to make adjustment work—if there were appropriate measures to support their activities. Accordingly, when public expenditures were cut, they called upon donors to attempt to influence recipient governments to protect and strengthen women's interests. In the context of health care, "privatisation special attention needed to be given to ensure women's continued use of the services despite their lack of access to a cash economy."[44] Donors were also enjoined to pay special attention to making "staff members capable of analyzing gender implications of macro-economic policies and their effects on the micro-economy, including the household level."[45] As we shall see, developing a gendered criticism of structural adjustment—but one that could be heard within DAC—would become an important part of the Group's mission in the next decade.

Thus, during the first decade of its existence the Group did have an impact on DAC, albeit less than it had hoped for. It was able to have WID-specific questions included in some DAC exams and country reports and some countries tried to develop WID-related statistical reporting practices, guided by DAC's recommendations. The openings provided by events such as the third UN conference in Nairobi helped by keeping gender issues on the global agenda. For the most part, however, the Group managed to achieve what it did internally largely because of the organizational skills its most active members brought to it, as it enjoyed only modest support from the Secretariat.[46]

The Expert Group in the "Golden Decade"

The 1990s were a golden decade for gender equality, as feminist activists were able to insert their concerns into the series of UN conferences that took place in the first half of the decade. They succeeded in linking gender to environmental issues (UN Conference on Environment and Development, Rio 1992), human rights (UN Conference on Human Rights, Vienna 1993), and population and reproductive rights (UN Conference on Population and Development 1994) with the culmination of their efforts in the fourth UN conference for women in 1995.[47] North-South tensions had abated over the course of the three previous UN conferences on women, and activists had honed their skills in the art of transnational advocacy. In this, the transnational feminist movement benefited not only from the help of allies in the UN but also received "substantial support from western foundations and *European and Canadian bilateral donor agencies.*"[48] DAC's Expert Group played a part here, providing support for the inclusion of women from the South in the preparatory conferences leading up to the Beijing conference.[49]

The Group's preparations for Beijing also led to strengthening its ties with the UN agencies. Up to this point, its main links to other international organisations had been with the World Bank and the IMF.

In 1993, however, the Group invited Gertrude Mongella, Secretary-General for the fourth UN Conference on Women, to address its annual meeting. It also held a seminar just prior to the UN Council for the Status of Women meeting in 1994. Collaboration with UN agencies continued after Beijing, initially in the form of annual seminars jointly sponsored by the Group and the UN Inter-Agency Network on Women and Gender Equality. These connections with the UN arguably strengthened the position of those within the Group favoring a critical feminist approach to development.

The challenges to neo-liberal structural adjustment also created openings for the Group within the DAC. The 1995 World Summit on Social Development in Copenhagen amplified earlier criticism of the Washington Consensus. DAC maintained a low profile at the Summit, as it was in the process of working out its version of a post-Washington Consensus that would allow it to stake out its place within the changing development landscape.

The DAC's new discourse, first articulated in *Development Partnerships in the New Global Context* (1995), reiterated its earlier commitments to sound economic policy frameworks, good governance, and participatory development, combining these with a concern for environmental sustainability and human rights. More importantly, it was here that the DAC began to enunciate several themes that would be elaborated on in its better-known document, *Shaping the Twenty First Century: the Contribution of Development Cooperation* (1996). These themes defined poverty reduction as an over-riding objective and identified six international development goals, one from each of the 1990s UN conferences, as medium-term objectives. Strongly backed by a core of DAC donors[50] and the World Bank under Wolfensohn's leadership, UN Secretary-General Kofi Annan would later accord these a central place in the Millennium Summit and the subsequent Millennium Development Goals (MDGs).

These shifts in the development discourse created openings for the Group, which seized the opportunity to secure DAC's official commitment to gender equality as a strategic development objective. *Gender Equality: Moving Towards Sustainable, People-d Development* (1995) drew explicitly on the more critical GAD discourse, stressing the need to identify the structures underpinning gender disparities in each partner country and to go beyond a narrow focus on technical aspects to acknowledge the socio-cultural dimensions of development.

Also picking up on Beijing's call for gender mainstreaming, *Gender Equality* called for a broadening of responsibility for promoting gender equality to include the DAC and all its subsidiary bodies as well as the donor agencies and for the adoption of a DAC Gender Plan."[51]

As in the earlier documents, *Gender Equality* sought to cast its argument in ways that would be heard by DAC. Thus it drew on earlier tropes such as "structural adjustment cannot succeed unless women are fully taken into account as economic actors" and women having an important role to play for environmental sustainability. It also drew on themes that spoke to DAC's new organizational discourse, including the stress on people-centered development while gender equality was identified as central to effective poverty reduction. Such efforts were important. As the Director of the OECD's Development Cooperation Directorate had made it clear, all chairs of DAC subsidiary bodies had to ensure that their work programs advanced the strategy outlined in *Shaping*. This injunction gained added force from the fact that the experts in the Group—or at least the members of the Bureau—knew the OECD had launched a broader organizational review in response to budgetary pressures.[52] In other words, the Group's survival and even that of DAC itself hinged on the ability of DAC and its subunits to work together.

Although the Group agreed on the need to work with the *twenty first Century* targets, it sought to do so in a way that incorporated gender equality. One of the challenges it faced was the DAC's reduction of gender equality to a singular focus on girls' education. Why was equal education for girls the only gender equality identified by DAC?[53] Eyben suggests that those delegates, like the Japanese representative who feared *Gender Equality's* radical potential, used the occasion to limit its impact:

> At the closed meeting of (all male) senior officials in The Hague in 1996, when DAC finalised the selection of the international development targets that were to evolve into the Millennium Development Goals, it was the Japanese representative who ensured that the target with reference to gender equality should be restricted to parity in education…Others at this meeting, despite the briefings they had had from gender specialists in their own ministries to propose a broader gender target, agreed to the Japanese proposal with little…resistance.[54]

When the Group got its first opportunity to discuss *Shaping*, the narrowed definition of gender equality did not go unnoticed. The Canadian representative presented a detailed critique of the document's general silence on gender equality and pointed out that the document "does not supersede or replace commitments made in...Rio, Vienna, Jomtien, Cairo, Copenhagen and Beijing."[55] In other words, *Shaping* was rightly seen as having narrowed the agendas set at these UN Conferences to items DAC considered to be manageable.

The Group sought to restore a broader perspective through the production of the revised *Guidelines on Gender Equality and Women's Empowerment in Development Co-operation.* The new Guidelines, adopted in 1998, reminded donors that "equal treatment in the context of inequality can mean the perpetuation of disparities."[56] Thus achieving gender equality requires changes in both institutional practices and deeper social structures. Recalling the DAC's and its members' commitment to gender mainstreaming, it enjoined donors to use the new gender equality marker in reporting through DAC's Creditor Reporting System. The latter is a three-tier system which sorts donor projects into those which have gender equality as a principal objective, those where it counts as simply significant objective, and those where gender is not targeted. To receive one of the first two ratings, gender equality must be explicitly promoted through measures which: "(a) reduce social, economic or political power inequalities between women and men, girls and boys, ensure that women benefit equally with men from the activity, or compensate for past discrimination or (b) develop or strengthen gender equality or anti-discrimination, legislation or institutions."[57]

Even while they asserted a broad gender equality agenda, the new *Guidelines* were carefully positioned as central to achieving the broad vision of development outlined by DAC Members in *Shaping the Twenty First Century.* The document picked up *Shaping's* emphasis on local ownership and underlined the importance of "local ownership of interventions for gender equality and support for strengthening local capacity for effective action on issues of inequality between women and men."[58] It recognized the importance of policy dialogue, while stressing that all agenda items in such dialogues incorporate gender equality and include local women's organizations and gender equality advocates in the process. Of particular importance, however, was the way in which the Guidelines picked up on—and sought to rework—the priority areas laid out in *Shaping.*

The *Guidelines* tackled *Shaping's* narrow focus on equal access for girls and boys to primary and secondary education by pointing out that such efforts needed to be complemented by support for the development of curriculum and educational material reflecting a gender equality perspective.[59] Poverty reduction was also central to DAC's new strategy, but *Shaping*—like the subsequent MDGs—was largely blind to the gendered nature of poverty. The *Guidelines* sought to address this by calling for macroeconomic strategies that tackle "the root causes of the preponderance of women among the impoverished," and promote "equal access to and control over economic resources and opportunities."[60] While *Shaping* talked about the importance of reducing maternal mortality, this had not been seen through a gender equality lens. The *Guidelines* accordingly called for "policies and programmes grounded in the recognition of sexual and reproductive health and rights of women and men, and recognition of the links between equality and the exercise of these rights." It also identified the need for "strategies that target men as well as women for activities related to child health, fertility regulation and safe sex practices and recognition of men's rights and responsibilities in these areas."[61] In other words, men and women together should share the tasks associated with intergenerational reproduction.

Of particular importance, the *Guidelines* picked up on a glaring silence in *Shaping*—the way in which macroeconomic structural adjustment policies and associated public expenditure reviews contributed to poverty and served to exacerbate gender inequalities. Here the Group was able to draw on the work of a task force it had created in 1994, whose members included leading feminist development economists Diane Elson, Anne Marie Goetz, and Ingrid Palmer.[62] Drawing on this work, the *Guidelines* pointed out that "to date neither DAC members nor their partners have given sufficient attention to the gender dimension of macro-economic policy."[63] To rectify this, DAC and its members should "(1) use program expenditure reviews to assess the impact of budgetary allocations on women and men; (2) enhance the ability of economic planners to assess the gender impact of economic policy; and (3) develop accounting mechanisms to make visible women's unpaid labour, such as time use surveys."[64]

The Guidelines were approved at the May 1998 High Level DAC Meeting and the Group was given a new name—the Working Party on Gender Equality—that better reflected its current orientation. The Group also dodged the bullet that killed the other unit within the OECD that focused on gender issues, the Working Party on the

Role of Women in the Economy.[65] In the latter case, the broader organization's embrace of gender mainstreaming was used as a justification for eliminating the working party. Some of the same thinking may have been behind the debate at DAC's high-level meeting in 1998 which considered three options: turn the group into an informal network; merge it with the Poverty Network; or extend its mandate for another year while DAC reflected on its options.[66] The latter was accepted, with the proviso that the Group modifies its work program to closely reflect DAC priorities, especially that of poverty reduction.

The Group's subsequent meeting reflected strong member support for its continuation:

> An overwhelming majority of members speaking in the names of their governments, as well as the UNDP and the World Bank, spoke in favour of the continued promotion of gender equality through a DAC subsidiary body. The WP-GEN was described as a renowned of excellence, a supporter and promoter of innovative, cutting-edge analysis, and a group whose strategic support for DAC policies improves the quality of development co-operation. Its expertise with partnership approaches was highlighted. . .Most members also favoured maintaining the status of a formal working party as opposed to its transformation into an informal group, on the grounds that the latter would have less political weight. It was feared that a change in status might lower the gender profile in development co-operation at a time when some members still need external support to counter risks of marginalisation in their aid agencies.[67]

The Group in fact survived with a renewed mandate until 2004 when it, along with all but two DAC working parties, was dissolved and reconstituted as a network (GenderNet), under which status it continues to operate.[68]

Conclusions

Historian Carol Miller identifies the following determinants of a development organization's receptiveness to feminist arguments: (1) the extent the organisation is vulnerable to external pressures for change in its ways of thinking about and carrying out development assistance; (2) the degree of fit between WID/gender concerns and the organization's mandate and procedures; and (3) the existence and capacity of internal

WID/gender policy advocates.[69] Although development formed part of the OECD's mandate from the outset, the issue of women in the development process only began to enter into its calculations in the aftermath of the first UN conference on women in 1975, which brought to the fore the gender dimension of North-South and East-West tensions. In other words, it was as "Warden of the West" that DAC was initially open to the establishment of the Expert Group on Women in Development. By this time, moreover, the DAC had embraced a softer development discourse centered on basic needs, more conducive to WID than the earlier Rostowian version. While these conditions created a potential space for the incorporation of gender, aid femocrats in key donor agencies took advantage of this opening.

Thus informal meetings at the OECD headquarter in Paris enabled femocrats in DAC donor agencies to develop a common strategy for the West and to influence the 1980 Platform for Action emerging out of the second UN conference for women. The Group's formalization in 1981 in turn provided a means for working out a common position in advance of the next UN conference in Nairobi, where the West—and its support for neo-liberal structural adjustment—would come under fire from an articulate group of Southern feminists (DAWN), a point also articulated by feminist economists—and feminist movements—in the North. Learning from this encounter, the Group sought to bring these ideas into DAC and its members' practice, but in doing so, it had to learn to frame its arguments in ways consistent with DAC's (shifting) official discourse. The Group has been fairly effective at inserting women (and later gender) into DAC's major governance instruments, such as the DAC Exam and DAC's Creditor Reporting System. During the "'golden years" of 1990s, when transnational women's movements were able to insert gender equality into a series of UN conferences, the Group was able to persuade DAC to declare gender equality a strategic development objective. By this time, however, the OECD had begun to work out its place in a changing environment, one in which the East-West conflict had lost its old salience but also one in which new actors and new tensions were coming to the fore.

While DAC began to pick out some of the emerging features such as enhanced South-South cooperation, the series of high-level conferences that marked the first decade of the new millennium revealed that the changes were much deeper than it had realized. The new actors included not only the wealthier countries of the South, whose growing importance DAC began to recognise in the 1990s, but also major philanthropies such as the Gates Foundation. DAC retains a significant role in the new Global Partnership for Effective Development Co-operation, sharing responsibility for the provision of secretarial support with the UNDP. The "non-DAC" donors and "partner" countries, however, have gained a more prominent place within the Partnership, reflecting the changing global context. While the Group's successor GenderNet has forged stronger links with the UN agencies that now regularly send representatives to its meetings, it is by no means clear whether the new actors share its commitment to gender equality. Nevertheless, there are some grounds for optimism as the Sustainable Development Goals adopted in 2015 as successors to the MDGs reflect the broader definition of gender equality that the Group had earlier fought for.

Notes

1. See the chapter by Patricia Hongler in this volume.
2. Matthias Schmelzer, "A Club of the Rich to Help the Poor? The OECD, 'Development' and the Hegemony of Donor Countries," In *International Organizations and Development 1945–1990*, ed. Marc Frey, Söhnke Kunkel and Corinna Unger (Basingstoke: Palgrave Mamillan, 2014): 12.
3. See inter alia Irene Tinker, "Introduction" to *Developing Power: How women Transformed International Development*, ed. Arvonne S. Fraser and Irene Tinker (New York: Feminist Press at NYU 2004): xxii.
4. On the changed development landscape see Charles Gore, "The New Development Cooperation Landscape: Actors, Approaches and Architecture," *Journal of International* Development 25 (2013): 769–786. The research for this chapter drew primarily on files culled from the OECD archives, with particular attention to the official minutes and key documents, backed by public accounts provided by several key individuals involved in the Group. Rosalind Eyben, who represented the UK's Department for International Development (DfID) and chaired the Group for several years, has provided the best documented accounts. See "Battles Over Booklets: Gender Myths in the British Aid Programme," *IDS Bulletin* 53: 4 (2009): 73–82; "Struggles in Paris: The DAC and the Purposes of Development Aid," *European Journal of Development Research* 25: 1 (2012): 78–91; and "Gender mainstreaming, organisational change and the politics of influencing", in *Feminists in Development Organizations: Change from the Margins*, ed. Rosalind Eyben and Laura Turquet (Bourton on Dunsmore: Practical Action

Publishing, 2013). Two original members of the Group, Arvonne Fraser and Geertje Lykclama à Nijeholt have also published their accounts. See Arvonne Fraser, "Seizing Opportunities: USAID, WID and CEDAW," and Geertje Lycklama, "Toward Empowerment: Influencing the Netherlands Aid Program," both of which appeared in *Developing Power*. I also interviewed Canadian Diana Rivington, who was a member for most of the 1990s and chaired the executive between 1999 and 2000.

5. See Eyben, "Battles," 75 on DAC's impact on DfID; for Japan see Sue Ellen Charlton, "Little Progress, Small Niches: The WID Mandate in Japanese Foreign Aid," in *Feminists Doing Development: A Practical Critique,* ed. Marilyn Porter and Ellen Judd (London: Zed Books, 1999): 42–56. On Korea, see Eun Mee Kim and JaeEun Lee, "Gender Empowerment in South Korean Development: Lessons for Foreign Aid," *International Studies Review* 12:11 (2011): 55–72. Liam Swiss, *Developing consensus: The globalization of development assistance policies* Ph.D. Dissertation, Sociology, McGill University, Montreal Canada 2009 examine the impact on all 22 members of the DAC.
6. As Sawer notes, "'femocrat' is a term invented in Australia to describe feminists who take up women's policy positions in government. Many of these were recruited from outside into middle-level or more senior positions in the bureaucracy and were appointed because of expertise and advocacy skills developed in the women's movement," Marian Sawer, *Sisters in Suits: Women and Public Policy in Australia* (Sydney: Allen and Unwin, 1990): 22.
7. A term coined to refer to the policies at the heart of the structural adjustment measures promoted by the Washington-based World Bank and the IMF. See John Williamson, "What Washington Means by Policy Reform," In *Latin American Readjustment: How Much Has Happened,* ed. J. Williamson (Washington: Institute for International Economics, 1989).
8. Helmut Führer "The Story of Official Development Assistance: A History of DAC/DCD in Dates, Names and Figures" Paris: OECD, 1996.
9. Schmelzer, "A Club of the Rich."
10. Eyben, "Struggles in Paris," 81.
11. John Toye, "Assessing the G77: 50 years after UNCTAD and 40 years after the NIEO," Third World Quarterly *2014, 35* (10), 1762.
12. This shift was in line with changes in the OECD's broader discourse as well as changes in the field of development, notably the World Bank's incorporation of social concerns under McNamara. See Rianne Mahon "The OECD's Search for a New Social Policy Paradigm: From Welfare State to (Gendered) Active Society" in *Analyzing Social Policy Language:*

Comparative and Transnational Perspectives Daniel Béland and Klaus Petersen eds. (Bristol, Policy Press 2014). While McNamara is credited with developing this approach, Führer's brief history of the DAC suggests that such concerns were already on DAC's agenda in 1973.

13. Ken Masujima "'Good Governance' and the DAC: Ideas and Organizational Constraints," in *Global Institutions and Development: Framing the World* Morten Bøas ad Desmond O'Neill eds. (London: Routledge 2004): 155.
14. For the term guerilla bureaucrats see Swiss, *Developing consensus* p. 138. See also Eyben "Struggles in Paris."
15. Masujima, "'Good Governance'," 154.
16. For more detail on the latter see Rianne Mahon "Articulating a Feminist Agenda Within the OECD: The Working Party on the Role of Women in the Economy" *Social Politics* 2015 22(4), 585–610.
17. Jane S. Jaquette and Kathleen. A. Staudt "Women, Gender and Development", in *Women and Gender Equity in Development Theory and Practice* Jane S. Jaquette and Gale Summerfield, eds. (Durham: Duke University Press 2006).
18. On this see Tinker "Introduction."
19. Ibid., 71.
20. Fraser, "Seizing Opportunities," 170.
21. Fraser, "Seizing Opportunities," 171
22. Fraser, "Seizing Opportunities," 171.
23. Sweden, Denmark, Norway, the Netherlands, Canada—and in the 1990s, the UK—exercised much of the leadership as members of the Group's executive.
24. Jaquette and Staudt, "Women, Gender and Development." 26. Both are political scientists but prior to her professorial career, Jaquette served as political analyst in USAID's WID Office (1979–1981).
25. Lycklama, "Toward Empowerment": 185.
26. OECD Historical Archives (hereafter OECD-HA) DAC/WID(85)1 Annex A Guiding Principles to Aid Agencies for Supporting the Role of women in Development, 1985, 7.
27. Ibid: 4–5.
28. See for example Lourdes. Benería and Gita Sen "Accumulation, reproduction and women's role in economic development: Boserup revisited," *Signs* 1981, 7 (2).
29. For more on DAWN got to http://dawnnet.org/feminist-resources/about/history. (04.10.2016).
30. Peggy Antrobus, 'A Caribbean Journey: Defending Feminist Politics' in *Developing Power*: 145.

31. An influential member of DAWN, Devaki Jain, made a presentation to the group in 1983 on her new work, 'Development as if women mattered: Can women build a new paradigm' New Dehli: Institute of Social Studies Trust.
32. OECD-HA DAC/WID/M(86)1/Prov Summary Record of the Meeting DAC Expert Group on Women in Development 27–28 January 1986, p. 3.
33. As the report by the Aid Evaluation group would note, however, "the most revealing finding is that women are addressed infrequently by evaluators and the human element of development assistance is generally overlooked in evaluation." OECD-HA DAC/WID(88)1 Report of the Chairperson of the Expert Group, 5.
34. Eyben, Struggles in Paris," 95. On Eyben, see also note 4.
35. OECD-HA DAC/WID(88) 1, Report of the Chair of the Expert Group.
36. OECD-HA DAC/WID/M(85)1(Prov), Summary record of the meeting of DAC Expert Group on Women in Development held 29–31 January 1985, 3.
37. OECD-HA DAC/WID(87) 2, Methodology for Statistical Reporting of Women-Oriented Aid Activities, 3.
38. DCD/DAC/WID/M(90)1/PROV, Summary Record of the 7th Meeting of DAC Expert Group on Women in Development 17–18 May 1990, 5.
39. OECD_HA DAC/WID(88)2, Draft Revised Guiding Principles to Aid Agencies for Supporting the Role of Women in Development. Note by the Task Force, 1.
40. Ibid., 7.
41. Ibid., 2.
42. The Group was well aware of UNICEF's position, which was discussed at the Group's meeting in 1987, followed by a seminar on the topic at the 1988 meetings and the establishment of a Task Force on Women and Structural Adjustment which included representatives on both sides of the debate.
43. Masujima, "Good Governance", 156.
44. OECD-HA DAC/WID/M(90)1(Prov).
45. Ibid., 4.
46. Eyben, "Gender Mainstreaming," 87.
47. Gulay. Caglar, Elisabeth Prügl and Suzanne Zwingel, "Introducing feminist strategies in international governance' in *Feminist Strategies in International Governance*, G. Caglar, et al., eds. (London and New York: Routledge 2013), 9.
48. Nuket Kardam, "The Emerging Global Gender Equality Regime from Neo-liberal and Constructivist Perspectives in International Relations", in *International Feminist Journal of Politics* 6:1 2004, 97. Emphasis added.

49. The Group launched what it called its "facilitation initiative," which involved the gender units in certain donor countries taking responsibility for supporting the participation of women's groups in Africa, Asia, and Latin America in their respective preparatory conferences for Beijing.
50. The Utstein Group was made up of the UK, the Netherlands, Norway, and Germany. For more on this see Sakiko Fukuda-Parr and David Hulme "International Norm Dynamics and the 'End of Poverty': Understanding the Millennium Development Goals" *Global Governance* 17 2011, 22.
51. Ibid., 6.
52. OECD-HA DCD/DAC/WID/M(96)1/Prov, 6–7.
53. While this indicator was taken from the Education for All conference at Jomtien, the organisation could have chosen other indicators such as those dealing with reproductive health from the UN conference on Population.
54. Rosalind Eyben, Rosalind "The Road Not Taken: International Aid's Choice of Copenhagen over Beijing" *Third World Quarterly* 27: 4 2006, 600.
55. OECD-HA DCD/DAC/WID/M(97)1/Prov Summary record of the 14th meeting of DAC Expert Group on Women in Development held 31 October 1997, 3.
56. Ibid., 6
57. http://www.wikigender.org/index/hph/Gender_Equality_Marker_Systemoldid=31629 (consulted August 2016).
58. OECD-HA DCD/DAC/WID(97)9, *DAC Guidelines on Gender Equality and Women's Empowerment in Development Co-operation*, Draft submitted for approval to the Expert Group meeting to be held 2–3 October 1997, 6–7.
59. Ibid., 21.
60. Ibid., 20.
61. Ibid., 21.
62. Chaired by the Dutch representative, the Task Force included the representatives of Canada, Denmark, the European Commission, Germany, Sweden, the UK, and the World Bank.
63. OECD-HA DCD/DAC/WID(97)9, *DAC Guidelines on Gender Equality and Women's Empowerment in Development Co-operation*, Draft submitted for approval to the Expert Group meeting to be held 2–3 October 1997, 19.
64. Ibid., 20.
65. See Mahon "Articulating A Feminist Agenda" op cit. for more detail on the latter's demise.

66. OECD-HA DCD/DAC(M)3/Prov, 6.
67. OECD_HA DCD/DAC/WID(99)1/Prov, 6–7. Note: the one negative voice was that of the Portuguese representative. Interview with Diana Rivington 28.10.15.
68. See www.oecd.org/dac/gender-development (10.2016).
69. Carole Miller (1998) "Gender advocates and multilateral development organizations: Promoting change from within" in *Missionaries and Mandarins: Feminist Engagement with Development Institutions* Carol Miller and Shahra Razavi eds. (Geneva: UNRISD 1998), 138.

Index

M. Leimgruber and M. Schmelzer (eds.), *The OECD and the International Political Economy Since 1948*, DOI 10.1007/978-3-319-60243-1

FSC
www.fsc.org
MIX
Papier | Fördert
gute Waldnutzung
FSC® C083411

Kolibri 360 GmbH
Ferdinand-Jühlke-Straße 7
99095 Erfurt, Deutschland
produktsicherheit@kolibri360.de